No Ordinary People
Twenty-One Friendships of C.S. Lewis

Copyright © 2021 Joel D. Heck

Winged Lion Press
Hamden, CT

All rights reserved. Except in the case of quotations embodied in critical articles or reviews, no part of this book may be reproduced or transmitted in any form or by any means, electronic or mechanical, including photocopying, recording, or by any information storage or retrieval system, without written permission of the publisher. Contact Winged Lion Press www.WingedLionPress.com

WINGED LION PRESS

ISBN 13   978-1-935688-22-8

Advanced Praise

When we think of C. S. Lewis, many pictures come to mind: Lewis the creator of Narnia and deep space, Lewis the indefatigable Christian philosopher and "bonny fighter" for the faith, Lewis the erudite historian of medieval and Renaissance literature, Lewis the lover of long walks and nude bathing; yet no picture of Lewis is complete without Lewis the friend. **He was a genius at friendship, as well as a gifted interpreter of the moral psychology of friendship, and his friendships reached beyond the delights of the Inklings fellowship. In introducing us to the larger constellation of Lewis's friendships** – male and female, celebrated and little known, likeminded and worlds apart – **Joel Heck has performed the great service of making us all better friends of C. S. Lewis.**

>Carol Zaleski, Co-author with Philip Zaleski of *The Fellowship: The Literary Lives of the Inklings: J.R.R. Tolkien, C. S. Lewis, Owen Barfield, Charles Williams*

"It's true: we are known by the company we keep, and these taut, clear, informative character sketches provide significant insight into C. S. Lewis while at the same time offering a window into essential details of Lewis's world. **Joel Heck has produced a resource that I expect to consult again and again. Indispensable.**"

>Diana Pavlac Glyer, Professor, The Honors College at Azusa Pacific University and Author of *The Company They Keep* and *Bandersnatch: C. S. Lewis, J. R. R. Tolkien, and the Creative Collaboration of the Inklings*

As a young atheist, C. S. Lewis mightily resisted John Donne's maxim, "No man is an island," asserting his "monstrous individualism" and his hatred of "interference," both human and divine. Yet God drew Lewis out of himself through experience, books, and many friends. This insightful study explores twenty-one of the friendships that supported and challenged Lewis, as he recovered faith and turned his prodigious talents to its exposition and defense.

>Angus Menuge, Ph.D, Professor and Chair of Philosophy, Concordia University. Co-editor, *The Inherence of Human Dignity, vol 1: Foundations of Human Dignity.*

Joel Heck has penned the book I wish I had written, and given his almost encyclopedic knowledge of all things Lewisian, he has done it very well indeed. Along the way, Heck fills in some aspects of Lewis's career that have been, hitherto, little known or written about, such as the fact that Lewis served as the General Editor of Thomas Nelson's Medieval and Renaissance Library. However, the major value of the book is seen in its focus on some of Lewis's lesser-known friendships, revealing how each of these enriched Lewis as a man and as a scholar. **The chapters on Austin Farrer and Alec Vidler alone are worth the price of the book. Heck's work also functions as an excellent rehabilitation of the classical idea of friendship itself and shows us how such friendship is possible even in the modern world. To top it all off, Heck has illustrated the book with delightful photographs, some seldom if ever seen in other books on Lewis. Well done!**

Will Vaus, Pastor & Author of *The Hidden Story of Narnia*

While some of C.S. Lewis's acquaintances are well-known names that carry their own glowing legacies, there are many others who have become lost in Lewis's shadow over time. Joel D. Heck has done a great service in spotlighting these names in his book, often using obscure and unpublished sources to give each individual their own story. **This work is a gift to future Lewis scholarship, and to all those interested in the people who inspired, encouraged, and challenged Lewis in his daily life and work.**

Laura Schmidt, Archivist
Marion E. Wade Center

Joel Heck's *No Ordinary People* is no ordinary book. Readers will be treated to thoughtful discussions of 21 people and how he or she engaged with Lewis. **In the end, we come away with a broader and more nuanced understanding of Lewis's many friends** and how each influenced the most popular Christian writer of the 20th century.

Don King, Author of *The Complete Poems of C.S. :Lewis*

Table of Contents

FOREWORD 1

INTRODUCTION 3

SECTION I
SIDE BY SIDE FRIENDS
Griffiths, Dyson, Farrer, Greeves, Janie Moore,
Warren Lewis, Sister Penelope

CHAPTER 1
Alan Richard Griffiths, 11
Chief Companion on the Road to the Christian Faith
Griffiths and Lewis traveled similar roads from atheism to Christianity and at approximately the same time, sharing their insights with one another as they made this spiritual journey. Griffiths was an atheist when Lewis, Griffiths' tutor for a degree in English literature at Oxford University, first met him.

CHAPTER 2
Hugo Dyson, A Roaring Cataract of Nonsense 29
Dyson was a member of the Inklings, known for his expertise in Shakespeare and his ability to quote Shakespeare at length. He was also loud, outgoing, clever, and boisterous. He had more of an influence on Lewis's conversion to Christianity than did J. R. R. Tolkien.

CHAPTER 3
Austin Farrer, A Hawk among Sparrows 47
First, Chaplain at St. Edmund Hall and then at Trinity College, Oxford, and later Warden at Keble College, Farrer was an Oxford graduate who returned to Oxford for an academic and pastoral career. He had a close relationship with Lewis, especially in the later years, and he became the most frequent speaker at the Oxford Socratic Club, of which Lewis was President. Many collections of his sermons have been published as books.

CHAPTER 4
Arthur Greeves, No Ordinary Person 73
Arthur Greeves was Lewis's lifelong friend and a Belfast neighbor to whom Lewis wrote more letters during his life than to anyone else. Arthur's artistic talent, love for the world of nature, and unpretentious personality combined with a love of Norse mythology that resonated with Lewis. Arthur is a prime example of Lewis's claim that "there are no ordinary people."

CHAPTER 5
Janie Moore, The 'Mother' of C. S Lewis 89
The relationship between Lewis and the woman he called his "mother" has been the subject of much speculation, but without much supporting data. This chapter pieces together some comments Lewis made in his writings with a plausible account of what happened between them, while looking both at Janie Moore's strong points (which are often glossed over) and her weak ones.

CHAPTER 6
Warren Hamilton Lewis, His Brother's Brother 113
The Lewis brothers were lifelong friends, although they had their disagreements early in life. We know a lot about C. S. Lewis because of the extensive diaries of Warren, but few people know much about the life of Warren Lewis and his career with the Royal Army Service Corps or the seven books he wrote, undoubtedly with the encouragement and support of his brother.

CHAPTER 7
Sister Penelope, Elder Sister in the Faith   135
This Anglican nun, Penelope Lawson, was librarian at the convent of the Anglican community of St. Mary the Virgin at Wantage, corresponded with Lewis, eventually getting Lewis to write the Introduction to one of her books, *The Incarnation of the Word of God: Being the Treatise of St Athanasius De Incarnatione Verbi Dei.* she authored several books, including *Windows on Jerusalem: A Study in the Mystery of Redemption, They Shall Be My People, The Morning Gift,* and *The Coming of the Lord: A Study in the Creed.* She is the woman to whom Lewis sent a copy of *Perelandra* for safe keeping during the war.

CHAPTER 8
R. E. Havard, Lewis Family Physician   165
When the Lewis family doctor died, Robert Emlyn Havard took over his practice, came to the Lewis household to help treat his illnesses, later joined the Inklings, and spent a lot of time outside his medical profession with Lewis and the Inklings.

CHAPTER 9
A. K. Hamilton Jenkin, The Cornwall Enthusiast   177
A fellow undergraduate shared Lewis'ss love of literature and writing. He was Lewis'ss first lifelong friend made at the University. These two Univ. students stayed in touch for most of their lives and spent a lot of time together during their university years. Jenkin became known for his writings on his home county of Cornwall.

Section II
Opponents, But Friends
Clarke, Weldon, Joad, Vidler, Haldane

Chapter 10
Arthur C. Clarke, Lewis, & Science Fiction 195
Clarke was becoming famous for his writing about science, space travel, and science fiction, but much younger than Lewis when Clarke first initiated some correspondence between them. Lewis highly praised Clarke's book *Childhood's End*. Clarke was the first person to recommend satellites for use in telecommunication, long before satellites were launched. Although an atheist, he corresponded with Lewis for more than a decade before moving to Sri Lanka, and Lewis once offered the young Clarke some tips on effective writing.

Chapter 11
Harry Weldon and the Resurrection 213
Harry Weldon was an agnostic, possibly an atheist, who once admitted to Lewis that the evidence for the resurrection was surprisingly strong in the case of Jesus. That admission shocked the atheist in C. S. Lewis and led to a reappraisal of the historicity of the New Testament Gospels.

Chapter 12
C. E. M. Joad, Agnostic, Intellectual Scallywag, and Convert 225
Joad was a British philosopher and prolific author who popularized philosophy for the average British citizen, read Lewis, and came back to the Church of England late in life, in part, under the influence of Lewis's writings.

CHAPTER 13
J. B. S. Haldane, AKA Edward Rolles Weston   251
    The atheist Haldane, mathematician and originator of Haldane's Dilemma, once debated Lewis, sort of, at the Oxford Socratic Club. Lewis read Haldane, usually in disagreement but sometimes in agreement.

CHAPTER 14
Alec Vidler:
C.S. Lewis was his Permanent Opposition   263
    Vidler was the editor of *Theology*, for which Lewis wrote on occasion, and the theologian with whom Lewis disagreed in "Modern Theology and Biblical Criticism," when Lewis brought his formidable literary skills to bear on New Testament theology. But they were friends and respected one another as colleagues.

SECTION III
Co-Workers and Fellow Pilgrims
Aldwinckle, Dunbar, Bradbrook, Brewer,
Bryan, Shelley, Maureen Moore

CHAPTER 15
Stella Aldwinckle, Atheists, and Agnostics   289
    Aldwinckle is best known for Chairing the Oxford Socratic Club, which she helped to birth, and her desire for Christ to be made known to as many people as possible. She and Lewis worked closely in leading the Oxford Socratic Club, of which Lewis was the President for twelve years.

CHAPTER 16
Nan Dunbar, Statius, and C. S. Lewis   307
> Dunbar was a young Classics scholar at Cambridge University with whom Lewis corresponded during his years teaching in Cambridge. He treated her as an equal, and, in the Classics, as his superior. They met during Lewis's later teaching career in Cambridge, while Dunbar taught at Girton College, Cambridge, for two years.

CHAPTER 17
Muriel Bradbrook, C. S. Lewis, & Shakespeare   317
> Like Dunbar, Bradbrook taught at Girton College, where she spent her entire career. She was another Shakespeare scholar whom Lewis respected a great deal

CHAPTER 18
Derek Stanley Brewer and C. S. Lewis   325
> Derek Brewer's career ended as the Master of Emanuel College, Cambridge, but it began with an interview for a scholarship to Magdalen College, conducted largely by C. S. Lewis who later became Brewer's tutor. Brewer took a degree in English under Lewis and early in his career was one of three English Fellows at the University of Birmingham to ask Lewis to serve as the General Editor for Nelson's Medieval and Renaissance Library.

CHAPTER 19
F. C. Bryan and the Oxford Socratic Club   335
F. C. Bryan was a Baptist minister who spoke both at a meeting of the Socratic Club and at two Socratic retreat-like weekends on the Christian faith. He had a unique ability to communicate biblical truths to college students, which made his Socratic connection very appropriate.

CHAPTER 20
Mary Shelley and Progressive Schools   345
Mary Shelley (distantly related to the author of *Frankenstein*) was one of Lewis's correspondents over quite a few years. She was once an atheist, a teacher in a progressive school, and later a Christian through the influence of Lewis. Lewis became the godfather of her older daughter Sarah with whom he corresponded.

CHAPTER 21
Maureen Moore, Baronetess of Hempriggs   363
Maureen Moore, the daughter of Janie Moore, who lived in the same household with her mother and C. S. Lewis, trained as a musician and later married Leonard Blake and became Lady Dunbar of Hempriggs, since she was in line to be the next Baronetess. She was one of the few people who lived in the same household with Lewis and knew his personal style rather than his professional style, but she also benefited from his tutoring in Latin and his attempts to help her get the musical education that enabled her later career in music.

Index   375

Foreword

Books by C. S. Lewis still sell far better than books about C. S. Lewis, but Lewisiana continues to flow from the pens of various Lewis scholars and fans. When one thinks that the market may have been glutted with material about Lewis, another person comes up with a new idea that generates a great deal of interest and contributes to our understanding of Lewis and his world. This volume offers a new perspective and, hopefully, will have that type of impact.

Many thanks are due to the Marion E. Wade Center for the availability of their extensive resources, particularly to Laura Schmidt, Archivist, for her reading of this manuscript as it neared the final stages of its preparation. In addition, her helpful input on various aspects of the bibliography helped to bring this manuscript to completion. My thanks also go to Marjorie Lamp Mead, Associate Director of the Wade Center, for allowing me to field test in lecture format several of the chapters in this manuscript and to incorporate some photographs from the Wade Center's extensive holdings. Many others read earlier versions of some of the chapters, so my thanks go to Steven Beebe, Crystal Hurd, Charles Huttar, Don W. King, Louis Markos, Angus J. L. Menuge, Steve Mueller, Joe Ricke, Jerry Root, Stephen Thorson, Sarah Watrers, and especially to Will Vaus, who gave the nearly final manuscript a thorough reading and made many fine suggestions. At the University where I am employed, I also thank Jeffrey Utzinger for his support and encouragement over the several years of writing that brought this book to publication.

This book would not be possible without the three volumes of *Collected Letters* of C. S. Lewis that have come out in 2000, 2004, and 2006, thanks to the tireless efforts of the now sainted Walter Hooper. The diaries of both Lewis brothers, including the unpublished portions of Warren Lewis's diaries, contributed a significant amount of information, as did so many of the books and essays by C. S. Lewis. Many more resources, too numerous to list, made important contributions. "Chronologically Lewis," begun in 2004 after a word of advice from Peter Schakel, offers the framework for this book, providing approximately 1,300 pages, more than 700,000 words, and more than 4,400 footnotes, all based on more than two hundred sources. This book could still have been written without the chronology, but it would have looked a lot different.

Introduction

C. S. Lewis was one of the Inklings, that group of Christian writers who lived in and near Oxford, England, during the 1940s and 1950s, who met regularly to talk, drink beer, and read books, poems, plays, and articles that members of the group were writing. Lewis had so many friends that many have come to think of him as that most friendly person who seemingly had time for everyone. While he did not start out as the ultimate mixer—hardly anyone does—he eventually became that kind of person. This book provides a glimpse into some of the friendships—some close and others casual—Lewis developed that are not well known, often not even on one's radar screen, but which provide us a closer look into the private life of one of the twentieth century's most engaging and effective writers.

The title—No Ordinary People—comes from Lewis's most famous essay, "The Weight of Glory." The essay was originally a sermon, delivered to a packed church at St. Mary the Virgin Church, Oxford. Near the end of that essay, he spoke these words:

> All day long we are, in some degree, helping each other to one or other of these destinations. It is in the light of these overwhelming possibilities, it is with the awe and the circumspection proper to them, that we should conduct all our dealings with one another, all friendships, all loves, all play, all politics. There are no ordinary people. You have never talked to a mere mortal.[1]

This book will demonstrate that Lewis lived what he taught, practiced what he preached, and that he was concerned about helping those people—all of his friendships—toward a heavenly destination. He had too many friends and acquaintances to describe them all, but each of them is illustrative of Lewis's concern for the people he knew. What he once wrote to Arthur Greeves in 1931 became a standard policy for him for the rest of his life: "I am glad that people become more and more one of the sources of pleasure as I grow older."[2]

In *The Four Loves*, C. S. Lewis wrote about *philia*, often translated as "friendship." Arthur Greeves, Alan Richard Griffiths, Hugo Dyson, and Austin Farrer serve as prime examples of this type of love. Alongside the other three loves—"affection," "Eros"

---

[1] *The Weight of Glory and Other Addresses*. New York: Simon & Schuster, 1980, 39.

[2] *Collected Letters, Vol. II*, 25.

or "romantic love," and "charity"—Lewis celebrates friendship, in part because the world ignores it.³ That's why this book is needed—to restore an appreciation for friendship in a world where so many relationships are belittled, ignored, or sexualized. Lewis regrets the necessity "to rebut the theory that every firm and serious friendship is really homosexual."⁴ That's why Lewis claims that he wrote the chapter on friendship as a rehabilitation.⁵ He believed that the old idea of friendship was a better idea, so he wrote the chapter to encourage others to return to that old idea, to prize friendship as a gift, and to engage in friendships with others.

However, not all of Lewis's friends were of the philia type. "Friends, side by side, [are] absorbed in some common interest."⁶ Friendship is "pleasure in cooperation, in talking shop, in the mutual respect and understanding of men who daily see one another tested …."⁷ Friendship is so important, he writes, that life "has no better gift to give."⁸ But only one-third of the friendships described in these pages were the side-by-side type of friendship. Some were friends, even though they held different views on important topics, and others—people like Haldane, Vidler, and Clarke—are better described as acquaintances. Some were co-workers and fellow pilgrims on the journey through life, such as Bradbrook, Aldwinckle, Brewer, and Neylan. While the philia type of friendship enriched Lewis's life, Lewis appreciated both the opponents, whose opposition Lewis at times relished,⁹ and his fellow pilgrims, who taught him much that he did not know and, consequently, can also teach us.

J. R. R. Tolkien and Others

No more important friendship happened in the life of Lewis than his friendship with J. R. R. Tolkien, whom he met in 1926 at a meeting of the Oxford University English faculty.¹⁰ Soon thereafter

---

³ *The Four Loves*. Harcourt Brace & Company, New York, 1988, 56.
⁴ *The Four Loves*, 60.
⁵ *The Four Loves*, 60, 77.
⁶ *The Four Loves*, 61.
⁷ *The Four Loves*, 64.
⁸ *The Four Loves*, 72.
⁹ Lewis once mentioned a friend who had described himself as "hungry for rational opposition." Those words, Lewis writes, also described him when he sat down to read Tillyard. C. S. Lewis and E. M. W. Tillyard, *The Personal Heresy*, 49.
¹⁰ The date was May 11, 1926, and the meeting of the Oxford English

Twenty-One Friendships of C.S. Lewis

Tolkien invited Lewis to participate in the Kolbitár, a group that met regularly to read Icelandic literature. Subsequently, Lewis and Tolkien met separately from the Kolbitár. When weekly meetings became the norm, they invited Warren Lewis and then another person and still another. Soon the Inklings were born. But this group did not exhaust Lewis's capacity for meaningful relationships.

Many other friendships are not as well known, but they all tell us something about Lewis. These are friendships between C. S. Lewis and various individuals with whom Lewis interacted, but who are little known outside of Lewis scholars. Many of Lewis's friends are already well-known, especially Tolkien, Charles Williams, Dorothy L. Sayers,[11] Joy Davidman, and Owen Barfield, largely because they participated in the Inklings (although Sayers and Davidman did not). Others, however, have been largely ignored. Their stories fill out the life of C. S. Lewis and his ways of drawing other people to the Christian faith, strengthening them in the faith, or influencing them in some way through their contact with him. Some of them—Arthur C. Clarke, Sister Penelope, and Austin Farrer's wife Katharine—became better writers through their contact with Lewis. To the extent that we read Lewis and follow his advice on writing, we will become better writers too. Lewis's correspondence with them provides one of the major sources of information about these friendships. Readers will find a wide range of relationships from the highly educated Oxford and Cambridge academics to the little educated and rather plain Arthur Greeves, from the intelligent and controversial philosopher C. E. M. Joad to the artistic Mary Shelley, and from close friends Hugo Dyson and Austin Farrer to the formidable opponent J. B. S. Haldane.

Some, like Hugo Dyson and Arthur Greeves, are rather well-known. Others, like F. C. Bryan and Nan Dunbar, although known in a few circles, are new to most readers of Lewis. In the process of writing these chapters, I discovered connections between Lewis and others that I had never seen before. I saw the generous amounts of time he gave to many of them, his conviction that there are "no

---

faculty took place at Merton College, Tolkien's college, beginning with tea at 4:00 p.m. See "Chronologically Lewis" for that date: http://www.joelheck.com/chronologically-lewis.php

[11] See, for example, Marsha Daigle-Williamson, "C. S. Lewis and Dorothy L. Sayers: Correspondence," *CSL: The Bulletin of The New York C. S. Lewis Society*, Vol. 48, No. 4 (July/August 2017), Whole No. 480, 1-8.

ordinary people," his desire to help them in any way he could, and his wide-ranging interests. In the process, I have grown in my respect for Lewis, whose friendships show his tolerance for other viewpoints, his engaging personality, his respect for both men and women, his commitment to the Christian faith, his appreciation of the character and talents of any other person, and his deep thinking. For Lewis, there truly were no ordinary people.

This book demonstrates how Lewis corresponded with, shared table fellowship, advised, and interacted in many other ways with a wide variety of people. He probably saw his contacts with other people in much the same way that he saw the letters of those who wrote to him. Some have stated that he answered every letter that he ever received.[12] Likewise, it seems, he opened the door of fellowship to nearly anyone who would desire to enter. In this book, we see how each of these twenty-one people had a positive impact on Lewis, even as Lewis had a positive impact on them. Many more people could have been chosen for this book, but we have limited our choices to twenty-one.

Lewis related well to people he disagreed with (if they gave him the chance), with people thirty years his junior or the same age, with men and women, with atheists and skeptics, with close friends, colleagues, and family members. He connected with people of his denomination (the Church of England), other denominations (Baptist and Catholic), clergy or laypeople, or people with no religion. While his father is an exception to this rule (since they were at odds with one another for many years), his lifelong friendship with his brother—and the significant reasons why they were both at odds with their father—still paints a powerful picture of friendship.

In his friendship with Nan Dunbar, we see the English Fellow with an interest in the Classics but deferring to the expertise of Dunbar and respecting her scholarship. In his friendship with Alec Vidler, we see a conservative scholar corresponding with a liberal scholar on a friendly basis while seeing the scholarly strengths that Vidler had to offer. In his relationship with C. E. M. Joad, we see an English Fellow whose training in philosophy enabled him to communicate with Joad,

---

[12] A letter Lewis wrote to Mary Neylan illustrates his commitment to people, not just letter-writing, when he states, "You may put out of your head any idea of 'not having a claim' on any help I can give. Every human being, still more every Christian, has an absolute claim on me for any service I can render them without neglecting other duties." *Collected Letters, II*, 482.

Twenty-One Friendships of C.S. Lewis

respect Joad's expertise to explain philosophy on a lay level and invite him to reconsider the Christian faith. In each of these friendships, we see an aspect of Lewis that we don't see in the same way anywhere else.

This book has three sections. The first section looks at Lewis's side-by-side friendships of the *philia* type. The second section explores Lewis's friendships with people who took opposing views on various topics but with whom Lewis remained cordial. The third section concludes with his relationships with co-workers and fellow pilgrims.

Only three of the twenty-one people on these pages were Inklings—Warren Lewis, the brother of C. S. Lewis, Hugo Dyson, and R. E. Havard—and even these three are among the least known of that group.[13] That makes this book much different from Diana Glyer's *The Company They Keep* or those books that describe Lewis as a spiritual mentor.

Each chapter describes the relationship between that person and Lewis, often beginning with a short introduction that explains why that person knew Lewis. Although the life story of these twenty-one people is not the center of that chapter, in most cases a brief biographical sketch follows the short introduction, followed by a description of that person's relationship with Lewis and lessons we can learn from their friendship.

Finally, while Lewis's home, undergraduate studies, and academic career were largely in all-male environs, he had significant relationships with some important women.[14] This book looks at seven women with whom Lewis interacted and whom he highly respected—Nan Dunbar, Muriel Bradbrook, Mary Shelley, Stella Aldwinckle, Janie Moore, Maureen Moore, and Sister Penelope. All of these friendships speak about the respect Lewis had for women and the amount of time he spent working with women.

---

[13] The forthcoming biography of Warren Lewis by Don W. King will rectify the lack of knowledge about Warren.

[14] Lewis's mother died when he was nine years old, leaving him to grow up in an all-male household. In addition, Oxford University only slowly and grudgingly opened both its faculty ranks and its student population to women during the twentieth century.

SECTION I
SIDE BY SIDE FRIENDS

Alan Richard Griffiths
Photo used with permission of Prinknash Abbey

Chapter 1

ALAN RICHARD GRIFFITHS
Chief Companion on the Road to the Christian Faith

Two atheists—a teacher and his student—saw evidence for the existence of God in many places and found themselves kindred spirits in a growing understanding of that truth. The spiritual journeys of C. S. Lewis, the Oxford don, and Alan Richard Griffiths, the student, were so similar that Lewis once described Griffiths as his "chief companion"[1] on that journey. Griffiths described their early relationship as "acquaintanceship ripened into friendship," adding that between 1929 and 1932, "I was probably nearer to Lewis than anyone else."[2] Journeying together creates a certain kind of intimacy that is available nowhere else.

On the Journey

Griffiths became acquainted with Lewis when he enrolled at Magdalen College to study Honour Moderations[3] (without Lewis) and then English Literature (with Lewis). Griffiths read English with Lewis as his tutor from 1927 until 1929.[4] By the time Griffiths first met Lewis, no later than Michaelmas term in the autumn of 1927, Lewis had moved beyond atheism to belief in a Universal Spirit, but

---

[1] C. S. Lewis, *Surprised by Joy*, 234. In view of this friendship, Lewis later dedicated *Surprised by Joy*, the autobiographical account of his conversion to Christianity, to Griffiths.

[2] Alan Bede Griffiths, "The Adventure of Faith," *C. S. Lewis at the Breakfast Table and Other Reminiscences*, edited by James T. Como, New York: Harcourt Brace & Company, 1992, 11. This book chapter is Griffiths' own recollection of his relationship with C. S. Lewis, pages 11-24 in the volume edited by James Como. Griffiths told his own story in *The Golden String*, a story that supports this close relationship between the two men. Alan Griffiths, *The Golden String*, Springfield, IL: Templegate Publishers, 1980, 56f. [Wade has CSL's copy of this book - https://vufind.carli.illinois.edu/vf-whe/Record/whe_832158/Description]

[3] A study of Greek and Latin texts, which Griffiths began to study in October 1925.

[4] See Walter Hooper's footnote in C. S. Lewis, *Collected Letters*, I, 834, n. 82.

not belief in God.[5] When the Great War[6] between Lewis and Barfield caused Lewis to write his major work, the *Summa*,[7] against Barfield's Anthroposophy, in the summer of 1928, Lewis lent it to Griffiths. This writing convinced Griffiths to become an Idealist.[8] The *Summa*, writes Griffiths, outlined Lewis's idea of the Universal Spirit behind all phenomena.[9]

Between 1929 and 1932 both Griffiths and Lewis were being drawn to the Christian faith.[10] The discovery of a passage in Berkeley's *Principles of Human Knowledge* charmed Griffiths both for its style and its content. Griffiths was reading a lot of philosophy, and Lewis, who had previously read that work, had recommended the book to him. The charming passage described everything existing either in the mind of a person or in the mind of an eternal Spirit.[11]

---

[5] This is an Idealist position. Alan Griffiths, "The Adventure of Faith," in James Como, *C. S. Lewis at the Breakfast Table*, 1992, 13, 16.

[6] A decade-long argument between Lewis and Barfield about truth and imagination.

[7] *Summa* is Latin for "highest." The full title is *Clivi Hamiltonis Summae Metaphysices contra Anthroposophos Libri II*, that is, in English "The Highest Books of the Metaphysics of Clive Hamilton against the Anthroposophists." For a full description of the Great War between Lewis and Barfield, see Stephen Thorson, *Joy and Poetic Imagination: Understanding C. S. Lewis's "Great War" with Owen Barfield and its Significance for Lewis's Conversion and Writings*, Hamden, CT: Winged Lion Press, 2015.

[8] Alan Griffiths, "The Adventure of Faith," in James Como, *C. S. Lewis at the Breakfast Table*, 1992, 13.

[9] Ibid. This is the absolute Idealism of Hegel rather than the subjective Idealism of Berkeley and Hume, essentially pantheistic the position that the German philosopher G. W. F. Hegel had held.

[10] Alan Griffiths, "The Adventure of Faith," in James Como, *C. S. Lewis at the Breakfast Table*, 1992, 11. Many have wondered when Lewis entered the pantheistic stage of his spiritual journey, but this is most likely happening through the Idealism of Hegel, which was pantheistic. See *Collected Letters*, II, 145, where Lewis writes to Paul Elmer More, "To you it may be a matter of surprise that I could ever have found this hatred unintelligible: but you would not wonder if you had traveled the same route as I, which was from materialism to idealism, from idealism to Pantheism, from pantheism to theism, and from theism to Christianity."

[11] This is the exact passage: "Some truths there are so near and obvious to the mind that a man need only open his mind to perceive them. Such I take this important one to be: viz. that all the choir of heaven and all the furniture of the earth, in a word all the bodies which compose the mighty frame of the world, have not any subsistence without a mind, that their being is to be perceived and known; that consequently so long as

This passage turned on a light for Griffiths. He came to think that one could not conceive of things existing without a mind to know them and experience them by the senses. He therefore thought that things were ideas and the ideas came from universal mind or Spirit. He believed that "God was a mind, a pure Spirit, and the universe was the thought of his mind, while our own perception of things was simply a limited participation."[12] This insight probably happened between June 1929, when Griffiths completed his degree at Oxford, and April 1930, and it seems likely to have been shared with Lewis, with whom Griffiths shared his discoveries.[13]

In *Surprised by Joy*, probably referring to the weekend of February 8-10, 1930, Lewis describes a conversation with Owen Barfield and Alan Griffiths about philosophy as "a way," rather than a subject, for Plato. The Christian philosopher Boethius had viewed philosophy in the same way, and at this point Lewis may well have remembered how Boethius had respected Plato.[14] The seed planted in his mind by Boethius was growing.[15] Lewis was thinking of philosophy as an impersonal subject for him to teach, with an impersonal Mind behind it, and he thought philosophy was the same impersonal subject for Plato. Instead, Barfield and Griffiths corrected him, stating that for Plato philosophy was a way of life rather than a mundane subject to teach.

In *The Golden String*, Griffiths describes philosophy at this time as "a matter of passionate interest which I felt to hold the meaning of life for me."[16] This statement coincides with the incident with Barfield, Griffiths, and Lewis. The story fits well with the last steps in Lewis's spiritual journey to theism. Not only was he learning to live

---

they are not actually perceived by me or do not exist in my mind or that of any other created spirit, they must either have no existence at all or else subsist in the mind of some eternal Spirit." This quotation from George Berkeley's *A Treatise Concerning the Principles of Human Knowledge*, Part I, 6, is cited in Bede Griffiths, *The Golden String*, 48.

[12] Griffiths, *The Golden String*, 48f.

[13] Griffiths, *The Golden String*, 65, who states that he began his experiment in country living in April 1930. This seems to be the latest date for this realization. The earliest date seems to be after Griffiths graduated from Oxford University, which occurred during the summer of 1929. Email from Robin Darwall-Smith, February 19, 2014, on the dates Griffiths took his English exams.

[14] Chris Armstrong, Ibid., 144.

[15] Ibid., 145.

[16] Griffiths, *The Golden String*, 65. See *From Atheism to Christianity*.

philosophy, he had to face his denial of God's existence.

Living a philosophy became more real to Lewis in early 1930. On February 8-10, 1930, Barfield and Griffiths are mentioned together in Lewis's letters, and, therefore, this is likely the time about which Lewis wrote these words:

> The fox had been dislodged from Hegelian Wood and was now running in the open, "with all the wo in the world," bedraggled and weary, hounds barely a field behind. And nearly everyone was now ... in the pack; Plato, Dante, MacDonald, Herbert, Barfield, Tolkien, Dyson, Joy itself. Everyone and everything had joined the other side. Even my own pupil Griffiths ... though not yet himself a believer, did his share.[17]

Lewis was beginning to see that an academic discipline like philosophy needed to become personal. The same was true of the Christian faith. His adherence to Idealism (the Hegelian Wood, since Hegel had been an Idealist) had been shaken, and he was now able to consider other possibilities for the meaning of life. Lewis had been dislodged from the wood (i.e., the weakness of his position had been exposed), he was running out in the open (he was looking at other options), and the other side was closing in (a personal God was looking much more plausible).

As stated above, Griffiths stayed with Lewis briefly in 1930. Earlier in life, Griffiths had been caught up in naturalism[18] and D. H. Lawrence,[19] but he was reevaluating those positions, traveling a road quite similar to the one Lewis was traveling.[20] Lewis no doubt helped

---

[17] C. S. Lewis, *Surprised by Joy*, 225. The word "wo" may mean both "where" (in German) and "woe." The "where" fits the Hegelian context (Hegel was German; Lewis is escaping the Hegelian Wood) and the "woe" alludes to the story of Diana and Actaeon. In Greek mythology Actaeon accidentally came upon Diana, the goddess of the hunt, while she was bathing, was turned into a deer, and then hunted by his own dogs. Lewis, then, is the hunted/the Actaeon figure being pursued by Diana/the Divine. This is classic Lewis: myth and philosophy coming together directly in life metaphors in a powerful way.

[18] The belief that everything has come into existence through natural processes and that supernatural events are to be excluded.

[19] An English writer and poet (1885-1930) who especially explored human sexuality in his writings.

[20] *Collected Letters, I*, 881. Lewis had rejected Naturalism years earlier. Not only did Griffiths travel a similar road, but Lewis's brother Warren did as well. While this can be pressed too far, Warren avoided a church service on board a ship that was taking him to Belfast in April 1930, calling the parts of the service he overheard "lugubrious," according

Griffiths see why naturalism was a dead end. A few months later, Griffiths spent a night with Lewis, shortly after Lewis had admitted that God was God.[21]

Griffiths, now a theist, had come to believe in God at about the same time as Lewis.[22] At this time Griffiths and Lewis were reading and recommending to one another some of the same works that they found helpful. In 1931, Lewis wrote to Arthur Greeves about having read William Law.[23] This is probably the time when he and Griffiths shared with one another Law's *A Serious Call to a Devout and Holy Life*.[24] He may also have read English clergyman and philosopher Joseph Butler's *The Analogy of Religion* around the same time, since Griffiths read it and probably shared it with Lewis.[25] Butler argued that a return to the orthodox Christian religion was superior to the impersonal teachings of deism. Shortly thereafter, Lewis read William R. Inge's *Personal Religion and the Life of Devotion*, another book that showed the superiority of personal religion over impersonal religiosity.

Griffiths states this about himself and Lewis:

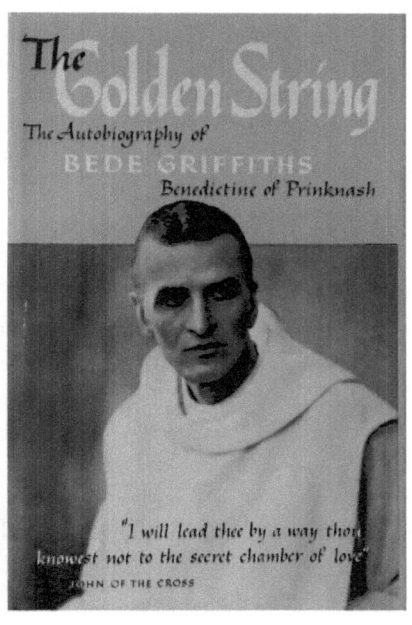

The Golden String
The Autobiography of Bede Griffiths

---

to unpublished diaries of Warren Lewis for the date April 13, 1930. Neither do Warren and his brother Jack attend church on the following Sunday, which is Easter Sunday, by which time Warren has arrived back in England. And yet, by June 1930, Warren has a conversation about the resurrection with the craftsmen who are making the stained-glass window that was to be dedicated to the Lewis parents and installed in their Belfast church, St. Mark's.

[21] C. S. Lewis, *Surprised by Joy*, 228. The visit took place during the week of June 9-13.

[22] C. S. Lewis, *Surprised by Joy*, 234f.

[23] *Collected Letters, I*, 961. May 18, 1931.

[24] Griffiths, *The Golden String*, 48.

[25] Griffiths, *The Golden String*, 48.

While I was reading philosophy I kept up a constant correspondence with him, and it was through him that my mind was gradually brought back to Christianity. During the following years [i.e., after Griffiths had graduated in 1929] we pursued the study of Christianity together, and first one of us and then the other would make the discovery of some masterpiece of Christian thought which we had not known before. I remember in particular how the discovery of William Law's *Serious Call* and Butler's *Analogy of Religion* excited us both. An unseen hand seemed to be leading us both to the same goal.[26]

Lewis respected mystical writers. The seventeenth-century mystic Jacob Boehme was one of them, and his book, *The Signature of All Things*, impressed him late in his spiritual journey. This book, Lewis writes, gave him "the biggest shaking up" since *Phantastes*. He had read Dean Inge, especially his essay "Institutionalism and Mysticism," Henry More's Defense of the Cabbala, a Jewish mystical work, and mystics Julian of Norwich, Teresa of Avila, and Walter Hilton.[27] Griffiths had a similar appreciation for mysticism and this undoubtedly influenced Lewis in the books he recommended and the conversations they shared, especially during those last months before Lewis became a Christian. Griffiths once wrote about Lewis, "There is no doubt that he had a profound kind of mystical intuition."[28]

As best we can tell, Griffiths became a Christian in March 1931 and Lewis in July of that same year.

ALAN RICHARD GRIFFITHS

Alan Richard Griffiths was born to Walter and Lilian Griffiths in Surrey, England, on December 17, 1906.[29] The family moved to the Isle of Wight in the English Channel when Alan was fourteen

---

[26] Griffiths, *The Golden String*, 48.

[27] An English Christian mystic who lived during the fourteenth century, best known for *The Scale of Perfection*.

[28] Alan Bede Griffiths, "The Adventure of Faith," *C. S. Lewis at the Breakfast Table and Other Reminiscences*, New York: Harcourt Brace & Company, 1992, 18.

[29] Shirley du Boulay, "Griffiths, Alan Richard [Bede Griffiths] (1906-1993)," *Oxford Dictionary of National Biography*, Oxford University Press, May 2007. Much of the biographical portion of this chapter comes from this article in the *Dictionary of National Biography*.

years old.[30] He was educated at Christ's Hospital,[31] Horsham, Sussex, the same school attended by F. C. Bryan, whose education is briefly described elsewhere in this book. After winning a scholarship to Magdalen College, he began his studies in the Michaelmas Term of 1925.[32] He took Honour Moderations and then, in 1927, read English Literature[33] with C. S. Lewis as his tutor.

Griffiths completed his degree in 1929 with second-class honors and left Oxford that summer.[34] In April 1930, he joined two friends—Hugh Waterman and Martyn Skinner—to purchase a cottage in the Cotswold village of Eastington, where they tried to live simply. They grew their own vegetables, milked cows, and used nothing from modern industry or factories. They lived off the land as much as possible.[35] While in the Cotswolds, Griffiths read the Bible extensively for the first time, an experience that changed his life. He became a Christian in 1931, the same year that Lewis did.[36]

Although he grew up in an Anglican family, his return to the Christian faith also included a switch to Roman Catholicism under the influence of John Henry Newman's *Essay on the Development of Christian Doctrine*.[37] In November 1931, he stayed at Prinknash Abbey, a Benedictine monastery about forty miles west of Oxford. He was received into the Roman Catholic Church at the abbey that Christmas Eve.[38]

---

[30] Walter Hooper, *C. S. Lewis: A Companion & Guide*, New York: HarperCollins, 1996, 670.

[31] Christ's Hospital was a school for those who came from poor families.

[32] On October 10.

[33] Bede Griffiths, *The Golden String*, Springfield, IL: Templegate Publishers, 1954, 30. He later writes that he "was a pupil of C. S. Lewis for two years...." Bede Griffiths, "Forty Years' Perspective," We Remember C. S. Lewis: Essays & Memoirs, David Graham, ed., Nashville: Broadman & Holman, 2001, 33.

[34] Alan Bede Griffiths, "The Adventure of Faith," *C. S. Lewis at the Breakfast Table and Other Reminiscences*, New York: Harcourt Brace & Company, 1992, 15.

[35] *Collected Letters, I*, 908.

[36] Griffiths, *The Golden String*, 92: the experiment in country life "lasted for less than a year," and near the end of that year he became a Christian. If they started in April 1930, they finished with the experiment at least by March. He probably became a Christian in March.

[37] Walter Hooper, *Companion & Guide*, 671.

[38] Walter Hooper, *Companion & Guide*, 671.

No Ordinary People

At Prinknash, Abbey Griffiths was made a postulant[39] one month later, and he then entered the novitiate as a Benedictine monk.[40] He took the name Bede, after the English monk, St. Bede "The Venerable" (672-735 A.D.).[41] On December 21, 1934, Griffiths became a full-fledged Benedictine monk at Prinknash Priory. Lewis attended the ceremony and spent the afternoon with him.[42] Griffiths took his solemn vows three years later,[43] and he was ordained a priest at Prinknash in 1940.[44]

After serving at two monasteries in the United Kingdom—in Farnborough beginning in 1947 and in Scotland at Pluscarden Abbey beginning in 1951—Griffiths moved to India with Father Benedict Alapatt in 1955. While at Farnborough he had begun to study Eastern thought, convinced that the church needed to understand Eastern spirituality to reach the Asian mind. When Griffiths left for India, he traveled to Bangalore, India, to "find the other half of my soul."[45]

Griffiths later left Bangalore to join a Syriac Rite monastery in the province of Kerala. While in Kerala, Griffiths wrote *Christian Ashram: Essays towards a Christian-Hindu Dialogue*,[46] a book that Lewis read in pre-publication form. The book explains how Indian Catholicism might develop in the future. In 1968 he moved again, this time to Tamil Nadu in south India. Griffiths studied Hindu thought, relating it to Christian theology, particularly as he pursued the contemplative tradition of both Christianity and Hinduism during the last four decades of his life. He wrote several books on Hindu-Christian dialogue, including *The Marriage of East and West*. He died on May 13, 1993.

---

[39] A candidate seeking admission into a religious order.

[40] On December 29, 1932.

[41] *Clive Staples Lewis*, 90. See also Alan Griffiths, "The Adventure of Faith," in James Como, *C. S. Lewis at the Breakfast Table*, 1992, 11, 18f.

[42] *Clive Staples Lewis*, 113. *The Golden String*, 140.

[43] On Dec. 21, 1937.

[44] On March 9, 1940. *The Golden String*, 168.

[45] Shirley du Boulay, "Griffiths, Alan Richard [Bede Griffiths] (1906-1993)," *Oxford Dictionary of National Biography*, Oxford University Press, May 2007. She cites Griffiths in his book, *Marriage of East and West*, 1-2

[46] The book was published in 1966 in India, and in 1967 it was published in the United States as *Christian in India*.

Disagreements

Over the three decades after they became Christians, Griffiths and Lewis wrote letters to one another about four dozen times and visited one another numerous other times. Having made the trek to Roman Catholicism,[47] Griffiths wanted Lewis to take that same route. Griffiths once claimed, "I doubt whether I was really anxious to convert him to Catholicism any more than I had wanted to convert him to Christianity."[48] In truth, however, he really was very anxious for Lewis to adopt Catholicism, and Lewis himself thought Griffiths anxious to convert him.

Lewis did not want to dispute over subjects about which he knew very little. On the other hand, Lewis was willing to debate those topics he knew, such as English literature, the Classics, and, for a time, philosophy.

The decision to stop the religious debate began with an Easter walking tour near Eastbourne. Owen Barfield, Cecil Harwood, and Sir Eric Beckett, a legal scholar of All Souls College, joined Griffiths and Lewis on that walk. Lewis wrote to his brother Warren, then serving in Shanghai, that Griffiths "engaged Barfield in a ... conversation of such appalling severity and egotism that it included the speaker's life history and a statement that most of us were infallibly damned."[49] That night, Griffiths was "quite intolerable" after dinner, like "a Calvinist Jesuit with strong leanings to the doctrine that the elect cannot sin."[50] Lewis no doubt felt responsible for inflicting Griffiths on Barfield.

The next letter from Lewis to Griffiths came two years later, where he thanks Griffiths for his "most welcome letter."[51] In that letter, Lewis especially addresses the differences between Anglicanism and Catholicism. Then he writes, "And while I am on the subject, I had better say once and for all that I do not intend to discuss with you in future, if I can help it, any of the questions at issue between our respective churches."[52]

---

[47] He had previously belonged to the Church of England.

[48] *The Golden String*, 19.

[49] On April 8, 1932. *Collected Letters, II*, 72.

[50] *Collected Letters, II*, 73. This is the same letter as in the previous footnote.

[51] *Collected Letters, II*, 133. The date of the letter is April 3, 1934.

[52] *Collected Letters, II*, 135. The date is April 4, 1934, and the letter also included a discussion of Pantheism, Neo-scholasticism, the virtuous pagan, and common ground between Christians of different persuasion.

Griffiths did not relent. Lewis had recently visited Griffiths at Prinknash Priory in Gloucester when Griffiths became a full-fledged Benedictine monk. During that visit differences had probably arisen again, and Griffiths later apologized. Lewis writes, "There was nothing to apologize for. My friendship with you began in disagreement and matured in argument and is beyond the reach of any dangers of that kind."[53] He also states, "… you must argue to the truth of your position, not from it. … But I still think it more profitable to adhere to our former agreement and to keep off the question."[54] While Lewis enjoyed debate, he did not want to debate denominationalism.

Again, two years later, Jack wrote to Griffiths about wanting to see Griffiths' review of *The Pilgrim's Regress*, fearing that his use of the term "Mother Kirk" might mislead Griffiths to think Lewis was more catholic than Anglican.[55] A month later, Lewis writes to Griffiths about the theological differences between them. In exasperation, he states,

> One of the most important differences between us is our estimate of the importance of the differences. You, in your charity, are anxious to convert me: but I am not in the least anxious to convert you. You think my specifically Protestant beliefs a tissue of damnable errors: I think your specifically Catholic beliefs a mass of comparatively harmless human tradition which may be fatal to certain souls under special conditions, but which I think suitable for you. I therefore feel no duty to attack you: and I certainly feel no inclination to add to my other works an epistolary controversy with one of the toughest dialecticians of my acquaintance, to which he can devote as much time and reading as he likes and I can devote very little. As well—who wants to debate with a man who begins by saying that no argument can possibly move him? Talk sense, man! With other Catholics I find no difficulty in deriving much edification from religious talk on the common ground: but you refuse to show any interest except in differences.[56]

Lewis had many friendly conversations with Tolkien and Havard, both Catholics, but with Griffiths it was different. Griffiths writes, "The result was that we agreed not to discuss our differences any more

---

[53] *Collected Letters, II*, 150. The date is Dec. 26, 1934.
[54] *Collected Letters, II*, 150.
[55] *Collected Letters, II*, 176. The date is January 8, 1936.
[56] *Collected Letters, II*, 178f. The date is February 20, 1936.

...."[57] While the end of such discussion undoubtedly disappointed him, Griffiths had probably been the cause.

Even then, however, Griffiths returned to the topic from time to time. In 1937, humor failed to dissuade Griffiths from the Anglican-Catholic debate. Lewis writes, "I received your statement that you do not think I am acting 'in bad faith' with some puzzlement: as if, in a conversation that had no apparent connection with money, you suddenly remarked 'I am not saying you are bribed.' One is of course glad to be acquitted: but quite in the dark as to how one came to be on trial."[58]

The next spring, Lewis wrote Griffiths about their different positions on reunion between Anglicanism and Catholicism. Lewis had read two articles about Griffiths' conversion, recently published in the Catholic periodical *Pax*.[59] Lewis concludes his letter with these words,

> I feel that whenever two members of different communions succeed in sharing the spiritual life so far as they can now share it, and are thus forced to regard each other as Christians, they are really helping on reunion by producing the conditions without which official reunion would be quite barren. I feel sure that this is the layman's chief contribution to the task.[60]

Lewis wrote in a cordial manner, and the discussion on reunion may have been Griffiths' attempt to approach the topic in two different ways—first, by writing about his own experience and, secondly, by writing on a denominational level rather than a personal level, so that Lewis didn't feel hunted.

Later that year, Lewis wrote quite bluntly, "On reunion I have no contribution to make: it is a matter quite above my sphere."[61] The following May, Lewis wrote to Griffiths, stating once again that he had no contribution to make on Christian reunion.[62] More than a dozen years later, Lewis's letter to Griffiths included this indication that Griffiths had raised the denominational question again: "I am no nearer to your Church than I was but don't feel v. inclined to reopen a

---

[57] Alan Bede Griffiths, "The Adventure of Faith," *C. S. Lewis at the Breakfast Table and Other Reminiscences*, New York: Harcourt Brace & Company, 1992, 25.

[58] *Collected Letters*, II, 217. The date is June 27, 1937.

[59] *Collected Letters*, II, 226. The date is April 29, 1938.

[60] *Collected Letters*, II, 226.

[61] *Collected Letters*, II, 234. The date is Oct. 5, 1938.

[62] *Collected Letters*, II, 256. The date is May 8, 1939.

discussion. I think it only widens & sharpens differences."[63] Griffiths couldn't let it go, but Lewis refused to be drawn in.

A Friendship Deepens

Once Griffiths accepted Lewis's unwillingness to discuss religious differences, the friendship deepened. Unwilling to carry a grudge, Lewis continued the correspondence for decades and occasionally met Griffiths face-to-face until Griffiths moved to India in 1955. Even then they continued their correspondence.

Their later letters discussed books they were reading or writing, world events, poetry, art, mysticism, natural law, the place of philosophy, prayer, and many other topics. Favorite authors that Lewis wrote about were Leo Tolstoy,[64] Charles Dickens,[65] Jane Austen, Sir Walter Scott, Thomas Merton, Blaise Pascal, and others. Lewis's view of the atonement, that the theory of how the atonement works matters much less than the fact of the atonement, i.e., that Christ by His death has forgiven us our sins,[66] also appears in these letters. He covered this topic in *Mere Christianity*, and, not coincidentally, Griffiths was one of the four clergy to whom Lewis sent his talks in Book II for critique.[67]

In 1934, Lewis wrote to Griffiths in response to his "most welcome letter." Lewis states of Pantheism, "our positions about Pantheism are exactly the same: for we both, in places, traveled the same road to Christianity, and the result of the arrival is certainly not any ingratitude or contempt to the various signposts or hostelries that helped on the journey."[68]

Lewis and Griffiths frequently wrote about Hinduism and Christianity, a topic of great interest to Griffiths and some interest to Lewis. Lewis stated his position on Hinduism, i.e., that the type of union Hindus were seeking with God was the opposite of what

---

[63] *Collected Letters, III*, 112. The date is April 23, 1951.

[64] On October 13, 1942, Lewis wrote to Griffiths, stating that *War & Peace* was the best novel, one he had read three times.

[65] On January 23, 1954, Lewis wrote to Griffiths about Charles Dickens being a great author on mere affection, and Sir Walter Scott having a civilized mind and a civilized heart with nobility and generosity flowing from him. He considered *Bleak House* to be Dickens' best book "for its sheer prodigality of invention." *Collected Letters, III*, 522f.

[66] See *Mere Christianity*, Book II, Chapter 4, "The Perfect Penitent," 53-56.

[67] *Mere Christianity*, II. See also *Collected Letters, II*, 502.

[68] *Collected Letters, II*, 133. April 4, 1934.

God intended. Lewis remarks that Griffiths was the one who once claimed that the choice was between Hinduism and Christianity,[69] a viewpoint that made its way into Lewis's *Mere Christianity*.[70] Lewis thanked Griffiths for the book, *Christ and India*, which Griffiths had sent him, and commented that the problem of Hinduism was India's hospitality to all gods, able to take any shape and retain none,[71] which was a far more open position on various gods that nearly any other religion was willing to take.

As Lewis grew older, he shared some of his most personal concerns with Griffiths. His last six letters to Griffiths mention his wife Joy as well as his own health. In late 1957, Lewis wrote about the new element of beauty, and one of tragedy, that had entered his life with his marriage, which had occurred just a few months earlier.[72] A couple of months later, he wrote to Griffiths about Joy's improvement in health, his love for her which started in *agape*, moving to *philia*,[73] then to pity, and then to *Eros*.[74] The cancer returned and Joy died in July 1960.

After Joy's death, Lewis wrote to Griffiths about grief as a process.[75] Later that month, he wrote about losing his wife, seeing the happiness of marriage more like lacking bread than lacking cake since he had grown accustomed to the happiness. Joy had become a central part of his life (like bread), not a pleasant add-on (like cake). He agreed with Bunyan in stating we must not mistake the decay of nature for the advance of grace, that is, the declining desire of our sexual nature is not necessarily the result of our growth in grace.[76] Eight months

---

[69] *Collected Letters*, II, 225, Lewis's letter of April 29, 1938, and *Collected Letters*, II, 770, Lewis's letter of April 15, 1947. Lewis also wrote on September 27, 1948.

[70] See Chapter 1, "The Rival Conceptions of God," in *Mere Christianity*, Book II: "What Christians Believe," especially 36.

[71] *Collected Letters*, III, 1042.

[72] The letter was written on August 1. Lyle W. Dorsett, *And God Came In*, New York: Ballantine Books, 1983, 127. See also William Griffin, *Clive Staples Lewis*, 388.

[73] *Philia* is the Greek word for love in the sense of friendship, while *agape* is the Greek word for love in the sense of unconditional favor, often translated "charity," and *Eros* is the Greek word for love in the sense of romantic love.

[74] *Collected Letters*, III, 884. On September 24, 1957.

[75] *Collected Letters*, III, 1300. On December 3, 1961.

[76] *Collected Letters*, III, 1303. The date of the letter is December 20, 1961.

later, Lewis wrote his last letter to Griffiths about his poor health and the results of a Hindu-Christian debate.[77] We don't have Griffiths' letter, but Griffiths seems to have written about the Hindu concept of an impersonal God, since Lewis states that Christians imply in the doctrine of the Trinity that God is not simply a Person (emphasis on the word a), but more than a Person.[78]

THE FUTURE STATE OF CHRISTIANITY

Lewis and Griffiths wrote about far more than denominational differences, Christian theology, and personal health. Both men had a deep passion for the salvation of souls and the future of the Christian church, since both men had lived some of their early years as non-Christians. They had experienced the Christian faith both from the outside and from the inside.

In 1936, Lewis had written to Griffiths about the current religious revival going on in the United Kingdom.[79] That religious revival included some examples in Lewis's life. For example, Lewis wrote to Griffiths about the fact that Mary Neylan, an ex-pupil of Lewis's, was close to becoming a Christian.[80] Lewis also hoped that Barfield might leave Anthroposophy for Christianity. That same year Lewis again wrote Griffiths about several topics, including the hints of Barfield moving away from Anthroposophy.[81] When Barfield was baptized in 1949, Lewis mentioned that baptism in a letter to Griffiths.[82] Lewis writes to Griffiths a few years later with encouragement, detailing the letters he gets from recent converts, his prayer list for the conversion of people to the Christian faith ("I have two lists of names in my prayers, those for whose conversion I pray, and those for whose conversion I give thanks. The little trickle of transferences from List A to List B is a great comfort."[83]), and the thought that they might be participating in a Christian Renaissance. These topics suggest the up side and the down side of this topic—there are hopeful signs for the future of Christianity, but one can't see the whole picture.

---

[77] *Collected Letters, III*, 1362. The date is August 4, 1962.
[78] See *Mere Christianity*, 162.
[79] *Collected Letters, II*, 176. The date is Jan. 8, 1936.
[80] *Collected Letters, II*, 392. On April 16, 1940.
[81] *Collected Letters, II*, 194f. The date is May 23, 1936.
[82] *Collected Letters, II*, 948.
[83] *Collected Letters, II*, 948. On June 27, 1949.

Twenty-One Friendships of C.S. Lewis

Lewis also wrote to Griffiths about how to reach atheists.[84] Lewis writes to Griffiths about his former pessimistic view of existence and Lewis's atheism. Lewis explains to Griffiths how he came to adopt atheism: "The early loss of my mother, great unhappiness at school, and the shadow of the last war and presently the experience of it, had given me a very pessimistic view of existence. My atheism was based on it...."[85] He notes his agreement with Lucretius on the universe's design, claiming that the argument from design is weak. He also writes that many Christians he knows are influenced by the argument from design.[86] The design argument cuts both ways, in favor of God because of the complex features of the world that point to purpose and complexity and against God because of the flaws in those very same features. He also argues that it is important to understand the Fall, which explains those flaws, and that we need a standard by which to judge certain things as bad. Both truths point to the existence of God.

A year before Griffith's death in 1993, John Swindells filmed ten hours of interviews, the basis of this account of his life and work

Griffiths' special concern was reaching the people of India with the Gospel, a concern that Lewis shared in his letters.[87] While Lewis agreed on this topic, he also saw some danger in underestimating the differences between Hinduism and Christianity. Lewis writes to Griffiths about the dangerous ground of Hinduism, especially whether or not Hinduism actually considers anything false.[88] The last

---

[84] *Collected Letters*, II, 746ff. The date is December 20, 1946.

[85] *C. S. Lewis: Collected Letters, II. Books, Broadcasts and War 1931-1949.* Edited by Walter Hooper. London: HarperCollinsPublishers, 2004, 747, written December 20, 1946.

[86] C. S. Lewis, "Is Theism Important?" *God in the Dock*, Edited by Walter Hooper, Grand Rapids: Eerdmans, 1970, 173.

[87] On January 16, 1954, Lewis writes the first of three letters this month to Griffiths about India, the type of missions to India, and India's ethos. *Collected Letters*, III, 408.

[88] On February 8, 1956. *Collected Letters*, III, 703f. Lewis also indicates that he had read Griffiths' *Christian Ashram: Essays towards a*

letter Lewis ever writes to Griffiths touches on a related topic, i.e., the results of a Hindu-Christian debate.'[89]

In Conclusion

Having journeyed nearly the same path to the Christian faith, the two men remained concerned about the spiritual journey of others, all around the world, especially Hindus, to the very end of their earthly pilgrimages. Over the years, Lewis supported Griffiths' adoption of Catholicism and monasticism, dialogued with Griffiths on numerous theological, literary, and philosophical topics, shared personal anguish in Joy Davidman's cancer, and touched on a wide range of additional topics. Though in agreement on many topics, they parted ways on denominationalism and other matters. Undoubtedly the common interests that Griffiths and Lewis had in spiritual matters, culminating in their conversion to the Christian faith sealed a relationship between these "chief companions" who had in common the most important thing of all—the center of their lives in their Christian faith.

Christian-Hindu Dialogue, a book dedicated to bridging the gap between Christian and Hindu religious beliefs. Likewise, on December 3, 1961, Lewis writes to Griffiths about the difficulty with Hinduism and high Paganism in the double task of reconciling and converting.

[89] *Collected Letters*, III, 1362. The date is August 4, 1962.

Twenty-One Friendships of C.S. Lewis

Hugo Dyson, 1971
©Douglas R. Gilbert

Chapter 2

HUGO DYSON
A Roaring Cataract of Nonsense

The Pub where the Inklings usually met
Author photo

Hugo Dyson was once so talkative, clever, and exuberant at an Inklings[1] meeting that C. S. Lewis described him as "a roaring cataract of nonsense."[2] The meeting included readings from Tolkien's manuscript of "the new *Hobbit*,"[3] a nativity play by Charles Williams, and part of Lewis's forthcoming book, *The Problem of Pain*, so there was much to discuss. Called "the most colorful of the Inklings,"[4]

---

[1] That collection of Oxford literary Christians who met weekly during the 1940s and 1950s to read works they were writing and discuss those writings and just about everything else.

[2] *Collected Letters, II*, 288. The meeting took place on November 9, 1939.

[3] The "new Hobbit" was later published as *The Lord of the Rings*.

[4] David Bratman, "Hugo Dyson: Inkling, Teacher, *Bon Vivant*," *Mythlore* Vol. 21, No. 4 (Winter 1977):19. The Inklings sometime in the 1930s and met until Lewis's death in 1963. The Thursday meetings were in the evenings to discuss things they were writing or enjoy one another's

Dyson brought intellect, humor, and personality to the group, and nearly everyone appreciated him, particularly on that night.

After their first meeting, Warren Lewis described Dyson more fully as "a man who gives the impression of being made of quicksilver: he pours himself into a room on a cataract of words and gestures, and you are caught up in the stream—but after the first plunge, it is exhilarating."[5] On another occasion, Warren wrote of Dyson: "Hugo in excellent and steadily improving spirits, which reached a climax in the Bird,[6] where I thought he was going to have hysterics."[7] Additionally, James Houston writes, "If you think that Lewis was witty and loquacious and always said the last word, you should have seen Dyson…. The wittiness, the intense enthusiasm of the man—he was alive to life in a remarkable way."[8]

H. V. D. Dyson

Hugo (or Henry Victor Dyson) Dyson was born in 1896 in Hove, Sussex and educated at Brighton College. After being trained at the military academy at Sandhurst, he served with the Royal West Kent Regiment in World War I,[9] fighting both in the Battle of the Somme and the Battle of Arras, the former a battle in which J. R. R. Tolkien fought and the latter a battle in which C. S. Lewis fought.[10]

After the war, Dyson studied English literature at Exeter College, earning his BA from that Oxford University college with distinction in 1921, a B.Litt. in 1924, and the MA in 1925. While an

---

conversation, and the last recorded one of these was October 20, 1949. The Tuesday meetings were during the day at local pubs primarily for conversation.

[5] *Brothers & Friends*, 97. The date is Feb. 18, 1933. This is Dyson's first appearance in Warren's diary and probably a description of their first meeting.

[6] The Eagle and Child pub, otherwise known as the Bird and the Baby, or just the Bird.

[7] *Brothers & Friends*, 210. The date is October 4, 1947.

[8] James Houston, "Reminiscences of the Oxford Lewis," in *We Remember C. S. Lewis: Essays & Memoirs*, David Graham, editor, Nashville: Broadman & Holman Publishers, 2001, 131.

[9] Humphrey Carpenter, *The Inklings: C. S. Lewis, J. R. R. Tolkien, Charles Williams and their friends*, London: HarperCollins*Publishers*, 1978, 256. For a thorough biography of Dyson, see David Bratman, "Hugo Dyson: Inkling, Teacher, Bon Vivant," *Mythlore* Volume 21, No. 4 (Winter 1977):19-34.

[10] Walter Hooper, *Collected Letters, I*, 988.

undergraduate, he attended the meeting of the Exeter College Essay Club in 1918 when Tolkien read "The Fall of Gondolin,"[11] a part of Tolkien's mythology later incorporated into *The Silmarillion*.

Dyson taught English at the University of Reading from 1924 until 1945, when he received a fellowship from Merton College, Oxford, to serve as Fellow and Tutor in English Literature. In 1925, he married Margaret Robinson, the daughter of a clergyman from Wantage. He retired in 1963 but returned as emeritus fellow in 1969, teaching the newly introduced modern literature class. Many of the writers he discussed in this course of study had been his friends.

Dyson's two major works dealt with the era of Alexander Pope. Lewis once stated in a letter to his brother that Dyson's "special period is the late 17th century" and that Dyson was very much intrigued by Warren Lewis's library, which centered in the same period.[12] Since Dyson was also a Shakespeare scholar, his interest has been described more broadly as comprising "the Elizabethans through the eighteenth century."[13]

Dyson wrote the introduction of his first book, *Poetry and Prose* (1933), a collection of the works of Alexander Pope. In addition to the works of Pope, Dyson added to this book his own notes to explain certain parts of Pope's writings.[14] Dyson's major work, *Augustans and Romantics, 1689-1830* (1940),[15] a survey of contemporary English literature from that same era, was written mostly by Dyson but with contributions by several other scholars.[16] Dyson also wrote "'The

---

[11] Diana Pavlac Glyer, *The Company They Keep: C. S. Lewis and J. R. R. Tolkien as Writers in Community*, Kent, Ohio: The Kent State University Press, 2007, 235. For the date, see *The Letters of J. R. R. Tolkien*, 163.

[12] Warren's interest, however, was French history rather than English literature. *C. S. Lewis: Collected Letters, II. Books, Broadcasts and War 1931-1949*. Edited by Walter Hooper. London: HarperCollinsPublishers, 2004, 16.

[13] Diana Pavlac Glyer, *The Company They Keep*, 235.

[14] Diana Pavlac Glyer, *The Company They Keep*, 235.

[15] Although the term is seldom used any more, the Augustans, named for the Roman poets of the age of Caesar Augustus, especially, Ovid, Horace, and Virgil, included Alexander Pope, Jonathan Swift, John Dryden, Richard Steele, William Law, Henry Fielding, Oliver Goldsmith, Daniel Defoe, Joseph Addison, Samuel Johnson, and others. The Augustans all wrote their style of literature, which featured bold political writing, personal expression in poetry, the novel, and especially satire, during the reigns of Queen Anne, King George I, and George II, i.e., approximately from 1700 to 1745.

[16] In his review of this book, one in a series of five volumes of

Old Cumberland Beggar' and the Wordsworthian Unities" in 1945, an interpretation of William Wordsworth that David Bratman calls "his finest essay."[17] In addition, his address to the British Academy in 1950, "The Emergence of Shakespeare's Tragedy," demonstrates his Shakespearean bona fides.[18] Although he did not publish a great deal,[19] his scholarship impressed Lewis, who stated in the Preface to *The Allegory of Love*, "The untiring intellect of Mr. H. Dyson of Reading, and the selfless use which he makes of it, are at once spur and bridle to all his friends."[20] One suspects that Dyson's talkativeness and love for the social moment distracted him from the quiet work of scholarly writing, resulting in fewer publications than one would expect from a distinguished literary career.

In a letter to his brother, Lewis describes Dyson:

> He is far from being a dilettante as anyone can be: a burly man, both in mind and body, with the stamp of the war on him, which begins to be a pleasing rarity, at any rate in civilian life. Lest anything should be lacking, he is a Christian and a lover of cats.[21]

If Dyson was not a dilettante, then he was very much the scholar. And if he loved cats, as did Lewis, he must have understood that aloofness that is characteristic of both cats and some people. But Dyson was anything but aloof.

As an expert on Shakespeare and due to his relaxed style, Dyson was asked during the early 1960s to host some televised lectures and plays about Shakespeare. This television experience resulted in a small part in the film *Darling* during 1965, where he played the role of Professor Walter Southgate, a major literary character who would die in the film. Dyson died in 1975 at the age of 79 and was buried in the

---

introductions to English literature, Charles Williams calls it "of the best throughout." He concludes that the book "is not only intelligent, it should be the cause of intelligence in others." Charles Williams, "Uncommon Fairness," *Time and Tide* 21 (December 28, 1940):1274-1275.

[17] David Bratman, "Hugo Dyson," 22.

[18] Diana Pavlac Glyer, *The Company They Keep*, 235.

[19] Dyson's review of Charles Williams' *The Figure of Beatrice: A Study in Dante* was published in *The Spectator*, September 3, 1943,

[20] C. S. Lewis, *The Allegory of Love: A Study in Medieval Tradition*. Oxford: Oxford University Press, 1936, viiif.

[21] *C. S. Lewis: Collected Letters, II. Books, Broadcasts and War 1931-1949*. Edited by Walter Hooper. London: HarperCollinsPublishers, 2004, 17. The date of the letter is Nov. 22, 1931.

cemetery of St. Cross Church, Oxford.[22]

C. S. LEWIS AND HUGO DYSON

Lewis and Dyson met for the first time in 1930 when Lewis entertained both Dyson and Nevill Coghill for dinner one July evening, and Lewis was determined to get to know him better. "My feeling was apparently reciprocated," he writes, "and I think we sat up so late with the feeling that heaven knew when we might meet again and the new friendship had to be freed past its youth and into maturity in a single evening."[23] That meeting was so successful that Dyson did not leave Magdalen College until 3 a.m.

New Building at Magdallen College where Lewis entertained friends
Author photo

Hugo Dyson is best known for a midnight conversation with Lewis on Saturday, September 19, 1931, until 4 a.m. the following morning. While Dyson probably was no "cataract of nonsense" that evening, he undoubtedly had a lot to say. Tolkien was with them, and the three men talked about metaphor and myth, truth, paganism and Christianity, dying and rising, love and friendship, and poetry and books from midnight until 3:00 a.m. when Tolkien left, with Lewis and Dyson continuing to talk while "strolling up and down

---

[22] *Collected Letters, I*, 990.
[23] *Collected Letters, I*, 918. The letter was written on July 29, 1930. The letter could be interpreted to mean that Lewis had met him once previously: "... having met him once I liked him so well that I determined to get to know him better." If that is the case, the first meeting would have been brief, and this second one much lengthier.

the cloister of New Building"[24] until 4:00 a.m. Undoubtedly Tolkien's concept of myth—that myth contains the stuff of both history and divinity[25]—was the centerpiece in that conversation, since Lewis himself identifies his understanding of myth in a Tolkienian way.

Dyson is the forgotten man in that exchange. One can easily imagine the garrulous Dyson at least as much engaged in the conversation as either Lewis or Tolkien, and, in fact, since Tolkien left an hour before the conversation was over, Dyson probably had a lot more to say than Tolkien. That night Dyson slept in the spare bed in Lewis's rooms at Magdalen College, so they had still more time for conversation. The very next day Dyson came to the Lewis home for lunch, and Maureen Moore, Mrs. Moore, and Lewis then drove Dyson to Reading, where Dyson taught. Dyson probably talked non-stop during the 26-mile trip. Nine days after that September 19 conversation, Lewis came to believe that Jesus was the Son of God.

While Tolkien is mentioned more often as an influence on Lewis's conversion, Hugo Dyson probably had a greater impact than Tolkien. After all, Dyson stayed the night, not Tolkien; Dyson came to lunch the following day, not Tolkien; Dyson was driven to Reading the next day, not Tolkien; and Dyson was simply more talkative than Tolkien. Lewis himself once wrote to Griffiths, listing Dyson first, "Dyson and Tolkien were the immediate human causes of my own conversion."[26] Then, in early November, Lewis traveled to Reading to spend time with Dyson. Lewis and Dyson were much closer at this time in life than Lewis and Tolkien, even though the latter two lived in Oxford while Dyson lived in Reading.

Three days after the midnight conversation, Lewis wrote to Arthur Greeves. He writes that he considers Greeves and Barfield friends of the first rank, but Dyson and Tolkien to be friends "of the

---

[24] The cloister is the porticoed walkway on the ground floor of New Building. *They Stand Together: The Letters of C. S. Lewis to Arthur Greeves.* Edited by Walter Hooper. New York: Macmillan Publishing Co., 1979, 421.

[25] See especially Tolkien's essay "On Fairy-Stories," in *Essays Presented to Charles Williams.* Grand Rapids: Eerdmans, 1947, 1966 (first paperback edition), especially pages 52 and 56.

[26] *Collected Letters, II,* 501.

2nd class,"[27] and he meets Dyson "four or five times a year."[28] Dyson is discussed far more in this letter than Tolkien, which also suggests the greater influence of Dyson on Lewis's conversion. His letter of October 1 to Arthur Greeves further confirms Dyson's role, since Lewis writes twice about "Dyson and Tolkien"[29] rather than "Tolkien and Dyson." He tells Arthur that his long talk with Dyson and Tolkien had a great deal to do with his coming to believe in Christ. His next letter explains:

> Now what Dyson and Tolkien showed me was this: that if I met the idea of sacrifice in a Pagan story I didn't mind it at all: again, that if I met the idea of a god sacrificing himself to himself ... I liked it very much and was mysteriously moved by it: again, that the idea of the dying and reviving god (Balder, Adonis, Bacchus) similarly moved me provided I met it anywhere except in the Gospels. The reason was that in Pagan stories I was prepared to feel the myth as profound and suggestive of meanings beyond my grasp even tho' I could not say in cold prose "what it meant."
>
> Now the story of Christ is simply a true myth: a myth working on us in the same way as the others, but with this tremendous difference that it really happened: and one must be content to accept it in the same way, remembering that it is God's myth where the others are men's myths...."[30]

---

[27] *They Stand Together: The Letters of C. S. Lewis to Arthur Greeves.* Edited by Walter Hooper. New York: Macmillan Publishing Co., 1979, 421. Lewis had known Arthur Greeves since his teen years, enjoying many of the same things, especially Norse mythology (see the chapter on Arthur Greeves), and Barfield was Lewis's intellectual equal more than anyone he knew, arguing with Lewis for years over many points of philosophy and profoundly influencing Lewis's thinking about the spiritual world and the nature of myth. For those reasons, Greeves and Barfield were friends of the first rank. Dyson and Tolkien shared Lewis's love of English literature as well as the profession of Fellows in English literature. The interests of Dyson and Tolkien were both professional and personal, while the interests of Greeves and Barfield had little to do with a common profession.

[28] *They Stand Together: The Letters of C. S. Lewis to Arthur Greeves.* Edited by Walter Hooper. New York: Macmillan Publishing Co., 1979, 421. In fact, they were good enough friends that Lewis later dedicated *Rehabilitations and Other Essays* to Dyson.

[29] *They Stand Together: The Letters of C. S. Lewis to Arthur Greeves.* Edited by Walter Hooper. New York: Macmillan Publishing Co., 1979, 425, 427.

[30] *They Stand Together: The Letters of C. S. Lewis to Arthur Greeves.*

We notice, once again, that Dyson is mentioned first, probably because of his greater influence on Lewis.

Social occasions with Lewis and Dyson were numerous and often hilarious. Warren writes that as they left the Mitre Tap one morning after consuming two glasses apiece of Bristol milk,[31] a boy fell on the cobblestone street outside the pub, leading Dyson to say, "Don't do that my boy: it hurts you and distresses us."[32] One month later, the Lewis brothers took the train to Reading and spent the evening and part of the next day with Dyson.[33] A few months later, the Lewis brothers went to dine at Exeter College as guests of Dyson and Tolkien.[34] Later that same year, Dyson dropped in at Magdalen, "burst" in, to use Warren's word, with "Dyson in his most exuberant mood—more 'boisterously at ease in Zion' to quote Tweedlepippin, than I had ever seen him."[35] Then, Dyson stated, when Warren offered him whiskey, "'It would indeed be unpardonable rudeness to your brother to leave any of this' and emptied the remains of the decanter into the glass."[36] On another occasion, Dyson turned up at College in the morning, so the Lewis brothers and Dyson spent a quarter of an hour in the buttery drinking beer, with Dyson again described as being "in his most exuberant mood."[37]

Dyson's participation with Lewis in the "Cave" confirms his fun-loving nature. The "Cave" refers to the Cave of Adullam, to which David fled for refuge against King Saul (1 Sam. 22:1). One such "Cave" took place in 1940, including Lewis, Tolkien, Leonard Rice-Oxley, Herbert Brett-Smith, and Dyson at The Golden Cross Inn in Oxford. In this context, the Cave was an event that Lewis described as a social diversion, a gathering of likeminded friends who are "anti-junto" (i.e., opposed to those who dominated the English School of Oxford University), with a smattering of the bawdy.[38]

Edited by Walter Hooper. New York: Macmillan Publishing Co., 1979, 427.

[31] A beer originating in the city of Bristol during the seventeenth century.

[32] *Brothers & Friends*, 98. The date is Feb. 18, 1933.

[33] *Brothers & Friends*, 99. The date is March 18, 1933.

[34] *Brothers & Friends*, 105f. The date is July 26, 1933.

[35] *Brothers & Friends*, 124. The date is November 17, 1933.

[36] *Brothers & Friends*, 125. The date is November 17, 1933.

[37] The unpublished portion of Warren Lewis's diary for March 10, 1934.

[38] *C. S. Lewis: Collected Letters, II. Books, Broadcasts and War 1931-*

Twenty-One Friendships of C.S. Lewis

In Oxford, Dyson lectured in summer classes in the University Extension Courses and did some examining, so he occasionally came into Oxford and would often visit the Lewis brothers while he was there. Dyson arrived one morning at Magdalen College, and Warren wrote, "I had an interrupted morning, but as the interrupter was Dyson, I really couldn't regret it. He was in—even for him—vivacious spirits and we had a longish chat while J,[39] the indefatigable, celebrated the last hour of term by taking a pupil. ... I was sorry not to see more of Dyson, but he was lunching with someone and had to go off ...."[40]

In 1934, C. S. Lewis and his brother Warren went to Exeter College, where Dyson was giving a dinner to celebrate the end of exams for his extension class. The Lewis brothers dined with Dyson, C. L. Wrenn, Nevill Coghill, Brett-Smith, and Tolkien. The evening was very high spirited.[41] A couple of days later, Dyson arrived at The Kilns to stay with the Lewises. Both the dinner and the weekend make it clear that Dyson and the Lewises were good friends.[42]

In the summer of 1938, Lewis met Charles Williams at Shirreff's, a favorite London restaurant of Williams at the bottom of Ludgate Hill. Dyson and Warren Lewis were also present. Lewis called it "a certain immortal lunch,"[43] showing the high regard he had for his three companions. Williams gave Lewis a copy of his recently released book, *He Came Down from Heaven*,[44] and the four of them spent two hours conversing in St. Paul's churchyard in an "almost Platonic discussion."[45] Lewis mentions the meeting almost in passing, but the fact that Dyson was among those present suggests that Dyson's presence was important to that meeting.

Numerous other social occasions, about which we know very little, also indicate the importance of Hugo Dyson to Lewis, and one

---

1949. Edited by Walter Hooper. London: HarperCollinsPublishers, 2004, 26 The date is March 13, 1940.

[39] Warren's abbreviation for Jack, his brother.

[40] The date is December 8, 1934. *Brothers & Friends*, 165f.

[41] The unpublished diary of Warren Lewis for July 19, 1934.

[42] The unpublished diary of Warren Lewis for July 24, 1934.

[43] *Image and Imagination: Essays and Reviews by C. S. Lewis*. Edited by Walter Hooper. Cambridge: Cambridge University Press, 2013, 115. The restaurant is no longer in existence. The date was July 4, 1938.

[44] Colin Duriez, *Tolkien and C. S. Lewis: The Gift of Friendship*, 86. See also *Image and Imagination*, 115.

[45] *Image and Imagination: Essays and Reviews by C. S. Lewis*. Edited by Walter Hooper. Cambridge: Cambridge University Press, 2013, 115.

can imagine much talk and tomfoolery on those occasions.

TEAM-TEACHING ON SHAKESPEARE

Lewis and Dyson teamed with other Oxford Fellows to offer three different series of lectures on English literature. The first series began in the Michaelmas Term of 1936, when Lewis, Nevill Coghill, Charles Leslie Wrenn (then Lecturer in English Language in Oxford[46]), and Dyson began a nine-week lecture series[47] on *Hamlet*. Lewis, Dyson, and Coghill did another nine-week lecture series, beginning in January 1937, this time adding Tolkien to their number. The topic, once again, was *Hamlet*.[48] A third lecture series, this time more broadly on Shakespeare, took place in the Michaelmas Term of 1938. For this series, in addition to Lewis and Dyson, lectures were also given by Lascelles Abercrombie, Miss Ethel Seaton, Nevill Coghill, Leonard Rice-Oxley, John Bryson, and Edmund Blunden.[49]

Although Shakespeare was not one of Lewis's strengths, he was by no means uninformed about the Bard. His only publication on Shakespeare, "*Hamlet*: The Prince or the Poem?" was read to the British Academy in 1942 as the Annual Shakespeare Lecture.[50] Another one of his papers, "The Renaissance and Shakespeare: Imaginary Influences,"[51] was delivered in Stratford one day before the start of World War II. Because the war began on September 1, the second address, probably the second half of this paper, was cancelled. Nevertheless, Lewis's limitations with Shakespeare led him to exclude Shakespeare's dramas, as indicated in the title of one of his major literary works, *English Literature in the Sixteenth Century Excluding Drama*.

---

[46] Walter Hooper, *C. S. Lewis: Companion & Guide*, New York: HarperCollins Publishers, 1996, 742.

[47] This record appears in the lecture lists from Cambridge University. Lewis probably did not lecture each week, since Coghill, Wrenn, and Dyson were also part of the lecture series. The other dates, all of them Fridays, were October 23, 30, November 6, 13, 20, 27, December 4 and 11.

[48] The dates were all Fridays again, January 22, 29, February 5, 12, 19, 26, March 5, 12, and 19, 1937.

[49] Lewis probably did not lecture on each of the dates, since this was apparently a lecture series to which each Don contributed part. The dates are October 14, 21, 28, November 4, 11, 18, 25, December 2, 9, and December 16, 1938.

[50] The essay was published that year in the *Proceedings of the British Academy*, Vol. XXVIII (*Selected Literary Essays*, xviii).

[51] This paper has not been preserved.

Dyson's expertise, however, provided greater depth in Shakespearian studies, as did the other Fellows who participated, allowing the other scholars to focus on some specific aspects of Shakespeare's works in these series of lectures.

Dyson among the Inklings

Dyson participated in an occasional meeting of the Inklings.[52] Since he taught in Reading until 1945, he was not local; but even after he moved to Oxford he did not always attend. When in attendance, he much preferred talking rather than listening to someone read a poem or article or book he was writing.[53] After all, as shown earlier, he did not write much. He was also known to dislike for Tolkien's *The Lord of the Rings*,[54] then in the process of being written. Christopher Tolkien described Dyson on one occasion as "lying on the couch, ... lolling and shouting and saying, 'Oh God, no more elves'."[55] Warren Lewis once wrote of an Inklings meeting that Dyson "came in just as we were starting on the '[new] Hobbit,' and as he now exercises a veto on it—most unfairly I think—we had to stop."[56] Warren also writes about Dyson, "He really can be very irritating at times."[57] As Philip and Carol Zaleski write, "He bristled at anything he disliked,"[58]

---

[52] We know of at least fourteen Inklings meetings attended by Dyson, although David Bratman counts ten meetings during the war that Dyson attended and eight meetings after the war. Given the hundreds of Inklings meeting that took place between 1933 and 1963, the dozen or so meetings that Dyson attended truly qualifies as "occasionally." Bratman, "Hugo Dyson," 27f.

[53] See Humphrey Carpenter, *The Inklings: C. S. Lewis, J. R. R. Tolkien, Charles Williams and their friends*, London: HarperCollins*Publishers*, 1978, 195.

[54] David Bratman, "Hugo Dyson: Inkling, Teacher, Bon Vivant," *Mythlore* Volume 21, No. 4 (Winter 1977): 28. Bratman notes, "If Hugo Dyson is remembered for one thing by Inklings readers, it's as the guy who didn't like *The Lord of the Rings*."

[55] Derek Bailey (Director) and Judi Dench (Narrator) (1992). *A Film Portrait of J. R. R. Tolkien* (Television documentary). Visual Corporation. Cited in Diana Glyer, *The Company They Keep*, 88.

[56] *Brothers & Friends*, 200. This was the Inklings meeting of April 24, 1947.

[57] *Brothers & Friends*, 218. The date is March 4, 1948.

[58] Philip & Carol Zaleski, *The Fellowship: The Literary Lives of the Inklings*, New York: Farrar, Straus and Giroux, 2015, 358.

adding the further comment, "His mind outran his manners."⁵⁹ At times Lewis tried to keep Dyson in check, more than once stating, "Shut up Hugo. Come on Tollers."⁶⁰ However, Dyson was not alone in his distaste for Tolkien's stories, and eventually Tolkien gave up reading them to the group altogether.

One of the most memorable Inklings meetings took place on March 11, 1948, which Warren Lewis described as "a red-letter Inkling."⁶¹ The Inklings met in the New Room, a private dining room in the old part of Magdalen College, and Lewis brought sherry and arranged dinner for the occasion. The main attraction was a ham that a Johns Hopkins University surgeon, Dr. Warfield Firor, had sent. Due to shortages of meat and other items in the years after the war, Firor frequently sent packages of food, especially full-sized hams, to Lewis, and Lewis often shared these packages with others since he was receiving regular gifts from several American admirers. In one letter, Lewis humorously called the good doctor "Firor-of-the-Hams, a sort of Fertility god."⁶²

On this occasion, Lewis had invited the Inklings to enjoy the ham with him. In addition to the ham, Lewis arranged for soup, fish, and a pate savory from the college kitchen. Tolkien and Dyson each contributed two bottles of Burgundy from Merton College, and David Cecil brought two bottles of port. The wine flowed freely that night, and one can imagine the boisterousness of the evening. Eight people were present: Lewis, Tolkien, Dyson, Warren Lewis, R. E. Havard (whose nickname, "Humphrey," was given by Dyson⁶³), Christopher

---

⁵⁹ Philip & Carol Zaleski, *The Fellowship: The Literary Lives of the Inklings*, New York: Farrar, Straus and Giroux, 2015, 358.

⁶⁰ Tollers was the nickname of J. R. R. Tolkien. Christopher Tolkien in *A Film Portrait of J.R.R. Tolkien*, 1996.

⁶¹ *Brothers & Friends*, 218.

⁶² *Collected Letters, II*, 909.

⁶³ Oral history interview excerpts with Dr. Robert E. Havard, July 26, 1984, OH/SR-14, The Marion E. Wade Center, Wheaton, Illinois. Used by permission. This oral history interview was done by Lyle W. Dorsett. Havard states, "There was a man—Dyson, Hugo Dyson from Reading who was referring to me and couldn't remember my name. And he said, 'Oh, you know, that's that Humphrey or something.' And the name for some reason took on and stuck and I was known to the Inklings as Humphrey from that time on. And still am by those who survived." Alan Jacobs states that Dyson forgot Havard's real name on one occasion and called him "Humphrey," and Havard remained Humphrey from that time on. Alan Jacobs, *The Narnian: The Life and Imagination of C. S. Lewis*, New York: HarperCollins, 2005, 195, note. Humphrey

Reuel Tolkien, David Cecil, and Colin Hardie. After dinner they went to Lewis's rooms for a raffle of an American dinner suit, won by Colin Hardie, who waived his claim in favor of Christopher Tolkien. The suit did not fit Hardie, but it fit Christopher. Each of the eight signed a thank you note to Dr. Firor,[64] including their current position along with their signature and stating that they had drunk to Firor's health. The memorable evening lasted until 1:00 a.m., and Lewis wrote Firor a thank you note the next day, including with his note the signatures from the previous night.

Other Inklings meetings included Dyson from time to time.[65] In one 1940 meeting, Dyson came to hear Adam Fox read his latest poem on Blenheim Park in winter. However, Lewis wrote to his brother, then serving in the war, that Dyson "was in his usual form and, on being told of Charles Williams' Milton lectures on 'the sage and serious doctrine of virginity,'" stated of Williams, "The fellow's becoming a common chastitute."[66]

Another Inklings meeting took place in Lewis's rooms at Magdalen. Tolkien notes that he attended "a full assembly" of the Inklings that evening. Lewis read excerpts from his book *The Great Divorce*, and Warren Lewis read from his forthcoming book on Louis XIV.[67] Dyson was in attendance, "rather tired-looking, but reasonably noisy."[68] In a later letter, since *The Great Divorce* was originally entitled

---

Carpenter says Dyson called Havard "Humphrey" either "in pure error of because it alliterated with his surname." Humphrey Carpenter, *The Inklings: C. S. Lewis, J. R. R. Tolkien, Charles Williams and their friends*, London: HarperCollins, 1997, 130.

[64] One can still see a copy of this note hanging on the wall of the Eagle and Child in Oxford. The original is fol. 86 of MS. Engl. Let. c. 220/1. It is also visible at https://www.facebook.com/divinitysta/photos/dr-judith-wolfe-and-two-st-marys-students-tom-miles-ma-3rd-year-and-greg-chilson/863965453708613/

[65] The certain, or at least likely, dates for his attendance include Feb. 29, 1940; March 14, 1940; August 2, 1940; May 25, 1944; October 18, 1945; August 8, 1946; April 24, 1947; September 25, 1947; February 24, 1948; March 11, 1948; March 18, 1948; February 4, 1949; October 20, 1949; and January 30, 1951.

[66] *Collected Letters, II*, 360. The date is February 29, and in attendance were Lewis, Adam Fox, Dyson, and Tolkien.

[67] Warren Lewis, *The Splendid Century: Some Aspects of French Life in the Reign of Louis XIV.*

[68] *The Letters of J. R. R. Tolkien*, edited by Humphrey Carpenter, Boston: Houghton Mifflin Harcourt, 1995, 83. The letter is dated May 25, 1944.

Who Goes Home?, Tolkien humorously suggested that it should have been called *Hugo's Home*.[69]

Another Inklings meeting explains Dyson's talkativeness as well as a major reason why he seldom attended the Inklings meetings—he talked so much that he was delayed on numerous occasions. Dyson had invited Warren Lewis to dine with him at Merton College that evening. Warren wrote of Dyson,

> He was in high spirits when I met him, and his spirits rose steadily for the rest of the evening. I was more than ever struck with his amazing knowledge of Shakespeare; I don't suppose there is a man in Oxford—with the possible exception of Onions—who can quote so happily, e.g., tonight, apropos of J: "O cursed spite that gave thee to the Moor": poor SPB's whole catastrophe epitomized in nine words![70]

After the dinner, because of the conversations Dyson engaged in, it took them forty minutes to get from Hall to the gate. Dyson and Warren Lewis then attended the Inklings meeting with Stanley Bennett, Lewis, Havard, Tolkien, and Gervase Mathew, but it was one that Warren did not enjoy, calling it "mere noise and buffoonery: though Hugo as improvisatore was very funny at times."[71]

In 1949, Dyson attended the last recorded Thursday meeting of the Inklings.[72] Warren notes that the Inklings enjoyed a ham supper in Lewis's rooms with Lewis, Dyson, and others. He includes two stories that are "too good to be 'lost in memory's flow.'"[73] He writes that Dyson "bellows uninterruptedly for about three minutes, and as he shows no sign of stopping, two guests at the bottom of the table begin a conversation: which being observed by Hugo, he raises his hand and shouts reproachfully—'Friends, friends, I feel it would be better if we kept the conversation general.'" Then, Warren writes, "He is to lecture this term on Henry V, and the other day in Merton was bombarding the History Tutor with questions about the period, finishing up with—'What I want is not facts, but ideas.' Gared,

---

[69] Ibid., 84. This letter is dated May 31, 1944.

[70] *Brothers & Friends*, 193. The Shakespearian reference from *Othello* to "the Moor" was a pun on C. S. Lewis's relationship with Mrs. Janie Moore. SPB stands for Smallpiggiebotham, Warren's nickname for his brother. The date is August 8, 1946.

[71] *Brothers & Friends*, 193.

[72] The exact date is October 20. The Tuesday meetings continued until Lewis's death.

[73] *Brothers & Friends*, 230.

intervening with his lisping drawl:—'An admirable summary of your disabilities, Dyson.'"[74]

WALKING TOURS AND DINNERS

In 1940, Lewis, Barfield, Dyson, Harwood, and Walter Field took a walking tour that began in Minehead, Somerset. Dyson and Field hit it off, but Field cornered Dyson with a story about an incident, leading Lewis later to write, "It was a novelty to hear Dyson reduced to comparative silence,"[75] a rarity for Dyson.

Dyson joined the Lewis brothers on walking tours and other sorts of trips more than once, but he showed his penchant for being a bit scatter-brained in 1946. Lewis invited his brother Warren and Dyson to travel with him to Liverpool, where Lewis would be participating in a BBC-radio program known as *Brains Trust*.[76] While Lewis participated in his *Brains Trust*, Warren Lewis and Dyson walked through parts of Liverpool, watching the ships, taking the ferry, visiting pubs, and reading. After losing track of Hugo several times on that trip, Lewis stated of Dyson that he "should always have a collar and lead when one travels with him."[77] During that same trip, Dyson sang and told stories, stating that "if I stopped I should become hysterical."[78] When they arrived at the Woodside Hotel in Liverpool, Hugo, "announced that we had blundered into a meeting of the Liverpool sabotage gang."[79]

Also in 1946, Lewis, Dyson, Derek Brewer and Tom Stock (the latter two undergraduates of Magdalen and pupils of Lewis), Philip Stibbe (an undergraduate at Merton College and pupil of Dyson), and Peter Bayley (an undergraduate of University College) dined together to celebrate the end of term. These six met and dined together once a term for three or four terms either at Magdalen College, Merton College, or in the upper room of the Roebuck Inn in Market Street.[80]

---

[74] *Brothers & Friends*, 230.

[75] *Collected Letters, II*, 382. The date of the letter is April 11, 1940.

[76] A BBC radio broadcast of a conversation on current topics with a narrator and several distinguished guests and experts on those topics.

[77] *Brothers & Friends*, 186. The date of the outbound trip is March 18, 1946.

[78] *Brothers & Friends*, 186.

[79] *Brothers & Friends*, 186.

[80] Derek Brewer, "The Tutor: A Portrait," in *C. S. Lewis at the Breakfast Table*, 58. See also Peter Bayley, "From Master to Colleague," in *C. S. Lewis at the Breakfast Table*, 79. The Roebuck Inn was a pub, or

No Ordinary People

These events involved Lewis and Dyson (and their pupils), but not Tolkien. Tolkien had small children at home, whereas Dyson and Lewis did not.

Dyson was also present when Lewis was given a farewell dinner prior to beginning his new position in Cambridge. The English faculty of Oxford University hosted Lewis at Merton College, and the evening included, in addition to Dyson and Lewis, Warren Lewis, J. R. R. Tolkien, Christopher Tolkien, John N. Bryson, David Cecil, F. P. Wilson, Nevill Coghill, J. A. W. Bennett, R. E. Havard, and an unnamed young man.[81] Dyson loved to gather with friends for food, libations, and talk.

The Final Farewells

After Lewis died on November 22, 1963, Walter Hooper arranged for an annual "Inklings Party" for Lewis's friends. The first such event seems to have occurred in 1966. On Friday evening, July 22, 1966, Hugo Dyson was among those who attended the event at Wadham College, along with Warren Lewis, Walter Hooper, J. R. R. Tolkien, Colin Hardie, Austin Farrer, R. E. Havard, Clyde Kilby, Owen Barfield, Roger Lancelyn Green,[82] Maurice Bowra, and Jean Wakeman. Several people chatted with Warren, most certainly Dyson among them, and spoke highly of both the *Letters*, which Warren had recently edited from his brother's correspondence, and Warren's memoir of his brother in that same volume.

While this Inklings Party appears to have been an annual event, the diary of Warren Lewis only records the events in 1966, 1968, 1969, and 1971. Warren describes these events in his diary with some horror, but Dyson undoubtedly enjoyed the social gatherings, the conversations, and the reminiscences of his deceased friend. Where we have records of who attended, Dyson always appears on the list.[83]

---

public house, in Oxford, named in 1610 after the arms of Jesus College.

[81] *Brothers & Friends*, 243. The date was December 9, 1954.

[82] Walter Hooper, " 'Warnie's Problem': An Introduction to a Letter from C. S. Lewis to Owen Barfield," *Journal of Inklings Studies*, Vol. 5, No. 1 (April 2015), 16. Barfield and Green paid for the event.

[83] In addition to the people listed above for the 1966 gathering, other attendees included Hugo's wife Margaret, George Sayer, Cecil Harwood, Colin Hardie, Pauline Baynes, Ruth Pitter, Gervase Mathew, Mary Neylan, Katharine Farrer, Roger Lancelyn Green's son and daughter, Leonard and Maureen Blake, the publisher Jock Gibb, Christopher Tolkien, Christopher Tolkien's wife Baillie, and Reginald R. Macan,

Twenty-One Friendships of C.S. Lewis

CONCLUSION

Hugo Dyson, the roaring cataract of nonsense, showed himself an impressive Shakespeare scholar, a loyal friend (ranking behind only Arthur Greeves and Owen Barfield), an occasional writer, a great humorist and storyteller, witty, an enjoyable if at times scatter-brained traveling companion, as well as a loud and voluminous waterfall of verbal foolishness. In truth, C. S. Lewis appreciated all those characteristics, even though he felt it necessary at times to keep Dyson in check. Above all, Dyson was an Inkling, a devout Christian, even more influential in Lewis's conversion to Christianity than Tolkien, and an at least occasional cataract of common sense.

---

former Master of University College.

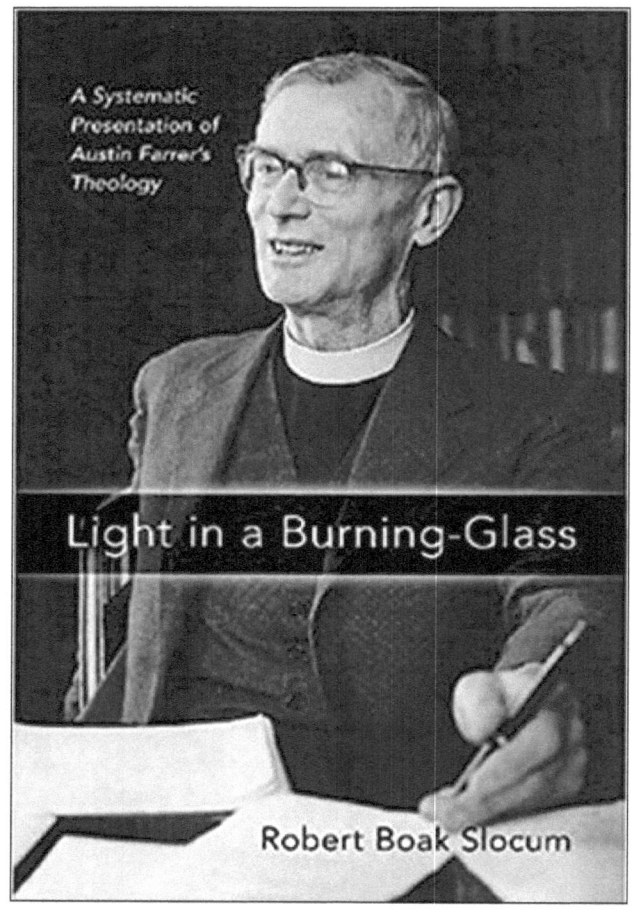

LIGHT IN A BURNING GLASS:
A Systematic Presentation of Austin Farrer's Theology
reprinted by Wipf and Stock in 2019

Chapter 3

AUSTIN FARRER
A Hawk Among Sparrows

"Austin Farrer was, by common consent, one of the most remarkable men of his generation. He possessed the qualities of originality, independence, imagination and intellectual force to a degree amounting to genius."[1] So stated Basil Mitchell, Oxford University philosopher and, after Lewis, the second president of the Oxford Socratic Club. Richard Harries, Bishop of Oxford, called Farrer "the greatest mind produced by the Church of England" in the twentieth century.[2] American philosopher Edward Henderson[3] wrote, "Austin Farrer was a philosopher and theologian of the highest order."[4] Gresham Professor of Divinity and Anglican priest Gordon Phillips described Farrer as "a scholar, a wit, a saint, a philosopher, and a man of prayer.... He was a hawk among sparrows."[5] I. M. Crombie wrote, "His especial genius lay in his ability to penetrate through the cloud of detail to the essential structure of a problem or the essential features of some doctrine."[6] Amidst all these superlatives, C. S. Lewis offered his own description—friend—perhaps the best compliment of all.

AUSTIN MARSDEN FARRER

Austin Marsden Farrer was born on October 1, 1904, in Hampstead, London, England, one of three children and the only son of Augustus John Daniel and Evangeline Farrer. Augustus Farrer was a Baptist minister and a lecturer in church history, the history of

---

[1] This quotation is from the book cover of Austin Farrer's *The Brink of Mystery*, London: SPCK, 1976.

[2] https://www.giffordlectures.org/lecturers/austin-marsden-farrer

[3] From Louisiana State University, co-author with Brian Hebblethwaite of *Divine Action: Studies Inspired by the Philosophical Theology of Austin Farrer*, London: T. & T. Clark, 1990.

[4] Philip Curtis, *A Hawk Among Sparrows: A Biography of Austin Farrer*, London: SPCK, 1985, 190.

[5] Philip Curtis, *A Hawk Among Sparrows*, 230f.

[6] I. M. Crombie, "Farrer, Austin Marsden (1904-1968)," rev. *Oxford Dictionary of National Biography*, Oxford University Press, 2004; online edition, May 2005.

religion, and elementary Hebrew at Regent's Park College, London. At home his father would read aloud books of the Victorian era, especially those written by Jane Austen and Sir Walter Scott, but, like Lewis, he would not read Thackeray.[7] Austin was educated at Acton Collegiate School and then St. Paul's School in London from 1917 to 1923,[8] where he eventually became the School Captain.[9] At St. Paul's, the school associated with Christopher Wren's St. Paul's Cathedral, he earned the top scholarship to Balliol College, Oxford.[10]

After the family attended a succession of Baptist churches during his early years, Austin left the Baptist church and was confirmed in the Anglican Church in 1924 during his years at Balliol.[11] In attendance at his confirmation was Thomas E. Bleiben, later the Vicar at Holy Trinity, Headington Quarry, the home church of C. S. Lewis.[12] One of the reasons for this denominational change appears in a letter from Austin Farrer's father to his son, where he states, "With you I protest against the view that the Eucharist is a mere bare commemoration—but there is no priestly miracle. Christ promises us a special grace if we take the sacrament according to His word."[13]

As Lewis did earlier in the century, Farrer earned First Class Honors in three different sets of exams, the first two as an Oxford undergraduate. After a first in both Honour Moderations[14] in 1925—which helped him win an S. S. Clarke Traveling Exhibition[15]—

---

[7] Philip Curtis, *A Hawk Among Sparrows*, 7. On Lewis, for example, he wrote to Arthur Greeves on February 20, 1917, "Why is it I can't appreciate Thackeray?" *Collected Letters*, I, 281. In reality, however, Lewis was both appreciative and critical of Thackeray: "No doubt Thackeray was the genius: but Trollope wrote the better books. All the old things I objected to in Thackeray I object to still." *Collected Letters*, II, 82.

[8] Philip Curtis, *A Hawk Among Sparrows*, 4.

[9] This was the top student leadership position. Philip Curtis, *A Hawk Among Sparrows*, 14.

[10] St. Paul's School had been founded in 1509 by Reformer John Colet, Dean of St. Paul's Cathedral. Philip Curtis, *A Hawk Among Sparrows*, 9, 12.

[11] Philip Curtis, *A Hawk Among Sparrows*, 24.

[12] Philip Curtis, *A Hawk Among Sparrows*, 24. Bleiben was Vicar of Holy Trinity from 1936 to 1947.

[13] Philip Curtis, *A Hawk Among Sparrows*, 22f.

[14] Greek and Latin language and literature.

[15] A scholarship and a visit to Greece. Philip Curtis, *A Hawk Among Sparrows*, 25.

and in Greats in 1927,[16] Farrer enrolled at Cuddesdon Theological College,[17] earning his third First, this time in Theology, in 1928.

By 1927, when he began his studies at Cuddesdon, he had adopted an Anglo-Catholic outlook on church life, while struggling to understand what God was like and how God was active in the world.[18] In 1928, Farrer was ordained a deacon, and in 1929[19] he was ordained a priest at All Saints' Anglican Church in Dewsbury, West Yorkshire, which has a tradition that Robin Hood died in Dewsbury and was buried in nearby Kirklees Park.[20] He served in Dewsbury from 1928 to 1931, the first year of those three years as a curate.[21] While at Dewsbury, Farrer continued to read theology, including Emil Brunner's *The Mediator*.[22] Farrer accepted a good deal of Brunner's position, leading him to reject some of the beliefs of Idealism[23] and restate his understanding of the relation between God and the created world. This set the stage for Farrer's later book, *Finite and Infinite*.[24]

Farrer returned to Oxford in 1931 to serve St. Edmund Hall as chaplain and tutor in philosophy and theology. Besides leading worship, he developed relationships with students through walks in the Parks or along the Cherwell River, through teas and lunches, and in tutorials. "Conversation flowed easily about everything under the sun," writes one of his former students, "but rarely, if ever, did one finish the walk without receiving from him some illuminating yet

---

[16] Ancient history and classical philosophy.

[17] A theological college in the Church of England is the equivalent of a seminary in the U.S. There he would earn a graduate degree.

[18] Philip Curtis, *A Hawk Among Sparrows*, 27, 34f.

[19] On Dec. 22, 1929. Philip Curtis, *A Hawk Among Sparrows*, 75.

[20] Philip Curtis, *A Hawk Among Sparrows*, 58.

[21] A curate is an Anglican clergyman serving a curacy in the first placement after ordination, as an assistant to a priest. The implication is that this priest is still in training, a position that usually, but not always, lasts for four years. In Farrer's case, clearly, the curacy lasted for just one year.

[22] Philip Curtis, *A Hawk Among Sparrows*, 79. Later Farrer expressed his disagreement with Rudolf Bultmann in an essay he wrote for *Kerygma and Myth*, London: SPCK Press, 1953. The essay was entitled "An English Appreciation." Philip Curtis, *A Hawk Among Sparrows*, 141.

[23] Idealism is a philosophy which states that matter is in some sense unreal, that everything we know is in the mind of the knower and, therefore, mental. Idealism was a prominent philosophy held by many philosophers in the teens and 1920s. C. E. M. Joad, *Great Philosophies of the World*, London: Thomas Nelson & Sons Ltd, 1937, 75f.

[24] Philip Curtis, *A Hawk Among Sparrows*, 80.

seemingly casual comment, beginning a train of thought which in retrospect led to a growth in the understanding of life."[25] He also visited students in the hospital and worked with the Student Christian Movement. He interviewed undergraduates for their degrees and conducted examinations.

During his years at St. Edmund Hall, Farrer twice traveled to the European continent to further his understanding of philosophy and theology, attending lectures by both Karl Barth (with whom he was not impressed) in Bonn, Germany, and Emil Brunner in Zurich, Switzerland. During those St. Edmund years he met Katharine Newton, who later became his wife.[26] They apparently became engaged in 1933 while Katharine was studying Greats at Oxford University.[27]

In 1935, Dr. Herbert Blakiston, President of Trinity College, interviewed Farrer to succeed Chaplain Kenneth Kirk. About Blakiston, Farrer once said that, when bearded, Blakiston "was a very tame lion,"[28] words

Austin Farrer during the St. Edmund years.
By permission of the Principal and Fellows of St Edmund Hall

---

[25] Philip Curtis, *A Hawk Among Sparrows*, 84.

[26] Philip Curtis, *A Hawk Among Sparrows*, 96. Katharine was born to Frederic Henry Joseph and Edith Grace Newton on September 27, 1911 in Chippenham, Wiltshire, England. *Contemporary Authors*, Volume 85, "Seeking the Secret Place," 1-43, Austin Farrer, 1957-2000, 43 The Marion E. Wade Center, Wheaton, Illinois.

[27] Philip Curtis, *A Hawk Among Sparrows*, 107.

[28] Philip Curtis, *A Hawk Among Sparrows*, 114. C. S. Lewis is famous for saying of Aslan, the lion of Narnia, that he was not a "tame lion." See, for example, *The Lion, the Witch and the Wardrobe*. New York: Macmillan Publishing Company, 1950, 180. French writer Jeanne Leroy wrote a book, published in 1893, entitled *Le Roman d'Arlette*, which was reviewed in *The Saturday Review* on Jan. 20, 1894. The reviewer states that Arlette,

similar to those used by C. S. Lewis about Aslan. Beginning with the Michaelmas Term of 1935, Farrer became Chaplain and Fellow of Trinity, a position he held for the next two-and-a-half decades.[29] Farrer led chapel worship, celebrated the Lord's Supper at Sunday worship, packed the chapel with worshippers at Sunday Evensong, preached, interacted with students in numerous settings, participated in Trinity's mission in the East End of London, and carried out many other activities. He had seven or eight Bible study groups each week and several discussion groups. He also examined students in divinity.[30] From 1937 to 1942, he held the Speaker's Lectureship, for which he developed his thoughts on both the book of Revelation and the structure of Mark's Gospel.[31]

Many years later, Lewis wrote about the nature of Farrer's priesthood at Trinity College, "No author is so free from labored *bonhomie*, emotional rhetoric, or conventional pietisms of phrase. He writes everywhere as one who both has authority and is under authority. This is what constitutes his priestliness, and this dictates everything else in the book."[32] Farrer himself stated, "To be a loyal churchman is hobbyism or prejudice unless it is the way to be a loyal Christian—to see through the Church to Christ as a man sees through the telescope to the stars."[33] Stephen Willink, college organist in the 1950s concurred, "We laid at his feet our doubts and enthusiasms and never doubted that even the most intractable personal problems once submitted to his scrutiny, would be robbed of its terrors."[34] These comments demonstrate a pastoral concern for the spiritual well-being of his students and the effectiveness of his ministry.

In New Testament circles, Farrer was known for his work on the Gospel of Mark, especially the attempt to explain the similarities between the three synoptic Gospels—Matthew, Mark, and Luke. Farrer believed that Mark was written first, then Matthew, who used Mark as a source, while Luke used both Mark and Matthew to write

---

the chief character, has a tame lion who plays with her. Perhaps Isaiah's account of the lion lying down with the lamb also influenced Lewis. See Isa. 11:6-9.

[29] Philip Curtis, *A Hawk Among Sparrows*, 106.

[30] Philip Curtis, *A Hawk Among Sparrows*, 113, 127.

[31] Philip Curtis, *A Hawk Among Sparrows*, 119f.

[32] Austin Farrer, *A Faith of Our Own*, Preface by C. S. Lewis. Cleveland: The World Publishing Company, 1960, 8.

[33] *A Faith of Our Own*, 24.

[34] Philip Curtis, *A Hawk Among Sparrows*, 129f.

his Gospel.[35] At the death of Oliver C. Quick, the Regius Professorship of Divinity became vacant, and Farrer's name was widely rumored as Quick's successor. His challenge to New Testament conventional thinking, however, brought a negative reaction from scholars both in the US and in the UK. As a result, Leonard Hodgson was chosen. Farrer also thought that the Gospel writers deliberately chose events in the life of Jesus that echoed events from the lives of Moses, Joseph, Elijah, and other Old Testament figures,[36] a view that, Farrer felt, explained the sequence of events in each of the Gospels.

On April 15, 1937, Farrer married Katharine Newton, the daughter of clergyman F. H. J. Newton, Vicar of Rickmansworth, at St. Mary's Church, Ashwell, Hertfordshire. Kenneth Kirk, whom Farrer had succeeded as Chaplain and Fellow of Trinity College, officiated at the wedding. Philip Curtis describes Katharine as "talented and high strung," "never physically robust," and having "the fragile beauty of porcelain."[37] Katharine graduated in Honour Moderations and Greats from St. Anne's College, Oxford in 1933,[38] and was later known as a mystery novelist—the author of *The Missing Link* (1952), *The Cretan Counterfeit* (1954), and *Gownsman's Gallows* (1957), all of them set in Oxford and featuring Inspector Richard Ringwood of Scotland Yard. Ringwood was modeled after Katharine's husband Austin. Katharine and Austin had one child, a daughter Caroline.

During his years at Trinity, Austin Farrer gave two series of lectures which later turned into books. The Bampton Lectures, which he gave in 1948, are annual lectures[39] on Christian theological topics, given at St. Mary the Virgin, the university church of Oxford University, since 1780. These lectures were published as *The Glass of Vision: The Making of St. John's Apocalypse*, which expressed Farrer's belief that religious truth can be communicated only through images.[40]

---

[35] https://www.giffordlectures.org/lecturers/austin-marsden-farrer

[36] Philip Curtis, *A Hawk Among Sparrows*, 119ff. That is, Farrer understood the Gospels to be related to Old Testament stories typologically. This does not mean that Farrer considered either the Old Testament stories or the New Testament stories non-historical.

[37] Philip Curtis, *A Hawk Among Sparrows*, 144.

[38] Walter Hooper, ed. Biographical Appendix, *Collected Letters: Narnia, Cambridge and Joy 1950-1963*, III, London: HarperCollinsPublishers, 2006, 1665. When Katharine graduated, St. Anne's was known as the Society of Oxford Home-Students, which became the St. Anne's Society in 1942 and St. Anne's College in 1952.

[39] Later biannual lectures.

[40] I. M. Crombie, "Farrer, Austin Marsden (1904-1968)," rev. *Oxford*

Farrer delivered the Gifford Lectures on "The Freedom of the Will" at the University of Edinburgh in 1957, later published as *The Freedom of the Will*. Farrer argued that the human will was free, while giving determinism its full weight and describing creativity and invention as the primary actions of the will.[41]

Trinity College, Oxford
Author photo

Farrer wrote many books, several of them compilations of his sermons, including some that were published after his death. He is best known for *Finite and Infinite: A Philosophical Essay*. The book was, in part, a response to the Logical Positivists. Farrer's basic argument is that we can discern the existence of God by looking at this world, especially the human beings in this world. The character, will, intellect, choice, initiative, voluntary actions, impulse, desire, duty, and other features of human beings must have originated from a source that is higher, more complex, and more intelligent than these human beings. For example, Farrer writes, "Our sense of duty finds itself at home only in a world where existence is the expression of the divine will."[42] Farrer proposes a "ladder of ascent" from lower creatures to successively more highly developed animals to human

---

Dictionary of National Biography, Oxford University Press, 2004; online edition, May 2005.

[41] https://www.giffordlectures.org/lectures?page=3 Determinism is a biological and evolutionary concept, while free will is decidedly biblical and Christian.

[42] Farrer, 298.

beings and then to God.[43] He writes that one must "...look for God at the beginning of the series..."[44] as well as at the end. The Creator is "the foundation."[45] Farrer's comparison of a dog to a human as the finite is to the infinite is also echoed in Lewis's writings.[46] Just as the dog sees a finger pointing and sniffs the finger rather than look in the direction the finger is pointing, so also humans think they understand religion as only psychological.[47]

In a later chapter, Farrer expresses himself as Lewis did in his essay "Transposition": "The relation of Absolute to finite mode is like that of a higher mode to a lower. As amoeba to frog and frog to man, so man to God—except that the distance is not finite but infinite, and God not only higher but highest." Lewis explained that concept in his essay "Transposition" the year after Farrer's book was published.[48] Farrer also wrote that we can see "the finite acts as a splintered image of God ...."[49] In the Preface, Farrer states, "Eighteen to sixteen years ago I sat down and wrote this book,"[50] which means that the thoughts behind this 1943 publication originated in the mid-1920s and undoubtedly influenced Lewis.

Farrer was trying to demonstrate the existence of God "from general considerations of reason."[51] Logical Positivists had declared religious statements, as well as statements of aesthetics, irrelevant because they were unverifiable. For the atheist or Logical Positivist, Farrer argued, the lack of order or hierarchy supports their position, while evidence of hierarchy supports the theist.[52] This statement from

---

[43] See especially Chapter IV, "The Ladder of Ascent." See also C. S. Lewis, *Mere Christianity*, New York: HarperCollinsPublishers, 1980. 164, for a discussion of various levels of initiative.

[44] Farrer, 283,

[45] Farrer, 2.

[46] Farrer, 91, 94.

[47] See C. S. Lewis, "Transposition," in *The Weight of Glory and Other Addresses*, New York: Simon & Schuster, 1980, 88.

[48] Farrer, 34.

[49] Farrer, 263.

[50] In a footnote, Farrer admits that in the book he discusses "a debased and puerile wing of Logical Positivism." *Finite and Infinite*, 105, n. 1.

[51] Farrer, 1. C. S. Lewis made a similar claim: "We are not taking anything from the Bible or the Churches, we are trying to see what we can find out about this Somebody on our own steam." *Mere Christianity*, New York: HarperCollinsPublishers. Copyright 1980. Chapter 5, "We Have Cause to Be Uneasy," 29.

[52] Farrer, 9.

Farrer best illustrates his position on order, or what some would call Intelligent Design:

> It is with a delighted surprise that the theologian stumbles across so much intelligibility in the universe; in whatever direction he pushes his studies, the angels have been before him ... a pre-established harmony is well known to be the happiest argument for theism—it would have been so unlikely to have been an accident.[53]

To be intelligible is not the normal order of things, Farrer states. Things that show order must have a mind behind them.[54] Nor can wish-fulfillment invalidate belief in God. As Farrer states, "... the fact that a belief satisfies cravings is no evidence against its truth: e.g. belief in the existence of police-protection."[55]

Farrer described God as "supra-personal" rather than "infra-personal," echoing, or perhaps anticipating, Lewis's description of God as "beyond personality."[56] Farrer refutes the argument from the skeptics that evil in the world makes the existence of God unlikely when he writes, " 'I believe in God because the world is so bad' is as sound an argument as 'I believe in God because the world is so good.'"[57] In fact, Farrer writes, our ability to make free moral choices is further evidence for the existence of God: "Moral effort may appear to be the essence of freedom. We are not free because we can choose how to act for the best, but because we can choose whether to act for the best or not."[58] These similarities between the thinking of Lewis and Farrer demonstrate the basis of their friendship and the reasons why Farrer later became a frequent speaker at the Oxford Socratic Club.[59]

In his last position, Farrer was Warden of Keble College, Oxford, a position he held from 1960 until 1968. During his time at Keble College, Farrer was an effective administrator, a frequent writer and speaker, a winsome preacher, and a member of the Church of England's Liturgical Commission. He preached his last sermon for Rev. Robin

---

[53] Farrer, 18. See also Farrer, 276, where Farrer writes, "From this point we may develop the famous argument from design."

[54] Farrer, 19.

[55] Farrer, 5.

[56] Farrer, 35.

[57] Farrer, 278.

[58] Farrer, 164.

[59] Farrer's book even contains a mention of Samuel Alexander's *Space, Time and Deity*. Farrer, 245.

No Ordinary People

Anstey at St. Andrew's, Headington, on Sunday, December 22, 1968, appropriately, on "The Ultimate Hope."[60] He died one week later at the age of sixty-four on Dec. 29, 1968. Katharine died a little more than three years later, on Palm Sunday, March 26, 1972.

AUSTIN FARRER, KATHARINE FARRER, AND C. S. LEWIS

In 1931, Austin Farrer came to Oxford. We do not know when Farrer and Lewis first met, but they probably met when Farrer began to serve as chaplain and tutor at St. Edmund Hall (1931-1935). The first time they were together, as far as we know with certainty, was when Farrer came to speak to the Oxford Socratic Club in 1942, the first year of the Club's existence. The Socratic Club was an undergraduate society devoted to debating what Lewis called "the pros and cons of the Christian Religion."[61] The Socratic was organized during the autumn of 1941 and held its first meeting on January 26, 1942. On May 13 of that year, the Socratic Club met and heard Farrer and Robert Eisler address the topic "Did Christ Rise from the Dead?" Eisler is the Austrian Jewish historian of art and culture, who fled Austria for Oxford during World War II. He had had previous contacts with Oxford and therefore was known to the Oxford academic community. Farrer answered the Socratic question about the resurrection of Christ with a "yes," while Eisler answered "no."

Keble College Quad
Author photo

Other than Lewis himself,[62] Farrer spoke more often at the

---

[60] Philip Curtis, *A Hawk Among Sparrows*, 168.

[61] C. S. Lewis, "The Founding of the Oxford Socratic Club," *God in the Dock*, Edited by Walter Hooper, Grand Rapids: Eerdmans, 1970, 127.

[62] Hooper lists twenty-seven instances when Lewis addressed the Socratic Club, although ten of these were talks and seventeen of them seem to be impromptu responses. There is some ambiguity about how to categorize some of his talks. I am indebted to Josiah Peterson for pointing this out. See Josiah Peterson, "C. S. Lewis & the Socratics: How to Talk to Those who Disagree with You," *CSL: The Bulletin of The New*

Socratic Club—nineteen times—than any other speaker in the Club's history. He spoke in defense of the Christian faith, all but one of them while Lewis was the President of the Socratic. Farrer explains: "I was occasionally called upon to stop a gap in the earlier programmes of Lewis's Socratic Club. Lewis was president, but he was not bound to show up."[63] That Farrer was the stopgap in a time of need speaks well of Farrer's abilities, since only a very capable person would be asked to step in on short notice. And, as Stella Aldwinckle once stated, "Austin Farrer was one of the outstanding ones."[64] Farrer was willing to step in because he believed that "rational argument does not create belief, but it maintains a climate in which belief may flourish."[65] He also believed that lack of argument destroys belief.[66] Farrer was Lewis's "go-to" person for theology, especially where theology crossed paths with philosophy.

With one major exception, most of what we know about the interaction between Farrer and Lewis comes from these Socratic Club meetings, since we only have two letters that Lewis wrote to Farrer, one of them to both Austin and his wife Katharine. That exception comes from the second of four series of BBC talks during World War II. Lewis sent those talks to four clergymen to get their perspective—an Anglican, a Roman Catholic, a Methodist, and a Presbyterian. Farrer was likely the Anglican.[67] The letters from Lewis to Farrer were few because the two men had frequent occasion to meet face-to-face since both lived in Oxford and taught at Oxford University. That

---

York C. S. Lewis Society, Vol. 51, No. 3 (No. 497), May/June 2020, 2, 4. Walter Hooper, "Oxford's Bonny Fighter," *Remembering C. S. Lewis: Recollections of Those Who Knew Him*, James Como, ed., San Francisco: Ignatius Press, 2005, 293-308. The Appendix shows that eleven of Farrer's nineteen talks were responses.

[63] Austin Farrer, "The Christian Apologist," *Light on C. S. Lewis*, edited by Jocelyn Gibb, New York: Harcourt, Brace & World, Inc., 1965, 25. Stella Aldwinckle probably invited him to fill a gap.

[64] Stella Aldwinckle, "Memories of the Socratic Club," *C. S. Lewis and His Circle: Essays and Memoirs from the Oxford C. S. Lewis Society*, Roger White, Judith Wolfe, and Brendan Wolfe, eds., 193.

[65] Austin Farrer, "The Christian Apologist," 26.

[66] Austin Farrer, "The Christian Apologist," 26.

[67] "I tried to guard against this [i.e., the idea that his talks were peculiar to one person or one denomination] by sending the original script of what is now Book II to four clergymen (Anglican, Methodist, Presbyterian, Roman Catholic) and asking for their criticism." *Mere Christianity*, Preface, XI. While Lewis nowhere states that Farrer was the Anglican, he is the most likely candidate.

Farrer never joined the Inklings can be attributed to his preference for philosophy and theology rather than literature.

Lewis wrote far more letters to Austin Farrer's wife Katharine, fifteen in all, than he wrote to Austin Farrer. In this exchange of letters, Lewis served as a literary midwife, especially dealing with the books and poems that Katharine was writing. Lewis gave his opinion when she requested it, encouraging her often, and his advice helped her to become a more effective writer. Lewis read all three books in her detective trilogy.[68]

We also learn about her husband through the letters Lewis wrote to Katharine Farrer. One letter tells us the opinion Lewis had of Austin's writing. In that letter, Lewis calls Austin's article "The Queen of Sciences" perhaps the "only bright spot in that issue" of *The Twentieth Century*.[69] One year later, Lewis writes to Katharine Farrer about her poem, "Summer's Term," but also with some glowing words of praise for Austin's *Short Bible, Arranged by Austin Farrer, D.D.*[70] In a letter to Sister Penelope, Lewis states of Farrer's printed lectures, which he had recently read, "I think he is α +."[71] A couple of years later, he mentions Farrer in another letter to Sister Penelope, writing very positively about Austin Farrer's recently published *Glass of Vision*.[72]

Most of all, we learn about Katharine Farrer in these letters, especially the books she was writing. As stated above, she wrote three detective novels, *The Missing Link* (1952), *The Cretan Counterfeit* (1954), and *Gownsman's Gallows* (1957). In the latter two cases, she seems to have requested Lewis's advice, asking him to give her some candid literary critique.

---

[68] Lewis warned Katharine Farrer, "... I'm no good on the specifically detective side." He apparently read little in this genre of detective stories, but he was willing to offer his critique anyway. *Collected Letters*, III, 640. The date of the letter is August 6, 1955.

[69] Austin Farrer, "The Queen of Sciences," *Twentieth Century*, Vol. 157, 489-94. The date of Lewis' letter is June 20, 1955. *Collected Letters*, III, 620.

[70] Austin Farrer, *A Short Bible*, ed. with general introduction, Fontana, 5-15 (published in the US as *Core of the Bible*, Harper, 1957). The date is May 20, 1956. *Collected Letters*, III, 754.

[71] The date is August 1, 1949. *Collected Letters*, II, 961. That is, alpha plus, which means an excellent academic mark at the top of First Class Honors.

[72] The date of the letter is January 10, 1952. *Collected Letters*, III, 158. The book was originally published in 1948.

Twenty-One Friendships of C.S. Lewis

Lewis started reading Katharine's *The Missing Link* the same year it was published and finished it one day later.[73] He tells her that he "thoroughly enjoyed the book" and offers numerous compliments about parts of the book. He then suggests that the dialogue needs improving, explaining why he makes that critique and offering some additional suggestions.[74] The next time, having seen the value of his professional advice, she seems to have requested his critique for *The Cretan Counterfeit*. He provides that critique, writing about the pluses and minuses of her book, liking its "thick-woven texture," the actual writing, the invention, and "a fine prodigality of characters."[75] While she was writing her third novel, *Gownsman's Gallows*, she sent him the book manuscript. He writes back with both praise and advice. He thinks her manner attractive and her characterization sometimes very good, but he wants to see more of two of her characters. He also offers some critique about the complexity of her plot and the tension between her genre and her real interests and powers.[76] In return, Lewis seems to have asked for Katharine's help when he was writing *Till We Have Faces*. After she sent him her comments, he writes about her helpful critique and his "native tendency to be too argumentative," giving her a further explanation of the character of Psyche in response to her critique.[77]

Katharine was also involved in the life of Lewis in other ways. When Joy went to answer the telephone on the evening of October 18, 1956, Katharine Farrer, not Lewis (as portrayed in the television movie "Shadowlands"), was calling her. Katharine once said that on the evening of October 18, she knew something was wrong with Joy, telling her husband, "I *must* ring her!"[78] As Joy went to answer the telephone, her left femur broke and the tragic story of "Shadowlands" moved toward its dramatic conclusion.[79]

Even after Lewis's death, the Farrers were supportive of Lewis's legacy. Walter Hooper organized a Socratic gathering the following February in the parlor of Wesley Memorial Church in memory of

---

[73] Specifically, on June 9, 1952.

[74] *Collected Letters*, III, 197f.

[75] The date is February 3, 1954, the same year in which the book was published. *Collected Letters*, III, 423f.

[76] The date is July 9, 1955. *Collected Letters*, III, 630f.

[77] The date is August 6, 1955. *Collected Letters*, III, 639f.

[78] Walter Hooper, ed. Biographical Appendix, *Collected Letters*, III, 1666.

[79] *Out of My Bone*, 297.

No Ordinary People

Lewis. Tributes to Lewis were delivered by Farrer, Owen Barfield, and Colin Hardie.[80] Farrer also attended several "Friends of C. S. Lewis" parties, organized annually by Walter Hooper. One of those took place on July 22, 1966, when Wadham College hosted Hooper's "Inklings Party."[81] Farrer was present to honor the memory of Lewis, as were Lewis's brother Warren, close friends J. R. R. Tolkien, Hugo Dyson, Owen Barfield, Colin Hardie, and Robert "Humphrey" Havard. Also present were Clyde Kilby, Jean Wakeman, Maurice Bowra, and others. After Farrer's death in 1968, Katharine attended two similar events.[82]

COMMON GROUND IN FAITH AND IMAGINATION

Lewis and Farrer became close friends, chiefly because they were both Christians, committed to the truths of Scripture, but also because they were prolific writers, Oxford academics, and people concerned for the spiritual well-being of souls. Farrer stated of Lewis—and it was true of Farrer as well—that "pastoral concern continues to rule his pen."[83] That concern—as well as their views of myth and the intersection between theology and imagination—manifested itself on specific issues, one of which was a talk Farrer gave at a Winter Theological Conference in 1943. On December 13-17, 1943, the Fellowship of St. Alban and St. Sergius met at Springfield St. Mary in Oxford on the subject "The Unity of Theological Experience." Farrer gave the opening address for the conference, presenting a lecture on "Historic Facts of God's Revelation and their Apprehension."[84] That topic became a Socratic Club address, "Can Myth Be Fact?" which

---

[80] Walter Hooper, "Oxford's Bonny Fighter," *C. S. Lewis at the Breakfast Table*, 173.

[81] Walter Hooper, " 'Warnie's Problem': An Introduction to a Letter from C. S. Lewis to Owen Barfield," *Journal of Inklings Studies*, Vol. 5, No. 1 (April 2015), 16.

[82] These latter two events are summarized on the appropriate dates in "Chronologically Lewis" and in the unpublished diary of Warren Lewis. The dates are November 22, 1969 and another in May 1971.

[83] Austin Farrer, "The Christian Apologist," *Light on C. S. Lewis*, edited by Jocelyn Gibb, New York: Harcourt, Brace & World, Inc., 1965, 34.

[84] "Program for Fellowship of St. Alban and St. Sergius Winter Theological Conference," Springfield St. Mary, Oxford, December 13-17, 1943. Rev. H. Carpenter, Warden of Keble College, Oxford, served as Chairman of the Conference. The Marion E. Wade Center holds a copy of the three-page conference schedule, cw-MISC.

Farrer delivered two years later.⁸⁵ On that Monday evening at Oriel College, Farrer describes myth as "a traditional tale which purports to describe real happenings."⁸⁶ As stated above, Farrer was known as an Oxford philosophical theologian who held that religious truth can best be communicated through images,⁸⁷ a position expressed in this talk and no doubt appreciated by Lewis. He goes on to state that many of those myths—such as those of Greek mythology—do not lay claim to historical fact, although they illustrate some important truth, some universally accepted idea. Nevertheless, the Christian myth, the story of redemption, though similar in outline to other myths, has its basis in historical fact.

The word "mythical" can suggest false or imaginary, but Christians insist that the Christian redemptive myth happened, that it was not imaginary or legendary. They also believe that it reflects profound spiritual truth. Lewis believed that the story of Christ was true myth, that the resurrection really happened, and that it is quite reasonable for this myth to bear a pattern like the myths of the dying and rising god.⁸⁸

But this understanding of myth did not arise first for Farrer in the 1940s. He had written to his father on this topic while studying theology at Cuddesdon, trying to avoid the rationalism of liberal Protestantism, which denied both the miraculous and the sacramental: "Christ is the poem that was history. His Eucharist the myth become bread. The sacramental ministry is on the one side human, on the other part of the divine mythus⁸⁹ which is Christ's living body."⁹⁰

On the Incarnation, Lewis writes, "The heart of Christianity is a myth which is also a fact. The old myth of the Dying God, *without ceasing to be myth*, comes down from the heaven of legend and imagination to the earth of history. It *happens*—at a particular date, in a particular place, followed by definable historical consequences."⁹¹

---

⁸⁵ May 28, 1945.

⁸⁶ *Socratic Digest*, No. 3, 1945, 83. In the *Socratic Digest*, we have the full text of Austin Farrer's talk that evening.

⁸⁷ http://www.oxfordbiblicalstudies.com/article/opr/t94/e2123

⁸⁸ See C. S. Lewis, "Myth Became Fact," *God in the Dock*, Edited by Walter Hooper, Grand Rapids: Eerdmans, 1970, 63-67.

⁸⁹ I.e., myth, or mythos.

⁹⁰ Philip Curtis, *A Hawk Among Sparrows*, 1985, 45f.

⁹¹ C. S. Lewis, "Myth Became Fact," *God in the Dock*, 66. H. A. Hodges also held a similar view. See Philip Curtis, *A Hawk Among Sparrows: A Biography of Austin Farrer*, London: SPCK, 1985, 32f.

Likewise, the crucifixion is both myth *and* fact: "a historical Person crucified ... *under Pontius Pilate*. By becoming fact it does not cease to be myth: that is the miracle."[92] While similarity in ideas does not by itself prove who borrowed from whom, Farrer's earlier remarks at Cuddesdon suggest his thought as the predecessor to that of Lewis. While Lewis had had an article published in 1944 in *World Dominion*[93] entitled "Myth Became Fact," Farrer's thinking goes back to the 1920s.

Likewise, the similarity between theology and poetry finds common ground between Farrer and Lewis. In a letter to his father during his years at Balliol and Cuddesdon, Farrer asks, "Is religion poetry?" and then replies, "Certainly not. But God being in his ultimate reality unknowable, our experience of him *clothes itself with* creature-elements."[94] Lewis later wrote his essay, "Is Theology Poetry?"[95] He delivered that essay to the Socratic Club almost two decades after Farrer asked almost the same question.[96] Lewis's answer was much the same: theology is certainly not poetry because "belief spoils a system for the imagination,"[97] even though Christians enjoy their theology. At the same time, Farrer also wrote, "Nearly all [worldviews] have certain poetical merits whether you believe them or not."[98]

Both Farrer and Lewis were Anglican Christians, Farrer by choice and Lewis since birth. Farrer and Lewis became close enough friends for Lewis to dedicate *Reflections on the Psalms* to Farrer. Both men were close to classical scholar and Inkling Colin Hardie and poet Martyn Skinner,[99] and both saw problems with the radical conception of God expressed at that time by the popular Anglican Bishop John Robinson.[100] Like Lewis, Farrer wrote an article for Alec Vidler's

---

[92] C. S. Lewis, "Myth Became Fact," *God in the Dock*, 67.

[93] *World Dominion*, Vol. XXII (September-October 1944). See also *God in the Dock*, 14.

[94] Philip Curtis, *A Hawk Among Sparrows*, 48.

[95] See *The Weight of Glory and Other Addresses*. New York: Simon & Schuster, 1980, 90-106.

[96] He gave that talk on Nov. 6, 1944.

[97] "Is Theology Poetry," *Socratic Digest*, Austin, TX: Concordia University Press, 2012, 78.

[98] "Is Theology Poetry," *Socratic Digest*, 76.

[99] Philip Curtis, *A Hawk Among Sparrows*, 146.

[100] Philip Curtis, *A Hawk Among Sparrows*, 192. See also C. S. Lewis, "Must Our Image of God Go?" *God in the Dock*, Edited by Walter Hooper, Grand Rapids: Eerdmans, 1970, 184-185.

Theology. Farrer's article, "Theology of Morals," was published in May 1939 as part of the series of articles that inaugurated Vidler's editorship.[101] Both men disliked the administrative side of college life.[102] Both appreciated the role of the imagination and utilized their understanding of the imagination to speak and write powerfully, and both were ardent in their defense of the Christian faith. Not surprisingly, these two men, joined together by their proximity to one another in Oxford, found much common ground.

The Socratic Farrer

As stated above, Farrer spoke more frequently at the Socratic Club than any other person except Lewis himself.[103] Here we summarize some of the issues Farrer addressed at the Socratic, especially since they were occasionally published in the *Socratic Digest*.[104] Both men combined a mastery of philosophy, theology, and literature. Farrer's forte was theology, while Lewis's was literature, and therein we see each man's uniqueness as well as his common ground with the other man.

A survey of the titles Farrer addressed at the Socratic Club shows his interest in the relationship of the Christian faith to modern science. In 1944, Dr. David Evans and Farrer spoke on the topic "Is Belief in a Personal God Compatible with Modern Scientific Knowledge?" Evans approached the topic from a scientific point of view, answering the question with a "yes," and Farrer replied from a philosophical and theological perspective, also stating "yes."[105] In 1945, philosopher Prof. H. H. Price and Farrer answered the question, "Has Man a Soul?" The evasive Price tells the audience not to expect a plain "yes" or "no," and he follows through on that prediction with his usual inexactness.

---

[101] Philip Curtis, *A Hawk Among Sparrows*, 135.

[102] Philip Curtis, *A Hawk Among Sparrows*, 139.

[103] Appendix I provides an overview of the nineteen addresses that Farrer gave to the Socratic Club between 1942 and 1958, eleven of them responses to the primary speaker.

[104] All published issues of the *Socratic Digest* have been reprinted by Concordia University Press and are available in a print-on-demand format at Lulu.com.

[105] Notes by Stella Aldwinckle. Stella Aldwinckle was founder of the Oxford University Socratic Club which began in 1942 and for which C. S. Lewis served as president. The Stella Aldwinckle Papers, Box 8, Folder 383. The Marion E. Wade Center, Wheaton College, Wheaton, IL.

In response Farrer states that while the biologists say they can show there is no extra "soul stuff" in the physical human body, belief in immortality (and, therefore, the existence of the soul) depends on faith in the creative power of God.[106] In 1946, scientist Dr. C. H. Waddington and Farrer spoke on the topic "Can Science Provide a Basis for Ethics?"[107] Waddington states that ethical inquiry is very important, and he proceeds to demonstrate this. Farrer says that Waddington is not incorrect, but that his position is incomplete.[108]

Both Farrer and Lewis were concerned that the doctrines of Scripture be easily understood.[109] In 1942, Farrer spoke on the topic "How Was Jesus Divine?" Farrer calls this a mystery, but one that has some similarities to our experience in the act of prayer. Prayer itself is a mystery, he states, because we are expressing our will or desire even as God is doing the same in us. Both our human nature and God's divine nature appear in this act of prayer. He concludes by saying, "Our incomplete acts of union with God are themselves the beginnings of the working of this adoption in us."[110]

In 1943, Farrer addressed the topic "Can We Know That God Exists?" He states that our way of knowing God is more like knowing a person than knowing a carpet. God is known through His creation and in our souls. We do not know God through cause and effect since that would make God part of our natural universe. An argument that upholds the existence of God should be judged as to whether it "lights up more of reality" than other arguments. Nothing is self-explanatory;

---

[106] Notes by Stella Aldwinckle. The Stella Aldwinckle Papers, Box 8, Folder 384. The Marion E. Wade Center, Wheaton College, Wheaton, IL.

[107] Notes by Stella Aldwinckle. The Stella Aldwinckle Papers, Box 8, Folder 370, and Box 9, Folder 406. The Marion E. Wade Center, Wheaton College, Wheaton, IL.

[108] Notes by Stella Aldwinckle. The Stella Aldwinckle Papers, Box 8, Folder 385. The Marion E. Wade Center, Wheaton College, Wheaton, IL. The summaries of their talks are incomplete and therefore difficult to describe.

[109] See, for example, "God in the Dock," *God in the Dock*. Edited by Walter Hooper, Grand Rapids: Eerdmans, 1970, 243, where Lewis writes, "Our problem is often simply one of translation. Every examination for ordinands ought to include a passage from some standard theological work for translation into the vernacular. The work is laborious but it is immediately rewarded. By trying to translate our doctrines into vulgar speech we discover how much we understand them ourselves."

[110] Austin Farrer, "How Was Jesus Divine?" *Socratic Digest*, No. 1, 1942-43, 25.

all finite things are grounded in infinity.

Farrer addressed the same topic with similar arguments four years later in his message, "Does God Exist?"[111] He was not attempting to prove the existence of God, but to show how an argument for the existence of God works.[112] The argument for the existence of God, he claims, is a unique type of argument. "Since the Divine Being is unique, he can only be known by a sort of acquaintance: he must impress us *in and through* finite things, very likely, without our fully conscious appreciation of the fact."[113] The reason there is something rather than nothing must presuppose a Divine Being. He also states, "Yet we all know that we are called,"[114] and that sense of calling he attributes to God. Furthermore, our limited understanding of certain ideas suggests that there is a Mind whose understanding is not so limited, and that Mind is God.[115]

Several years later, the Socratic Club met to hear the topic "'Very God and Very Man': Why Talk Like This?" David Edwards, Fellow of All Souls College, Oxford, spoke, and Austin Farrer responded. Edwards asks why we talk like this, i.e., why we use the words "very God of very God" in the Nicene Creed. History is ambiguous about what happened, he states, but these words are the best way to describe the object of Christian experience. Our job is to expound, not justify, the formula. Christ's deity is known by being exercised, i.e., it is practical. To be the Son is to know the Father. The Trinity is unintelligible without the Incarnation. Only this conception of God delivers the Christian goods of constancy and charity. Austin Farrer continues by saying that heaven was not emptied of the Son when the Son became incarnate. Each person of the Trinity cares for the other by existing. Sonship is not a physical Sonship. The Trinity is not the application of a natural human relation, but the application of our true relation to God.[116]

Not every address to the Socratic Club by Austin Farrer was recorded, but we catch the topics of concern to Farrer in the few

---

[111] The date is Oct. 13, 1947. Austin Farrer, "Does God Exist?" *Socratic Digest*, No. 4, 118-123.

[112] Austin Farrer, "Does God Exist?" *Socratic Digest*, No. 4, 121.

[113] Austin Farrer, "Does God Exist?" *Socratic Digest*, No. 4, 118.

[114] Austin Farrer, "Does God Exist?" *Socratic Digest*, No. 4, 121.

[115] Austin Farrer, "Does God Exist?" *Socratic Digest*, No. 4, 122.

[116] Notes by Stella Aldwinckle. The Stella Aldwinckle Papers, the Wade Center, 8-365, attendance list book for Socratic Club meetings. Also 8-391. The date is January 26, 1953.

addresses we have. The Socratic Farrer spoke frequently, not only because he was a good speaker, but also because he had studied both theology—the study of God as revealed in His Word—and philosophy—the primary method by which topics were addressed at the Oxford Socratic Club.

The Pastoral Farrer

Finally, Austin Farrer's closeness to Lewis shows itself in his presence at several important events in the life of Lewis. He was present at the Oxford Registry Office in Oxford on April 23, 1956, when the superintendent registrar joined Lewis and Joy Gresham in marriage,[117] thereby enabling Joy to remain in England.

When Joy died in 1960, Farrer was asked to read the funeral service.[118] She had received absolution from Farrer earlier that day, and she had specifically asked him to read the funeral service over her when it was held at the Oxford Crematorium chapel. Days later, Lewis wrote to the Farrers, "She loved you both very much. And getting to know you both better is one of the many permanent gains I have got from my short married life."[119]

On the morning of the day that Lewis nearly died in July 1963, Farrer gave him communion.[120] At 3:00 p.m. Lewis woke up and asked for tea. After Lewis died on Nov. 22, 1963, Vicar Ronald Head said a requiem for him at his home church, Holy Trinity,[121] four days later, followed by the funeral service at 11:00 a.m.[122] Vicar Head led the service, and Austin Farrer read the Scripture lesson. On November 30, an official memorial service for Lewis was held

---

[117] The superintendent registrar was Cecil W. Clifton. *Clive Staples Lewis*, 376. See also *A Love Observed*, 122.

[118] The date she died was July 13, 1960. Douglas Gresham, *Lenten Lands: My Childhood with Joy Gresham and C. S. Lewis*, New York: HarperCollins Publishers, 1988, 128.

[119] Walter Hooper, ed. Biographical Appendix, *Collected Letters, III*, 1666.

[120] The date is July 15, 1963. Roger Lancelyn Green and Walter Hooper, *C. S. Lewis: A Biography*, New York: HarperCollins, 1974, 302.

[121] Ronald Head, "C. S. Lewis as a Parishioner," *C. S. Lewis and His Circle: Essays and Memoirs from the Oxford C. S. Lewis Society*, edited by Roger White, Judith, Wolfe, and Brendan N. Wolfe, Oxford: Oxford University Press, 2015, 185.

[122] James Dundas-Grant, "From an 'Outsider'," in *C. S. Lewis at the Breakfast Table*, 233.

at Magdalen College, Oxford, and Austin Farrer also spoke at that service.[123] In his remarks, Farrer spoke about Lewis's intense awareness and intellectual imagination. Farrer stated that Lewis ...

> had more actuality of soul than the common breed of men. He took in more, he felt more, he remembered more, he invented more. The reflections on his early life ... record an intense awareness, a vigorous reaction, a taking of the world into his heart, which must amaze ... [Lewis had] a capacity for experience beyond our scope.... If it is a crime to think about all you strongly feel and feel the realities about which you think, then the crime was certainly his. It was this feeling intellect, this intellectual imagination that made the strength of his religious writings.... He paid you the compliment of attending to your words. He did not pretend to read your heart. He was endlessly generous .... When he had entered into any relationship, his patience and his loyalty were inexhaustible.... But it is not the work of Lewis's pen; it is the work of God's fingers that we are to praise.[124]

---

[123] Carpenter, *The Letters of J. R. R. Tolkien*, 341. Brown, *A Life Observed*, 222.

[124] Austin Farrer, *The Brink of Mystery*, London: SPCK, 1976, 45-47.

Appendix I: Austin Farrer at the Socratic Club

Austin Farrer spoke every year at the Socratic Club between 1942 and 1954 except for 1949. In many of those years he spoke twice. His popularity at the Socratic speaks of his skill in speaking, not only with meaningful and engaging content but also with rhetorical skill.

Date	Topic	Speaker/Respondent
May 13, 1942	"Did Christ Rise from the Dead?"	Austin Farrer Robert Eisler
Nov. 2, 1942	"How Was Jesus Divine?"	Austin Farrer
May 10, 1943	"Immortality"	Austin Farrer
Nov. 1, 1943	"Can We Know That God Exists?"	Austin Farrer
May 1, 1944	"Explaining' the Universe"	Peter B. Medawar Austin Farrer
Oct. 30, 1944	"Is Belief in a Personal God Compatible with Modern Scientific Knowledge?"	Dr. David Evans Austin Farrer
May 28, 1945	"Can Myth Be Fact?"	Austin Farrer
Nov. 12, 1945	"Has Man a Soul?"	Prof. H. H. Price, Philosophy, New College, Oxford Austin Farrer
Feb. 11, 1946[1]	"Can Science Provide a Basis for Ethics?"	Waddington Dev. Biology, Genetics Austin Farrer
Jan. 27, 1947	"Is Dogma the Shackling of Thought?"	Austin Farrer R. Nicol Cross, Harris Manchester College
Oct. 13, 1947	"Does God Exist?"	Austin Farrer W. L. Walsh
June 7, 1948[2]	"Biblical Thought and the Language of Philosophy"	Austin Farrer P. J. Thompson

Twenty-One Friendships of C.S. Lewis

Date	Topic	Speaker/Respondent
Nov. 6, 1950	"Is Theology a Science?"	Rev. G. C. Stead, Fellow and Chaplain, Keble College Austin Farrer
May 14, 1951[3]	"Images and Symbols"	Valerie Pitt, English, University College o South Wales Austin Farrer
Feb. 11, 1952[4]	"The Nature of Meaning"	Owen Barfield Austin Farrer
Jan. 26, 1953[5]	"'Very God and Very Man': Why Talk Like This?"	David Edwards[6] Austin Farrer
Nov. 26, 1953[7]	"Creation Myths"	P. H. Nowell-Smith, Trinity College, Oxford Austin Farrer
June 2, 1954[8]	"Poetry, Language and Ambiguity"	Dorothy L. Sayers Austin Farrer
May 22, 1958[9]	"Should religious assertions be regarded primarily as moral assertions?"	Richard Bevan Braithwaite, Cambridge University Austin Farrer

Appendix II: Selected Works of Austin Farrer[125]

The works of Austin Farrer are listed in chronological order.

Finite and Infinite: A Philosophical Essay. Westminster: Dacre Press, 1943.

The Glass of Vision: The Making of St. John's Apocalypse. Westminster: Dacre Press, 1948.

A Rebirth of Images. Westminster: Dacre Press, 1949.

A Study in St. Mark. Westminster: Dacre Press, 1951.

St. Matthew and St. Mark. London: Dacre Press, 1954.

Faith and Logic. London: Allen & Unwin, 1957.

The Freedom of the Will. London: Adam & Charles Black, 1958.

Lord I Believe: Suggestions for Turning the Creed into Prayer. London: Faith Press, 1958.

Said or Sung: An Arrangement of Homily and Verse. London: Faith Press, 1960.

A Faith of Our Own. Cleveland, OH: World Publishing Company, 1960.

Love Almighty and Ills Unlimited: An Essay on Providence and Evil. New York: Doubleday, 1961.

The Revelation of St. John the Divine. Oxford: Oxford University Press, 1964.

Saving Belief. London: Hodder and Stoughton, 1964.

The Triple Victory: Christ's Temptation According to St. Matthew. London: Faith Press, 1965.

A Science of God?[126] London: Geoffrey Bles, 1966.

Faith and Speculation. London: A & C. Black, 1967.

A Celebration of Faith. London: Hodder and Stoughton, 1970.

Reflective Faith: Essays in Philosophical Theology. London: SPCK, 1972.

---

[125] A complete chronological list of Farrer's extensive writings appears in *A Hawk Among Sparrows*, 250-257. This Appendix is an incomplete list, especially featuring books mentioned earlier in the chapter.

[126] Published in the U.S. as *God Is Not Dead*. New York: Morehouse-Barlow, 1966.

Twenty-One Friendships of C.S. Lewis

The End of Man. London: SPCK, 1973.
The Brink of Mystery. London: SPCK, 1976.
Interpretation and Belief. London: SPCK, 1976.

"Lewis's in Snow" watercolor by Arthur Greeves, Easter 1917
Used by permission of the Marion E. Wade Center,
Wheaton College, Wheaton, IL.

Chapter 4

ARTHUR GREEVES
No Ordinary Person

The friendship of C. S. Lewis with Arthur Greeves is one major reason why Lewis once wrote that "there are no ordinary people."[1] The two men were opposites in many ways—Lewis a brilliant Oxford academic and Greeves the plain-spoken and artistic Belfastian who rarely worked a regular paying job. Despite their differences, Greeves had a positive influence on Lewis in his appreciation of nature and the arts, and Lewis encouraged Greeves in his artistic and creative writing ability. But for his friendship with C. S. Lewis, we would know nothing about Arthur Greeves.

Lewis wrote more letters to Joseph Arthur Greeves than to any other person. The first letter is dated June 5, 1914, written from Malvern College, where Lewis was attending a prep school to prepare for the university. They met for the first time at least seven years earlier[2] but had a significant encounter two months prior to that letter when they bonded immediately. The last letter—the 296th letter—was written on Sept. 11, 1963, about two-and-a-half months before Lewis's death, and more than forty-nine years after the first letter.[3]

ARTHUR GREEVES AND C. S. LEWIS

Lewis and Greeves became well-aquainted for the first time at Bernagh,[4] as the Greeves family home was known, across the street from Little Lea, the Lewis home, on Circular Road in Belfast,

---

[1] "The Weight of Glory," *The Weight of Glory and Other Addresses*. New York: Simon & Schuster, 1980, 39.

[2] *Collected Letters, I,* 3f.

[3] There were probably more than 296 letters, since on Oct. 1, 1931 Lewis wrote about some of his letters written earlier to Arthur, which Arthur had temporarily sent to him, "I am suppressing and will return to you in a day or two." *They Stand Together*, 424. By "suppressing" Lewis meant that he was sending those letters back at once and keeping them from his brother Warren. One can easily understand why letters devoted to either Lewis's sadism or his relationship with Mrs. Moore might have been destroyed.

[4] Possibly Irish for "gap." See http://www.ulsterplacenames.org/landscape_in_irish-language_names.htm.

Northern Ireland. Lewis's account of their meeting—and their mutual love for Norse mythology—is memorably recorded in *Surprised by Joy*. Arthur was confined to bed while recuperating from an illness, and he was lonely. Arthur sent a message to Lewis, inviting him to visit. He accepted, and this is how the scene unfolded:

> I found Arthur sitting up in bed. On the table beside him lay a copy of *Myths of the Norsemen*.[5]
>
> "Do *you* like that?" said I.
>
> "Do *you* like that?" said he.
>
> Next moment the book was in our hands, our heads were bent close together, we were pointing, quoting, talking—soon almost shouting—discovering in a torrent of questions that we liked not only the same thing, but the same parts of it and in the same way; that both knew the stab of Joy and that, for both, the arrow was shot from the North. Many thousands of people have had the experience of finding the first friend, and it is nonetheless a wonder; as great a wonder ... as first love, or even a greater. I had been so far from thinking such a friend possible that I had never even longed for one; no more than I longed to be King of England. If I had found that Arthur had independently built up an exact replica of the Boxonian world I should not really have been much more surprised. Nothing, I suspect, is more astonishing in any man's life than the discovery that there do exist people very, very like himself.[6]

They were kindred spirits. Later, Lewis called him "the most faithful of friends."[7] Throughout their lifetimes they shared other interests, including Icelandic sagas[8]; the books of Jane Austen, Charles Dickens, H. G. Wells, George MacDonald, Rider Haggard, Naomi Mitchison, J. G. Lockhart, and many other authors; classical music

---

[5] By H. A. Guerber (1908), subtitled *From the Eddas and Sagas*.

[6] *Surprised by Joy: The Shape of My Early Life*. San Diego: Harcourt Brace Jovanovich, 1955, 130f. Later, Lewis writes about this moment as though it were frequently typical of friendship: "The typical expression of opening Friendship would be something like, "What? You too? I thought I was the only one." C. S. Lewis, *The Four Loves*, Harcourt Brace & Company, New York, 1988, 65.

[7] C. S. Lewis, Introduction, *They Stand Together*, edited by Walter Hooper, New York: Macmillan Publishing Co., 1979, 25. *The Lewis Papers*, Vol., X, 218-220. The date is approximately 1935.

[8] See *They Stand Together*, 75, where Lewis mentions the purchase of a copy of a book which Arthur owned about Icelandic sagas. The date is June 1, 1915.

(Arthur could play the piano); stage plays and Richard Wagner's operatic works; a love of nature; long walks; a love of art (Arthur was an accomplished artist) and the outdoor beauty of County Down. After Lewis's discovery of George MacDonald's Faerie Romance *Phantastes*, Arthur was the first person Lewis told about the book. "I have had a great literary experience this week," he writes, three days after he purchased the book. In addition to enthusing about some parts of the story—Anodos and the terrible ash tree as well as the episode of Cosmo—he states, "You simply MUST get this at once."[9] The one who had said, "Do *you* like that?" also frequently said, "Share this experience with me also."

Lewis and Greeves shared their innermost secrets, including Lewis's early sadistic devotion to the lash and his questionable relationship with Mrs. Moore. Portions of Lewis's letters to Arthur Greeves were blacked out, but technology has been able to determine the original wording behind those intentional smudges. That wording shows itself to be an eroticism that is sometimes associated with whipping or being whipped.[10]

Arthur Greeves and Mrs. Moore are undoubtedly the two people, mentioned in a letter during the Kirkpatrick years, to whom Lewis is referring when he writes to Arthur about "the two people who matter most to me in the world."[11] Lewis's mother Flora had died in 1908, or she would have been one of the two people who mattered most to him. That his father Albert was not one of these surprises no one, given the strained relationship between father and son. Nor was Lewis as close to his brother Warren at this time as he would later become. A postscript from Lewis to Greeves demonstrates both the closeness of their relationship and the alienation between father and son when Lewis writes, "Haven't heard from my esteemed parent for some time; has he committed suicide yet?"[12]

The general statement in one of his letters to Arthur—"I love someone."[13]—undoubtedly also referred to a romantic relationship

---

[9] *They Stand Together*, 92f. The date is March 7, 1916.

[10] Lewis addresses this matter in one of the blacked-out portions of a letter to Arthur, dated May 29, 1918, and it is probably a response to Arthur's previous letter. *They Stand Together*, 217. See also *They Stand Together*, 224.

[11] *They Stand Together*, 204. The letter is dated Dec. 14, 1917.

[12] *They Stand Together*, 254. The date is June 2, 1919, right in the middle of his staunch atheism.

[13] *They Stand Together*, 208. The date of the letter is Dec. 12, 1918.

with Mrs. Moore. There was no one else in Lewis's life that could have qualified as the "someone" whom Lewis loved, and there was no one but Arthur with whom he could have shared this secret. That explains a comment Lewis later made, that Arthur "carried the innumerable secrets of my own furtive and ignoble adolescence locked in a silence ...."[14] That relationship with Mrs. Moore probably also explains his statement, "I believe in no God, least of all in one that would punish me for the 'lusts of the flesh.'"[15]

Lewis's early love for Richard Wagner's music once took him to Theatre Royal in London's West End to hear "The Valkyrie,"[16] the second part of Wagner's Ring cycle. In his next letter to Arthur, Lewis enthuses about the opera with phrases like "the glorious love-music of the orchestra ... simply swept you away," "it was simply heaven," "all his music is splendid," and "I was so full of delights."[17]

In Lewis's years with W. T. Kirkpatrick,[18] Arthur Greeves became Lewis's confidant. In many of those letters, Lewis addressed Greeves as Galahad,[19] evidence of an appreciation both for the friendship of Greeves and the Arthurian writings of Sir Thomas Malory. With Arthur, Lewis could share the beauty of the landscape of Surrey, the books he was reading, his new appreciation for Shakespeare,[20] the things he was writing (such as his unsuccessful attempt at writing opera in *Loki Bound*[21] and various attempts at poetry), the music he

---

[14] *The Lewis Papers*, Vol. X, 219. The date is approximately 1935.

[15] *They Stand Together*, 221. The date is June 3, 1918.

[16] The date is June 14, 1918. *Collected Letters, I*, edited by Walter Hooper, London: Harper Collins Publishers, 2000, 381.

[17] *They Stand Together*, 222. The date is June 17, 1918.

[18] Lewis studied with Kirkpatrick from Sept. 19, 1914 to April 25, 1917.

[19] Lewis calls Arthur "Galahad" forty-six times between May 4, 1915 and June 17, 1918. Galahad was the greatest knight of the King Arthur stories who was renowned for his gallantry and purity. In one letter, Lewis writes "...you are Galahad the spotless whose 'strength is as the strength of ten, because your heart is pure.' " Lewis apparently appreciated the purity of Arthur's character, perhaps in contrast to Lewis's own rebellious nature. *Collected Letters, I*, 127.

[20] See *They Stand Together*, 239. The date of the letter is Dec. 2, 1918.

[21] An irreverent opera in the tradition of ancient Greek tragedy. Lewis was writing this tragedy in 1914, but he never completed it. The only part of this which has survived consists of 119 lines reproduced in the unpublished *Lewis Papers*, vol. IV, 218-20. *Loki Bound* owes its origin especially to the *Poetic Edda* and the *Prose Edda* of Nordic mythology. *Collected Letters, I*, 249.

was hearing, and the languages he was learning. He once wrote to Arthur, "When one has read a book, I think there is nothing so nice as discussing it with someone else."²² Lewis once encouraged Arthur to write something creative by commenting, "Ink is the great cure for all human ills."²³ Lewis no doubt encouraged Arthur in numerous other ways, even enabling Arthur to believe that he was capable of writing the musical score for Lewis's *Loki Bound*, and Arthur returned the favor.

They were not always in agreement. Lewis once wrote, "You don't admit my arguments, and yet make no endeavor to answer them."²⁴ Less than a month later, Lewis continued his verbal assault on Arthur's argumentative powers, asking Greeves to "talk sense the next time you do me the honor of arguing with me."²⁵ Arthur certainly knew that Lewis was intelligent, and that he stood little chance of arguing successfully against Lewis. Therefore, Arthur did not engage in head-to-head epistolary combat in his letters. One also understands why Lewis would describe his own besetting sin as pride.²⁶ In the year of his conversion to Christianity, while Warren was beginning to organize the *Lewis Papers*,²⁷ Lewis disarmingly mentions the most striking feature of his early letters—"their egotism." He states, "I seem to be posturing and showing off in every letter."²⁸

They also disagreed in their appreciation of *Beowulf* compared to Malory,²⁹ in their understanding of beauty and nature,³⁰ in their views of the divinity of Christ (for a time),³¹ as well as other areas of disagreement, both literary and musical. But they had more

---

[22] *They Stand Together*, 94. The date is March 7, 1916.

[23] *They Stand Together*, 104. The date is May 30, 1916.

[24] *They Stand Together*, 73. The letter is dated May 25, 1915.

[25] *They Stand Together*, 77. The letter is dated June 8, 1915.

[26] *They Stand Together*, 339. The date is Jan. 30, 1930.

[27] *The Lewis Papers* are a collection of family papers in the Lewis family from 1850-1930, compiled by Warren Lewis and consisting of letters, diaries, poems, brief essays, and various other documents. *The Lewis Papers* are held at the Marion E. Wade Center, Wheaton, Illinois.

[28] *They Stand Together*, 424. The letter is dated Oct. 1, 1931.

[29] *They Stand Together*, 145. The letter is dated Nov. 1, 1916.

[30] *They Stand Together*, 216f. Here, on May 29, 1918, and elsewhere Lewis describes the position of Idealism, which holds that we can never see trees or other material objects as they really are.

[31] See *They Stand Together*, 502-505. Lewis seems to have prevailed in this controversy. These are three letters dated Dec. 11, 1944, Feb. 5, 1945, and Dec. 26, 1945.

agreements than disagreements.

Arthur's artistic talent had some influence on Lewis. While studying with Kirkpatrick, Lewis wrote, "You are going to help me to improve my drawing next hols."[32] Undoubtedly Arthur did. And Arthur's book recommendations were also seriously considered. For example, Arthur's recommendation led Lewis to read David Lindsay's *A Voyage to Arcturus*, a book that profoundly influenced Lewis's writing of his adult fiction.[33]

Lewis did not send any letters to Greeves for about three-and-a-half years between April 1923 and December 1926. Walter Hooper attributes this to a cooling-off period, when a two-week visit to Oxford and Arthur's rude behavior resulted in numerous awkward moments.[34] Lewis once described Arthur as impatient, a grumbler, self-indulgent, and unworldly.[35] But Arthur had many positive qualities as well, including generosity. During Lewis's years of poverty, just before Lewis became a Fellow of Magdalen College in 1925, Arthur sent

Circular Road from the driveway of Little Lea
Arthur's home was located just to the left of the house in view
Author photo

---

[32] *They Stand Together*, 80. The letter is dated July 24, 1915.

[33] *They Stand Together*, 470. The date of the letter is Dec. 26, 1934. The Ransom Trilogy, sometimes known as the Space Trilogy, consist of three books, *Out of the Silent Planet* (1938), *Perelandra* (1943), and *That Hideous Strength* (1945).

[34] *All My Road Before Me*, 258. The date is July 13-25, 1923. Lewis complained that Arthur insisted on butter rather than margarine, put his bare feet on the dining table, stayed in pajamas until noon, and acted in other unusual ways.

[35] *The Lewis Papers*, Vol. X, 218-220. The date is uncertain, but approximately 1935.

some money from time to time to help Lewis make ends meet, just as he did years later for William McClurg (see below).

Lewis once wrote about Arthur, "If I had to write his epitaph, I should say of him what I could say of no one else known to me—'He *despised* nothing.' Contempt—if not the worst, surely the most ludicrously inappropriate of the sins that man commits—was, I believe unknown to him."[36] Arthur was no ordinary person.

JOSEPH ARTHUR GREEVES

Who was Arthur? Joseph Arthur Greeves was born on August 27, 1895,[37] the same year as Warren Lewis, the older brother of C. S. Lewis. Greeves was the youngest of five children[38] of Mary Margretta Gribbon and Joseph Malcolmson Greeves. Arthur's father Joseph was the director of J. & T. M. Greeves, Ltd., flax spinners,[39] so he was a wealthy man.

As a child, Arthur was diagnosed, probably incorrectly,[40] as having a weak heart, with the result that he spent much of his life in what was perceived as delicate health.[41]

This may have led Arthur into his besetting sin, which Lewis once described as indolence.[42] This poor health resulted in only occasional work, but Arthur did work for a time during his younger years at his brother Thomas' firm, Greeves & Morton: Linen Merchants.[43]

Arthur was easily influenced. Lewis once wrote, "He could be

---

[36] *The Lewis Papers*, Vol. X, 220. The date is approximately 1935.

[37] Arthur Greeves Diaries, 1-9.

[38] The other four children were named Thomas Jackson Greeves (1886-1974), Mary Elizabeth Greeves (nicknamed Lily, 1888-1977), William Edward "Willie" Greeves (1890-1960), and John Greeves (1892-1969). See http://www.sinton-family-trees.uk/ft_main.php?rin=3229.

[39] "Greeves, Joseph Arthur," C. S. Lewis *Collected Letters, I*, edited by Walter Hooper, London: Harper Collins Publishers, 2000, 993. This is a biographical note on Greeves by Walter Hooper.

[40] Zaleski calls it a misdiagnosis. Philip Zaleski and Carol Zaleski, *The Fellowship, The Literary lives of the Inklings: J. R. R. Tolkien, C. S. Lewis, Owen Barfield, Charles Williams*. New York: Farrar, Straus and Giroux, 2015, 49.

[41] Lewis once wrote of Arthur's "real and supposed ill health," an indication that there was some truth to poor health being both real and imagined. December 1929, *The Lewis Papers*, Vol. X, 219. The date is approximately 1935.

[42] *They Stand Together*, 339. The letter is dated Jan. 30, 1930.

[43] Introduction, *They Stand Together*, 19.

persuaded to read, or at least begin, any book: to adopt (for a time) any canons of taste."[44] Arthur was "easily drawn into the follies of any and every coterie."[45] All of the Greeves children possessed what Lewis called simplicity, or naivete,[46] often an endearing personal quality.

The Greeves and Lewis families lived in the same Belfast neighborhood on Circular Road in Strandtown, Belfast, just south of Belfast harbor. In mid-April 1914, while home due to illness, Arthur invited Lewis to visit. Arthur was eighteen years old and Lewis fifteen. His home was located almost directly across the street from the Lewis home. Arthur had previously attempted to reach out to Warren and Jack, but for some reason they had never responded. This time Jack accepted.[47] Then occurred the exchange described at the beginning of this chapter. Lewis once called Greeves his "oldest and most intimate friend,"[48] since Arthur was one of the first friends outside of the family that the young Lewis made.

Arthur was raised in the Plymouth Brethren tradition and later influenced by the Quaker tradition, i.e., the Society of Friends, as well as Unitarianism[49] and the Baha'i religion.[50] Greeves returned to the Quaker tradition at the end of his life.[51] Greeves attended Campbell College from 1906-1912, one term of which coincided with Lewis's only term at that school—Autumn of 1910 (without the two boys ever meeting[52]).

When he was in his mid-twenties, Arthur considered three career possibilities—to enroll at Oxford University, to study painting at the Slade School of Fine Art at University College, London, or to take up

---

[44] *The Lewis Papers*, Vol. X, 219. The date is approximately 1935.

[45] *The Lewis Papers*, Vol. X, 219. The date is approximately 1935.

[46] *The Lewis Papers*, Vol. III, 304.

[47] *Surprised by Joy: The Shape of My Early Life*. San Diego: Harcourt Brace Jovanovich, 1955, 130.

[48] *The Lewis Papers*, Vol. III, 305, cited in *They Stand Together*, edited by Walter Hooper, New York: Macmillan Publishing Co., 1979, 18. The date is 1933.

[49] See *They Stand Together*, 502-505, where Lewis is defending the deity of Christ against what Arthur appears to have written in opposition to that position. Two letters are dated Dec. 11, 1944, and Feb. 5, 1945.

[50] Introduction, *They Stand Together*, edited by Walter Hooper, New York: Macmillan Publishing Co., 1979, 29.

[51] Introduction, *They Stand Together*, 37.

[52] *Surprised by Joy*, 130. Lewis states that they attended Campbell College at the same time, but never met.

poultry farming.[53] Despite Arthur's efforts in June to resurrect his knowledge of Latin[54] so he could pass Oxford Responsions[55]—or perhaps because of this failed effort—he decided against Oxford. His artistic talent led him to the second option. Arthur enrolled at the Slade School of Fine Art at University College, London, with the term that began on January 3, 1921,[56] where he studied drawing and painting.[57] He continued at the Slade until the end of 1923,[58] earning a Certificate in Painting from Life[59] for his efforts.

After earning his Certificate, he set up a studio in the Paddington area of London for the next few years.[60] He later studied art in Paris and in 1936 exhibited two of his paintings with the Royal Hibernian Academy in Dublin, Ireland.[61] Those

---

[53] *They Stand Together*, 270f. The letter is dated April 11, 1920.

[54] See Lewis's advice to Arthur about Latin in Lewis's letter of June 6, 1920. *They Stand Together*, 276. Later that month, in a letter dated June 19, he gave Arthur advice about John Milton, Francis Bacon, English, writing, and, once again, Latin. *They Stand Together*, 280, 282.

[55] Entrance exams to the university.

[56] University College London Calendar, 1920-1921. http://www.ucl.ac.uk/library/about/records-office/contact

[57] First Entry Form, Robert Winckworth, Archives Assistant, UCL Records, University College London. Arthur lived at 66 Torrington Square, London, upon entrance to the Slade School. http://www.ucl.ac.uk/library/digital-collections/collections/records

[58] The term ended on December 15. University College London Calendar, 1923-1924. http://www.ucl.ac.uk/library/digital-collections/collections/records

[59] Email, dated Nov. 17, 2017, from Robert Winckworth, Archives Assistant, UCL Records, University College London. Painting from Life was one of the fields of study at the Slade, along with Figure Drawing, History of Art, Fine Art Anatomy, Decorative Design, Sculpture, Perspective, Head Painting, Painting from the Cast, Wood Engraving, Lettering, and Drawing of Heads from Life. http://www.ucl.ac.uk/library/digital-collections/collections/records This certificate would be the equivalent to a professional certification rather than an undergraduate or graduate degree.

[60] *They Stand Together*, 292f. This letter from Lewis on April 22, 1923 seems to have been written to Arthur while Arthur was living in London. Among other topics, it addresses the arts and Arthur's painting. Arthur's address was 119 Westbourne Terrace.

[61] Nancy-Lou Patterson, "Joseph Arthur Greeves (1895-1966)," *The C. S. Lewis Readers' Encyclopedia*, edited by Jeffrey D. Schultz and

No Ordinary People

two landscape paintings were entitled "Ballinroy" and "Above Ballysallagh."⁶² Greeves expressed his love of nature through the artistic landscape scenes he painted, and he helped Lewis to appreciate the beauty of the outdoor world through his ability to notice even the slightest features of nature. Lewis once wrote, "What he called the 'Homely' was the natural food both of his heart and his imagination. A bright hearth seen through an open door as we passed, a train of ducks following a brawny farmer's wife, a drill of cabbages in a suburban garden—these were things that never failed to move him, even to ecstasy ...."⁶³ Arthur's love for the seemingly ordinary and God's creation was not lost on Lewis.

Arthur also taught Lewis to look at people with a similar sense of awe. Lewis writes, "He continued to feel—indeed he taught me to endeavor to feel with him—at once a human affection and a rich aesthetic relish for his antediluvian aunts, his mill-owning uncles, his mother's servants, the postman on our roads, and the cottagers whom we met in our walks."⁶⁴ Perhaps in that sense of awe which Arthur felt in other people we see the beginnings of Lewis's belief that there are no ordinary people.

A local novelist, Forrest Reid, and Arthur had become acquaintances through their mutual love of art. They were well enough acquainted to help the Lewis brothers sell the contents of Little Lea soon after the death of their father Albert Lewis. Forrest Reid was the author of sixteen novels, including *Following Darkness* (1912) (which inspired James Joyce's *A Portrait of the Artist as a Young Man*), *Uncle Stephen* (1931), Reid's autobiography *Apostate* (1926), *Peter Waring* (1937), and other books. Reid lived in Belfast from 1924 until

---

John G. West Jr., Grand Rapids: Zondervan, 1998, 190. Walter Hooper notes that Arthur was a member of the Royal Hibernian Academy. *Collected Letters, I*, 995. See also the Hibernian records of exhibited artists. See Ann Stewart, *Royal Hibernian Academy of Art—Index of Exhibitors*.

⁶² Ann M. Stewart, *Royal Hibernian Academy of Art—Index of Exhibitors* (alphabetical listing of exhibited artists and their works) of the Royal Hibernian Academy. Manton Publishing, 1987. Kate McBride, Academy Coordinator, Royal Hibernian Academy, 15 Ely Place, Dublin, Ireland D02 A213. The catalogue numbers of the paintings are 188 and 204.

⁶³ *They Stand Together*, edited by Walter Hooper, New York: Macmillan Publishing Co., 1979, 25. *The Lewis Papers*, Vol., X, 218-220. The date is uncertain, but approximately 1935.

⁶⁴ *The Lewis Papers*, Vol. X, 219. The date is approximately 1935. See also *Collected Letters, I*, 974, where Lewis writes about homeliness as Arthur's chief lesson for Lewis.

his death in 1947.[65] In 1944, Reid was awarded the James Tait Black Memorial Prize for his last novel *Young Tom* (1944).

When in 1930, Lewis encouraged Arthur to submit some of his attempts at writing to a friend for his critique, he gave them to Forrest Reid. Lewis then had the difficult task of writing an encouraging letter to lift Arthur's spirits, because Reid's verdict on Arthur's writings was quite discouraging.[66] The encouragement seems to have worked, since Arthur was later engaged in writing a detective story.[67] Arthur Greeves painted several portraits of Reid, which are owned by the Royal Belfast Academical Institution.[68]

Forrest Reid
by Arthur Greeves,
displayed at The Royal Belfast
Academical Institution,
Used by permission

In 1936, Arthur took a summer trip to the United States to visit William Moncrief McClurg, whom he had met years earlier in Belfast.[69] Arthur and his four aunts had provided financial assistance to McClurg, which had enabled him to study medicine at the Kirksville College of Osteopathy and Surgery at Kirksville, Missouri. McClurg later set up his medical practice in New England. At the invitation of McClurg, Arthur traveled to New England in 1936, and the two men purchased a used car. They drove through the Adirondack Mountains in New York, stayed at Hurricane Lodge in Keene, New York, and then traveled through Long Island, Vermont, and Cape Cod,

---

[65] Much of the biographical information in this paragraph appears in the *Wikipedia* article about him.

[66] This is the letter of Aug. 18, 1930, along with which he included a part of his diary. *They Stand Together*, 378-384.

[67] *They Stand Together*, 440, 449, 462. These letters, which mention Arthur's detective story, are dated, respectively, March 27, 1932, Feb. 4, 1933, and Sept. 1, 1933. In 1926 and 1927, Greeves was writing a play entitled *Trees*, which was never published. See *They Stand Together*, 296, 298.

[68] Some of this biographical information, including the identification of Arthur Greeves as the painter of the Forrest Reid painting shown in this article, comes from "The Instonian Profile," *Sea-Horse*, Spring 2014, 12.

[69] We don't know how they met or the circumstances under which they met, except that McClurg had taken some science classes in Belfast, which motivated him to study medicine.

Massachusetts. At Cape Cod they visited an artists' colony so that Arthur could enjoy some of the paintings and mingle with the local artists. McClurg later established a medical practice as an osteopathic physician in London.[70] The two men kept in touch with one another, and Arthur spent a holiday with McClurg in London in 1961.[71]

After the death of his mother in 1949, Arthur moved to Silver Hill, a cottage in Crawfordsburn, County Down, where Lewis stayed at times, especially during the summers of 1958 and 1959 when Lewis and his wife Joy visited.[72] Arthur died in his sleep on August 29, 1966 at the age of seventy-one.

Religious Differences

"During the earlier years of our acquaintance," writes Lewis, "he was (as always) a Christian, and I was an atheist. But though (God forgive me) I bombarded him with all the thin artillery of a seventeen-year-old rationalist, I never made any impression on his faith—a faith both vague and confused, and in some ways too indulgent to our common weaknesses, but inexpungable. He remains victor in that debate. It is I who have come round. The thing is symbolical of much in our joint history. He was not a clever boy, he was even a dull boy; I was a scholar. He had no 'ideas.' I bubbled over with them. It might seem that I had much to give him, and that he had nothing to give me. But this is not the truth. I could give concepts, logic, facts, arguments, but he had feelings to offer, feelings which most mysteriously—for he was always very inarticulate—he taught me to share. Hence, in our commerce, I dealt in superficies, but he in solids. I learned charity from him and failed, for all my efforts, to teach him arrogance in return."[73]

Lewis's arrogance and Arthur's charity are borne out in another statement Lewis made in a letter to Arthur in 1916: "Indeed Arthur if I could get a little of your diffidence, and you a little of my conceit we should both be very fine fellows.[74]

---

[70] *They Stand Together*, 481, n. 3.

[71] *They Stand Together*, 555. The date of Arthur's letter is May 6, 1961.

[72] *Collected Letters, I*, 995.

[73] *They Stand Together*, edited by Walter Hooper, New York: Macmillan Publishing Co., 1979, 25. *The Lewis Papers*, Vol., X, 218-220.

[74] *They Stand Together*, 120. The date is July 11, 1916.

Their religious differences in the early years appear in several of Lewis's letters. Arthur had not liked Lewis's portrayal of Christianity in his long poem, "The Quest of Bleheris."[75] Later that year, Lewis made the claim that "all religions, that is, all mythologies ... are merely man's own invention—Christ as much as Loki."[76] That same month, Lewis writes to Arthur, "I am quite content to live without believing in a bogey who is prepared to torture me forever and ever if I should fail in coming up to about an almost impossible ideal...."[77] Writing from a hospital in early 1918, where he was recovering from war injuries, Lewis writes to Arthur, "The gods hate me—and naturally enough considering my usual attitude towards them."[78] Ironically, Lewis's first Christian book, *The Pilgrim's Regress*, would be written during a two-week stay in Belfast with Arthur, the Christian whose faith Lewis had rejected early in life.[79] Lewis gave him a complimentary copy, and he dedicated the book to Arthur.

In 1929, with his conversion to theism less than a year away, Lewis shared the discovery of George MacDonald's *The Diary of an Old Soul*, just as he had shared the discovery of MacDonald's *Phantastes* thirteen years earlier. He strongly advised Arthur to read it, describing MacDonald as an author who seems to know everything.[80] Then, two months later, Lewis writes to Arthur about John Bunyan's book, *Grace Abounding*. He found himself intrigued with one sentence in Bunyan's book: "I could not find that with all my soul I did *desire* deliverance."[81] There Bunyan was feeling himself united to Christ and yet somewhat hesitant to be wholeheartedly united, but Lewis didn't understand what Bunyan meant. He wondered what Arthur thought of "the darker side of religion."[82] A few sentences later Lewis writes about that darker side—sin, death, and judgment, "There must be something in it: only what?"[83] When Lewis became a Christian a year

---

[75] *They Stand Together*, 124. The letter is dated July 18, 1916.

[76] *They Stand Together*, 135. The date of the letter is Oct. 12, 1916.

[77] *They Stand Together*, 137f. The letter is dated Oct. 18, 1916.

[78] *They Stand Together*, 209. The date of the letter is Feb. 21, 1918.

[79] This happened during August 1932.

[80] *They Stand Together*, 313. The letter is dated Oct. 10, 1929.

[81] *The Complete Works of John Bunyan, with an Introduction*, Classic Reprint Series, London: Forgotten Books, 2017. *Grace Abounding to the Chief of Sinners*, 41.

[82] *They Stand Together*, 319. The letter was written in 1929 in serial form, this entry on Dec. 22.

[83] *They Stand Together*, 320. The date of the letter is also Dec. 22, 1929.

later, Arthur was the first person to whom he wrote, describing how it had happened.[84]

Some weeks after he became a theist, Lewis writes a letter to Arthur, explaining how much he appreciates Arthur's letters. First, he writes, things from Belfast carry a sweetness about them; second, Arthur is "the only person whom I can write to or be written to with full understanding"; and, third, the common ground between them represents "the deepest stratum in my life."[85] Clearly, whatever had bothered Lewis about Arthur was forgiven, and the two men—though living in vastly different worlds—had come to appreciate one another all the more.

For example, a discussion on good and evil and its relationship to God appears in a later letter. Lewis agrees with Arthur, but he also advances the argument. In one sense, God is pure Light and no darkness. Agreeing with Arthur, Lewis writes that God includes evil in the sense that he understands it.[86] In his letter, Arthur had stated, "God must have a potentiality of His opposite—evil." Lewis replied with a counter-argument, that God has no opposite; God is beyond good and evil.[87] There can be good without evil, but evil cannot exist without good.[88] We can be in the same position as the dog, which, while being taken for a walk, goes around a post and must turn back in order to go forward. The dog really wants to go forward but does not realize that the best way to do that is to retreat. In the same way, we at times resist God's leash even while God affirms our desire to go forward.[89]

Conclusion

Arthur Greeves profoundly influenced C. S. Lewis. Arthur's humility must have rubbed off on Lewis, and we remember that Lewis called him Galahad as a compliment to his purity. In addition, Lewis

---

[84] See *They Stand Together*, 423-428. These two letters are dated Oct. 1 and Oct. 18, 1931. The story is told in detail elsewhere, including my book *From Atheism to Christianity: The Story of C. S. Lewis* (Concordia Publishing House, 2017).

[85] *They Stand Together*, 370. The letter is dated July 29, 1930.

[86] *They Stand Together*, 462f. But this summary, of course, greatly simplifies Lewis's letter, which is too long and complicated to summarize fully. The letter is dated Sept. 12, 1933.

[87] *They Stand Together*, 462.

[88] *They Stand Together*, 463.

[89] Ibid.

gained from Arthur's appreciation of the homely and the simple, his generosity (he would "offer me assistance in my lean times," writes Lewis[90]), his charity, his love of nature, his artistic talent (which combined with his love of nature to produce landscape paintings), and his detachment from the things of this world. None of these characteristics are lofty or pretentious. They remind us that "there are no ordinary people."[91]

---

[90] *The Lewis Papers*, Vol. X, 220. The date is approximately 1935.

[91] C. S. Lewis, "The Weight of Glory," *The Weight of Glory and Other Addresses*. New York: Simon & Schuster, 1980, 39.

"Jack" with Maureen and Mrs. Moore on holiday in Cornwall, 1917
Used by permission of the Marion E. Wade Center,
Wheaton College, Wheaton, IL.

Chapter 5

JANIE MOORE
The "Mother" of C. S. Lewis

One of the longest and most unusual friendships that C. S. Lewis ever had was with Mrs. Janie Moore, a woman twenty-six years his senior and the mother of his good friend Paddy. Some speculate that the relationship began as an infatuation, quickly moved to a sexual relationship, and then changed significantly when Lewis became a Christian in 1931. Others describe the later stage of that relationship as a test of Lewis's Christian faith, as he steadily met every challenge of a most demanding relationship. At one point in his life after his conversion, he began to refer to Mrs. Moore as his "mother,"[1] something that, given her age, seems reasonable.

Rarely has this relationship been explored in any depth or with a broad attempt to look at the entire picture of Janie Moore's life. This chapter will do just that, examining the nature of a friendship that displayed *philia*,[2] but perhaps also *Eros*.[3]

PADDY MOORE

A few months after his arrival in Oxford, Lewis joined the Officers' Training Corps[4] (OTC) in preparation for joining the war effort on the continent. Paddy Moore joined E Company of No. 4 Officer Cadet Battalion, the same one that Lewis joined. Since their names were close together in the alphabet, they ended up as roommates at Keble College. Soon thereafter Lewis met Paddy's mother. Lewis wrote to his father about Mrs. Moore, stating, "I like her immensely."[5] Paddy and Lewis were given a month's leave before their deployment to France, and they spent three weeks at Paddy's home and Lewis then spent just one week with his father in Belfast.[6]

---

[1] This began no later than Nov. 9, 1941. See *Collected Letters*, II, 496, for the first documented use of the term *mother*.

[2] Friendship.

[3] Intimacy, including the physical, sexual aspect of the relationship.

[4] Alister McGrath, *C. S. Lewis, A Life: Eccentric Genius. Reluctant Prophet*, 56. The exact date is May 7, 1917.

[5] The date is August 27, 1917. *Collected Letters*, I, 334.

[6] Hooper, *Companion & Guide*, 713. See also *The Lewis Papers* V:233.

After their deployment to France, they never saw one another again. They had promised that if one of them did not return from the war, the other person would look after the parent of the deceased one.[7] When Paddy died in the war, Lewis kept that promise and took care of Paddy's mother, Janie Moore, and Paddy's sister, Maureen.[8]

Paddy fought against the German Spring offensive that began on March 21, 1918.[9] This strategy included a series of German attacks along the Western Front and marked the deepest advances by either side since 1914. The Germans knew that they had to win before the United States fully engaged in the war and changed the odds in favor of the Allies, so they made one last prolonged attempt to do so.[10] Despite the surprise attack and the advantage in numbers, early successes by the Germans were not sustained. All the German gains were lost, the Hindenburg line collapsed, and this major contributing factor, along with other dynamics, led eventually to the November 11 Armistice.

Early in the German offensive, undoubtedly in Operation Michael,[11] the main part of the offensive, Paddy Moore died in battle. The Germans had launched their offensive against the British Fifth Army and the right wing of the British Third Army. Paddy was reported missing on March 24, only three days after the fighting had begun.[12] He may have been one of the 7,512 British soldiers who died

---

The leave began on September 29, 1917.

[7] Walter Hooper, ed., *All My Road Before Me: The Diary of C. S. Lewis*, San Diego: Harcourt Brace Jovanovich, 1991, 4. Hooper recalls that Maureen Moore told him about this promise.

[8] Paul McCusker makes this point in "What do we make of Lewis's relationship with Mrs. Moore?" *Women and C. S. Lewis*, edited by Carolyn Curtis and Mary Pomeroy Key, Oxford, England: Lion Books, 2015, 41.

[9] This major offensive was called the Kaiserschlacht, i.e., "Kaiser's Battle." It was also known as the Ludendorff Offensive, so named for General Erich Ludendorff.

[10] The US had officially entered the war on April 6, 1917 but was slow in mobilizing. US troops started arriving on the Western front in the summer of 1918.

[11] Michael was the code name for the main attack, which came against the British forces. These forces held the territory between Amiens, France, and the English Channel.

[12] Paul McCusker and Michael Ward state that he died at Pargny. Michael Ward, "Lady Dunbar 1906-1997," *VII: An Anglo-American Literary Review*, Volume 14 (1997):5. Paul McCusker, "What do we make of Lewis's relationship with Mrs. Moore?" *Women and C. S. Lewis*, edited by Carolyn Curtis and Mary Pomeroy Key, Oxford, England: Lion Books, 2015, 44.

on the first day. His death was confirmed in April, and in December he received the Military Cross posthumously for "conspicuous gallantry and initiative."[13] Mrs. Moore, of course, was devastated. After receiving a letter of sympathy from Albert Lewis, Mrs. Moore wrote back, confirming the promises that her son and Lewis had made, "Jack[14] has been so good to me. My poor son asked him to look after me if he did not come back."[15]

JANIE KING MOORE

Janie King Askins was born in Pomeroy, Northern Ireland, on March 28, 1872,[16] the oldest of six children of Rev. William James Askins,[17] Rector of Dunleer, County Louth, Ireland, and Jane King Askins.[18] The Askins family had moved to Dunany, Ireland in 1871, where Rev. Askins served as Vicar of Dunany and Dunleer until his death in 1895.[19] Her siblings, from oldest to youngest, were Edith ("Edie"),[20] John Hawkins,[21] William James,[22] Robert[23] (known as Rob in Lewis's diary), and Sarah.[24] Both John and Robert became doctors, and William James, the namesake of his father, became a clergyman of the Church of Ireland.

---

[13] *Collected Letters*, I, 1020. Hooper, *Companion & Guide*, 713. See also Michael Ward, "Lady Dunbar 1906-1997," *VII: An Anglo-American Literary Review*, Vol. 14 (1997):5.

[14] Jack is the name by which most of the friends and family of C. S. Lewis called him.

[15] *The Lewis Papers*, VI:44f.

[16] https://www.findagrave.com/memorial/156508230/janie-king-moore

[17] 1842-1895.

[18] 1846-1890. Her mother had the same name as Janie.

[19] Much of the biographical information is based on Walter Hooper, *C. S. Lewis: A Companion & Guide*, New York: HarperCollins Publishers, 1996, 712-715. Janie was baptized on July 21, 1872 and grew up in Dunany. Walter Hooper, ed., *All My Road Before Me: The Diary of C. S. Lewis*, San Diego: Harcourt Brace Jovanovich, 1991, 3.

[20] 1873-1936.

[21] 1877-1923. She lost this brother, Dr. John Askins in 1923, nursing him in her home until his death. This is the brother who died after weeks of raving and needing to be restrained and sedated. The date of his death is April 6. Hooper, *Companion & Guide*, 714.

[22] 1879-1955.

[23] 1880-1935.

[24] Later, Sarah Horan. See *All My Road Before Me*, 17.

After her mother died in 1890, Janie did most of the work of raising her brothers and sisters. When her father died in 1895, Janie took on many more responsibilities for raising them. This early work of mothering undoubtedly shaped her life as the sustainer of a household and quickly became the glue that held the family life together. Warren Lewis writes in his diary, "Her mother died when she was a schoolgirl at Lincoln, and the next few years she spent in 'bringing up' her brothers and sisters, and fighting their battles against a tyrannical and oppressive father."[25] Later, however, she seems to have taken this to an extreme and alienated many of those around her by running too tight a ship in the Lewis household.

On August 1, 1897, Janie married Courtenay Edward Moore,[26] a civil engineer and the son of Courtenay Moore,[27] Rector of Mitchelstown in County Cork, and Jessie Mona Duff.[28] The daughter of a clergyman married the son of a clergyman, and one would expect this combination to succeed. It did not. Janie and her husband separated in 1907, and she moved to Bristol where her brother Robert was a government medical doctor and where her sister Edie also lived. Her god-daughter Vera Henry once remarked that "she would never go anywhere with him [her husband] or do anything he wanted her to do but was always messing about with hers."[29] They had two children—Edward Francis Courtenay "Paddy" Moore[30] and Maureen Daisy Helen Moore.[31]

---

[25] *Brothers & Friends*, 238. The date of the diary entry is January 17, 1951.

[26] 1870-1951.

[27] Rector Moore was a writer of articles for the *Journal of the Cork Historical and Archaeological Society*, which he helped to found (see John Hayes, "C. S. Lewis and a Chronicle of the Moores," *Irish University Review*, Vol. 39, No. 1, [Spring-Summer 2009]:96), having written "Some Account of Kingston College, Middletown, Co. Cork," Vol. 4, No. 38 (April-June 1898): 107-115. The article is a miscellaneous recounting of some of the events and people who worked at Kingston College.

[28] Walter Hooper, ed., *All My Road Before Me: The Diary of C. S. Lewis*, San Diego: Harcourt Brace Jovanovich, 1991, 3. For six years Canon Moore edited the *Irish Ecclesiastical Gazette*, the newspaper of the Anglican communion in Ireland, and he was a director of the Mitchelstown and Fermoy Light Railway Company. John Hayes, "C. S. Lewis and a Chronicle of the Moores," *Irish University Review*, Vol. 39, No. 1, [Spring-Summer 2009]:96.

[29] The unpublished diary of Warren Lewis for January 17, 1951.

[30] November 17, 1898 to March 24, 1918.

[31] Maureen was born on August 19, 1906 and died on February 15,

Twenty-One Friendships of C.S. Lewis

Janie came to know Lewis through her son. Since Paddy was a cadet in the OTC, Janie and her daughter Maureen moved to Wellington Square in central Oxford to be close to him. After his deployment in October 1917, she apparently moved back to Bristol. While recovering from war wounds, Lewis was transferred to a convalescent home in Bristol, where he could be near Mrs. Moore. After the war, Lewis returned to Oxford University. Mrs. Moore and her daughter Maureen moved back to Oxford, found a house to rent, and from this time on they shared a house with Lewis.[32] Already in May 1919, Lewis's father and brother—Albert and Warren—were corresponding, unhappily, about Lewis's relationship with Mrs. Moore.

Mrs. Moore met Warren Lewis, then on a six-month leave from the Royal Army Service Corps, for the first time in 1922.[33] About that meeting, Warren wrote, "I am glad to have met Mrs. M and Maureen, not only intrinsically but because it gives me a larger share in J's[34] real life."[35]

In 1930, Janie King Moore, Lewis, and his brother Warren jointly purchased an eight-acre property, The Kilns, in Headington Quarry. She lived there with the Lewis brothers until her death two decades later. In his diaries Lewis calls her "Minto" or "D." "D" was Lewis's nickname for Mrs. Moore.[36] Mrs. Moore went into the Restholme Nursing Home in Oxford in April 1950, and Lewis visited her nearly every day until her death.[37] She died of influenza on January 12, 1951

1997. See the chapter on her life elsewhere in this book.

[32] Hooper, *Companion & Guide*, 713. The house was located at 28 Warneford Road, and Lewis resumed his studies in January 1919. Warren Lewis writes, "... as soon as his first year as an undergraduate was over ... he set up a joint ménage with her and her daughter Maureen." W. H. Lewis, "Memoir of C. S. Lewis," *Letters of C. S. Lewis*, San Diego: Harcourt Brace & Company, 1966, Revised Harvest edition 1993, 32.

[33] He had returned from a year of service in Sierra Leone, arriving in Liverpool on April 7, 1922. The met on August 5.

[34] Warren's abbreviation for his brother Jack, a lifelong nickname.

[35] *Brothers & Friends*, 12.

[36] Some think it stands for Diotoma, who allegedly is the source of Plato's idea of love and may be an allusion to a sexual relationship. Walter Hooper states that the "D" stood for the Greek letter delta (Δ), which Warren could not reproduce on his typewriter. Walter Hooper, ed., *All My Road Before Me*, 10. Minto may have been a nickname that resulted from a favorite candy she liked.

[37] See, for example, *Collected Letters*, III, 78. "I visit her, normally, every day ...."

at the age of 78. Three days later she was buried in the Holy Trinity Churchyard, Headington, Oxfordshire.[38] Her husband, with whom she was never reconciled, died in Terenure, a suburb of Dublin, later that year.[39]

C. S. LEWIS AND MRS. MOORE

Mrs. Moore was in many ways a typical homemaker. She participated in family activities such as badminton, and on at least one occasion she went golfing with Maureen.[40] She enjoyed playing Bridge, with Lewis often one of a foursome. Lewis frequently read books to her,[41] but sometimes he read from his diary or the *Times*. She made numerous contacts with people about getting Maureen a good musical education.[42] She sometimes served as a sounding board for Lewis, for example, when he was considering the Reading University faculty position for which he had been interviewed[43] or when the family needed to make decisions about their finances.[44] In addition to her domestic duties of preparing meals, serving tea, and doing laundry, she often made marmalade, strawberry, gooseberry, or plum jam,[45] probably to use as gifts for various friends and acquaintances. She frequently recruited Lewis to help her at various stages in the preparation of the jam.

Criticisms of Janie Moore

When Mrs. Moore died in 1951, Warren wrote, "And so ends the mysterious self-imposed slavery in which J has lived for at least

---

[38] https://www.findagrave.com/memorial/156508230/janie-king-moore

[39] The date is on June 9. Hooper, *Companion & Guide*, 714. See also John Hayes, "C. S. Lewis and a Chronicle of the Moores," *Irish University Review*, Vol. 39, No. 1, [Spring-Summer 2009]:99.

[40] *All My Road Before Me*, 224. The date is March 25, 1923. See also page 420. The dates are July 1 and 2, 1926.

[41] *All My Road Before Me*, 16, 21.

[42] *All My Road Before Me*, 25.

[43] *All My Road Before Me*, 54, 56.

[44] See "Chronologically Lewis" for January 26, 1927.

[45] See, for example, *All My Road Before Me*, 15, 61, 228, 306. Lewis was not happy to be involved, once stating, "... I cd. willingly have every fruit tree in England burnt down." *All My Road Before Me*, 71. The plum jam she made for Mrs. Raymond, perhaps as a way of raising some money: *All My Road Before Me*, 95f.

thirty years."⁴⁶ In a letter to one of his correspondents later that year, Lewis himself explains, "I have lived most of ... my private life in a house which was hardly ever at peace for 24 hours, amid senseless wranglings, lyings, backbitings, follies, and *scares*. I never went home without a feeling of terror as to what appalling situation might have developed in my absence. Only now that it is over do I begin to realize quite how bad it was."⁴⁷ So domineering was Mrs. Moore that one writer attempted to make the case that she was the model which Lewis used for the Queen of Underland in the Narnian chronicle *The Silver Chair*.⁴⁸

Indicative of Mrs. Moore's faulty perception of events, Warren also writes,

> On getting in from my walk I found Minto in the early stages of an attack of hysteria, moaning "Oh, Maureen's hurt, there's been an accident, Maureen has had an accident etc., etc." and urging me to go out with Paxford and investigate—which I immediately did. On reaching St. Clement's I was much relieved to find Maureen perfectly alright, and very angry when I learnt that her first act had been to ring up the house and say (a) that there had been an accident, (b) that she was quite alright, and (c) that she wanted Paxford with the car papers. What had happened was that, in avoiding a van which pulled out without warning, she had swerved into another car, injured its rear hub, and burst one of her own front tires. Very odd, this characteristic of Minto's to make melodrama out of every happening, and to suppress or falsify any favorable evidence in her possession....⁴⁹

Another example of Mrs. Moore's misperception came during the last year of her life. Warren writes, "After finishing the mail I bussed up to Restholme, where I had a very nasty fright: found M in tears, who handed me a letter from Maureen, sobbing out with difficulty 'Very bad news: killed.' I tore the letter open and found nothing but a half-sheet of the usual feminine *petits riens*.⁵⁰ Astonishing how even in a state of semi-imbecility, Minto retains the power of importing a

---

⁴⁶ *Brothers & Friends*, 236. The date of the diary entry is January 17, 1951. "J" is Warren's abbreviation for his brother Jack.

⁴⁷ The recipient of this letter was Mrs. Mary Van Deusen. *Collected Letters, III*, 108.

⁴⁸ Michael C. Kotzin, "Mrs. Moore as the Queen of Underland," *Mythlore*, Volume 3, Number 3, Issue 21 (Summer 1979):46.

⁴⁹ The unpublished diary of Warren Lewis for November 14, 1934.

⁵⁰ French for "little things" or "little nothings" or "little trifling."

hideous plausibility to her wildest mare's nests!"[51]

Mrs. Moore had a wide variety of health problems, including poor circulation, varicose veins, indigestion, headaches, neuritis, toothaches, sore back, sore ankles, irritation of the bladder, and other ailments. The frequent, almost daily, reports on her health in Lewis's diary during the 1920s suggest that she was a hypochondriac. Already in May 1922, she had pains in her arm that seemed of uncertain origin.[52] Her health problems increased as the years passed, she had a mild stroke in 1944,[53] and her increasingly poor health undoubtedly contributed to her sometimes erratic and demanding behavior. After her death Warren states as much:

Janie Moore's tombstone
Author photo

> The last three or four years of Minto's life were obviously very nearly unbearable owing to her hate, and malice.... Looking back over this miserable period I feel that the charitable, probably the true explanation of her horrible behavior was that for some years before her death her brain was slowly giving way.[54]

Whether or not this was true, health problems were major factors in her disagreeableness. Her health had been failing for quite some time, when Warren wrote, four years before her death, "Minto has been within measurable distance of death—threatenings of pneumonia."[55]

In his "Memoir of C. S. Lewis," Warren Lewis describes her impact on his brother:

> She was a woman of very limited mind, and notably domineering and possessive by temperament. She cut down to a minimum his visits to his father, interfered constantly

---

[51] *Brothers & Friends*, 233. for June 16, 1950.

[52] *All My Road Before Me*, 40.

[53] *Collected Letters, III*, 1555.

[54] *Brothers & Friends*, 270. The date is February 6, 1967. She may have been dealing with dementia.

[55] *Brothers & Friends*, 198. for March 17, 1947.

with his work, and imposed upon him a heavy burden of minor domestic tasks. In twenty years I never saw a book in her hands; her conversation was chiefly about herself, and was otherwise a matter of ill-informed dogmatism: her mind was of a type that he [Jack] found barely tolerable elsewhere. The whole business had to be concealed from my father of course, which widened the rift between him and Jack; and since an allowance calculated to suit a bachelor living in college was by no means enough for a householder, Jack found himself miserably poor. Nevertheless he continued in this restrictive and distracting servitude for many of his most fruitful years, suffering the worries and expense of repeated moves, until in 1930 we all settled at The Kilns, Headington Quarry.[56]

Mrs. Moore was demanding. Whenever they moved to another rental house or apartment, Lewis was involved in painting, staining, cleaning, hanging pictures, and moving boxes and furniture. Mrs. Moore sent him on shopping trips for food and other items, walking the dogs, digging the hen run,[57] running errands to deliver messages, and checking out possible living spaces to rent, in addition to requiring his help in the kitchen and around the house at a moment's notice. This made writing more difficult for Lewis since he was often summoned in the middle of his writing to help with some domestic task. Lewis himself once stated that "he had to write by snatches, between walking the dog and peeling the potatoes."[58] Warren notes that Mrs. Moore would sometimes tell visitors, "He is as good as an extra maid in the house."[59]

Warren once wrote in his diary about differing opinions of an upcoming Easter holiday, "Minto of course want[ed] absolute subordination of everyone and everything to her own desires."[60] Five months later, while on holiday in Kilkeel, County Down, Warren opens another window into Minto's mind, stating, "Something wrong with Minto at breakfast this morning, who made a flat and emphatic denial of every statement made by everyone, thus extinguishing all

---

[56] W. H. Lewis, "Memoir of C. S. Lewis," *Letters of C. S. Lewis*, 32f.

[57] That is, preparing the ground for hens to peck for food.

[58] David Wesley Soper, *Exploring the Christian World Mind*, London: Vision Press, 1964, cited in Colin Duriez, *Tolkien and C. S. Lewis: The Gift of Friendship*, Mahwah, NJ: HiddenSpring, 2003, 40. Duriez does not give a page number in Soper's book.

[59] W. H. Lewis, "Memoir of C. S. Lewis," *Letters of C. S. Lewis*, 37.

[60] The unpublished diary of Warren Lewis. The date of the diary entry is March 10, 1934.

conversation."⁶¹ During that same holiday, Warren writes, "I then and there registered a determination that no pressure short of the certainty of an open rupture with J will ever induce me to go on any expedition of which Minto is a member in the future."⁶² The irritability of Mrs. Moore and her insistence on getting her own way were increasingly on display throughout her life.

Not surprisingly, mother and daughter did not always get along either. Lewis once wrote about a spat over how Maureen washed the dishes after a meal. While not specifically criticizing Mrs. Moore, his account states, "Maureen offered to wash up after supper. Like a fool (or a knave) I acquiesced and she began, not according to D's fundamental principles. D rushed into the scullery and took the implements out of her hands and a violent altercation followed, Maureen claiming to be judged by results, and D saying that if every servant had to learn her ways she didn't see why her daughter shouldn't." Mrs. Moore apparently wanted the dishes done her way, and Maureen didn't think *how* one did the dishes mattered as much as *that* they were done. This disagreement was followed by another argument, once again apparently Mrs. Moore's fault.⁶³ Mrs. Moore's unusual relationship with her daughter led her to say, when Maureen was about to go out with a friend, "If I don't hear from you by eleven o'clock tonight, I'll know there has been an accident."⁶⁴ The disagreements of a mother with her daughter happen in almost every family, but Mrs. Moore's claim on one occasion that her life would be shortened by five years, if Maureen did not leave the home, strikes one as over the top.⁶⁵

Mrs. Moore had a strange relationship with the family handyman Paxford, whom she regarded highly, although with few reasons for regarding him so. Her citing Paxford about two radios illustrates this unfounded trust:

> Maureen: "Well, the A set certainly has the better tone."
>
> Minto: "Oh, no dear, Paxford says the B set has a lovely tone: he says the A set is tinny."
>
> Maureen: "Well, it blurs the sound: you can't hear the 'underneath of any of the music.'"

---

⁶¹ The unpublished diary of Warren Lewis. The date is August 5, 1934.

⁶² *Brothers & Friends*, 153. The date is August 15, 1934.

⁶³ *All My Road Before Me*, 396.

⁶⁴ The unpublished diary of Warren Lewis for November 6, 1933.

⁶⁵ The unpublished portion of Warren Lewis's diary for June 6, 1931.

Minto: "Paxford and I were saying it was so clear."

Maureen: "Then it's easier to find stations on the A set."

Minto: "Paxford says the B set is easier: Paxford says he got 40 stations on it: he made it work beautifully."

Maureen (trying the B set, which emits a series of siren-like whoops and then a muffled jazz band): "It doesn't seem particularly easy to get ANY station on the B."

Minto: "Ask Paxford dear: he'll show you how to work it in the morning."

Myself: (internally) "Bugger Paxford" (aloud) "Well goodnight. I'm off to bed."

Minto: "Goodnight Pax Warnie. Paxford says—" (I close the door and go to bed).

Moral: If you want to get anyone disliked, see that you include his name in every sentence you frame.[66]

Her negative opinions about other people will not surprise anyone since this is a common human failing. But her comment about Mr. Samuel Henry, who purchased Albert Lewis's law practice, as "an old swine" strikes one as petulant.[67] As a result of her inability to get along with her various landlords—nine of them in four years[68]—Mrs. Moore, Maureen, and Lewis moved frequently to a new location. On one occasion Mrs. Moore showed her temper after a cold evening in the drawing room. Lewis recorded the event in his diary, "After supper I begged D to let me wash up, but she asked rather savagely, 'Do you want me to die?'"[69] This outburst gives further credence to Warren's comments. But Warren was not living with his brother and Mrs. Moore during the early years, so he only saw the later years and the increasingly poor health of Mrs. Moore.

JANIE MOORE'S STRENGTHS

Walter Hooper writes, "Many of those who knew her regret that his [Warren's] account has been the dominant one and counted for so

---

[66] *Brothers & Friends*, 122. The date is October 20, 1933.

[67] The unpublished portion of Warren Lewis's diary for January 9, 1931.

[68] On July 4, 1923, Lewis notes that they had lived in nine different homes since 1919. *All My Road Before Me*, 252f.

[69] *All My Road Before Me*, 290. The date is February 24, 1924.

much. Owen Barfield knew her over many years and liked her."[70] In the Foreword to *All My Road Before Me* Barfield writes: "One of the things that make me welcome its [the diary's] appearance in print is that it will do much to rectify the false picture that has been painted of her as a kind of baneful stepmother and inexorable taskmistress ... If she imposed some burdens on him, she saved him from others by taking them on herself even against his protestations. Moreover she was deeply concerned to further his career."[71] That latter comment is accurate, since she was especially concerned that Lewis not compromise his undergraduate education by missing classes.[72] Lewis had long stretches, especially during his student years, when he had the opportunity to read and study.[73] "Her main virtue was kindness," wrote George Sayer, "especially to those in any sort of need. Her main fault, that of being too autocratic and controlling, was the almost inevitable result of having to take charge, at an early age, of a large house and family."[74] She once arranged for Lewis to have breakfast in bed,[75] and on other occasions encouraged him to continue his diary.[76] Lewis once wrote, "The maids have grown very fond of D and would hardly let us go."[77] Lewis also once stated that she "has a great knack of getting the best out of people."[78]

Minto also managed the household, preparing most of the meals, fixing tea, doing laundry, and many other household tasks. Occasionally she read a letter Lewis had written and offered her advice about the tone and contents of his letter,[79] and, of course, they

---

[70] Hooper, *Companion & Guide*, 714f. In *All My Road Before Me*, 65, Lewis writes on July 7, 1922, "D and Barfield hit it off splendidly...."

[71] Cited in Hooper, *Companion & Guide*, 715. See, for example, *All My Road Before Me*, 265, where Jack writes in his diary, "Poor D feels keenly (what is always on my mind) how the creative years are slipping past me without a chance to get to my real work....".

[72] See, for example, "Chronologically Lewis" for March 13, 1923.

[73] See, for example, *All My Road Before Me*, 28-43, where in May 1922 Lewis has extensive opportunities to devote time to his studies.

[74] George Sayer, *Jack*, 6, cited in Hooper, *Companion & Guide*, 715.

[75] See the unpublished portion of *All My Road Before Me* for February 19, 1923.

[76] *All My Road Before Me*, 264.

[77] *All My Road Before Me*, 22. On April 20, 1922. Later, however, on December 30, 1931, Warren wrote about the way that Minto handled the servants would make them maidless. *Brothers & Friends*, 92f.

[78] *All My Road Before Me*, 103.

[79] *All My Road Before Me*, 66.

discussed many important decisions together, including income tax.[80] Her good cooking is undoubtedly the reason why Warren once wrote, "Minto's cookery has unfitted me for the 'luxuries' of mess life."[81] Mrs. Moore and Lewis took frequent walks together,[82] and they attended an occasional play[83] or concert.[84] During the summer months, she planned their vacations, usually deciding where the family would spend their free time.[85]

Her daughter Maureen's interest in music may have come from Mrs. Moore, since they attended various musical events together, such as a Christmas Eve celebration in 1929, when they heard the first part of the *Messiah*. On another occasion, she went with Maureen, Warren, and a friend to hear the Oxford Bach Choir in the Sheldonian.[86] Mrs. Moore was anxious to further Maureen's possible career in music and did what she could to find music teachers for her.

In the early years when Warren was not yet living at The Kilns,[87] Mrs. Moore wrote letters to Warren quite frequently. She once wrote to Warren, causing him to write in his diary that he received a letter "from Minto containing an unexpected expression of affection which touched me greatly."[88]

She had the gift of hospitality, often opening her home to others in need of lodging, including Lewis's friends,[89] preparing

---

[80] See *All My Road Before Me*, 84, where they discuss when Lewis should travel to Belfast to spend time with his father at Christmas. See *All My Road Before Me*, 434, 439, on Lewis's "tax muddle."

[81] *Brothers & Friends*, 48. The date is May 16, 1930. He also wrote about her breakfast of sausage and bacon, "Minto fries these better than I have ever tasted them anywhere else." *Brothers & Friends*, 74.

[82] See *All My Road Before Me*, 268, where Lewis writes, "D and I went out for our usual little stroll before supper."

[83] Such as *Peer Gynt* on Feb. 10, 1925. *All My Road Before Me*, 350.

[84] For example, they were at the Oxford Playhouse on May 8, 1926. See also February 15, 1927, when they attended the O.U.D.S. performance of Shakespeare's tragedy *King Lear*. There were other similar theatrical performances she attended with friends and family.

[85] See March 1924, when they vacationed in Clevedon, and August 1925, when they vacationed for three weeks in Exmoor.

[86] The unpublished diary of Warren Lewis for March 5, 1933.

[87] Warren then still serving in the military, i.e., the Royal Army Service Corps (RASC).

[88] *Brothers & Friends*, 205, for July 9, 1947.

[89] For example, Leo Baker in 1922, see *All My Road Before Me*, 57f.

tea for frequent visitors,[90] and carrying out various other domestic tasks, such as making clothing[91] and making and hanging curtains.[92] Occasionally, she exercised that gift of hospitality by arranging to take an additional boarder to supplement the family income. That hospitality included animals, since she and Lewis always had pets—cats, dogs, and other animals. Frequent guests at mealtimes cut into their ability to make ends meet, but she was more focused on helping people than managing expenses.[93] In 1924, for example, she cared for the two sons of Mrs. Holmes, who was dying.[94] After the death of another friend's husband, she went to see the woman daily, sometimes going with her to the cemetery to visit her husband's grave.[95] Her advocacy for Maisie Hawes eventually rescued Maisy from a Cinderella-like home situation, where she was poorly treated and constantly doing housework for the family.[96] Mrs. Moore was a hard worker, sometimes insisting on continuing her work even when she was not feeling well.[97] Warren once wrote, "Anyone who works as hard as Minto does is surely entitled to her off days."[98]

Despite Warren's overall negative assessment of Janie Moore, he did not always think poorly of her. She and Lewis had invited Warren to make his home with them when he retired, and he accepted. In late 1929, Mrs. Moore wrote to Warnie, "I hope you will spend your leaves with us [here] or wherever we are. We hope someday to get a larger house, [where] things would be more comfortable for you, so please do think of our home as your home, and be assured always of a very hearty welcome."[99] When Warnie retired in 1932, he found that

---

[90] See, for example, *All My Road Before Me*, 432.

[91] See *All My Road Before Me*, 26, where she is in the process of making nightgowns for a friend. See also *All My Road Before Me*, 44, 48, where she is described as making a dress. See also 61 and 77, both in the month of July, the former July 1 and the latter July 29. One assumes either that she had an obsession with jam-making or used jars of jam as frequent gifts.

[92] *All My Road Before Me*, 25.

[93] See, for example, *All My Road Before Me*, 112-113, where Ivy and then Smudge arrive and share meals and, in Ivy's case, stays overnight.

[94] *All My Road Before Me*, 324. The exact dates were May 22-24.

[95] The woman was Mrs. Studer. *All My Road Before Me*, 452. The date is February 16, 1927.

[96] See especially *All My Road Before Me*, 85f.

[97] See, for example, *All My Road Before Me*, 245f.

[98] *Brothers & Friends*, 71.

[99] The date is October 27, 1929. *The Lewis Papers* X:197.

Mrs. Moore and Lewis had added two extra rooms to The Kilns just for him.[100]

After Warren retired from the Royal Army Service Corps, he moved into The Kilns. A year later he wrote, "When everything possible has been raked up against the household and the life, I can say with no reservations whatsoever, that the past twelve months has (*sic*) been incomparably the happiest of my life."[101]

In the early years, Warren once wrote,

> ... there is much that I like about Minto: she has always been charitable, even in the days of her greatest poverty: her kindness to animals is unfailing and extravagant: she loves flowers and woods and sunsets and birds: and if she makes great demands on J, she is also obviously very fond of him and looks after him meticulously: and finally, she accepted my intrusion into the house without the least sign of protest, although from the very nature of things it cannot have been entirely agreeable to her. And lastly of all, without being in any way intimate, we are on very good terms with each other.[102]

Despite the irritableness of Mrs. Moore, Lewis lived out his Christian faith in her presence. Mrs. Moore might well be the best example of this passage from "The Weight of Glory":

> And our charity must be a real and costly love, with deep feeling for the sins in spite of which we love the sinner …. Next to the Blessed Sacrament itself, your neighbor is the holiest object presented to your senses.[103]

Mrs. Moore was his neighbor, and, despite growing challenges with the passing years, Lewis treated her with the same courtesy and kindness that he treated everyone else.

Mrs. Moore's Atheism

Mrs. Moore is alleged to have been an atheist, and certainly she rarely attended a worship service during the years of her acquaintance with Lewis. Walter Hooper writes, "Mrs. Moore blamed God for her son's death, and Owen Barfield remembered her chiding Lewis and

---

[100] Hooper, *Companion & Guide*, 714.

[101] *Brothers & Friends*, 129. The date of this entry is December 21, 1933.

[102] *Brothers & Friends*, 128f. The date is December 21, 1933.

[103] C. S. Lewis, "The Weight of Glory," in *The Weight of Glory and Other Addresses*. New York: Simon & Schuster, 1980, 39f.

Warnie for going to those 'blood feasts' in their parish church every Sunday morning."[104] The death of a child has resulted in more than a few people turning their backs on God, and this is probably the reason for her atheistic stance. However, the status of her spirituality is worth reconsidering. Janie Moore was the daughter of a Church of Ireland clergyman, William James Askins. Her brother William James Askins was also a clergyman and later a Dean in the Church of Ireland. He served a church in Cavan County, Ireland, a border county along the southern edge of Northern Ireland, and later in Kilmore in southern Ireland. Janie Moore also married the son of a clergyman. While it is certainly not unheard of for the daughter of a clergyman to become a convinced atheist, it is at least unlikely, especially given some other indicators in her life.

For example, when Maureen was confirmed at Headington School,[105] an event that could only have happened with her mother's permission, Mrs. Moore was in attendance. When Maureen made her first communion a month later, Mrs. Moore was again present.[106] She also attended other occasional worship services. For example, in 1930, Warren took her and Maureen to the Electra Cinema to see King George V's funeral.[107] In 1934, while the family was on holiday in Kilkeel, Northern Ireland, Warren tells us, "Minto then went out shopping and returned about seven with the parson whom we heard preaching on Sunday, and who proved to be an old friend of her girlhood's days...."[108] She was sufficiently friendly toward him to bring him back to their lodging.

The strongest argument against the idea that Mrs. Moore was a thoroughly convinced atheist, however, is the thirty-plus years during which she shared the same house with the twentieth century's most famous Christian writer. Could she really have put up with his Christianity if she were not at least somewhat sympathetic to the Christian faith? Could he really have had no impact upon her when he became a theist in 1930 and a Christian in 1931? Could his Christian life truly have made no impression on her? Would she never have read any of his writings and been swayed by them?

---

[104] The "blood feasts," of course, refer to the Lord's Supper. Hooper, *Companion & Guide*, 714f.

[105] The date was Dec. 14, 1922. *All My Road Before Me*, 152.

[106] *All My Road Before Me*, 179.

[107] The exact date is January 30.

[108] The unpublished diary of Warren Lewis. The date is Aug. 8, 1934. Mrs. Moore had not attended the worship service the previous Sunday.

Twenty-One Friendships of C.S. Lewis

Warren once wrote, "...there is no doubt at all about what Minto *was*—an intensely selfish, very spiteful, untruthful, greedy, dishonest, low-minded woman, a bad daughter, a bad wife, a bad mother, a bad employer, and a bad friend: also an atheist, but this I ignore, for she was only an atheist in the famous Johnsonian sense."[109] The following quotation from Samuel Johnson is very likely what Warren had in mind.

> He that grows old without religious hopes, as he declines into imbecility, and feels pains and sorrows incessantly crowding upon him, falls into a gulf of bottomless misery, in which every reflection must plunge him deeper, and where he finds only new gradations of anguish and precipices of horror.[110]

That does not mean that she was a Christian, but it does mean that her irritable behavior (though probably exaggerated by Warren) led her to even more irritability. Most likely, Mrs. Moore's "atheism" was an atheism in behavior, particularly after the loss of her son in the war. Furthermore, in his reminiscences of Lewis as a parishioner, Ronald Head commented that Lewis "never failed to put Mrs. Moore's name on the list of the faithful departed on All Souls' Day."[111] Lewis apparently thought she had been a believer, or he wouldn't have put her name with "the faithful departed."

Sexual Intimacy?

The relationship between Lewis and Mrs. Moore has been much discussed, and most writers think that they were sexually intimate in the early years.[112] When Lewis writes to Arthur Greeves in 1917

---

[109] The unpublished diary of Warren Lewis. The date of the diary entry is January 17, 1951. Warren made a similar comment on June 17, 1933, so this was not a passing opinion, *Brothers & Friends*, 104.

[110] Samuel Johnson, *The Rambler*, No. 69.

[111] Ronald Head, "C. S. Lewis as a Parishioner," *C. S. Lewis and His Circle: Essays and Memoirs from the Oxford C. S. Lewis Society*, edited by Roger White, Judith Wolfe, and Brendan N. Wolfe, Oxford: Oxford University Press, 2015, 185.

[112] See, for example, Paul McCusker, "What do we make of Lewis's relationship with Mrs. Moore?" *Women and C. S. Lewis*, edited by Carolyn Curtis and Mary Pomeroy Key, Oxford, England: Lion Books, 2015, 42. See also John Blake, "The C. S. Lewis you never knew," December 1, 2013, at http://religion.blogs.cnn.com/2013/12/01/the-c-s-lewis-you-never-knew/, where Blake cites Warren Rochelle, Professor of English at the University of Mary Washington in Virginia, who stated, "She gave him a lover for a while, but no one can prove it." See also Jerry Walls,

about the two who "matter most" to him in the world, he is probably referring to Arthur and Mrs. Moore.[113] When, two months later, he writes to Arthur that he loves someone, he is most likely referring to Mrs. Moore.[114] At the time, he was at odds with his father and his brother. There is no other clear candidate. Just a few months after that, he states that Mrs. Moore "has certainly been a very, very good friend to me."[115] Walter Hooper writes that "the rapidity and depth of Lewis's involvement, the initiatives taken by Mrs. Moore to assure it, her acquiescence in Lewis's lies and his readiness to lie in the first place … together invite such words as 'affair,' 'mischief,' and 'blackmail,' all used by Albert [Lewis] in discussing the liaison."[116] Hooper concludes that sexual intimacy between Janie Moore and Lewis was "likely."[117]

Already in October 1917 Lewis was writing to Arthur Greeves about excluding mention of Mrs. Moore in his letters, so fearful was he that his father might see one of those letters and learn about her. He writes that he will "not to refer to the subject,"[118] which apparently is Mrs. Moore. On one occasion, Lewis writes to his brother about getting the help of his friend Rodney Pasley in order to keep his father from knowing the true extent of his relationship with Mrs. Moore.[119] Lewis received money from his father under the pretense that he needed it for college expenses, which is true, but the money also supported both Mrs. Moore and her daughter Maureen. Had he known that his son was supporting three people with the stipend he intended for his son, Albert Lewis would not have understood, regardless of the nature of the relationship between Lewis and Mrs. Moore. Years later, Lewis wrote to Rhona Bodle, "I treated my own father abominably and no sin in my whole life now seems to be so serious."[120] Whatever Lewis's feelings for Mrs. Moore at the beginning, over time she became a mother to him and in most letters

---

"Sinful, Scandalous C. S. Lewis, Joy, and the Incarnation." Houston: https://christianthought.hbu.edu/2013/12/09/sexy-sensational-c-s-lewis-and-the-incarnation/#more-1717 (December 9, 2013).

[113] *Collected Letters*, I, 348. The date is December 14, 1917.
[114] *Collected Letters*, I, 355. The date is February 12, 1918.
[115] *Collected Letters*, I, 387. The date is June 20, 1918.
[116] Walter Hooper, Introduction, *All My Road Before Me*, 9.
[117] Ibid.
[118] *Collected Letters*, I, 339. See also *All My Road Before Me*, 161.
[119] *Collected Letters*, I, 571. This letter was sent on August 7, 1921.
[120] *Collected Letters*, III, 445. The date is March 24, 1954.

from about 1941 onwards he speaks of her as his "Mother."[121]

While Lewis became an atheist too early for his relationship with Mrs. Moore to be the cause, his atheism allowed him to enter into that relationship and to maintain it through the 1920s. Lewis once wrote of his time at Cherbourg House, when he became an atheist, that the feeling of guilt was something that he hardly knew, unless its consequences were severe.[122] Furthermore, he himself once stated, "When I came first to the University I was as nearly without a moral conscience as a boy could be,"[123] and he claimed to be living at this time without ethics.[124] Perhaps that's why Lewis once expressed his frustration with "the tiresome convention of bathing things,"[125] at a time when swimming in the nude was his preferred practice. In 1930, probably within days of his conversion to theism, Lewis wrote to Arthur Greeves about absolute chastity, very possibly reflecting a change in his relationship with Mrs. Moore.[126] His conscience may have convinced him to cut off the sexual side of that relationship while still keeping his promise to Paddy.

Since *The Pilgrim's Regress* is Lewis's allegorical autobiography, the brown girls that John, the main character in the book, fathered probably also reflect some early sexual indiscretions on Lewis's part. His reference in *Regress* to the temptation of the brown girls also suggests that sexual activities were a part of Lewis's past, and a person who claimed to be living without ethics is far less likely to save sex for marriage.[127] After all, the main character in *Regress* stands for Lewis himself. Likewise, in his long narrative poem *Dymer*, the character Dymer displayed the same sexual ethic as John. It is liberating for a person to be able to dispense with guilt feelings, but there are both good ways and bad ways to do so. Denial of guilt is one of the bad ways. There were too many reasons for Lewis's adoption of atheism to attribute it to just one reason, but, as is so often the case, his

---

[121] The first clear reference to Mrs. Moore as his mother appears in a letter to Sister Penelope on Nov. 9, 1941. See *Collected Letters, II*, 496.

[122] *Surprised by Joy*, 69.

[123] *The Problem of Pain*, 29.

[124] *Early Prose Joy*, 23.

[125] *Collected Letters, I*, 304. The date of that letter to Arthur Greeves was May 13, 1917.

[126] *Collected Letters, I*, 913. The date of that letter to Arthur Greeves was July 8, 1930.

[127] *The Pilgrim's Regress: an allegorical apology for Christianity, Reason, and Romanticism*. Grand Rapids: William B. Eerdmans, 1958, 13.

relationship with Mrs. Moore was one reason to maintain his atheism. By denying the existence of God and the need for a personal ethic, he could excuse his behavior.

Later, Lewis wrote about a conversation with fellow undergraduate Leo Baker, "We talked of group marriage as a remedy for monogamy. I pleaded that it was better than prostitution and a thousand times better than [an] *affaire de coeur*,[128] but he didn't think much of it."[129] Clearly traditional marriage, and even marriage itself, was not on Lewis's radar screen. That Christmas, Lewis spent three weeks with his father, writing almost every day to Mrs. Moore. The frequency of such letter-writing is more consistent with intimacy than mere acquaintance.

A month later, Lewis writes, "D and I were alone, Maureen being at lunch in Headington …"[130] Was this—and other statements about being alone—Lewis's way of quietly expressing their sexual relationship in his diary, but in a way that would not be understood by another set of eyes? Why would he need to state that they were alone?

Lewis also once wrote about Valerie Evans, Maureen's teenage friend, "Valerie is prettier than ever: but the knowledge of this fact is rapidly spoiling her. Her main interest is now dress and she has adopted—perhaps innocently and unconsciously … all those provocative little mannerisms which underline the fact that blind nature made her for one purpose. If only pretty women would realize with how many and with *what* people they share the power of attracting in this way!"[131]

Late in his journey toward theism, Lewis became aware of the moral law within him and his personal "zoo of lusts,"[132] probably because he had not placed restrictions on his sexual nature. But it is also likely that he set aside that aspect of his relationship with Mrs. Moore after he became a Christian. He saw pride as his besetting

---

[128] French: "matter of the heart."

[129] *All My Road Before Me*, 76. This is for July 27, 1922.

[130] *All My Road Before Me*, 182. The date is January 19, 1923. The word "alone" appears more than one hundred times in his diary. On October 9, 1922, Lewis wrote, "We get very little time to ourselves now, and the presence of our guest is very burdensome." The presence of a paying guest caused them a problem. *All My Road Before Me*, 116.

[131] *All My Road Before Me*, 345f. Lewis groups July 17-29, 1924, together in this diary entry, so we can't be certain which of those thirteen days he meant by this entry.

[132] This writer certainly understands that the word "lust" means far more than sexual desire.

sin, rather than sins of the flesh, and reproved himself especially over the way he had postured himself toward his lifelong friend Arthur Greeves. Later he would state that spiritual sins are far worse than the sins of the flesh[133] and say that "a cold, self-righteous prig who goes regularly to church may be far nearer to hell than a prostitute." [134] Having been guilty of both sins, he knew from experience which was worse.

Around 1926, Lewis writes the poem "Infatuation."[135] This poem seems to reflect the time when Lewis was in a close relationship with Mrs. Moore, but one that he recognized as infatuation. The opening stanza ends with the statement that "she" came in by stealth, suggesting that Mrs. Moore was the initiator of their relationship. "Infatuation" may have a double meaning, where Lewis writes about love, rather than about a person, and personified love as though it were a person. At one point he distinguishes love from the person about whom he wrote (Stanza 5 "love can reach/That other soul of hers."). She interrupts his reading, she loves, and she could take his name. Might Mrs. Moore, living in the same house as an aspiring young poet, have asked him to write a poem about the two of them? Though much of the poem is obscure, Lewis appears to be writing about Mrs. Moore. This explains why Lewis himself once wrote to Arthur Greeves, "There is room for other things besides love in a man's life."[136]

Many years later, when Lewis wrote *Mere Christianity*, he wrote about the difficulty of chastity:

> We may indeed be sure that perfect chastity ... will not be attained by any merely human efforts. We must ask for God's help. Even when you have done so, it may seem to you for a long time that no help, or less help than you need, is being given. Never mind. After each failure, ask forgiveness, pick yourself up, and try again. We learn, on the one hand, that we cannot trust ourselves even in our best moments, and, on the other, that we need not despair even in our worst, for our failures are forgiven.[137]

---

[133] *Mere Christianity*, 102.

[134] *Mere Christianity*, 103.

[135] George Sayer assigned the date of 1926 to this poem, *Jack*, 182.

[136] *Collected Letters, I*, 353. The date is February 2, 1918, and Lewis is writing from No 10 British Red Cross Hospital in Le Tréport, France.

[137] *Mere Christianity*. New York: HarperCollinsPublishers. Copyright 1980, 101.

No Ordinary People

A man who could write about the difficulty of living the chaste life will not surprise us when we learn that, more likely than not, he did not live such a life, especially in the years before his conversion.

The love of his life seems to have been Janie Moore, initially, but that changed in 1931 when Jesus Christ became the center of his life and brought about major changes. Not only did his relationship with Mrs. Moore change, a change that she resented, but it provided him with a primary area of Christian service in continuing to provide for her and care for her even in her disagreeableness. If Lewis was intimately involved with Mrs. Moore in his early years, the fact that he took care of her after his conversion to Christianity, is to his credit and the credit of the God who changed his life.

Conclusion

Mrs. Moore was the mother of Paddy, daughter of a clergyman, an intimate partner and "mother" of C. S. Lewis, a test of his Christian faith, an atheist primarily due to the loss of her son Paddy, and an irritant to both Warren Lewis and Lewis himself. She was also a hard worker with the gift of hospitality and a heart for others. In retrospect, she was far more the latter than the former. Lewis's loyalty to her and to the memory of his good friend Paddy Moore speaks of strong character in difficult circumstances. The man who, as a part of his Christian duty, answered every letter he ever received was the same man who kept his promise to Paddy Moore. As Paul McCusker writes, "When any feelings of familial affection had deserted Lewis, he still did his duty by her."[138]

---

[138] Paul McCusker, "What do we make of Lewis's relationship with Mrs. Moore?" *Women and C. S. Lewis*, edited by Carolyn Curtis and Mary Pomeroy Key, Oxford, England: Lion Books, 2015, 47.

Twenty-One Friendships of C.S. Lewis

"Jack" with Warnie Lewis at Annagassan, Ireland, 1949
Used by permission of the Marion E. Wade Center,
Wheaton College, Wheaton, IL.

Chapter 6

WARREN HAMILTON LEWIS
His Brother's Brother

Many people have lived unhappily in the shadow of a more famous relative, but Warren Lewis thrived under the influence of his brother, C. S. Lewis, and made his own mark as a military officer, writer, gentleman, and Inkling. The brotherhood of Warren and C. S. Lewis provided not only social support for both brothers, but it laid the foundation for their success as writers.

Warren Hamilton Lewis was born in Dundela Villas, on the outskirts of Belfast, Northern Ireland, on June 16, 1895, the son of Albert James Lewis and Flora Augusta Hamilton. He died on April 9, 1973.

Childhood

Albert and Flora valued education highly and passed this value to their sons. During the early years, Flora taught the boys at home, especially reading. Flora, who taught Latin, French, and math to Jack, must also have done the same with Warren, since he became quite fluent in French. This later helped him to read and write late seventeenth and early eighteenth-century French history.[1] His maternal grandfather, Rev. Thomas Hamilton, baptized both brothers.

Their childhood included writing stories. While Jack wrote about Animal-Land, Warren wrote stories about India. These two imaginary lands were later combined into the land of Boxen. The stories of talking animals were illustrated with occasional drawings, and the Lewis brothers invented a history to support the stories they were writing.

At the age of nine Warren crossed the Irish Sea to attend Wynyard School, a boarding school in Watford, Hertfordshire. Flora took him to Wynyard, where he would survive the unusually ineffective supervision of Headmaster Robert Capron. Although undoubtedly exaggerating, Warren once wrote, "I cannot remember one single piece of instruction that was imparted to me at Wynyard."[2]

---

[1] Lewis, *Surprised by Joy: The Shape of My Early Life*. San Diego: Harcourt Brace Jovanovich, 1955, 4.

[2] *Lewis Family Papers*, Vol. III, 40. Flora Lewis died during his years

The great tragedy during the Wynyard years, however, was the death of his mother.³ After four years at Wynyard, Warren began classes at Malvern College⁴ in Malvern, Worcestershire. He enjoyed his years there, rising to prefect in May 1913 and left in July of that year.⁵

At the age of sixteen, Warren started his first diary, a small Collin's Pearl Diary whose first entry is January 1, 1912. After little more than a month of keeping his diary, he stopped. Six years later, Warren resumed his efforts, and continued his somewhat sporadic diary-making for the rest of his life. Those diaries, comprising the years 1918–1972, are the primary source for biographical information about him.

Royal Military College, Sandhurst

Warren decided on an Army career near the end of his years at Malvern.⁶ He left Malvern College with plans to attend the Royal Military College (RMC).⁷ His father then made arrangements for him to study with W. T. Kirkpatrick, the man who had taught Albert and would later tutor his younger brother, so that Kirkpatrick could prepare Warren for Sandhurst.⁸ Warren's four months of private study with W. T. Kirkpatrick during the autumn of 1913 accomplished its goal.⁹ Warren wrote of his time with Kirkpatrick:

> When I went to Bookham I had what would now be called "an inferiority complex," partly the result of Wynyard, partly of my own idleness, and partly of the laissez faire methods of

at Wynyard on August 23, 1908.

³ Due to their father's emotional response to his wife Flora's death, Albert inadvertently alienated his two sons. The emotional distance that the two boys had from their father subsequently caused them to develop a close friendship after their mother's death. That closeness, reflected in their common interest in writing, would last their entire lives.

⁴ The equivalent of high school in the American educational system.

⁵ Walter Hooper, "Warren Hamilton (Warnie) Lewis," 1011.

6 The actual date that he decided was May 24, 1913.

⁷ He left Malvern on July 29. Examination for Admission to the Royal Military Academy, or the Royal Military College. Army Personnel Centre.

⁸ *Brothers & Friends*, xiii.

⁹ Warren started with Kirkpatrick on September 10, 1913. During the years between 1878 and 1899, more than two-thirds of the annual average of 330 new cadets had studied with a crammer before taking the army examination for entrance to Sandhurst. Thomas, *The Story of Sandhurst*, 151f.

Twenty-One Friendships of C.S. Lewis

Malvern. A few weeks of Kirk's generous but sparing praise of my efforts, and of his pungent criticisms of the Malvern masters restored my long lost self-confidence: I saw that whilst I was not brilliant or even clever, I had in the past been unsuccessful because I was lazy, and not lazy because I was unsuccessful.[10]

Warren was probably influenced toward a military career by George Harding, who married Warren's cousin Hope Ewart and had been a member of the Army Service Corps since 1901.[11]

Warren took the entrance exam for Sandhurst in November, received a green light on his health in the Report of the Medical Board[12] on January 17, and on February 4, 1914, he entered the Royal Military College. He had placed twenty-first out of 201 candidates on the entrance exam.[13] He was a Prize Cadet, one of the top twenty-five scores on the exam, which earned him a scholarship and entitled him to enter at a lower rate of tuition.[14] After a nine-month period of training,[15] shortened from eighteen months because of the war, Warren was commissioned to the Royal Army Service Corps (RASC) as a 2nd Lieutenant.[16] He left the RMC on October 1. A comment later in life about enjoying the *Odyssey* because in it there were no battles may indicate one reason why he chose the Service Corps rather than the Infantry or the Artillery.[17] World War I had begun on August 4, 1914.

While the records of the Royal Military College contain little

---

[10] *The Lewis Papers*, Vol. IV, page 62, cited in Hooper, Volume 1, 1012.

[11] George Harding retired in 1928 with the rank of Colonel.

[12] Report of Medical Board, Register No. 100/L/4050, January 17, 1914.

[13] By comparison, Churchill studied with a crammer and failed to enter Sandhurst three times before he was finally successful. He graduated 8th out of 150 in 1895. Thomas, *The Story of Sandhurst*, 154, 157. Field-Marshal Montgomery entered Sandhurst 72nd out of 170 candidates and left 36th of 238. Smyth, *Sandhurst*, 139.

[14] £80 instead of the usual £150.

[15] The course of study seems to have been three terms and approximately eighteen months at the time that Warren was there, since author John Smyth entered Sandhurst in January 1911 and left in summer 1912, Smyth, *Sandhurst*, 141–147. More than five thousand cadets passed through Sandhurst during World War One with an average length of study at six months. Hugh Thomas, *The Story of Sandhurst*, 178.

[16] On September 29, 1914.

[17] *Brothers & Friends*, July 13, 1966, 262.

information about Warren, we learn something about the College at that time from histories and, thereby, about Warren. In addition, we learn that military service was an honorable and acceptable activity in the Lewis family, both from Warren's military service, his brother's service in World War I, and from his brother's writings.[18]

Colonel John Gaspard Le Marchant conceived the idea of educating officers for the British Army in late 1798.[19] The subsequent effort resulted in the establishing of the Royal Military College by Royal Warrant on June 24, 1800 and the founding of the school by the end of 1802. The College is located on five hundred acres on the north side of the London-Southampton coach road, southwest of London and near the village Blackwater and the hamlet Sandhurst.[20] RMC was to become "the premier school of military education in Britain."[21]

Photo, left, of Sandhurst gun carriage and cadets, 1915.
Photo, right, Sandhurst cadets of that time with their bicycles.
Photos used with permission of the Royal Military Academy

Throughout its history, the RMC had a mixture of military subjects (rifle-shooting, riding, fencing, military surveying, topography, etc.) and general subjects (mathematics, history, Latin, French, German, etc.), with wartime sometimes resulting in the elimination of the non-military subjects. "At times of war, or during war scares," writes Hugh Thomas, "the course has been very short indeed—as it was at the time of Crimea. But in all essentials the Royal Military College has been

---

[18] Jack once wrote to Mrs. Johnson, in a letter dated November 8, 1952, "When Our Lord Himself praised the Centurion He never hinted that the military profession was in itself sinful. This has been the general view of Christendom. Pacifism is a v. recent & local variation." *Collected Letters, III*, 247. See also Jack's essay, "Why I Am Not a Pacifist" in *The Weight of Glory and Other Addresses*. New York: Simon & Schuster, 1980.

[19] Hugh Thomas, *The Story of Sandhurst*, 15f.

[20] Thomas, *The Story of Sandhurst*, 28, 33, 35.

[21] Thomas, *The Story of Sandhurst*, 82.

the same since 1874."²² This explains why Warren's course of study was shortened from the normal two- or three-year program. In 1918, some cadets were hurried through in as little as two months.²³

Sandhurst graduates have distinguished themselves on the field of battle and elsewhere, including Field-Marshal Viscount Bernard Montgomery, to whom the German High Command surrendered their forces at the end of World War II; Field-Marshal Viscount Allenby (later High Commissioner of Egypt; the Allenby Bridge, which crosses the Jordan River near Jericho in Israel is named after him); Sir Douglas Haig, commander-in-chief of British Armies in France; King Hussein of Jordan; and Sir Winston Churchill, who came in 1893, graduated in 1895, and later served as the Prime Minister of Great Britain during World War II. After World War II, the Royal Military College, Sandhurst, was combined with the Royal Military Academy, Woolwich, to become the Royal Military Academy, Sandhurst.²⁴

The Army

Shortly after graduation and deployment, Warren was sent to France to serve with the 4th Company, 7th Divisional Train British Expeditionary Force in the supply and transport side of the Army. This involved providing transportation, food and water, clothing and furniture, fire service, some involvement in disciplinary measures, staff clerks, administration of barracks, and similar items, but not ammunition or military equipment.²⁵ Some of Warren's early transfers and promotions, about which little else is known, appear below:

- In September 1915, Warren was transferred to 3rd Company 7th Divisional Train, France.
- On September 24, 1916, he was promoted to the rank of lieutenant.
- On October 1, 1916, he was promoted to the rank of

---

[22] Thomas, *The Story of Sandhurst*, 126.

[23] During World War I, 5,131 cadets passed through Sandhurst with an average length of course at six months. Since Warren was there for nine months and cadets at the end of the war were there for two months, this indicates that the length of stay gradually shortened during the war. Thomas, *The Story of Sandhurst*, 178, 180.

[24] Thomas, *The Story of Sandhurst*, 223.

[25] Warren was sent on November 4, 1914. "Royal Army Service Corps," *Wikipedia*, accessed June 13, 2008.

temporary captain.

- On November 13, 1916, he was appointed officer commanding 4th Company 7th Divisional Train in France.
- On November 21, 1916, Warren was transferred to the 32nd Divisional Train.
- On November 29, 1917, Warren attained the rank of captain.
- On December 23, 1917, he attended the Mechanical Transport School of Instruction in France.
- On March 4, 1918, Warren graduated from the Mechanical Transport School of Instruction first in his class. Other training courses included six months at the London School of Economics and a War Course in 1931.[26]

In mid-April 1918, Warren's brother was wounded in battle during a German offensive, so Warren visited him on April 24 in Liverpool Merchant's Mobile Hospital, Étaples, France, riding his motorcycle to see him. Lewis biographer George Sayer tells us that this incident ended an estrangement between the brothers, caused by differing opinions of Malvern College.[27] Warren had enjoyed Malvern College, while his brother had detested it. In May 1918, Warren began serving with the 31st Divisional Mechanical Transport Company in France. On November 10, 1918, the war ended, and the Armistice was signed the next day.

After the war, Warren served briefly in Belgium[28] until reassigned to England. On November 18, 1919, Warren was posted to Aldershot, the military headquarters in England, for the 2nd Regular Officer's Course. In subsequent years, Warren also served in the following places:

- 487 Company, Southern Command, Salisbury, England

---

[26] The course at the School of Economics took place from October 4, 1926 to March 23, 1927. Army Form B.199A. Army Personnel Centre.

[27] George Sayer, *Jack*, 131. Sayer's comment indicates that he thought Warren rode a bicycle, but it is quite certain that Warren's "bike" was a motorbike. None of Warren's diaries mention a bicycle, but they make frequent mention of motorcycles, or motorbikes. The problem arises because Warren shortens the word motorbike to bike.

[28] He began to serve on April 11, 1919, for the 6th Pontoon Park, Namur, Belgium.

Twenty-One Friendships of C.S. Lewis

(June 1920 to January 1921)

- Freetown, Sierra Leone, West Africa (March 9, 1921 to March 23, 1922)
- Colchester, England as the Officer in charge of Supplies (October 4, 1922 to December 1925)
- Woolwich, England (December 30, 1925 to March 1927)
- Shanghai, China (April 11, 1927 to April 1930)[29]
- Bulford, England (May 1930 to October 1931)
- Shanghai, China (October 9, 1931 to December 14, 1932).[30]

Warren later called the three years at Colchester "the happiest three years of my Army life,"[31] in part because of the proximity of his brother, who was then living in Oxford. One minor feature of that happiness was a visit from Jack in July 1924, after which they traveled together to Oxford on Warren's motorcycle.[32]

During his first tour of duty in Shanghai, Warren received a telegram stating that his father had died.[33] A leave allowed him to return home to help settle Albert's estate. The leave was taken at the end of this tour in Shanghai, traveling by ship to England. The trip took longer than usual because Warren spent an entire day in Japan, visiting Kyoto, including the Park of the Imperial Palace, the old town, the Chion In temple, and the Dibutsu Buddha temple. Then he visited Kobe, Japan, and a day later toured Yokohama. On the return trip, Warren visited the Imperial Palace in Tokyo, followed by the Tombs of the Shoguns. The next day he visited Kamakura, where the real Dibutsu Buddha is located, the one in Kyoto being only a copy. For five days, then, the *Tai Yin*, Warren's ship, meandered its way past Japan, allowing the passengers to see the sights of Japan from the ship.

---

[29] This China tour was quite dangerous because of hostilities in the area, and this caused much distress to both his father and his brother. *Collected Letters II*, 698.

[30] J. E. Treble letter, November 1979. Army Personnel Centre.

[31] *Brothers & Friends*, February 6, 1967, 269. In his diary, Jack reports that Warren gave a favorable report of Colchester, confirming this impression. *All My Road Before Me*, 157, an entry dated December 23, 1922.

[32] A visit on July 3 and 4, 1924. *All My Road Before Me*, 341.

[33] Albert Lewis died on September 25, 1929, and Jack sent him a telegram to that effect.

Along the way, he spent a day in San Francisco, a day in Los Angeles, a day crossing the Panama Canal, two days in New York, and a day in Boston, before stepping ashore at Liverpool on April 16.[34]

Warren disembarked at Liverpool in mid-April 1930. Later that month, he and Jack visited Little Lea, did some packing, and left behind their childhood home.[35] A month later, Warren was assigned to Bulford, not far from Oxford, which allowed him to spend weekend leaves with his brother. During his time in Bulford and while on leave, he began the task of editing *The Lewis Papers*.[36]

While Jack rarely traveled outside of the United Kingdom, Warren's military career taught him to appreciate other parts of the world. He visited China, Japan, the United States, France, Sierra Leone, and several other countries on his trips between the UK and China or Sierra Leone. Another difference between Jack and Warren is the latter's interest in the architecture of the big city, especially in the United States (which he had seen on his 60-day journey from Shanghai to Liverpool in 1930). He was impressed by the tall buildings of Los Angeles and New York, writing, "I like the sheer soaring sweep of them,"[37] and he called the skyscrapers of New York "an illustration of Avalon perhaps, in a modern edition."[38] He especially liked Boston for its English flavor: "Boston, superficially at any rate, is simply a very pleasant English city which has had the misfortune to be dumped down on the Eastern American seaboard."[39]

Warren left for his last tour of duty in China in 1931, arriving in Shanghai on November 17. This tour was completed when he applied for leave, which was added to the end of his service. He sailed home on the *Automedon*,[40] retiring from the Royal Army Service Corps on

---

[34] Greater detail of Warren's travels can be read in "Chronologically Lewis," located at my website at www.joelheck.com, or in the original account in Warren's diaries, which are kept at the Marion E. Wade Center in Wheaton, Illinois.

[35] The brothers moved into a new home, The Kilns, in Oxford on October 10 and 11, 1930.

[36] *The Lewis Papers* are the unpublished memoirs of the Lewis family from 1850-1930. These papers are held at the Marion E. Wade Center in Wheaton, Illinois.

[37] *Brothers & Friends*, March 20, 1930, 26.

[38] *Brothers & Friends*, April 4, 1930, 30.

[39] *Brothers & Friends*, April 6, 1930, 31.

[40] Army Form B.174. Leave of Absence. Automedon was the name of Achilles' charioteer in Homer's *Iliad*. The *SS Automedon*, a British passenger and cargo steamer, was sunk on November 11, 1940 by a

Twenty-One Friendships of C.S. Lewis

December 21, 1932 with the rank of Captain, after eighteen years, two months, and twenty days of service.

Warren was recalled to active service shortly after the beginning of World War II, posting to Le Havre, France, and then evacuated from Dunkirk (although not part of the "Miracle at Dunkirk" later that month) in early May 1940. During this time, due to his length of service and the performance of his duties, he attained the rank of Major.[41] He was transferred to the Reserves on August 16, 1940 and joined the 6th Oxon (Oxford City) Home Guard Battalion as a private soldier, sometimes serving on his boat, the *Bosphorus*, especially during the summer of 1941.[42] After his transfer, he was awarded medals for his service.[43]

Reconversion and Spiritual Life

Like his brother, and probably in reaction against his father's religion, Warren ceased to become a practicing Christian at some unknown point in his youth. Toward the end of his military service, he began to reconsider the truths of the Christian faith. Even earlier, during his time in Sierra Leone, he had planned to read the entire Bible and must have been successful or at least come close, having resolved to read five pages per day and having gotten past Leviticus, the major stumbling block for most Bible readers.[44] Warren seldom started a reading project he did not finish.

In 1922, his brother's diary notes that Warren[45] had stated that reality never came up to our dreams. Warren was expressing what his brother later described as Joy, a longing for another world. During his Army service, while on his way home to settle his father's estate, Warren stood in front of the Great Buddha of Kamakura, Japan,[46] and

---

German ship, the *Atlantis*, during World War II. For a picture of the ship, visit https://www.wrecksite.eu/wreck.aspx?134952.

[41] The exact date of this promotion is January 27, 1940. Army Form B.199A. Army Personnel Centre.

[42] *Collected Letters*, II, 486, 504. He was no longer in the Reserves as of March 29, 1947.

[43] On August 5, 1944. Army Form B.199A. Army Personnel Centre.

[44] *Brothers & Friends*, March 8, 1921, 8.

[45] *All My Road Before Me: The Diary of C. S. Lewis, 1922-1927*. New York: Harcourt Brace, 1991, 162. The date is December 29, 1922.

[46] This event in Kamakura took place on March 4, 1930. Warren visited Japan and the United States, particularly San Francisco, Los Angeles, New York, and Boston on this trip. *Brothers & Friends*, March

as a result became more deeply convinced of the truth of the Christian religion, apparently because of the spiritual nature of his encounter with this Dibutsu Buddha into whose face he stared for ten minutes.[47] Then, while on his first walking tour in January 1931, he commented to his brother that he was beginning to think that the religious view was true.[48]

Eventually Warren returned to the Christian faith, probably in May 1931, which he described as "the full revolution—indifference, skepticism, atheism, agnosticism, and back again to Christianity."[49] On Christmas Day, 1931, Warren took Communion at the Bubbling Well chapel in Shanghai, the first time he had communed in many years and the same day that his brother communed for the first time since childhood.[50] his brother returned to the Christian faith on September 28, 1931, about a week before Warren left for his last tour of duty in China. The two brothers returned to the Lord's Table at the same time and to the Christian faith within a few months of one another.

Warren later wrote about the great peace that descended on him when he sat in a church sanctuary and about his intent to pray for Minto.[51] Minto, of course, was Mrs. Janie Moore, Jack's adopted "mother" and the mother of his wartime friend Paddy Moore. Later, Warren writes of the miraculous elements in the Bible: "As a Christian, the mentality of the Believer who picks and chooses the miracles in which he will believe is to me at any rate baffling. If you believe that sundry dead people were brought to life in the same flesh which they were going to be buried in, why should not Balaam's ass have spoken, or the sun stood still for Joshua?"[52] He wrote in his diary about Chesterton's *Everlasting Man*, reflecting his views by relishing Chesterton's "trouncing of the Evolutionists which is really admirable."[53] Warren's preferences in worship practice were similar to those of his brother. He once wrote that he "should like no hymns at all."[54]

---

and April, 1930, 22–32.
[47] *Brothers & Friends*, 20.
[48] *Collected Letters, I*, 948.
[49] *Brothers & Friends*, 80. The date of the diary entry is May 13, 1931.
[50] Carpenter, *The Inklings*, 46. *Brothers & Friends*, 92.
[51] *Brothers & Friends*, August 14, 1933, 114; September 14, 1933, 120.
[52] *Brothers & Friends*, November 7, 1933, 123.
[53] *Brothers & Friends*, March 20, 1934, 144.
[54] *Brothers & Friends*, August 15, 1946, 193.

He and his brother became active in their local parish church in Oxford—Holy Trinity, Headington Quarry. Warren served for several years as a vestryman of Holy Trinity,[55] and the two brothers were regular worshippers for the rest of their lives.

THE KILNS AND WALKING TOURS

In 1930, Warren, his brother, and Mrs. Moore purchased The Kilns in Headington Quarry. Two months earlier, Warren had considered the advantages and disadvantages of living with his brother and Mrs. Moore. Finally, he concluded that "a closer intimacy with J[56] and a correspondingly fuller intellectual life: a healthier life too, by the cutting out of those hours spent in social and ceremonial drinking"[57] favored the decision.

Warren and his brother went on eight annual walking tours during the 1930s, the first of them in the midst of winter 1931.[58] This was the first walking tour that Warren ever took, and he enjoyed it, mostly because he had his brother's full attention. On these tours the brothers would walk cross country for several days, enjoying nature, staying overnight in local inns, and eating meals in pubs. Jack must have known that Warren would enjoy walking tours, because he wrote to Warren in detail about a walking tour that he took with Owen Barfield, Walter Field, and Cecil Harwood in 1927. No walking tour for the brothers occurred in 1932, due to Warren's last tour of duty in China (see the appendix on page 133 for a list of their walking tours).

Later, after his brother's death, Warren wrote in his diary that those walking tours were the most satisfying remembrance of life with Jack.[59] When, in 1940, Warren was involved in the war effort, Jack wrote to him stating that it seemed "almost brutal to describe a

---

[55] See a letter by C. S. Lewis dated January 26, 1953, *Collected Letters, III*, 286. A vestryman is a layman who serves on a vestry, the equivalent of a church council, which manages the temporal affairs of the church.

[56] That is, Jack, Warren's abbreviation for his brother.

[57] The unpublished diary of Warren Hamilton Lewis, dated May 25, 1930. The Marion E. Wade Center, Wheaton, Illinois. WHL Diaries collection: https://archon.wheaton.edu/index.php?p=collections/controlcard&id=1959 J was Warren's abbreviation for his brother Jack.

[58] The Marion E. Wade Center has the walking tour maps of Warren Lewis: https://archon.wheaton.edu/index.php?p=collections/controlcard&id=1963

[59] *Brothers & Friends*, April 8, 1966, 256.

January walk taken without you,"[60] and he prayed in that same letter that God might bring the two brothers together again soon.

One year into the experiment of living at The Kilns, Warren reviewed the past year. He pronounced it "the happiest of my life,"[61] in spite of some reservations about Minto. In that same diary entry, Warren described his daily post-military routine: 7:45 tea, 8:10 got up, shaved, bathed, dressed, took the dog for a walk, had breakfast, walked to London Road, caught the 9:30 bus to Rose Lane, worked on *The Lewis Papers* in College, came with Jack by car to The Kilns for lunch, worked on the grounds of The Kilns or walked until tea time at 4, piano practice under Maureen's tutelage until six, 7:00 supper, took the dog for a walk, read and wrote until 11:00, made fires, made the dogs' beds, said prayers, read two evening lessons in bed, read poetry for about 20 minutes until midnight, then to sleep.[62] In the summer Jack and Warren had more time for walking than in term time, and Warren was able to work longer at College and less at home.

Mrs. Moore

One would expect that someone like Warren would have been able to sort out the nature of the relationship between Jack and Mrs. Moore. However, on one occasion, Warren brought up the subject of Minto and Jack and was so firmly put down that he never brought it up again. Jack had promised Paddy that if he survived the war and Paddy didn't, he would take care of Paddy's mother, and that seems to be accurate. The article on Janie Moore elsewhere in this volume addresses other evidence.

Mrs. Moore should receive her due, for without her support, Warren would very likely never have lived with his brother while she was alive. During her younger years she was far from the irritable person she later became. And surely she must take some credit for the summary statement that Warren wrote in 1933: "I can say with no reservations whatsoever, that the past twelve months has [*sic*] been incomparably the happiest of my life."[63]

---

[60] *Collected Letters, II*, 316, January 9, 1940.

[61] *Brothers & Friends*, December 11, 1933, 129.

[62] The unpublished diary of Warren Hamilton Lewis dated December 21, 1933.

[63] *Brothers & Friends*, December 11, 1933, 129.

Eventually Warren became exasperated by the way his brother was constantly at the beck and call of Mrs. Moore, calling the last three or four years of her life "very nearly unbearable."[64] When Mrs. Moore died in 1951, Warren wrote, "And so ends the mysterious self-imposed slavery in which J has lived for at least thirty years."[65] He went on to marvel that his brother was able to accomplish so much "in the intervals of washing her dishes, hunting for her spectacles, taking the dog for a run, and performing the unending futile drudgery of a house which was an excruciating mixture of those of Mrs. Price and Mrs. Jellaby."[66] She was the one that made Warren always seem like a boarder at The Kilns.

His Brother's Brother

During Warren's service with the RASC, the letters between the two brothers demonstrated the camaraderie they had had for many years, including the terms APB and SPB, Archpigiebotham and Smallpigiebotham. These affectionate monikers were terms of endearment as well as indications of their sense of humor. Jack even wrote in his letters to Warren about "the true nature of PBism," i.e. Pigiebothamism, "pure, unadulterated, orthodox, high flying Pigiebotianism," and "Pigiebotian moments."[67] That friendship made possible the living arrangements at The Kilns and their continued collaboration on various projects such as the "public works"[68] on the lands surrounding The Kilns.

As indicated earlier, after retirement Warren began to edit *The Lewis Papers*. He enjoyed many other activities with his brother, including the annual walking tour, meetings with the Inklings, attendance at many social events, and travel to Magdalen College on many days to read in Jack's rooms. As a member of the Inklings, Warren also spent time with his brother's friends. He was well read and would use the literary knowledge gained by his reading to engage in conversation, as he had done in his letters to Jack from abroad.[69] Later

---

[64] *Brothers & Friends*, February 6, 1967, 270.

[65] *Brothers & Friends*, January 17, 1951, 236.

[66] Mrs. Price and Mrs. Jellaby are characters from Charles Dickens's novel *Nicholas Nickleby*. *Brothers & Friends*, 236f.

[67] *Collected Letters*, I, August 2, 1928, 775, January 12, 1930, 870.

[68] This is a term used by Warren to describe cutting back the foliage, building a path, or other landscaping.

[69] For example, *Collected Letters*, I, 790, n. 17.

he would write, "He and I, born of the same parents, he so brilliant, I so much the reverse. How and why?"[70] While he exaggerates the differences between them, the distinction is true.

During his time at The Kilns, Warren helped his brother with his growing correspondence, especially after the serializing of *The Screwtape Letters* in *The Guardian* and their release in book form in 1942. Jack's appearance on the BBC in the early 1940s further boosted his fame. The letter typing began in 1943[71] and continued for the next two decades. Warren once estimated that he had typed 12,000 letters for his brother.[72]

The Kilns, Headington Quarry
Author photo

One of the characteristics of the Lewis family was a fondness for tobacco and alcohol. For Warren, alcohol was a major pastime during his military service which became a serious drawback, causing him much difficulty throughout his life. The irony is that Warren, the alcoholic, outlived his younger brother by almost a decade. His years in the Army turned his moderate use of alcohol into a more frequent practice, eventually serving as a remedy to bouts of depression or as a method of dealing with setbacks, and later his abuse of alcohol caused Jack to cancel at least one Irish holiday.[73] He especially turned to drink in 1963 after the death of his brother.

---

[70] *Brothers & Friends*, July 4, 1967, 275.
[71] West, 76.
[72] *Brothers & Friends*, September 9, 1967, 279.
[73] Summer 1949. See *Collected Letters, II*, 952f.

Twenty-One Friendships of C.S. Lewis

Author and Inkling

Many of those who read extensively eventually become writers. This helps to explain why Warren, one of the original Inklings, that group of Oxford intellectuals who met weekly, beginning in 1933, to discuss wide-ranging ideas and to read books, essays, poems, and plays they were writing, also became a writer. Warren frequently mentions their meetings in his diary, those who attended, and the topics they discussed or manuscripts they read. Warren and Jack had a lot in common, including a love of poetry and an appreciation of authors such as Wordsworth, Chesterton, Virgil, and Homer. He once wrote, "A book, a good chair, my pipe and a good bed to go to when night falls, and I'm about as happy as one can be in this very trying world."[74] As they read books together in their sitting room, they would often read interesting passages to one another as they met them.[75]

Warren's writing benefited from his brother's encouragement. In 1931 between his two tours of duty in China, Warren gave Jack an essay he had written on the Duke of Marlborough. Jack read the essay and encouraged Warren to continue writing.[76] But much of Warren's writing style was developed by his childhood training under Annie Harper, the brothers' governess,[77] by what he read, and by his regular diary entries. This passage about Salisbury Cathedral and the surrounding area illustrates his flowing prose, his attention to detail, and his ability to visualize what he had seen:

> After this I walked for a long time in the Close which was gloriously still and restful, and a wonderful blend of colour—the old grey houses, the green of the trees, a lot of lilac, and splendid flaming beds of tulips in many of the gardens: at the bottom of the Close were some magnificent horse chestnuts in bloom. The Cathedral was all I remembered it and more: it is wonderful the way its perfect symmetry leads the eye upwards by front and roof and flying buttress to that soaring spire.[78]

---

[74] Glyer, 250.

[75] *Collected Letters, II*, 337.

[76] *Brothers & Friends*, June 6, 1931, 81.

[77] In *Surprised by Joy*, Jack writes about his childhood education, which was probably the same that Warren had received before going off to school: "I, meanwhile, was going on with my education at home; French and Latin from my mother and everything else from an excellent governess, Annie Harper." *Surprised by Joy: The Shape of My Early Life*. San Diego: Harcourt Brace Jovanovich, 1955, 11.

[78] *Brothers & Friends*, May 24, 1930, 51.

No Ordinary People

Warren once wrote that in earlier life he had formed the habit of deliberately fixing in his mind various bits of scenery.[79] Those that he committed to memory stayed with him and undoubtedly improved his writing ability. In addition, the work he did in completing the editing of *The Lewis Papers* between 1933 and 1935 enabled him to grow as a writer.

Warren's special area of expertise was seventeenth century French history, eventually writing seven books in that field.[80] That French period became an interest in 1919, when he read the diaries of St. Simon.[81] He wrote in his diary, "I saw in a shop window an abridgement of St. Simon's Memoirs, bought it as a change from French novels, and became a life-addict to the period."[82]

Warren's first published work was an essay entitled "The Galleys of France." He included the essay in his first book published six years later. Edited by his brother, *Essays Presented to Charles Williams* included that essay, along with J.R.R. Tolkien's seminal essay, "On Fairy-Stories," C. S. Lewis's "On Stories," and essays by Owen Barfield, Dorothy L. Sayers, and Gervase Mathew. In this essay, Warren uses colorful detail and sweeping but accurate generalizations. His writing makes you almost feel as though you were there. What a surprise to learn that along with the criminals, deserters, purchased slaves, and smugglers, the French sent the Huguenots to the oars of its galleys and the whip of the petty officer, there to row until they died.

His first book, *The Splendid Century: Some Aspects of French Life in the Reign of Louis XIV*, was published in 1953,[83] and Warren included words of thanks to Jack and Gervase Mathew "for their patience in listening to several chapters of it in manuscript."[84] The United States edition came out the next year in New York and was reviewed in the

---

[79] *Brothers & Friends*, February 26, 1934, 143. See also *All My Road Before Me*, 162, where Jack notes Warren's comment that nearly everyone is insensible toward beauty.

[80] He also compiled the unpublished *Lewis Papers* and he published *Letters of C. S. Lewis*, which includes a brief biography of Jack.

[81] *Brothers & Friends*, 2, n. 2. This note mentions a letter to his father, dated March 3, 1919. St. Simon is Louis de Rouvroy, Second Duke of Saint-Simon (January 16, 1675–March 2, 1755), was a French soldier, diplomat and famous diarist, the author of *Memoirs on the Reign of Louis XIV, and the Regency*, which has appeared in several editions.

[82] Hooper, 1012.

[83] For a brief synopsis of each of these books on French history, see the article by Richard C. West in the Bibliography.

[84] Page x, cited in Glyer, 127.

New York Times. Warren was delighted.[85] Like so many other writings, his book was read to the Inklings. Tolkien remarked about Warren's reading to the Inklings, "Writing a book: it's catching."[86] Humphrey Carpenter writes that his "readability, wit and good sense almost equaled his brother's work."[87] Diana Glyer calls this book "a standard text in its field."[88] The last of Warren's seven books on French history was published in 1963. In the years after his brother's death, he edited the *Letters of C. S. Lewis*. One of the most powerful pieces of writing, however, was the portion of his diary in which he described, in great detail, the last days together with his brother and the day of Jack's death.[89]

Warren's research style showed similarities to that of his brother, who preferred primary sources over secondary ones and who was meticulous and exhaustive in much of his research. Richard West writes, "Warren's lengthy bibliographies indicate that he read every relevant work available to him in the extensive resources of the Bodleian, so he was well-grounded in the scholarship on his chosen period. His footnotes ... show a distinct partiality for citing primary sources."[90]

THE PERSONALITY OF WARREN LEWIS

Warren Lewis was a well read and intelligent gentleman.[91] He was both a gentle man and a gentleman, impeccable in his manners, a thinker and writer, and a scholar. The obituary that ran in *The Times* one week after his death describes him as "deeply humble and a warm and delightful companion." His brother calls him "the most perfect gentleman anyone could hope to meet" and "the politest of men."[92] John Wain writes that he was "a man who stays in my memory as the most courteous I have ever met."[93] Such courtesy and gentlemanliness

---

[85] *They Stand Together: The Letters of C. S. Lewis to Arthur Greeves*, a letter dated April 2, 1954, 530. See also Glyer, 250, for the opinion of other reviewers.

[86] Tolkien, 71.

[87] Carpenter, 243.

[88] Glyer, 17.

[89] *Collected Letters, III*, 1484f. See also "Memoir of C. S. Lewis," in *Letters of C. S. Lewis*, 45f.

[90] West, 80.

[91] Mead, 4.

[92] *Collected Letters, III*, 1462.

[93] Wain, cited in Hooper, 1013.

resulted in what Diana Glyer calls his "generous hospitality."[94] Once, on a trip with Jack, Mrs. Moore, and Maureen, Mrs. Moore, who was being rather irritable, says to Maureen, "What is he [Warren] so politely and cleverly saying now?"[95] Apparently Warren could be a gentleman even in trying circumstances, and the following quotation from Warren's diary shows his gentlemanliness even in defeat: "After I had finished my diary I played a single of croquet with J. I was off my game and he was playing really well: he beat me by six hoops and thoroughly deserved his win."[96]

Gentleman Warren was also generous in praise, stating after the death of Charles Williams: "And so vanishes one of the best and nicest men it has ever been my good fortune to meet,"[97] and of Magdalen College Fellow Paul Benecke he writes, "the absolute best man I have ever known in my life."[98] He states of Tolkien's *The Lord of the Rings*, "…how near he is to real magic" and "The inexhaustible fertility of the man's imagination amazes me."[99]

Warren hadn't always been the consummate gentleman. Earlier in life, Warren responded sharply to his father's criticism of army life, stating, "It's all very well for you, living in the study and spending £1400 a year on yourself."[100] The strained relationship between father and sons explains, but does not excuse, this behavior. A few months later, Jack expressed unhappiness with Warren's cynicism, his rejection of that which is warm and generous, and his general dissatisfaction with the human condition.[101] But this, of course, is the young Warren, whose maturity was still developing.

Warren was both an inveterate optimist and a genuinely humble man. On one occasion, after a solitary walk, Warren writes, "A great wave of happiness suddenly swept over me, and I realized, I hope with gratitude, how very good life is."[102] Later that same year, he writes about his occasional negative comments against Minto, who must truly have been exasperating if his comments are anywhere near

---

[94] Glyer, 33.
[95] *Brothers & Friends,* August 7, 1934, 152.
[96] *Brothers & Friends,* August 23, 1922, 12.
[97] *Brothers & Friends,* May 15, 1945, 183.
[98] *Brothers & Friends,* September 28, 1944, 179.
[99] *Brothers & Friends,* October 10, 1946, 195; November 12, 1949, 231.
[100] *All My Road Before Me,* an entry dated December 30, 1922, 164.
[101] *All My Road Before Me,* an entry dated March 30, 1923, 226.
[102] *Brothers & Friends,* November 24, 1934, 163.

the truth, "I must be at least as exasperating to others as they are to me."[103] That optimism also translated into a good sense of humor. Jack once wrote to Arthur Greeves about an unwelcome visitor, stating that while the New Testament tells us to visit widows, he and Warren agree that nowhere does it tell us to let *them* visit *us*.[104]

Warren's gentlemanliness, kindness, and humility made it easy for him to get along with children. Jack once described himself as shy with children, but Warren was able to get on better with children.[105] Both brothers welcomed the evacuees from London during World II, and one guesses that Jack's writing of the *Chronicles of Narnia* owes something to Warren.

Warren often deferred to his strong-willed and brilliant brother, but he was generally more even-keeled. Jack once wrote, "... he is in so many ways better than I am. I keep on crawling up to the heights & slipping back to the depths: he seems to do neither."[106] Depression and alcohol were his besetting problems, both of them started, according to Warren himself, by insomnia.[107] But in spite of these challenges, Warren Lewis excelled as a military officer, a writer, a companion, and a gentleman.

After Jack

Jack's death left Warren almost immobilized. Nearly a year later he writes, "I seem to miss my dear SPB more rather than less as time goes on."[108] But it was not all sadness, for he also writes of his pleasant memories: "Oddly enough as time goes on the vision of J as he was in his later years grows fainter, that of him in earlier days more and more vivid. It is the J of the attic and the little end room, the J of Daudelspiels and walks and jaunts, the J of the early and middle years whom I miss so cruelly."[109] One of his regrets later in life was the lack of detail in his diaries, even though his diaries were quite extensive. Writing about his brother, Warren states, "Oh if only I could have known in time that he was to die first, how I would have Boswellised

---

[103] *Brothers & Friends*, December 9, 1934, 166.

[104] *Collected Letters: II*, 160. The date is December 7, 1935.

[105] *Collected Letters, II*, 171. A letter dated December 7, 1935.

[106] *Collected Letters, I*, 949. January 10, 1931.

[107] *Brothers & Friends*, 225. The date is March 4, 1949.

[108] *Brothers & Friends*, 254. The entry for September 1, 1964.

[109] *Brothers & Friends*, 255. The date is February 22, 1965. A Daudelspiel was a trip on a motorcycle, which Warren called his Daudel.

No Ordinary People

him!"[110]

After the death of his younger brother, Warren and the Millers—Len and Mollie—spent more time together; Mollie was the housekeeper at The Kilns for many years. Warren continued writing, producing the *Letters of C. S. Lewis*, which included his biography of his brother. Eventually his health began to fail. He developed circulation problems and later had a pacemaker installed. He died on April 9, 1973, at the age of seventy-seven. He is buried in the cemetery of Holy Trinity, Headington Quarry, in the same grave where his brother had been buried a decade earlier.

Warren Hamilton Lewis, older by three-and-a-half years, was as good a brother and companion as one could hope to have. His literary interests paralleled his younger brother, even though they did not scale the heights of C. S. Lewis. His military career, begun at the Royal Military Academy at Sandhurst, spanned more than eighteen years, providing a commonality with Jack's briefer military service. The walking tours continued the close bond begun in childhood and interrupted by Warren's military service, and the involvement of both men in the Inklings and at The Kilns further cemented that bond. His travel and service in other countries broadened both his outlook and that of his brother. Above all, however, the similar spiritual journeys of the brothers from formal Christianity to atheism and back to the Christian faith[111] provided the depth necessary to maintain this friendship across the decades until the day that God called them home.

The tombstone of the Lewis brothers

---

[110] *Brothers & Friends*, April 8, 1966, 256.

[111] On Warren's description of his spiritual journey, see *Brothers & Friends*, 80, cited earlier.

Appendix - Walking Tours

The eight walking tours of the Lewis brothers—just the two of them—appear below. Their ending coincided with World War II and the rapidly increasing fame of Jack with corresponding increases in demands for his time. While the distance traveled does not appear in Warren's diaries in each year, the distance was approximately fifty miles each year. An early January walk allowed Jack to return to Oxford in time for the start of the Hilary Term.

Date	Location	Distance
January 1–4, 1931	Wye Valley, Wales, near the English border	54 miles
January 3-6, 1933	Wye Valley, Wales	
January 1-6, 1934	Wye Valley, Wales	
January 3-5, 1935	Chiltern Hills, near Oxford	
January 13-16, 1936	Derbyshire, north of Oxford	
January 5–9, 1937	Dulverton, Somerset	
January 10–14, 1938	Wiltshire, which included Malmesbury, Chippenham, and Salisbury	51.5 miles
January 2–6, 1939	Welsh marshes, Malvern	42 miles

Sister Penelope

Chapter 7

SISTER PENELOPE
Elder Sister in the Faith

In the middle of World War II, C. S. Lewis sent a copy of *The Screwtape Letters* to an Anglican nun for safekeeping, fearing that the bombing of London (and, potentially, Oxford) might obliterate his book manuscript.[1] The Nazi Air Force bombing London on September 7, 1940 and continued almost nightly for the next nine months.[2] After the war, Lewis wrote, the manuscript "can be made into spills or used to stuff dolls or anything."[3] Eventually the manuscript was sold to raise money for remodeling the convent's chapel. Sister Ruth Penelope Lawson was that Anglican nun.

Ruth Penelope Lawson was born on March 20, 1890 in Clent, Worcestershire, to Laura Penelope Anstice and Rev. Frederick R. Lawson.[4] Clent, where Rev. Lawson was serving as Vicar of St. Leonard's Church of England,[5] is located about fourteen miles southwest of Birmingham, England, in the beautiful, hilly countryside of Worcestershire. She was born in the vicarage, the youngest child in the family, and called Clent home for the first eighteen years of her life. She later recalled with fondness the marigold and yellow azalea, the rhododendron and foxgloves, the Wych elms and beech trees, the gorse and the bracken.[6] She had two sisters—Mary Caroline and

---

[1] "in case the one the publisher has got blitzed." *Collected Letters, II*, 493. On October 9, 1941.

[2] Until May 10-11, 1941.

[3] *Collected Letters, II*, 493. On October 9, 1941.

[4] Walter Hooper, *C. S. Lewis: Companion & Guide*, New York: HarperCollins Publishers, 1996, 718.

[5] Frederick R. Lawson was Vicar of St Leonard from 1886 to 1908 according to the church warden of St Leonard, Clent, transmitted by Christine who works in the Belbroughton Fairfield Clent Church Office. Email on October 15, 2019. He came to Clent from Pershore in South Worcestershire. *Meditations*, London: The Faith Press, 1962, 20.

[6] A Religious of CSMV, *Meditations*, Leighton Buzzard, Great Britain: The Faith Press Ltd., 1962, pages 20, 22-23. "There was no end to the loveliness of Clent and it was always new. I loved every bit of it with my whole soul, although I did not know as yet that it was God I loved in it. It was my home for my first eighteen years ...." The term caterpillar is used to form an analogy. Sister Penelope thinks of the butterfly as our glorious future after this life is over, and "from birth to death we are as

Grace Elizabeth. Her brother Robert died in infancy, and her sister Mary, married to Tom Westmacott, died in a tragic riding accident in India in 1912.[7]

When she was six years old, her father took her to a missionary exhibition in Oldhill, near Birmingham, where she saw the kindly face of a priest who smiled at her. Enchanted by that smile and aware of the occasion, she "decided on the spot to be a missionary." From that smile at Oldhill came her first sense of a special vocation, the understanding of what she believed, and a conviction of how to teach it.[8]

Already in her fourth year, she was exiled, as she called it, from her home for months at a time to stay with an aunt because of concerns for her father's health. She later wrote, "I still feel about Clent as about no other place on earth, and the pain of leaving there is with me still. I can see that now as a type of my essential state as a member of a fallen race, exiled from my true home, a stranger and a sojourner on earth."[9]

In 1899 Penelope won a Victoria Scholarship, available to daughters of clergymen.[10] The scholarship enabled her to attend Worcester High School,[11] now called Alice Ottley School, where she developed a love for the Classics and an appreciation for the spiritual world.[12] Her teacher, Miss Ottley, taught her two things:

> The first was that it was my duty as a Christian to examine my conscience before Communion, and to confess to God specifically what I found amiss.... The other thing she taught me personally and unknown to herself, on the evening of March 15th, 1904. Our Confirmation was next day, and we

---

caterpillars." *Meditations*, 9.

[7] Vee Walker, *Major Tom's War*, London: Kashi House, 2018, 56. This historical novel describes events before and during World War I and includes relatives of Sister Penelope's family. Sister Penelope was Vee Walker's Great Aunt, and Major Tom (part of the title of the book) was her brother-in-law.

[8] *Meditations*, 17.

[9] *Meditations*, 23.

[10] Richard James, "A Timeline from 1890 to 1977+ of Selected Religious and Political Events in the British Isles Intertwined with the Family Tree, Life & Writings of Ruth Penelope Lawson," citing the *Worcestershire Chronicles*, December 6, 1902.

[11] Upper Tything, Worcester, which is about thirty miles southwest of Birmingham.

[12] Walter Hooper, *Companion & Guide*, 718. See also Sister Penelope's spiritual autobiography, *Meditations*.

had stayed on after school for a last class. I do not remember a word of what she said, and she had her back to the failing light, so I could not see her face. But, as she talked, I knew with overwhelming certainty that she was living in a world of most intense reality, to which I was, as yet a total stranger. I was outside it utterly, but it existed; and, like a dog on the wrong side of the door, I wanted desperately to be let in.[13]

She was confirmed on March 16, 1904. She studied German and Theology at Keble College, Oxford,[14] from 1909 to 1912 and then joined the Convent of the Community of St. Mary the Virgin (CSMV)[15] at Wantage as a Novice a few weeks after graduating from Keble College. Sister Penelope made her Profession in Life Vows of Poverty, Chastity and Obedience on March 25, 1915 at age twenty-five. She then worked for six years in the Community's training homes for girls and taught in schools in Wantage, Fulham, Abingdon, and Plymouth[16] (see photo, above).[17] When her friend Evie Winnington-Ingram married Tom Westmacott (who formerly had been married to Penelope's sister Mary) on September 21, 1918,[18] Sister Penelope was very likely present.

At Springfield St. Mary, Banbury Road, Oxford, she worked in a hostel for Oxford University students and then, in 1931, returned to

---

[13] *Meditations*, 27f.

[14] She studied under B. J. Kidd, the Warden of Keble College and lecturer in Church History, and R. W. Hunt. Walter Hooper, *Companion & Guide*, 718.

[15] Described in one website as "an Anglo-Catholic Community that grew out of the Oxford Movement." See https://www.pilgrimreaderbooks.com/product/37144/Also-the-Holy-Ghost-An-Essay-on-the-Bible-a-Religious-of-CSMV.

[16] From the inside cover of her book, *The Wood*, published in 1973 by Mowbray. According to the biography provided by Sister Elizabeth Jane CSMV, Sister Penelope taught at St. James Girls' School, Fulham; St. Mary's School, Wantage; St. Helen's School, Abingdon; St. Dunstan's Abbey School, Plymouth; and St. Katherine's School, Wantage between 1916 and 1929.

[17] Used with the permission of Vee Walker, author of *Major Tom's War*, London: Kashi House, 2018.

[18] Date supplied by Vee Walker, author of *Major Tom's War*, London: Kashi House, 2018. This compelling story describes war conditions during World War I along with the tragic death of Mary Lawson soon after her marriage to Tom Westmacott, Tom's war injuries, his convalescence under the care of Evie Winnington-Ingram, and the marriage of Tom and Evie after the war. The war heroism of French civilians and Major Tom also enhances the entire narrative with its several sub-plots.

Wantage where she served at St. Katherine's House nursing home. In 1933 she returned to St. Mary's Convent, Wantage, where she became the librarian,[19] serving in that capacity for the next decade. In 1939 she earned the Lambeth Diploma in Theology, the same year that she wrote her first letter to C. S. Lewis. Her special subject for the diploma was the Hebrew text of the Psalms and, as a result, she later taught classes on the Psalms for the Novices.[20] In 1940, she became a Licensed Teacher of Theology.[21]

Beginning in 1947 she lived and served at St. Michael's House, Wantage, which had become a care home that CSMV operated. She worked there until 1975, when she and other older sisters moved to St. Mary's Convent. She lived there until her death in 1977.

Late in life, Sister Penelope wrote about her last years, drawing inspiration from a picture of the Everest Expedition of 1953, which was given to her by someone on that climb. The photo was taken of the summit ridge that marked the end of their climb. Sister Penelope writes, "I keep that picture always within sight, because it seems to me old age is like that climb. Seen as an element in the descent to death, the pains and limitations of this last lap of life on earth appear as opportunities for fellowship with God. They are His precious gifts, the best His love can give, because they are material for penance for my sins and those of all the world, in union with our Lord's vicarious penitence."[22]

Over the years Sister Penelope published thirty-five works of theology (especially devotional works), translated seventeen volumes of the Church Fathers, wrote a series of plays covering biblical history, and penned book reviews for *Church Times*. She wrote anonymously in most cases, listing herself as "A Religious of CSMV," as was customary at that time.[23] Lewis had great respect for her scholarship and her

---

[19] http://merton.org/Research/Correspondence/y1.aspx?id=1140. She was librarian from 1934 to 1944.

[20] "Sr Penelope CSMV Biographical Sketch," from Sister Elizabeth Jane CSMV in an email of September 12, 2019.

[21] Will Vaus, "Some Ladies at Wantage: C. S. Lewis, Sister Penelope, & The Community of St. Mary the Virgin," *The Chronicle of the Oxford C. S. Lewis Society* Volume 6, Issue 3 (October 2009):25. See also "The Beginnings of C. S. Lewis's Correspondence with Sr Penelope CSMV." Sister Elizabeth Jane CSMV in an email of September 12, 2019.

[22] *Meditations*, 80.

[23] Clara Sarrocco, "The Kingliness of Friendship: C. S. Lewis and Sister Penelope, CSMV," *CSL: The Bulletin of the New York C. S. Lewis Society*, 2.

spirituality, having spoken of Sister Penelope as his "elder sister" in the Faith.[24] He kept the photograph of the Shroud of Turin, which she had sent him, on the wall of his bedroom for the rest of his life.[25]

When, years later, she asked Lewis if he wanted the *Screwtape* manuscript back, he replied, "If you can persuade any 'sucker' (as the Americans say) to buy the MS of *Screwtape*, pray do, and use the money for any pious or charitable object you like."[26] In her annotations to his letters she said:

> I wrote to him again begging him to let me send it back ... He would not have it, and would only have destroyed it if I had insisted ... Very reluctantly, when we were hard put to it for funds for doing up St. Michael's chapel, did I venture to ask him if I might dispose of it ... It is now in the Berg Collection in the New York Public Library.[27]

Scholarly Pen Pals

They Meet via the Postal Service

As the shadow of an impending world war fell on the United Kingdom, Sister Penelope wrote to Lewis for the first time. She had read a review of Lewis's *Out of the Silent Planet*,[28] which motivated her to read the book, and she ordered it for the CSMV library. Then she wrote to Lewis, stating that his book "has given and still gives me a joy and delight quite impossible to put into words." She also wrote:

> I am librarian here ... it is not easy to find the right type of story book for sisters who are resting or convalescing after illness. At ordinary times we do not read novels at all, as you may imagine; but the right novel at the right moment can have a real spiritual value. So I got yours, and never has any made me so happy.[29]

And again, she wrote,

---

[24] Hooper, 719.

[25] Ibid., 720. *Collected Letters, II*, 494, October 9, 1941 and *Collected Letters, II*, 495, November 9, 1941.

[26] This letter does not appear in *Collected Letters*. See Hooper, *Companion & Guide*, 720. The date of his letter is June 18, 1956.

[27] Ibid.

[28] E. L. Mascall, "Out of the Silent Planet," *Theology* 38 (April 1938):303-304.

[29] "The Beginnings of C. S. Lewis's Correspondence with Sr Penelope CSMV." Sister Elizabeth Jane CSMV in an email of September 12, 2019. The date of her letter is August 5, 1939.

> It provokes thought in just the directions where I have always wanted to think; and whenever it is most delightfully suggestive one senses the most profound scriptural basis ... There are bits—Augray's views about the different sorts of bodies, the relations of the unfallen creatures with Oyarsa, their social order, their peaceful awareness of the spiritual world—which are more lovely and more satisfying than anything I have met before.[30]

Along with her letter she sent a copy of her book, *God Persists: A Short Survey of World History in the Light of Christian Faith*.[31] Lewis's reply was the first of fifty-five letters[32] that he wrote to her. While he was grateful for her comments about *Out of the Silent Planet*, he feared that pride could make short work of his humility. He tells her that his impetus for writing the book was a student who took seriously the dream of interplanetary colonization and, probably exaggerating, "that a 'scientific' hope of defeating death is a real rival to Christianity."[33]

Lewis notes that only two out of sixty reviews knew that the fall of the Bent One in *Out of the Silent Planet* had a theological meaning, and then he makes one of his more famous statements:

> But if only there were someone with a richer talent and more leisure, I believe this great ignorance might be a help to the evangelization of England: any amount of theology can now be smuggled into people's minds under cover of romance without their knowing it.[34]

No one, except perhaps J. R. R. Tolkien, living in the United Kingdom at that time had a richer talent than Lewis for writing imaginative theology, but he probably did not know this in 1939! By this time, Lewis had probably made his first attempt at what eventually became the Narnia series and had failed,[35] which may explain why he didn't think he had such talent. Sister Penelope wrote back almost immediately,[36] sending another book, *Leaves from the Trees*, along with her letter.

---

[30] Walter Hooper, *Companion & Guide*, 718.

[31] *Clive Staples Lewis*, 162.

[32] I list fifty-five letters in an appendix, but some say there were fifty-six. For example, Clara Sarrocco's article states that there are fifty-six.

[33] *Collected Letters*, II, 262.

[34] Ibid.

[35] See the so-called Lefay fragment. See Edwin Brown, *In Pursuit of C. S. Lewis*, 90.

[36] *Collected Letters*, II, 262. August 24, 1939.

Twenty-One Friendships of C.S. Lewis

More important than the content of any single letter, however, is the extent of this correspondence, which lasted twenty-four years. Their letters were scholarly and academic, theological and devotional, full of humor and personal touches, and a model of letter-writing between two people with common interests. In addition, this correspondence paved the way for a later correspondence between Lewis and Nan Dunbar, who was herself a talented scholar with the same love of the Classics that Sister Penelope had.

Books—His, Hers, and Others

People who read and write a lot enjoy talking about what they are reading. Lewis once wrote, "When one has read a book, I think there is nothing so nice as discussing it with someone else."[37] Lewis had read the book she sent in her first letter, *God Persists*, within a few days of receiving it. He especially appreciated her treatment of the heathen, stating, "it was through *almost* believing in the gods that I came to believe in God."[38] He recommends that she read both George MacDonald and Charles Williams, since she wants to find fictional writings, like *Out of the Silent Planet*, for those who are convalescing.

He also encouraged her on other occasions to read George MacDonald.[39] A year later he called George MacDonald's *Phantastes*

Sister Ruth Penelope, third from left, age 27
Used with the kind permission of Vee Walker

---

[37] A letter to Arthur Greeves on March 14, 1916. *Collected Letters*, I, 173.
[38] Ibid.
[39] *Collected Letters*, II, 451. October 24, 1940.

a book that helped him understand how the better elements in mythology can prepare people for the gospel, especially when they do not know where they are being led.[40] Williams was also a topic of Lewis's letters more than once. Lewis writes to her about Charles Williams in 1941,[41] and he writes twice in 1945, the first time about how to get her plays published, since Williams was also a playwright, and the second time about Williams' recent death.[42]

Over the years, they wrote to one another about Samuel Johnson and Coventry Patmore,[43] Austin Farrer and Simone Weil,[44] Boethius and Chalcidius, Macrobius and Pseudo-Dionysus,[45] Homer (*The Odyssey*), which Lewis thought the best novel in the world,[46] Martin Buber,[47] Kathleen Nott,[48] George MacDonald, and Charles Williams. But more often they wrote about the books they were writing.

Lewis was clearly pleased with her letters. Her parallel between dog and man on the one hand and man and God on the other hand, he writes, is one he has often thought of, and he thinks that it illustrates the nature of grace. Apparently, Lewis thought that as man cares for his dog out of unmerited love, so God cares for us. They both had thought about animal suffering, so on this topic also he found in Sister Penelope a kindred spirit.[49]

In his next letter, Lewis writes to her about his portrayal of High Anglicanism in *The Pilgrim's Regress* as consisting of those harsh and dry scholastics who hated their father's religion, a view he later moderated, and the battle between supernatural religion

---

[40] *Collected Letters*, II, 453f. November 4, 1940. At the same time, however, he didn't have the same appreciation for MacDonald's poetry. See *Collected Letters*, III, 123. June 5, 1951.

[41] *Collected Letters*, II, 497. November 19, 1941.

[42] The letter was written on January 3, 1945 and the second on May 28, 1945. *Collected Letters*, II, 635, 656.

[43] *Collected Letters*, II, 497. November 19, 1941.

[44] *Collected Letters*, III, 158. November 6, 1957.

[45] *Clive Staples Lewis*, 391. W. H. Lewis, *Letters of C. S. Lewis*, Revised and Enlarged Edition, edited by Walter Hooper, San Diego: Harcourt Brace, 1993, 470f.

[46] *Collected Letters*, II, 516f. April 9, 1942.

[47] *Collected Letters*, II, 526. July 29, 1942.

[48] *Collected Letters*, III, 428. February 15, 1954.

[49] *Collected Letters*, II, 265. August 24, 1939. Lewis wrote a chapter on animal pain in his book, *The Problem of Pain*. Sister Penelope wrote an essay called "Consider the Dog: A Study in Right Relationship," later the first chapter in her book, *Leaves from the Trees*.

and modernism, expressing a strong preference for the supernatural. He has received a copy of her book, *Scenes from the Psalms*, and he appreciated learning about how psalms were sung in ancient Israel.[50]

The following year, Lewis writes to Sister Penelope, thanking her for a book she wrote, *Windows on Jerusalem: A Study in the Mystery of Redemption*.[51] A few months later he tells her about a book he is writing, i.e., *Perelandra*, and comments in his letter that he has just gotten Ransom to Venus. He states that the Eve of Venus, the unfallen first woman of that young world, needs to be a combination of a Pagan goddess and the Virgin Mary.[52] Soon thereafter, he sends her a pre-publication copy of *Perelandra*.[53] The following year, Lewis writes to Sister Penelope about problems with completing *Perelandra*: "I should have more joy of *Perelandra* at the moment than of 99 books that have had no hitch about them."[54]

Later that year, Jack writes to Sister Penelope about literary topics, having just finished reading her book *They Shall Be My People*, enthused about her Old Testament scholarship, which cuts the ground from the Old Testament critics, and his book *Miracles*, for which he has completed six chapters.[55]

Near the end of the war, Lewis writes to Sister Penelope, having just received a copy of her translation, *The Incarnation of the Word of God: Being the Treatise of St. Athanasius "De Incarnatione Verbi Dei."*[56] His introduction to the book, "On the Reading of Old Books," helped in the book's promotion. The book was dedicated to him.[57] Later that year, Lewis wrote to Sister Penelope about finishing the writing of *That Hideous Strength* and about Sister Penelope's book *Windows on*

---

[50] *Collected Letters, II*, 285f. November 8, 1939. He also returns her copy of *The Divine Journey* by James Gillman, which he has now read.

[51] *Collected Letters, II*, 480. The date of this letter is April 10, 1941.

[52] *Collected Letters, II*, 494-496. November 9, 1941.

[53] *Collected Letters, II*, 516f. April 9, 1942. *Perelandra* was published on April 20, 1943.

[54] *Collected Letters, II*, 554ff. February 20, 1943.

[55] *Collected Letters, II*, 590f. September 24, 1943. He also mentions the writing of *Miracles* a couple of weeks later. *Collected Letters, II*, 592. October 5, 1943.

[56] *The Incarnation of the Word of God: Being the Treatise of St Athanasius De Incarnatione Verbi Dei*. Translated and edited by A Religious of C.S.M.V.; London: Geoffrey Bles, 1944. Lewis wrote this letter on February 19, 1944.

[57] *Collected Letters, II*, 602f.

Jerusalem, which he has just reread.⁵⁸ Late in the war, Lewis wrote to Sister Penelope, briefly mentioning three of his books during this very prolific period in his writing—*The Great Divorce*, due out in August, *That Hideous Strength*, which was due in July, and *Miracles*, which was supposed to come out next year.⁵⁹

In the 1950s they had more discussions about books they were writing. On December 30, 1950, Lewis writes to Sister Penelope about her biblical plays, *They Shall Be My People*, thinking that they may be her most important writings. Lewis learns that he has been granted a year's leave to complete the writing of *English Literature in the Sixteenth Century*, which would begin with the Michaelmas term of 1951 and continue through the next two terms.⁶⁰ A year later Lewis writes to Sister Penelope about having finished the writing of his volume on English literature for the *OHEL* series.⁶¹ The book was finished in July 1952, and Lewis writes to Sister Penelope four months later, stating, "The OHEL is finished and gone to press. Joy, joy, my task is done."⁶²

One of Lewis's last letters to Sister Penelope came soon after the publication of *A Grief Observed*. The book was published in September 1961, and she wrote to him the following January. Lewis writes to Sister Penelope, congratulating her on identifying him as the author N. W. Clerk, author of *A Grief Observed*, but also asking her to keep that identity top secret. Their correspondence and her familiarity with his writing style probably led her to the conclusion that he was the author, especially since she knew about Joy's death in 1960.⁶³

---

⁵⁸ *Collected Letters, II*, 624. September 6, 1944.

⁵⁹ *Collected Letters, II*, 657. May 28, 1945.

⁶⁰ Alister McGrath, *C. S. Lewis—A Life: Eccentric Genius, Reluctant Prophet*, Carol Stream, IL: Tyndale House, 2016, 248. See also *Collected Letters, III*, 112. A letter to Warfield Firor on April 23, 1951.

⁶¹ Oxford History of English Literature.

⁶² Walter Hooper, *C. S. Lewis: Companion & Guide*, HarperOne, 1998, 480. On November 28, 1952. This letter does not appear in *Collected Letters*.

⁶³ He wrote the letter on February 1, 1962. Walter Hooper, "*A Grief Observed*: A Study of C. S. Lewis's Thoughts on the Subject," *VII*, Volume 30 (2013) 54. For the latter reference, see Jack L. Knowles, "That 'such a genius should be a beastly American': C. S. Lewis as Critic of American Literature," *VII*, Volume 23 (2006), 43. See also "Sr Penelope CSMV Biographical Sketch."

Twenty-One Friendships of C.S. Lewis

Advice on Effective Writing

Lewis and Sister Penelope also discussed effective writing and how to get their books published. Most of the advice traveled in one direction—from Lewis to Sister Penelope. They both had a passion for writing, and their literary friendship allowed them to talk about good writing, publishers, how to get a book published, and a variety of related topics. They both earnestly believed in what they were writing. Years after Lewis's death, an anonymous correspondent expressed such thoughts about Sister Penelope in these words:

> It is not just that you bring together basic doctrine in a clear, readable fashion in a way that reminds me of the late CS Lewis … but that your books are not restless: they seem to come from an inner centre of Peace. Perhaps they are the fruit of your contemplation, & as such bear the stamp, the odour, of the Object of your contemplation.[64]

She had acquired the certainty that Miss Ottley had demonstrated so many years before. Perhaps the advice of C. S. Lewis had something to do with it. One of Lewis's important pieces of advice came when he wrote to Sister Penelope about symbolism. He writes that "Symbolism exists precisely for the purpose of conveying to the imagination what the intellect is not ready for."[65] Six months later, Jack writes to Sister Penelope, giving her some advice that her style needs to be simpler and more concrete,[66] which is another way of stating that more concrete ideas, including symbolism, convey the author's intent more effectively.

Some years later, Lewis writes to Sister Penelope about a story she is writing, stating that he is "so excited" about her story. He writes about dialogue, Sister Penelope's style, and not letting "the cat out of the bag" too quickly, since in real life people do not see the end of the story until the end. Instead, create suspense and keep the reader reading. The basic plot is sound, he states, but it needs some tweaking. He tells her that the great thing about her story is that it has "narrative zest."[67] Weeks later, having taken his advice, she sends him an improved chapter. Lewis has more advice about her novel, this time including numerous comments about her specific choice

---

[64] Notes from Sister Elizabeth Jane, a member of the Convent of the Community of St. Mary the Virgin, in an email of September 12, 2019.

[65] *Collected Letters, II*, 565. March 25, 1943.

[66] *Collected Letters, II*, 590f. September 24, 1943.

[67] *Collected Letters, II*, 864. July 22, 1948.

of words.[68] Lewis's common practice of speaking the words he was writing appears in his advice: "In correcting dialogue it is useful to imagine it being acted on the stage or at least read aloud."[69]

A few years later, he offers some critique about Sister Penelope's book, *The Coming of the Lord: A Study in the Creed*, calling it the best theological book he has read in a long time. He makes some recommendations, such as a suggestion to use the word *foundation* or *basis* rather than *fundament* and to avoid confusing the post-Christian with the pre-Christian.[70]

Lewis also wrote to Sister Penelope about her series of plays, including one on Nehemiah which he found the least dramatic.[71] The script moved slowly and predictably, incorporating the story of Jonah, but ending merely with the need for regular observance of Jewish harvest feasts in the future.[72] He offered criticism when criticism was needed.

Getting Published

Advice on writing from an experienced writer is always good, but how do you get something published? Lewis explains that he simply writes to the publisher he "fancies best," then the next best and so on until he has a publisher.[73] He also writes about where she could get her translation of Athanasius' *De Incarnatione* published, recommending that she try both Geoffrey Bles Ltd. and J. M. Dent & Sons Ltd., his own publishers.[74] She had been rejected once, but Bles, probably with a good word from Lewis, agreed to publish the translation.

---

[68] *Collected Letters, II*, 873f. August 31, 1948.

[69] *Collected Letters, II*, 874. August 31, 1948.

[70] *Collected Letters, III*, 318. He makes the same point in "De Descriptione Temporum," *Selected Literary Essays*, 10. April 1, 1953.

[71] One of the eighteen plays in *They Shall Be My People* deals with the rebuilding of the walls of Jerusalem, a play entitled "A People That Dwells Apart." *They Shall Be My People: The Bible Traversed in a Course of Reading Plays*, 196-204. The play included an Isaiah, allegedly the author of Isaiah 40-66 who wrote in the fifth century B.C. and a line that suggested that the story of Jonah was a story and not history: "What it means is true." She also adopts 397 B.C. as the date of Ezra's ministry in Israel.

[72] *Collected Letters, II*, 592. October 5, 1943.

[73] Ibid.

[74] *Collected Letters, II*, 554ff.

Twenty-One Friendships of C.S. Lewis

Other letters from Lewis to Sister Penelope included his not so subtle advice on finding a publisher by simply throwing a manuscript at one publisher after another,[75] and how to deal with book rejections. Recently several publishers had rejected her book, *The Morning Gift*, which was apparently never published. He tells her that many good books were published after several rejections.[76] He declines to write a Foreword for *The Morning Gift*, because he has done too many of them.[77] In 1957, after years of publishing and corresponding, Lewis's last piece of advice dealt with literary agents (recommending Curtis Brown as the best) and, again, publishers (avoid working directly with them; use an agent).[78]

THEOLOGICAL DISCUSSION AND PERSONAL SPIRITUALITY

The same autumn that Sister Penelope started the correspondence, Lewis wrote to her, addressing the manner in which psalms are sung in worship settings, the first of many topics related to theology and personal spirituality.[79] In many letters these two pen pals requested prayers from the other person, and they touched on a wide range of spiritual topics, especially prayer.[80]

As stated earlier, one topic the two discussed was animal pain. Lewis's letter about Sister Penelope's dog being healed shows his interest in animals and animal pain.[81] Regarding animal suffering Lewis once wrote about her essay "Consider the Dog: A Study in Right Relationship," "I very earnestly hope that you are right ... about tails wagging as soon as trumpets sounding: *not* (as the anti-sentimental do vainly talk!) through sentiment, but because animal suffering raises quite terrifying problems about divine justice."[82] Sometime later, he reread "Consider the Dog" and wrote to her about

---

[75] *Collected Letters, II*, 911f. January 31, 1949.

[76] *Collected Letters, III*, 5f. January 12, 1950.

[77] *Collected Letters, II*, 961. August 1, 1949.

[78] *Clive Staples Lewis*, 387. W. H. Lewis, *Letters of C. S. Lewis*, Revised and Enlarged Edition, edited by Walter Hooper, San Diego: Harcourt Brace, 1993, 465. May 12, 1957.

[79] *Collected Letters, II*, 285f. November 8, 1939.

[80] *Collected Letters, III*, 279. January 9, 1953.

[81] *Collected Letters, II*, 656. May 28, 1945.

[82] *Collected Letters, II*, 265. August 24, 1939. See also "Consider the Dog: A Study in Right Relationship," Chapter 1 in *Leaves from the Trees*. Cambridge: W. Heffer & Sons, 1937, 1-5. But it is not certain that Lewis had read "Consider the Dog," since the pagination does not agree. She probably addressed this topic in several of her writings.

it, 'with great enjoyment.'"[83]

In that essay, Sister Penelope wrote about man as the link between God and the lower creation. "The glory of God," she writes, "can be known by the animals only through men."[84] Nooni, the small dog in her essay, is "utterly one of the family," able to take no for an answer, trusting the family completely.[85] She is patient and good-tempered.[86] "The words which express the utter trust we ought to have in God do express the utter trust she has in us, through whom … she has experienced some faint reflection of the Divine Dependability."[87] Sister Penelope concludes, "So Nooni and her like speak to us from Him, and tell us that right relationship with God consists in love, and in faith which means believing in the Beloved as utterly dependable, and issues in obedience even when the command is hard and one does not understand. … [W]hat they give us is sound as far as it goes; and coming as it does within the range of common experience might well be a starting-point both for improving our own relationship with God and for teaching others."[88] It's no wonder that Lewis enjoyed that essay; he loved animals too.

Nearly a year later, Lewis wrote to Sister Penelope about his plan to make his first private confession the following week to a personal guide, i.e. Father Walter Adams of the Society of St. John the Evangelist in Oxford. He feared that his confession might simply be "an orgy of egoism."[89] In November 1940, Jack made his first confession. A week and a half later, having made that confession without indulging in egoism, he writes to Sister Penelope again about that confession.[90] Since Sister Penelope, a fellow Anglican, was, like Adams, a member of a Religious Order, she would understand this experience. Very likely she suggested private confession to him in the first place.

The two wrote to one another about the human "trappings"

---

[83] *Collected Letters, II*, 495f. November 9, 1941. This certainly dealt with "Consider the Dog," since the dog's name, Nooni, appears both in this letter and in "Consider the Dog."

[84] "Consider the Dog," 1.

[85] "Consider the Dog," 2.

[86] "Consider the Dog," 3.

[87] "Consider the Dog," 4.

[88] "Consider the Dog," 4f. She also touches on a "theology of animals" in several places in *Meditations*, suggesting, for example, that the living creatures around the throne of heaven, described in Revelation 4, are animals. *Meditations*, 71.

[89] *Collected Letters, II*, 450-452. October 24, 1940.

[90] *Collected Letters, II*, 453f., November 4, 1940.

of religion,[91] very probably including the features of the Christmas season that Lewis disliked so much.[92] He also wrote about the need to stamp out "manmade" religion,[93] arguing that what man has decided doesn't necessarily follow from what God has revealed.

Lewis wrote on one occasion about the two natures of Christ, thinking that her way of writing suggested that deity had replaced the human soul in the man Jesus. He wasn't certain that he was reading her right or that his theology was correct, so he raised the issue rather than criticize her position.[94] His theology was correct, but whether or not she intended what he thought is impossible to answer without seeing her initial letter. He was correct, however, in seeing Christology of supreme importance for any theological writing.

They also discussed personal piety, such as how Christ was in the house during a trying time,[95] the cost of Mrs. Moore's nursing home care, which leads him to "cheerful insecurity" in the Lord,[96] and he asks her if Christ's invitation for us to grow is not perhaps because He knows that we need to advance just a little more in order to break down the assault of the Evil One.[97] He cites Thomas à Kempis who stated that if one wants to make peace one must have peace inside oneself.[98]

Two months before his death, Lewis writes to Sister Penelope about waking from his recent coma and about honoring Lazarus instead of Stephen as the first martyr.[99] Clearly Lewis knows that his life is nearing its end, and he writes wistfully about his recent near death experience and the last days that he sees ahead of him.[100] Other letters throughout the years addressed such topics as busy lives, which sometimes separate us from God, forgiveness,[101] his book on prayer,[102]

---

[91] *Collected Letters, II*, 497. November 19, 1941.

[92] "Christmas and Xmas in the Life of C. S. Lewis," *CSL: The Bulletin of The New York C. S. Lewis Society.* Vol. 48, No. 6 (November/December 2017):1-8.

[93] On May 28, 1945.

[94] *Collected Letters, II*, 526f. July 29, 1942.

[95] *Collected Letters, II*, 592. October 5, 1943.

[96] On December 30, 1950.

[97] On September 6, 1944.

[98] On January 3, 1945.

[99] *Clive Staples Lewis*, 444. W. H. Lewis, *Letters of C. S. Lewis*, Revised and Enlarged Edition, edited by Walter Hooper, San Diego: Harcourt Brace, 1993, 508f. September 17, 1963.

[100] For example, for Mrs. Moore. *Collected Letters, III*, 158. September 17, 1963.

[101] *Collected Letters, III*, 123. June 5, 1951.

[102] *Collected Letters, II*, 428. February 15, 1954. Sister Penelope's letter

the phrase "sinned *in* Adam," angels' bodies, and the existence of Hell.[103]

Miscellaneous Topics

The correspondence between Lewis and Lawson covered many other topics than the major ones listed above—books, writing, publishers, and spiritual matters. They wrote about personal health, family members and friends, travels, duties, the war, his new position as Professor of Medieval and Renaissance English at Cambridge University, and other matters.

Early in their correspondence, the war was an occasional topic, especially the service of Warren Lewis in France. Sister Penelope apparently had spoken to some women who were then serving in the war effort, the WAFS,[104] and Lewis wrote likewise about his talks to the RAF.[105] He also wrote about his forthcoming talks, "Beyond Personality," his fourth series to be broadcast on the BBC,[106] originally scheduled to raise the morale of the citizens of Great Britain. Both Lewis and Sister Penelope wanted to serve the war effort in ways appropriate to their vocations. In a passage from an essay entitled "Servants of the Lord," Sister Penelope wrote that the saving work of God "is in us, going on inside us, working in us like leaven in the lump; yet we are equally in it, included in, environed and conditioned by it, and, insofar as we are being faithful, we are part of the leaven ourselves and the saving mystery is working *through* each one of us, as well as in us. In that sense we are all the servants of the Lord." Lewis would have agreed.[107]

Sister Penelope once wrote that she "scented" a philologist, and Lewis agreed with her assessment, but he touted Tolkien as "a real philologist." He proceeded to discuss the origin of the word *hross*, which comes from the second syllable of walrus, a word Tolkien had

---

of October 22, 1940 states, "May I say that you yourself asked for my prayers in your first letter and you have them." "The Beginnings of C. S. Lewis's Correspondence with Sr Penelope CSMV." Sister Elizabeth Jane CSMV in an email of September 12, 2019.

[103] *Collected Letters, II*, 450-452. October 24, 1940.

[104] Sometimes called the Women of the Air Transport Auxiliary, the ATA.

[105] *Collected Letters, II*, 480. See also the letter of May 15, 1941, *Collected Letters, II*, 484f. *Collected Letters, II*, 493f. October 9, 1941.

[106] *Collected Letters, II*, 602f.

[107] *Meditations*, 52.

worked on for the Oxford English Dictionary.[108] Lewis also writes about the words *hnau, sorn-séroni,* and *handramit,* all invented words that appear in *Out of the Silent Planet.*[109]

Lewis's marriage and the tragic circumstances surrounding his wife's cancer consumed a significant part of his letters. In 1957 Lewis wrote to Sister Penelope about his marriage to Joy Gresham, Joy's cancer at the time of the marriage, the new beauty and happiness that had entered his life, and his new stepsons David and Douglas.[110] Just two months later he had the opportunity to write to Sister Penelope with the good news that Joy's illness seemed to be arrested.[111]

Later that year, Lewis writes to Sister Penelope about Joy's improvement, stating that she was improving "little by little till the woman who cd hardly be moved in bed can now walk about the house and into the garden," even though the sword of Damocles that hangs over everyone still hangs over them.[112] Marriage brought Lewis so much happiness that he felt comfortable enthusing about married life, having the kind of happiness at age fifty-nine that most men have decades earlier, and enjoying the good wine now.[113] Several letters to Sister Penelope she did not keep. One told of Joy's relapse, and two told about Joy's death. Sister Penelope wrote, "In one he said, 'They tell me she is in God's hands. She was in those here, and I saw what they did to her.' But she came through, as his last letter shows."[114]

Lewis's second last letter to her on June 23, 1962 mentions his work on the Commission to Revise the Psalter with "delightful colleagues,"[115] work that had begun in 1959 and was continuing at the

---

[108] Peter Gilliver, https://public.oed.com/blog/jrr-tolkien-and-the-oed/

[109] *Collected Letters, II,* 265. August 24, 1939.

[110] *Collected Letters, III,* 837. March 6, 1957.

[111] *Clive Staples Lewis,* 387. W. H. Lewis, *Letters of C. S. Lewis,* Revised and Enlarged Edition, edited by Walter Hooper, San Diego: Harcourt Brace, 1993, 465. May 12, 1957.

[112] *Clive Staples Lewis,* 391. W. H. Lewis, *Letters of C. S. Lewis,* Revised and Enlarged Edition, edited by Walter Hooper, San Diego: Harcourt Brace, 1993, 470f. November 6, 1957.

[113] Lyle W. Dorsett, *And God Came In,* New York: Ballantine Books, 1983, 137. February 12, 1958.

[114] "Overview of C. S. Lewis's Correspondence with Sr Penelope CSMV." Sister Elizabeth Jane CSMV in an email of September 12, 2019.

[115] *Clive Staples Lewis,* 429. See also Walter Hooper, *C. S. Lewis: Companion & Guide,* HarperOne, 1998, 112. See also my article on the Commission to Revise the Psalter in *Seven,* 2020 (Volume 37).

time of this letter.

They Meet in Wantage

Since Lewis and Sister Penelope lived only a few miles apart, they met on more than one occasion. They met (or may have met) on at least five occasions. In 1941,[116] 1942, possibly in 1948,[117] 1951,[118] and in 1953.[119]

One of those occasions stands out. At the instigation of Sister Penelope, the Mother Superior of CSMV invited Lewis to come to Wantage to talk to the Junior Sisters, and they planned his visit for the weekend of April 20-22, 1942. He accepted the invitation with a sense of humor, thinking it odd that he would be speaking to a group of nuns and wondering if he would find a dungeon or a chained skeleton in the guest house.[120] On that weekend, he spoke to the Junior Sisters three separate times on "The Gospel in our Generation,"[121] followed by discussion time. The purpose was to show the Sisters "how to present the Gospel to various classes of people, in parishes, schools, etc.," and the lectures were described as "excellent."[122]

St. Mary's Convent Guesthouse
Photo by Will Vaus

---

[116] *Collected Letters*, II, 484f. May 15, 1941. Lewis indicates that he hopes to visit her in Wantage at the end of term, which is probably the first time they met.

[117] *Collected Letters*, II, 862.

[118] *Collected Letters*, III, 124.

[119] *Collected Letters*, III, 279. January 9, 1953.

[120] *Collected Letters*, II, 480. The date of this letter is April 10, 1941.

[121] Richard James, "A Timeline from 1890 to 1977+ of Selected Religious and Political Events in the British Isles Intertwined with the Family Tree, life & Writings of Ruth Penelope Lawson."

[122] "CSMV St Mary's Convent Logbook Entry for 20th April 1942." Provided in an email from Sister Elizabeth Jane CSMV on October 29, 2019.

A few weeks later, Lewis writes to Sister Penelope about the recent visit to Wantage, asking her to commend him to those he met. He mentions the completion of *Perelandra* and requests permission to dedicate the book to the women at the Convent. The dedication was "To Some ladies at Wantage." Sister Penelope was amused that the Portuguese edition later translated this 'To some wanton ladies.' She had a delightful sense of humor and enjoyed telling the story of how, when she was a girl, she heard a missionary preach on the evils of alcohol. "Bring up your son to hate the bottle," he said, "and when he is a grown man he will never depart from it!" In that same letter, he also commends the audience at Wantage, which was better than the audience to whom he spoke recently on "*Hamlet*: The Prince or the Poem?"[123] That latter audience was the British Academy!

He also sends under separate cover another manuscript of *Perelandra* and requests it back with the Rev. Mother's permission for the dedication.[124] He received that permission, since the published book contained the dedication. The book was released by the Bodley Head of London on April 20, 1943, so this July letter probably contained a pre-publication copy of the book. He also asked that Sister Penelope commend him to four different nuns at the Convent, an indication of the fondness with which he recalled his speaking engagement in Wantage the previous April.[125] A year later, Lewis wrote that he would love to spend some time in Wantage again.[126]

Conclusion

C. S. Lewis and Sister Ruth Penelope Lawson carried on an extensive correspondence on a wide range of topics over the course of twenty-four years. They had literary interests, both as scholars and writers, which explains why he sent her a copy of the *Screwtape* manuscript during World War II. He valued her as his "elder sister" in the Christian faith, a factor that was more important to him than her virtues as a scholar and writer. Her insight into Scripture, especially the Psalms, and her personal piety meant more to him than the frequent banter between them about books, writing, and publishers.

Their friendship led to some helpful advice from the master of the English language to the Anglican nun. While her publications did not enjoy a reputation approaching that of Lewis, she wrote frequently, and her writings were accepted by a variety of publishers.

---

[123] *Collected Letters*, II, 519f. On May 11, 1942.

[124] *Collected Letters*, II, 526. July 29, 1942.

[125] *Collected Letters*, III, 1546. December 22, 1942.

[126] *Collected Letters*, II, 586f. The letter is dated August 10, 1943.

His advice probably advanced her writing career and reputation, and his Introduction to her most famous translation, Athanasius's *The Incarnation of the Word of God*, helped that book find a publisher and ensure its success.

Sister Penelope
Used by kind permission of CSMV

Twenty-One Friendships of C.S. Lewis

BIBLIOGRAPHY OF BOOKS BY SISTER PENELOPE [127]

Also the Holy Ghost: An Essay on the Bible. London: A. R. Mowbray; New York: Morehouse-Gorham, 1956. A layman's introduction to the Bible.

As in Adam: A Study in the Church. London: A. R. Mowbray, 1954.

The Coming: A Study in the Christian Faith. A reissue of two earlier books, *The Coming of the Lord* and *As in Adam.* 1974.

The Coming of the Lord: A Study in the Creed. New York: Morehouse-Gorham; A. R. Mowbray, 1953. Lewis called it "the best theological book by anyone I have read for a long time."

The Communicant's Pocket Book. London: The Faith Press, 1960.

Concerning Christian Joy. London: C. L. A.,[128] 1952.

God Persists: A Short Survey of World History in the Light of Christian Faith. London: A. R. Mowbray, 1939. Sister Penelope sent a copy of this book to C. S. Lewis when she wrote to him the first time.

Handbook to the Plays: They Shall Be My People. London: Oxford University Press, 1952.

The House of Mary: A Gospel Play for Passiontide and Easter. London: The Girls' Friendly Society, 1947. Second Edition, The Faith Press, 1960.

If Any Man Serve Me: Broadcast Readings for Holy Week. Pax House, 1942. These meditations were read during Holy Week of 1942.

In Face of Fear. London: S.P.C.K., 1962.

Leaves from the Trees. Cambridge: W. Heffer & Sons, 1937.

Light in the Night: A Book for Those in Bed. Oxford: A. R.

---

[127] Her articles, minibooks, Cistercian studies, and book reviews are not catalogued here.

[128] Church Literature Association.

Mowbray, 1938. S.C.M. Press, 1958.

Meditating on the Bible. London: C.L.A. n.d.

Meditations of a Caterpillar. London: The Faith Press, 1962. This collection of fourteen brief essays in ninety-two pages she called her "spiritual autobiography."

The Morning Gift. (unpublished) Sister Penelope wrote to Lewis in 1949 about how to get this book published. n.d.

A Pocket Book for Christians. London: S.C.M. Press, 1957.

Runners after God: The Call to the Religious Life. London: C.L.A., 1965.

Scenes from the Psalms Arranged for Use in Schools. London: S.P.C.K., 1939.

These Last Days: Time Seen through Christian Eyes. London: The Faith Press, New York: Morehouse Gorham, 1959.

This is Life: A Book for the Busy. London: SCM Press, 1960.

To See the Lord: A Study in Fulfillment. London: Church Union, 1958. C.L.A. Lent Book.

Windows on Jerusalem: A Study in the Mystery of Redemption. London: Pax House, 1941.

The Way to Pray. London: C.L.A., 1963.

The Wood for The Trees: An Outline of Christianity. Cambridge: W. Heffer & Sons, 1935. Third edition from The Faith Press, 1959. Fourth edition from Mowbrays, 1971. This book, her first, describes the Church of England as a true *via media*, a middle road between Protestantism and Catholicism. It was her first book, originally published by W. Heffer & Sons as *The Wood: An Outline of Christianity.*

The Work of God: A Study in the Divine Office of the Church. London: The Faith Press, 1964.

These Last Days: Time Seen Through Christian Eyes. London: The Faith Press, 1959.

They Shall Be My People: The Bible Traversed in a Course of Reading Plays. 2 vols. London: Oxford University Press, 1951. In 1952, Lewis promised to order a copy of the books and read them. These two volumes contain thirty-three plays approximately 10-15 pages in length each, dealing with various events in the history of God's people. In her Preface, Sister Penelope writes, "The Hero of this story is Almighty God Himself. It is a love story, the story of His love for man." Volume I covers the Old Testament in eighteen plays, while Volume II covers the New Testament.

This is Life: A Book for the Busy. London: S.C.M. Press, 1960.

Types and Shadows: A Quarry for Teachers. London: The Girls' Friendly Society (G. F. S.), 1941.

Translations

St. Anselm. *Prayers and Meditations.* London: Mowbray, 1952.

St. Thomas Aquinas. *The Golden Chain: Selections from the Catena of S. Thomas Aquinas for Lent and Easter.* London: Mowbray, 1956.

St. Athanasius: Letter to Marcellinus on the Psalms. London: Mowbray, 1949. Later reprinted as an Appendix to the second edition of Athanasius's *The Incarnation of the Word of God.* Introduction by C. S. Lewis.

An Augustinian: Meditations to the Holy Spirit. London: Mowbray, 1957.

Bernard of Clairvaux. *On the Christian Year: Selections from his Sermons.* London: Mowbray, 1954.

Bernard of Clairvaux. *On the Love of God.* London: Mowbray, 1950.

Bernard of Clairvaux. *On the Song of Songs: Sermones in Cantica Canticorum.* London: A. R. Mowbray, 1952.

Brother Bernard. *The Threefold Gift of Christ.* London: Mowbray, 1954.

Hugh of St. Victor. *The Divine Love.* London: Mowbray, 1956.

Hugh of St. Victor. *Selected Spiritual Writings.* Classics of the Contemplative Life. London: Faber & Faber; New

York: Harper & Row, 1962.

The Incarnation of the Word of God: Being the Treatise of St. Athanasius. London: G. Bles, the Centenary Press, 1944. New York: Macmillan. A translation. Lewis wrote the Introduction for this translation. His Introduction was later republished as "On the Reading of Old Books."

Lent with Saint Bernard: A Devotional Commentary on Psalm 91. London: Mowbray, 1953.

A Little Book on the Contemplation of Christ. London: Mowbray, 1951.

The Meditations of William of St. Thierry. London: Mowbray, 1954.

Origen. *The Song of Songs. Commentary and Homilies. Ancient Christian Writers*, vol. 26. Westminster, Maryland: Newman Press, Maryland & Longmans Green, 1957.

The Pastoral Prayer of St. Aelred of Rievaulx. Dacre Press, 1955.

Robert of Bridlington. *The Bridlington Dialogues: An Exposition of the Rule of St. Augustine for the Life of the Clergy.* Robert Bridlington. London: Mowbray, 1960.

Twenty-One Friendships of C.S. Lewis

APPENDIX I: LEWIS'S LETTERS TO SISTER PENELOPE

The major topics of each letter are listed along with the date.

1. August 9, 1939—pride and humility over Sister Penelope's comments on *Out of the Silent Planet*, smuggling theology, her book *God Persists*

2. August 24, 1939—philology, the dog-man and man-God relationships

3. November 8, 1939—the Numinous, *The Pilgrim's Regress*

4. October 24, 1940—angel bodies, the existence of hell, first confession

5. November 4, 1940—free will and *Phantastes*

6. April 10, 1941—the invitation to speak in Wantage, her book *Windows on Jerusalem*

7. May 15, 1941—Lewis coming to Wantage after term is over, BBC talks, RAF talks

8. October 9, 1941—the Shroud of Turin, returning the *Screwtape* manuscript

9. November 9, 1941—the Shroud of Turin, writing *Perelandra*, Mrs. Moore

10. November 19, 1941—grumbling, religion, plans for next April in Wantage

11. April 9, 1942—*The Odyssey*, *Perelandra*, and health

12. May 11, 1942—Miss Burton, *Perelandra* now finished

13. May 15, 1942—BBC talks, RAF talks

14. July 29, 1942—the rejection of Athanasius' *De Incarnatione*, Lewis recommends another publisher and requests permission to dedicate *Perelandra* to the sisters at Wantage

15. August 22, 1942—mythology, Henry More

16. December 22, 1942—*Perelandra*, gratitude

17. February 20, 1943—writing, Bles, Dent, publisher's request for a crib for *De Athanasius*, real creativity

18. March 25, 1943—biblical plays called *The Holy Seed*

(published later as *They Shall Be My People*), symbolism in writing

19. August 10, 1943—difficult circumstances at home, peace

20. August 16, 1943—willingness to read the plays that become *They Shall Be My People*

21. September 24, 1943—biblical plays, making a start on his book *Miracles*

22. October 5, 1943—critique of the biblical plays, finding a publisher, domestic crisis

23. February 19, 1944—the arrival of *De Incarnatione*, June Flewett

24. September 6, 1944—completion of *That Hideous Strength*, the invasion of Normandy

25. October 21, 1944—Muriel's health

26. January 3, 1945—Sister Penelope's plays, *That Hideous Strength*

27. May 28, 1945—Sister Penelope's scriptural plays, "religion," and the death of Charles Williams

28. January 31, 1946—Athanasius' *De Incarnatione*, Oxford students returning from the war, *That Hideous Strength*, Holst's "The Planets"

29. October 21, 1946—a spaceship for interplanetary flight

30. November 21, 1947—poems in *Punch* magazine, the domestic situation at The Kilns

31. April 8, 1948—*Miracles*, Sister Penelope's proposed book on the Psalms and another proposed story of hers

32. July 19, 1948—Sister Penelope's proposed geological romance, possibly meeting in Oxford

33. July 22, 1948—a book manuscript Sister Penelope sent

34. August 31, 1948—Lewis critiques a recent story (probably *The Morning Gift*) of Sister Penelope

35. January 31, 1949—how to find a publisher, comments from Bles

36. August 1, 1949—God's infinite now in prayer

37. August 16, 1949—an improved *Morning Gift*

38. January 12, 1950—*The Morning Gift* being rejected, rejections by publishers, writing a book on communication with Tolkien

39. December 30, 1950—a different plan for *The Morning Gift*, Mrs. Moore now in a nursing home, cheerful insecurity, adaptations of *Screwtape*

40. June 5, 1951—George MacDonald's poetry, "a plain called Ease," believing in forgiveness

41. January 10, 1952—Adam, Austin Farrer, Simone Weil, *They Shall Be My People*, *English Literature in the Sixteenth Century*

42. November 28, 1952—Lewis's *OHEL* volume is done

43. January 9, 1953—two Greek words for "when," Prayer, Mrs. Hooker, their recent meeting

44. April 1, 1953—*The Coming of the Lord*, some critique of the same

45. February 15, 1954—busy lives, Kathleen Nott's *The Emperor's New Clothes*

46. July 30, 1954—Lewis's new Chair at Cambridge University, fourteen days of *vivas*

47. June 18, 1956—the prophecies of Isaiah, selling the old *Screwtape* manuscript Lewis sent to Sister Penelope

48. March 6, 1957—marriage to Joy Davidman, Joy's sickness, *The Third Eye* by Lobsang Rampa, David and Douglas Gresham

49. May 12, 1957—Literary Agents, Joy now at home

50. November 6, 1957—Joy's cancer arrested, Lewis's osteoporosis, authors Lewis is reading

51. February 12, 1958—happiness in marriage as good wine

52. October 8, 1958—a letter Sister Penelope did not keep about Joy's relapse

53. February 1, 1962—*A Grief Observed*, N. W. Clerk, Thomas Merton

54. June 23, 1962—the Commission to Revise the Psalter,

the success of returning to Cambridge

55. September 17, 1963—conventional things, Lewis's recent coma, Lazarus as the first martyr, purgatory

Twenty-One Friendships of C.S. Lewis

APPENDIX II: BOOKS AND AUTHORS THEY DISCUSSED

Books by Sister Penelope
God Persists
Scenes from the Psalms
They Shall Be My People
Windows on Jerusalem: A Study in the Mystery of Redemption
The Incarnation of the Word of God: Being the Treatise of St. Athanasius "De Incarnatione Verbi Dei"

Books by C. S. Lewis
English Literature in the Sixteenth Century
A Grief Observed
Miracles
Out of the Silent Planet
Perelandra
That Hideous Strength
The Great Divorce
The Pilgrim's Regress
The Screwtape Letters

Other Authors
Boethius
Martin Buber, *I and Thou*
Chalcidius
Austin Farrer, *Glass of Vision: The Making of St. John's Apocalypse*
James Gillman, *The Divine Journey*
Samuel Johnson
George MacDonald, *Phantastes*, *The Diary of an Old Soul*
Macrobius
Kathleen Nott, *The Emperor's New Clothes*
Homer, *The Odyssey*
Coventry Patmore
Pseudo-Dionysus
Lobsang Rampa, *The Third Eye*
Simone Weil, *Waiting on God*
Charles Williams

R.E. Havard, at a C.S. Lewis Memorial Gathering
at Magdalen College, Oxford in July 1974
Used by permission of the Marion E. Wade Center,
Wheaton College, Wheaton, IL.

Chapter 8

R. E. HAVARD
Lewis Family Physician

In 1934, Robert Emlyn Havard became C. S. Lewis's new family physician. Havard soon became a member of the Inklings, and he joined the Lewis brothers on many social occasions. He was a close enough friend that one of the Chronicles of Narnia—*Prince Caspian*—was dedicated to Havard's daughter, Mary Clare. Writing from a physician's point of view, he wrote a short Appendix to Lewis's book, *The Problem of Pain*, about the observed effects of both physical and mental pain. He had originally read that paper to the Inklings, and Lewis included it with his book, which was released just eight months after Havard read his paper. His contributions to the Inklings' meetings were so well respected that he was invited to speak at the very first meeting of the Oxford Socratic Club.

Dr. Havard also made his way into another book that Lewis wrote. In *Perelandra*, the physician who would attend Ransom upon his return from Perelandra was named Humphrey, the nickname that the Inklings assigned to Dr. Havard. He once explained Einstein to Lewis,[1] and on another occasion he joined Lewis and Warren on Warren's boat, the *Bosphorus*, for a several-day pleasure tour up the Thames River. He frequently dined with the Lewises and was present on that night when the Inklings enjoyed one of the hams that the American physician, Dr. Warfield Firor, sent to Lewis during the period of rationing in England.[2] This remarkable physician became a friend of the Lewis brothers for good reasons.

Robert Emlyn Havard

R. E. Havard was born on March 15, 1901, in Faldingworth, Lincolnshire, a small town eleven miles northeast of Lincoln in the

---

[1] *C. S. Lewis: Collected Letters, Volume 2. Books, Broadcasts and War 1931-1949.* Edited by Walter Hooper. London: HarperCollinsPublishers, 2004, 638.

[2] Walter Hooper, editor. *Brothers & Friends: The Diaries of Major Warren Hamilton Lewis*, New York: Harper & Row, 1982, 218f., for March 11, 1948.

East Midlands.³ His father, the Rev. John Emlyn Havard, served as the Anglican Vicar of Faldingworth and Buslingthorpe from 1908 to 1930.⁴ During those early years, Havard attended Wolverley School in Kidderminster, then studied chemistry at Keble College and earned a First-Class degree in 1921. He was awarded the Bachelor of Medicine and B.Chem. from Queen's College, Oxford, in 1927.⁵ Havard became a Research Student at Guy's Hospital and in London Hospital. He then moved to Oxford as an Assistant House Surgeon at the Radcliffe Infirmary, and Demonstrator in the Biochemistry Department of Oxford University. After some time in Oxford, he taught at Leeds University in their Biochemistry Department.⁶

Havard married Grace Mary Middleton on December 29, 1931. Grace had earned the BA from St. Anne's College, Oxford, in 1929. Robert and Grace had five children: John Edward (b. 1932); Mark Emlyn (b. 1935); Mary Penrose Clare, to whom *Prince Caspian* was dedicated (b. 1936); Peter Laurence (b. 1939); and David Thomas (b. 1942).⁷

In 1934, the year that Havard met C. S. Lewis, Havard returned to Oxford to take over the medical practice of Dr. W. Wood with offices in Headington and St. Giles. The former office was located near the Lewis home, and the latter was located near the Eagle and Child pub. Queen's College gave him a Schorstein Research Fellowship, also in 1934, and he subsequently earned a doctorate in medicine.⁸ In 1943, Havard was called to the Royal Navy, where he served as a medical officer. Somehow Tolkien was able to get him returned to Oxford from the war. Writing to his son Christopher, Tolkien states, "the Useless Quack has returned to Oxford! Almost the only wire I have ever pulled that has rung a bell. But there he is, uniform, red-beard, slow smile and all, still in Navy, but living at home and working on his research Board (Malaria)."⁹

---

³ In 1770-72, John Marius Wilson's *Imperial Gazetteer of England and Wales* gives this description of Faldingworth: "a parish in the district and county of Lincoln; 2 miles WNW of Wickenby r. station, and 4 SW of Market-Rasen.... Pop., 365. https://www.visionofbritain.org.uk/place/12207.

⁴ Walter Hooper, *Companion & Guide*, 679.

⁵ Walter Hooper, *Companion & Guide*, 679f.

⁶ Hooper *Companion & Guide*, 680.

⁷ Hooper *Companion & Guide*, 680.

⁸ Hooper *Companion & Guide*, 680.

⁹ The date of the letter is March 1, 1944. Humphrey Carpenter, editor.

Twenty-One Friendships of C.S. Lewis

After the war Havard worked on that same malaria research project. He wrote papers on phosphate levels and human biochemistry for journals such as *Proceedings of the Physiological Society*, *The Biochemical Journal*, *Annals of Tropical Medicine and Parasitology*, and *Lancet*.[10] Grace Havard died on September 10, 1950. Robert retired in 1968 and later moved to a home for the aged on the Isle of Wight.[11] When the Tolkiens moved to 76 Sandfield Road, before Havard moved to the Isle of Wrignt, they became neighbors and closer friends of the Havards, who lived at 28 Sandfield Road. Havard died on July 17, 1985. He is buried at St. Philip Priory, Begbroke, about seven miles north of Headington Quarry.

HAVARD AND INKLINGS MEETINGS

In May 1934 Lewis became ill, and Dr. Robert E. Havard came to The Kilns for the first time to treat him. Havard became Lewis's physician, replacing Dr. W. Wood, who had died earlier in the year.[12] Havard wrote about that first visit, stating that they spent five minutes talking about the flu and the next half-hour or more discussing ethics and philosophy. Since Havard was "well-read and keenly interested in

---

The Letters of J. R. R. Tolkien, 68.

[10] Diana Pavlac Glyer, *The Company They Keep*, Kent, Ohio: The Kent State University Press, 2007, 237f.

[11] http://tolkiengateway.net/wiki/Robert_Havard

[12] William Griffin, *Clive Staples Lewis: A Dramatic Life*, New York: Harper & Row, 1986, 107. We know from Havard's "Philia: Jack at Ease," in *C. S. Lewis at the Breakfast Table*, Boston: Harvest Books, 1992, 215, that Lewis was ill and called for Havard at some point after the death of his previous doctor, Dr. W. Wood, who had died early in 1934. Havard thinks it was 1934 or 1935. Griffin states that Lewis called for Havard at the beginning of May, but we do not know for certain that he was ill until later in the month. Whether or not this was a mild illness that later got serious, we do not know. One cannot be certain that Griffin has the part of the month accurately. On June 3, Warren writes that Minto had two patients for more than a week, since Warren got the flu within twenty-four hours of Lewis. *Brothers & Friends*, 146. This seems to push the arrival of Havard and the advent of the flu to the second half in the month, closer to June 3. Then again, there are no diary entries by Warren between May 6 and June 3, so the flu could have come at any point between those two dates, and the fatigue that Warren saw in Lewis may have signaled the onset of the flu. Diana Glyer suggests that Havard did not become Lewis's physician until 1940, since the first databale reference—*Collected Letters, II*, 343—to such service comes from that year. Glyer, *The Company They Keep*, 238.

the processes of literature and in theology,"[13] he was eventually invited to attend the Inklings, which had only begun to meet the previous autumn. But he did not attend for some years. Havard first attended an Inklings meeting on February 1, 1940. About that meeting, Lewis writes, "We had the usual pleasant party on Thursday evening in college with the welcome addition of Havard, who has been bidden all along but has hitherto been prevented from attending by various accidents."[14] His attendance at Inklings meetings is documented at least thirty-one times,[15] but he undoubtedly attended many more times than that. Walter Hooper called him "one of the most faithful of the Inklings, rarely missing a meeting.[16]

The Inklings thought highly of Havard and demonstrated their appreciation by giving him several nicknames. Havard was known as Humphrey, The Red Admiral, and U. Q. or The Useless Quack. The Useless Quack nickname had nothing to do with Havard's medical expertise. Lewis used the name Humphrey for the doctor who made an appearance in *Perelandra*.[17] When Havard grew a ruddy beard while serving as a medical officer for the Navy, Lewis named him The Red Admiral. Havard stated that Warren's nickname for him— Hmphrey— was the result of an annoyance when Havard did not arrive with his car,[18] but another explanation from Havard is that Dyson could not remember his actual name on one occasion.[19]

---

[13] George Sayer, *Jack: A Life of C. S. Lewis*, Wheaton, IL: Crossway, 2005, 151.

[14] *C. S. Lewis: Collected Letters, II.* Edited by Walter Hooper. London: HarperCollinsPublishers, 2004, 343.

[15] These are the dates for which we know Dr. Havard attended: For 1940—February 1 and 22; March 14 (for which see *Collected Letters, II*, 365); April 25 (see *Collected Letters, II*, 404f.); and May 16 (see *Collected Letters, II*, 416); for 1941—January 7; for 1944 (see *The Letters of J. R. R. Tolkien, 47*)—April 13 and November 24; for 1945—January 30, October 18, and December 12; for 1946—March 28, April 2 and 11, August 8 and 15, September 5, October 24, and November 28; for 1947—April 24, October 23 and 30, November 11, 18, and 27; for 1948—January 1, March 11, 16, and 18, and April 8; for 1951—January 30.

[16] Hooper *Companion & Guide*, 680.

[17] See, for example, *Perelandra*. New York: Macmillan, 1944, 28.

[18] Robert E. Havard, "Philia: Jack at Ease," in *C. S. Lewis at the Breakfast Table, 222*. See also Hooper *Companion & Guide*, 680.

[19] Oral history interview excerpts with Dr. Robert E. Havard, July 26, 1984, OH/SR-14, The Marion E. Wade Center, Wheaton, Illinois. Used by permission. This oral history interview was done by Lyle W. Dorsett. Havard states, "There was a man—Dyson, Hugo Dyson from Reading

Nevertheless, the Inklings thought highly of Havard and his contributions to the discussions, or he would not have attended so frequently. He also offered good-hearted jabs and received them. Lewis, who once had the mumps, wrote to George and Moira Sayer about Havard's contribution to an Inklings meeting, "Humphrey kept on quoting me bits out of *The Problem of Pain*, which I call a bit thick."[20] Although Tolkien and others called him U. Q. Humphrey, or The Useless Quack, Tolkien also called him Honest Humphrey.[21] Tolkien once affectionately wrote a poem about him,

> Dr. U. Q. Humphrey
> Made poultices of comfrey,
> If you didn't pay his bills
> He gave you doses of squills.[22]

As indicated above, Havard attended his first Inklings meeting in 1940. At that meeting, Havard read a paper on the clinical experience of the effects of pain, which Lewis asked him to write for an appendix to *The Problem of Pain*.[23] In a letter to Warren, Lewis wrote that Havard wrote the paper "in order that I might use all or part of it as an appendix to my book."[24] He attended again three weeks later.[25]

---

who was referring to me and couldn't remember my name. And he said, 'Oh, you know, that's that Humphrey or something.' And the name for some reason took on and stuck and I was known to the Inklings as Humphrey from that time on. And still am by those who survived." Alan Jacobs states that Dyson forgot Havard's real name on one occasion and called him "Humphrey," and Havard remained Humphrey from that time on. Alan Jacobs, *The Narnian: The Life and Imagination of C. S. Lewis*, New York: HarperCollins, 2005, 195, note. Humphrey Carpenter says Dyson called Havard "Humphrey" either "in pure error of because it alliterated with his surname." Humphrey Carpenter, *The Inklings: C. S. Lewis, J. R. R. Tolkien, Charles Williams and their friends*, London: HarperCollins, 1997, 130.

[20] Lewis wrote to the Sayers on August 15, 1951, about a recent undated occasion. *C. S. Lewis: Collected Letters, III, Narnia, Cambridge and Joy 1950-1963*. Edited by Walter Hooper. London: HarperCollinsPublishers, 2006, 133f.

[21] Humphrey Carpenter, ed. *The Letters of J. R. R. Tolkien*, Boston: Houghton Mifflin Company, 2000, 109.

[22] Carpenter, *The Inklings*, 177. The footnote on page 176 references "MS (Estate of J. R. R. Tolkien)."

[23] Roger Lancelyn Green and Walter Hooper, *C. S. Lewis: A Biography*, Boston: Houghton Mifflin Harcourt Company, 1994, 187.

[24] *Collected Letters, II*, 343.

[25] *Collected Letters, II*, 358.

Havard was clearly a good writer, not only for medical journals, but for other purposes as well. Lewis once wrote about Havard's writing, "Havard read us an account of a mountain climb he had taken part in—a straight account in plain language, which made our hair stand on end."[26] Glyer affirms this, stating, "Havard ... was a gifted reader, writer, and supporter of his friends' work ...."[27]

The content of many Inklings meetings was recorded because of some significant events, such as a reading of *The Lord of the Rings* or *The Lion, the Witch and the Wardrobe* or because of a Firor ham feast. However, we know little of the exact dialogue, since the meetings were so spontaneous, and no one was taking notes or recording them. Occasionally the diaries and letters of Tolkien, C. S. Lewis, and Warren Lewis recorded the bare bones outline of a meeting as well as a story of two, but we usually get nothing more. When we do get meeting notes, we get very little information. Even rarer are mentions of contributions from Havard.

Havard's participation in the Inklings, however, included other occasions. On December 12, 1945, for example, Lewis, Tolkien, Warren, and, for part of the time, Dr. Havard attended an Inklings victory holiday at The Bull Hotel, Fairford,[28] possibly in celebration of the end of World War II. The occasion included a lot of walking around Quenington, Hatherop, Sunhill and Meysey Hampton, and lots of talking.

On March 11, 1948, the Inklings met in the New Room of Magdalen College to celebrate the generosity of Dr. Warfield Firor and enjoy the ham he had sent. Lewis brought sherry and burgundy, they raffled off an American dinner jacket suit, and they all enjoyed the ham. They also had soup, fish, and a savory from the college kitchen. Each of them signed a thank you note to Dr. Firor, including their current position. On the way home Warren suggested to Humphrey the idea of coming to Malvern with them, and Havard responded favorably.[29] Havard was to have joined them in Malvern several weeks later but was unable to do so. Eventually, in January 1949, he was able to travel to Malvern to be with them.[30]

---

[26] *Collected Letters, II*, 405. The date of this Inklings meeting was April 25, 1940.

[27] Glyer, *The Company They Keep*, 23, n. 23.

[28] *Brothers & Friends*, 184f.

[29] *Brothers & Friends*, 218f., and the unpublished diary of Warren Lewis.

[30] *Brothers & Friends*, 219.

Twenty-One Friendships of C.S. Lewis

On January 30, 1951, the Inklings met at the Bird and Baby, including Havard,[31] where the discussion included the possibility of Lewis being elected to the Poetry Chair. Just nine days later they learned that Lewis had lost the Chair to Cecil Day Lewis.[32]

SOCIAL GATHERINGS AND HOLIDAYS

Havard also met Lewis on many other occasions than Inklings gatherings. On August 26, 1939, for example, Lewis and Hugo Dyson met at Folly Bridge, just south of the Tom Tower, climbed down to Salter's Shipyard, and boarded Warren's *Bosphorus*. Because of military duty, Warren could not join them. So Havard joined them to provide the nautical expertise (although a medical officer, he had served in the Navy). "Our spirits were high," Havard comments, "at the prospect of a temporary break with politics and daily chores."[33] Together they traveled up the Thames, stopping for dinner at the Trout in Godstow and for the night at Rose Revived near Newbridge Farm, about twelve miles southwest of Oxford.[34] They spent several days traveling past Radcot, Lechlade, Inglesham, Godstow, and other places, talking about the Russo-German pact, the Renaissance, and many other topics. The trip illustrates the warmth between the Lewis brothers and their doctor, but it also demonstrates what Havard stated much later, i.e., that "seeing him so regularly two or three times a week, I came to know him well in all his moods."[35] Havard spent much time with Lewis, sharing many interests, meals, drinks, and conversation. They even went on holidays together at least once, i.e., in January 1949 when Lewis, his brother Warren, and Havard spent eight days together in Malvern.[36]

In addition, the following January, Havard came to The Kilns and skated on the pond.[37] That July, he came to The Kilns to see Lewis and, while there, they both listened to Hitler's speech over the radio in

---

[31] *Brothers & Friends*, 239, and the unpublished diary of Warren Lewis.

[32] *Brothers & Friends*, 239f.

[33] Carpenter, *The Inklings*, 68.

[34] Robert E. Havard, "Philia: Jack at Ease," in *C. S. Lewis at the Breakfast Table, 219*.

[35] Robert E. Havard, "Philia: Jack at Ease," in *C. S. Lewis at the Breakfast Table, 218*, 225.

[36] *Collected Letters, II*, 904. The date is January 5, 1949.

[37] The date is January 14, 1940.

the early evening. In August, Havard took Lewis to Tolkien's home, where they stayed until about 12:45 a.m. Then Havard dropped Lewis at College to change clothes and take his turn on patrol as part of the Home Guard.[38]

Since Havard drove a car and Lewis did not (although Warren did), Havard's car became a mode of transportation on numerous occasions. In 1948, for example, Havard provided transportation back home after the Lewis brothers saw the Walt Disney movie "Bambi." Since Havard and his family also saw the movie at that showing, he was gracious enough to offer them a ride,[39] and he provided such transportation, especially for Warren, after many an evening Inklings meetings.

Occasionally, Havard spent time with Warren when Lewis was not available. Warren went to supper with the Havards one evening in 1950. The other guests included Havard's brother-in-law, a man named Middleton, and Middleton's wife, a woman Warren calls "one of the most interesting and intelligent women I have met for a long time." (Middleton was the maiden name of Havard's wife Grace.) Mrs. Middleton was writing a book on the life of the Earl of Middleton (1608-1674). They also had interesting conversation, including amusing stories about life in the court of King George VI.[40] When the king's family entertained without ceremony, Mrs. Middleton stated, the favorite after dinner entertainment was "Twenty questions" with the King as the question master.[41] This gathering may have been one of the remaining wishes of Grace Havard, since she died less than three months later.[42] The Lewis brothers attended Mrs. Havard's Requiem Mass two days after her death.

As stated above, in 1951, while waiting to dine at the Royal Oxford, Lewis heard the news that he had lost the Poetry Chair to Cecil Day Lewis. He was with Tolkien, Owen Barfield, Humphrey Havard, David Cecil, J. A. W. Bennett, and Warren.[43] Then Lewis

---

[38] *Collected Letters, II*, 436. The date is August 16, 1940.

[39] *Brothers & Friends*, 221. The unpublished diary of Warren Lewis provides the additional detail that Havard and family were also at the same showing and drove them home. The date is August 13, 1948.

[40] George VI was King of the United Kingdom from December 11, 1936, until his death on February 6, 1952.

[41] The unpublished diaries of Warren Hamilton Lewis for June 17, 1960.

[42] The date is September 10, 1950. Hooper, *Companion & Guide*, 681.

[43] The date is February 8, 1951. *Clive Staples Lewis*, 319.

said, "Fill up! And stop looking so glum. The only distressing thing about this affair is that my friends seem to be upset."[44] Havard was also present when the English faculty gave Lewis a farewell dinner at Merton College before he took up his Chair of Medieval and Renaissance English at Cambridge University.[45] One of the last social occasions was in June 1963, when Lewis met Roger Lancelyn Green, Gervase Mathew, Humphrey Havard, Colin Hardie, and Walter Hooper at The Lamb and Flag at noon.[46] Lewis was in his last few months of life.

Et Cetera

A few additional connections between Lewis and Havard further illustrate the importance of this friendship. When Lewis dedicated his 1940 book, *The Problem of Pain*, to some of the Inklings, that included Williams, Dyson, Warren Lewis, Tolkien, and R. E. Havard.[47] When the Oxford Socratic Club met for the first time, Havard was the guest speaker. That first meeting was held on January 26, 1942, at Somerville College, and Havard spoke on "Won't Mankind Outgrow Christianity in the Face of the Advance of Science and of Modern Ideologies?"[48] When Lewis married Joy Davidman at the Oxford Registry Office on April 23, 1956,[49] Dr. Robert Havard and Dr. Austin Farrer were witnesses to the wedding.[50]

After Lewis died on November 22, 1963, Havard was among those who attended a Requiem mass for Lewis in a Catholic church, along with Tolkien, James Dundas-Grant, and others.[51] Havard probably also attended Lewis's funeral, which was held on November 26 at 11:00 a.m.[52] at Holy Trinity, Headington Quarry,[53] conducted

---

[44] *The Letters of J. R. R. Tolkien*, 351.

[45] The date is December 9, 1954. *Brothers & Friends*, 243.

[46] The date is June 17, 1963. Green and Hooper, 159.

[47] A letter to Alan Richard Griffiths. *Collected Letters*, II, 501.

[48] Green and Hooper, 215.

[49] *Clive Staples Lewis*, 376.

[50] *A Love Observed: Joy Davidman's Life & Marriage to C. S. Lewis*, Hancock, MI: North Wind Books, 2000, 122. See also "Certified Copy of an Entry of Marriage, Pursuant to the Marriage Act 1949."

[51] James Dundas-Grant, "From an 'Outsider'," in *C. S. Lewis at the Breakfast Table*, 233.

[52] Ibid, *233*.

[53] Douglas Gresham, *Lenten Lands: My Childhood with Joy Davidman and C. S. Lewis*, San Francisco: HarperOne, 2013, 4.

by Father Ronald Head.[54] Havard also attended at least two of Walter Hooper's "Inklings Party," held in memory of Lewis, at Wadham College in 1966[55] and at University College in 1968.[56] R. E. Havard was the Lewis family physician, to be sure, but he was also much more than that—an Inkling, a companion, a writer, and, especially, a friend.

---

[54] Alistair McGrath, *C. S. Lewis: A Life: Eccentric Genius, Reluctant Prophet*, London: Hodder & Stoughton, 2013, 359. Carpenter, *The Letters of J. R. R. Tolkien*, 341. Brown, *A Life Observed*, 221. Jeffrey D. Schultz and John G. West, Jr., eds. *The C. S. Lewis Readers' Encyclopedia*, Grand Rapids: Zondervan, 1998, 64.

[55] On July 22, 1966, and July 17, 1968. Walter Hooper, " 'Warnie's Problem': An Introduction to a Letter from C. S. Lewis to Owen Barfield," *Journal of Inklings Studies,* Vol. 5, No. 1 (April 2015), 16.

[56] The unpublished diary of Warren Hamilton Lewis for July 17, 1968.

Twenty-One Friendships of C.S. Lewis

A.K. Hamilton Jenkin, photo by Clyde Kilby in June 1975
Used by permission of the Marion E. Wade Center,
Wheaton College, Wheaton, IL.

Chapter 9

A. K. HAMILTON JENKIN
The Cornwall Enthusiast

During his college years, C. S. Lewis met Owen Barfield and A. C. Harwood, two undergraduate friends who maintained and deepened their friendship with him over decades. Leo Baker was another fellow undergraduate and lifelong friend whose name is familiar to some. Very few know about some of the other friends during the same period, Rodney Pasley, H. D. Ziman, George Fasnacht, Edward Watling, W. D. Robson-Scott, and others, especially A. K. Hamilton Jenkin, one of the most delightful and eccentric of Lewis's friends. Jenkin was the Cornwall enthusiast who made a name for himself during a literary career that produced eleven books and many articles about the history and culture of his native Cornwall.

Jenkin matriculated to University College, Oxford, in 1919, the same year that Lewis returned from the war and resumed his studies, and he, like Lewis, read English. Lewis and Jenkin became fast friends, and their literary careers each produced a long list of publications.

ALFRED KENNETH HAMILTON JENKIN

Alfred Kenneth Hamilton Jenkin[1] was born to Alfred Hamilton Jenkin and Amy Louisa (Keep) Jenkin on October 29, 1900, in Redruth, Cornwall,[2] about midway between Penzance and Truro. Perhaps the length of time the family had lived in Cornwall (more than a century) explains his enthusiasm for that part of England, which became not only a subject of frequent conversations but also a topic for the books he would later write.

When Jenkin came to Oxford University, he was calling St. Ives his home. St. Ives is located on the northern coast of Cornwall, and he worked there as both a journalist and a broadcaster.[3] Like Lewis, Jenkin completed his education at University College in 1922, earning

---

[1] From this point on, the author will refer to A. K. Hamilton Jenkin as Jenkin.

[2] Walter Hooper, *C. S. Lewis: A Companion & Guide*, London: HarperCollins, 1996, 682.

[3] Hooper, *Companion & Guide*, 683.

the BA, and then he wrote a thesis on Richard Carew (1555-1620), who had written a history of Cornwall, for a Bachelor of Letters in 1924,[4] followed by the MA

In 1926, Jenkin married Luned Jacobs, the daughter of the novelist and short story writer W. W. Jacobs, and the couple had two daughters, Jennifer Hamilton and Honor Bronwen. Jenkin and his wife divorced in 1934. During World War II, Jenkin met Elizabeth Lenton (nee Le Sueur) at Mullion Cove Hotel, where she was Managing Director. They married in 1948, and together they managed the Poldu Hotel, Mullion, while Jenkin continued his research into his next book, News from Cornwall (1951). When Elizabeth fell ill in 1954, they returned to the family home in Redruth, Trewirgie House.

In 1954 Jenkin was elected a Fellow of the Society of Antiquaries, of London. He was elected President of the Royal Institution of Cornwall for 1958 and 1959, and he was its Vice-President in 1977. Jenkin helped to form Old Cornwall societies, and he was elected President of the Federation of Old Cornwall Societies for the 1959 to 1960 term. In 1962 he was made the first Life Vice-President of the Federation, an honor he kept for the remainder of his life. At the Gorsedd (a Welsh word that means "throne") of Cornwall in 1978 he received a medal, which commemorated the fact that he was one of only two living Bards (a professional poet) whom Henry Jenner initiated at the first Gorsedd in 1928. Jenkin was awarded the honorary Doctor of Letters by the University of Exeter, a Cornwall institution, in 1978.[5]

Jenkin's first major book was *The Cornish Miner* (1927), a book that became the standard work on Cornish mining and which established his reputation as a historian. The miners of Cornwall mined copper and tin especially, but also silver, zinc, and arsenic at various stages of their history. At one point in the nineteenth century, there were more than two thousand active mines. Jenkin also wrote *Cornish Seafarers* (1932), *Cornwall and the Cornish* (1933), *Cornish Homes and Customs* (1934), *The Story of Cornwall* (1934), and *Cornwall and Its People* (1945). In the 1960s he published a 16-part series on *Mines and Miners of Cornwall* (1961-78), the result of sixteen years of research and visits to many Cornish mines.

---

[4] Hooper, *Companion & Guide*, 683. See also the unpublished portion of All My Road Before Me for March 11, 1924.

[5] Hooper, *Companion & Guide*, 683.

Twenty-One Friendships of C.S. Lewis

Elizabeth died in 1977,[6] and Jenkin died on August 20, 1980, at Treliske Hospital, Truro, in his native Cornwall. Jenkin willed his books and pamphlets to the Redruth public library and many other documents, photos, maps and manuscripts to the County Record Office in Truro, which he had helped to set up. [7]

JENKIN AND LEWIS—FROM ACQUAINTANCES TO FRIENDS

The first mention of Jenkin's name at Oxford University appears in the minutes of the 195th meeting of the Martlets on June 14, 1919.[8] The Martlets are one of the longest-standing undergraduate societies of Oxford University, one in which Lewis was involved both as an undergraduate and as an Oxford don for more than two decades and one which served as a precursor to the give-and-take of the Inklings and the Socratic Club. The Martlets are the only undergraduate society whose minutes are preserved in the Bodleian Library,[9] and the society remains in existence today. [10]

Lewis and Jenkin had met at earlier Martlet meetings, but they knew little of each other. Lewis was the secretary for the Martlets when they met that Saturday evening (he was later elected President), and this duty undoubtedly helped preserve something of his writing for future generations. Although Jenkin's name was not listed in the minutes, his attendance can be assumed since the meeting took place in his rooms. Five months later, Jenkin himself was the speaker, presenting a paper on the Cornish poet Robert Hawker.[11] Both Lewis and Jenkin were beginning to stretch their wings as writers, while the society became for them and the rest of the members a source of mutual encouragement.

A few additional contacts between the two precede their first sustained time together, an event that started to build a lifelong friendship. A Martlets meeting with their Cambridge counterpart in March 1920, a Martlets meeting later that year when Jenkin read a

[6] Hooper, *Companion & Guide*, 684

[7] Hooper, *Companion & Guide*, 683.

[8] Minutes of the Martlets. Ref. MS. Top. Oxon. d. 95 (1919-1923).

[9] C. S. Lewis: *Collected Letters, I*, . Edited by Walter Hooper. London: HarperCollinsPublishers, 2000, 430.

[10] See the "Sport, music and college facilities" section of the University College website at http://www.ox.ac.uk/admissions/postgraduate_courses/college_guide/university.html.

[11] The Martlets [Notes] Ref. MS. Top. Oxon. d. 95 (1919-1923). The date was November 5, 1919.

paper on Charles Dickens, and a November meeting in which Lewis read his paper to the Martlets on Narrative Poetry are three of those more formal contacts which set the stage for their friendship.[12]

Lewis and Jenkin spent significant time together for the first time on March 1, 1921. Prior to this, of course, they had crossed paths at meetings of the Martlets, but they had not gotten acquainted until this moment. Lewis had met Barfield and Harwood by this time, but they had not yet become fast friends, nor were they studying English literature, as Jenkin was and Lewis was a couple of years later. Lewis ran into Jenkin while going into College and they went to Jenkin's rooms on Merton Street. He describes Jenkin as "a little, pale person with a smooth green face, not unlike a lizard's,"[13] but Lewis later describes Jenkin as his "first lifelong friend" in Oxford.[14] They talked about Jenkin's passion, the county of Cornwall located in the far southwest corner of England. While some became bored with Jenkin's constant talk about Cornwall—its scenery, customs, history, language, and business—Lewis liked it.[15] Cornwall boasts a rugged coastland with spectacular cliffs, hundreds of sandy beaches, and the cities of Penzance (of Gilbert and Sullivan fame) and Land's End, the most southwestern point. Two Cornwallian books that influenced Jenkin were *The Survey of Cornwall* by Richard Carew[16] (1603) and *The Autobiography of a Cornish Smuggler* by John Cornish (1749-1809). Jenkin's zest for Cornwall taught Lewis to be enthusiastic about something.

Jenkin was not just passionate about Cornwall; he was passionate about everything. He taught Lewis to enjoy even the ugly things,[17] to surrender completely to whatever appeared before him, to "rub one's nose in the very quiddity of each thing, to rejoice in its being (so magnificently) what it was."[18] Arthur had taught Lewis something similar, but Arthur especially enjoyed the homely while Jenkin enjoyed everything he saw. This openness to what was in front of him helped

---

[12] See "Chronologically Lewis" for more detail about the meetings of March 9, 1920, October 20, 1920, and November 29, 1921.

[13] *C. S. Lewis: Collected Letters, I. 1905-1930.* Edited by Walter Hooper. London: HarperCollinsPublishers, 2000, 526.

[14] *Surprised by Joy: The Shape of My Early Life.* San Diego: Harcourt Brace Jovanovich, 1955, 199.

[15] *Collected Letters, I,* 527.

[16] Remember that Jenkin wrote a B.Litt. thesis on Carew.

[17] *Collected Letters, I,* 527.

[18] *Collected Letters, I,* 527.

Lewis to approach the Scriptures and all other types of literature with the same willingness to learn, to lay aside preconceptions, to see what was actually there rather than what one wanted to see.

ALL ROADS LEAD TO CORNWALL

Jenkin clearly loved Cornwall, so he talked about Cornwall on almost every occasion. On one occasion, for example, Jenkin arrived at The Kilns and stayed into the early evening. He engaged in conversation with Mrs. Moore and Lewis on a wide variety of topics, most of which Jenkin steered toward his native Cornwall. Lewis wrote that he and Mrs. Moore "were amused to notice again how in his conversation all roads lead to Cornwall."[19]

The next month, [20] Jenkin arrived at The Kilns as everyone was sitting down to supper. Jenkin was to have his *viva*, that is, his live examination for his degree before Oxford dons, three days later. Besides talk about Henry James' 1898 ghost story *The Turn of the Screw* and Jane Austen's *Emma*, conversation included mining in Cornwall fifty years ago, a subject on which Jenkin was becoming an expert. He said that some of the ladders that miners had to climb were four times the height of St. Paul's Cathedral.[21]

That fall, Lewis walked into town after tea with Jenkin and went to Jenkin's rooms. Jenkin read aloud an imaginative essay he had written about Cornish mining about which Lewis wrote, "It was all right, real plain and good and hard, but cunning prose too. He has undoubtedly found his feet at last: I think this is the real stuff. I was delighted at this." [22] That essay was probably Jenkin's "Spirit of the Mine," which benefited from having an audience and receiving feedback. He brought the essay back the next month, and Lewis read it to Mrs. Moore in its improved version and she liked it. [23] Lewis was already helping others to become better writers.

---

[19] *All My Road Before Me: The Diary of C. S. Lewis, 1922-1927*. Edited by Walter Hooper. New York: Harcourt Brace, 1991, 56. The date is June 25, 1922. Jenkin was what Walter Hooper once referred to himself as, i.e., "a single subject lunatic." For Hooper it was C. S. Lewis, and for Jenkin it was Cornwall.

[20] The exact date of Jenkin's arrival is July 9, 1922, which makes his viva on July 12.

[21] *All My Road Before Me*, 66.

[22] The unpublished portion of Lewis's diary for this date, Oct. 28, 1922

[23] The date is November 15, 1922. This comes from the unpublished portion of *All My Road Before Me* for this date.

The next month,[24] Lewis went to the College library to return two books. He met Jenkin, who led Lewis to King's rooms where the Martlets met that evening. The Rev. Dr. A. J. Carlyle spoke very entertainingly on the relation of history to literature. On the very next day, Jenkin entertained Lewis with conversation about Cornish legends, [25] an aspect of Cornwall apparently inspired by Carlyle's talk on the previous night.

A few days later, [26] Jenkin read to Lewis a new version of his article for *The Contemporary Review*, probably that same "Spirit of the Mine," now a nearly finished product. The article was finally published in early 1923. In the Spring of 1923, [27] Lewis and Jenkin talked most of the afternoon about all kinds of topics, chief among them Jenkin's article, "Spirit of the Mine," which The Contemporary Review had recently published. Jenkin's developing skill as a writer was evident from a press cutting about "Spirit of the Mine," since the writer mentioned "Mr Jenkin's valuable article." [28] During this month, Jenkin was Lewis's almost daily companion with nine recorded meetings between them, and writing was one of their major topics. Lewis and Jenkin had developed a friendship with their common bond of literature and their interest in writing. For Jenkin, the writing was only about Cornwall.

Later that Spring, Jenkin came in at supper time, and after supper Jenkin and Lewis sat in the drawing room. Jenkin showed Lewis an article of his which had been rejected by the *Daily Mail*, a description of a night in a mine. Jenkin had already moved on to his next article about Cornwall.[29]

Several years later, Lewis came to the library and was pleasantly surprised to meet Jenkin, who had come up to take his MA Lewis and Jenkin met that evening in Jenkin's former flat. They then had supper together at the George and caught up on one another's life. Lewis learned that Jenkin had written a book on mining in Cornwall, no doubt *The Cornish Miner* which by this time had been accepted for

---

[24] The precise date is December 6, 1922.

[25] The unpublished portion of *All My Road Before Me* for December 7, 1922.

[26] On December 10, 1922. This incident is recorded in the unpublished portion of *All My Road Before Me*.

[27] March 6, 1923, to be precise. *All My Road Before Me*, 214.

[28] An unpublished portion of Lewis's diary for this date in *All My Road Before Me*, 214.

[29] The date is May 29, 1923. *All My Road Before Me*, 238.

publication. It was published the next year, and Jenkin went on to write many more books about Cornwall.[30]

Enjoying Everything

Jenkin's most endearing quality was his appreciation of nearly everything he encountered. As noted earlier, Jenkin taught Lewis to enjoy everything, even the ugly things, to surrender completely to whatever appeared before him, and "to rejoice in its being (so magnificently) what it was."[31] One day Jenkin came to The Kilns after lunch, and he and Lewis cycled up Shotover to the bridle path to Horspath, where they sat and talked about the man on the street and many other subjects. Lewis was pleased with Jenkin's positive view of the man on the street, [32] something that Lewis himself championed, especially when he later wrote that there were "no ordinary people."[33]

After the start of term in 1922, Lewis bicycled to Merton Street and called for Jenkin, who had just come up from St. Ives for the Michaelmas Term. They biked along Parks Road and through Wolvercote and Port Meadow. At Wytham, they entered the village and found the place "so lonely, so wild, so luxurious, that we both thought of Acrasia's bower of bliss." Jenkin commented that natural beauty affected him as the suggested background of a happiness that was not there.[34]

A month later, Lewis bicycled to Jenkin's rooms one afternoon, and the two rode to the Botley Road and through Ferry Hinksey. They talked about the tenth century Old English poems "The Wanderer" and "The Seafarer," and many other subjects. When they got to Thessaly, they laid their bikes down and walked into the wood. They enjoyed the beauty, and Lewis appreciated Jenkin's delight in elementary pleasures, writing, "Jenkin's undisguised delight in the more elementary pleasures of a ramble always bucks me: one really would not be surprised if he suddenly said, 'Let's pretend to be Red Indians.' I got the real joy in this wood."[35]

---

[30] The date is June 24, 1926. *All My Road Before Me*, 417.

[31] *Collected Letters, I*, 527.

[32] The exact date is July 9, 1922. *All My Road Before Me*, 67.

[33] *The Weight of Glory and Other Addresses*. New York: Simon & Schuster, 1980, 39.

[34] The exact date is October 14. *All My Road Before Me*, 119.

[35] The date is November 7, 1922. *All My Road Before Me*, 134.

The next year, Lewis and Jenkin took another bike trip to Shotover and past Horspath Lane. At a gate on the Horspath Lane looking east, Jenkin said he always perceived rather than felt this kind of scenery to be beautiful.[36]

Two years later, Lewis wrote to Jenkin about the delight at the thought of seeing Jenkin. If he were to see Jenkin while Lewis was in a tutorial, he would "fling a book in my pupil's face and outstrip the winds in getting downstairs." [37] He told Jenkin that he especially appreciated him for "some smaller and yet more intimate connection with the feel of things, for a certain gusto and complete rightness of palate." [38] He also commented on the beauty of his surroundings, which he knew Jenkin would appreciate.

About a year later, Lewis wrote to Jenkin, his first letter in months: "I grow daily more and more doubtful in all subjects." Lewis was drawing closer to belief in God and wondering about the validity of some values he held. Lewis also stated, "You have as much of the gift of happiness as any man I know," [39] something Lewis did not yet have, but wished he did. Lewis expressed appreciation for Jenkin's writing ability, i.e., his "fine palate" for the topics he writes about.

COOL WATER AND A WELL-WORN SHOE

Perhaps the major reason for this friendship was as an antidote to the loneliness he felt in a household with no mother, a distant father, an alienated brother, and a life largely devoid of friends until his university years. He once wrote that at Cherbourg House, when he was twelve years of age, he made his first real friends. [40] Although he had made a friend in Arthur Greeves when he was fifteen, he still had few friends before attending the university. The university provided the opportunity for Lewis to make friends his own age, with similar interests in literature, and distant from a father who seemed too often to interfere rather than to understand. When Lewis returned to Oxford University after the war, he became friends with Jenkin. Amazingly, Lewis mentions Jenkin 198 times in his diary, *All My*

---

[36] The date is May 24, 1923. *All My Road Before Me*, 236.

[37] The date is November 4, 1925. *Collected Letters, I*, 652.

[38] *Collected Letters, I*, 653.

[39] The date is September 8, 1926. *C. S. Lewis: Collected Letters, II, Books, Broadcasts and War 1931-1949*. Edited by Walter Hooper. London: HarperCollinsPublishers, 2004, 669.

[40] C. S. Lewis, *Surprised by Joy*, 58.

Road Before Me, which encompasses about three years between 1922 and 1927 (he wrote off and on during those six years).

In Spring 1922, with their friendship about a year old, Lewis and Jenkin met in the High.[41] This was the first of eight meetings in this month alone, indicating that Lewis enjoyed Jenkin's company and literary interests.[42] There could have been more meetings, since we cannot assume that Lewis recorded every event of every day. After breakfast Lewis rode his bicycle to Merton Street to find Jenkin. Together they cycled through Marston to Elsfield and Beckley, where they called at Bee Cottage to see Harwood. They continued their ride until lunchtime. Other minor meetings between Lewis and Jenkin also took place in May and June, but the large number of contacts indicates that the friendship was deepening.

On the day of his *viva*,[43] Jenkin came to supper, apparently after the *viva* was completed, and afterwards Lewis finished Miss Wiblin's Latin lesson while Arthur talked to Jenkin.[44] They all had tea and cakes in the dining room. These were the people in Oxford with whom Jenkin felt most at home. He left afterwards for St. Ives, the coastal town in Cornwall where he was living.

Near the end of Michaelmas term in 1922, Jenkin came to tea. They talked about college food and Jenkin's upcoming vacation trip to Italy.[45] Jenkin seems to be more a man of means than Lewis, but at this stage in Lewis's life almost everyone had more resources than he did. The next day, Lewis and Jenkin went for a ride along the road beyond Cowley to Marsh Baldon. George Fasnacht came to tea, and Jenkin and Lewis conversed about poets Thomas Wade Earp and Wilfred Rowland Childe, the extinction of the planet, eugenics, Idealistic Nihilism (the theory that nothing exists), and Pasley's principle (i.e., "the same disgrace which now attaches to an illegitimate child shd. attach to a child too many"). They talked about almost everything.

Lewis and Jenkin even attended the Martlets when one of them was presenting a paper. This was after Jenkin's graduation from Univ., but apparently while staying on for the B.Litt. Therefore, on February 14, 1923, Jenkin attended the Martlets to hear Lewis's paper on

---

[41] "The High" is High Street in Oxford, a major street that runs between Carfax on the west at the center of the city and Magdalen Bridge on the east.

[42] The precise date is May 3, 1922. *All My Road Before Me*, 28f.

[43] That is, Wednesday, July 12, 1922.

[44] Arthur Greeves Diaries, 1-7. Held at The Marion E. Wade Center.

[45] *All My Road Before Me*, 149. The date is December 4, 1922.

Edmund Spenser.

Two days later, after his discussion class, Lewis walked to Merton Street and found Jenkin at home. He enjoyed Jenkin, stating, "It was delightful to see him again. We talked mainly about his Italian adventures."[46] The very next month, Lewis expressed a similar thought when Jenkin turned up. They went out together, riding to Garsington and back. He states, "Jenkin and I seldom say anything of importance on our jaunts these days, but it is like cool water to be out with him."[47] A year later, he expresses the same delight when Jenkin arrived unexpectedly. Lewis writes in his diary, "I was delighted to see him again."[48] That same year, Lewis wrote that "to talk with him was like slipping into a well worn shoe."[49]

Between February 21 and March 12, 1923, Lewis dealt with Doc Askins (John Askins), the brother of Mrs. Moore, because the Doc thought he was going mad or was about to have a nervous breakdown. Those problems delayed the next letter until April 21, 1923, when Lewis wrote to Jenkin, Lewis's first letter to Jenkin in six months. This was in part due to the problems with Doc Askins. He apologized for his failure to write, and for his inability to visit Jenkin, explaining the reasons as the Doc's funeral, his limited finances, and the many letters he had yet to write. A few days later, he received a card from Jenkin, very kindly acknowledging Lewis's apologies.[50]

JENKIN'S FAITH

During several of their visits together, Jenkin talked about his Christian faith and seemed interested in helping Lewis understand the faith better. About a year after the beginning of their friendship,[51] Lewis and Jenkin met in the High again. They walked down St. Aldate's and over the waterworks to Hinksey, immediately west of Oxford. They talked about the difficulty in finding people genuinely interested in literature, people who were not also amateurish about it. Later, at Jenkin's rooms, they had tea together and Lewis spoke to Jenkin about staying up for another year. He also talked about religion,

---

[46] The date is February 16, 1923. *All My Road Before Me*, 201.

[47] The date is March 4, 1923. *All My Road Before Me*, 212.

[48] The unpublished portion of *All My Road Before Me* for March 10, 1924.

[49] The date is June 14, 1924. *All My Road Before Me*, 333.

[50] *All My Road Before Me*, 232.

[51] *All My Road Before Me*, 28f. The date is May 3, 1922.

discovering that Jenkin's views were "traditional and rather different to mine." [52] Lewis had just completed his BA and was contemplating another year of studies to earn credentials in English literature. He was about to take exams in Greats in the following month. On this occasion, while Lewis was deep into atheism, Jenkin was apparently a witness to the message of the gospel. Less than a year earlier, Lewis had written to his brother Warren, "The trouble about God is that he is like a person who never acknowledges your letters and so in time you come to the conclusion either that he does not exist or that you have got his address wrong." [53]

A few days later, Lewis went into town to Jenkin's rooms. Jenkin claimed to have been surprised to hear of Lewis's removal from the Martlets (probably for failing to pay his dues—this was a time of poverty in Lewis's life). He took Lewis in his canoe for a short time, tied up the canoe in the shade, and read to Lewis about baptism from an eighteenth-century book that opposed baptism by immersion.[54] Jenkin seemed anxious to influence Lewis toward the Christian faith, even though a controversial matter like baptism by immersion is an odd topic to use for this purpose.

One afternoon that fall,[55] Lewis was starting back to work when Jenkin arrived. Lewis talked of Troilus and chivalry, and Jenkin attributed the knightly standard, including chivalry, to Christianity. For him, the typical example of the Christian ideal at work was the Apostle Paul. This led a discussion of Christianity, and Lewis, dismissively, stated that a person gets little definite teaching in the Gospels.[56] Jenkin was clearly attempting to influence Lewis toward Christianity. The very next day, Jenkin arrived at teatime and persuaded Lewis to come to his rooms. He showed Lewis one or two poems of John Donne, which Lewis liked, and he also read Lewis some ballads. The profound Christian content of Donne's poems further suggests that Jenkin was attempting to have a Christian influence on Lewis.

Several years later in 1926, Lewis left College to hurry to the Good Luck to have lunch with Jenkin. After lunch they sat in the garden of the Union and had a rambling conversation that Lewis considered to be of much profit.[57] Was it about spiritual matters? This

---

[52] *All My Road Before Me*, 28f.

[53] C. S. Lewis, *Collected Letters, I*, 555. The date is July 1, 1921.

[54] *All My Road Before Me*, 31f. The date is May 8, 1922.

[55] The date is October 18, 1922.

[56] *All My Road Before Me*, 121f.

[57] The date is June 25, 1926. *All My Road Before Me*, 417.

was the same period during which Lewis was growing "more doubtful in all subjects."[58]

A few years later, Lewis wrote to Jenkin, very disappointed about being unable to meet in London, but wanting Jenkin to come and stay with him. He says of Jenkin,

> You have a place in my mental world—you are a gap in my inner bookshelf—a drawn tooth in my psychic jaw—a *hiatus valde deflendusi*[59] in the manuscript of my mind—a broken lace in my spiritual boots—which no one else supplies. It seems hard that we should never meet.[60]

Lewis also writes about his definite religious outlook, though he explicitly states that it is not Christianity. With his adoption of theism less than four months away, Lewis is now aware that "there is another Party in the affair."[61] Lewis most likely told him this because he knew Jenkin's interest in Lewis's religious outlook, but also because his friendship with Jenkin was on the same level as that of Arthur Greeves or Owen Barfield.

In 1939,[62] Lewis wrote a lengthy letter to Jenkin on various topics, one of the last letters he ever wrote to Jenkin. Lewis had hoped to share a meal with Jenkin, Barfield, and Harwood this evening, but Jenkin's illness and problems on the Barfield-Harwood side had sabotaged this opportunity. It seems that at this time, nearly a decade later, Jenkin considered himself an atheist.[63] Lewis offered the just published *Out of the Silent Planet* to Jenkin, although he doubted if Jenkin would like a fantasy tale.

LITERATURE

This last category of common interests is brief, largely because Lewis and Jenkin shared so much of their literary passion in conversation, as a part of the Martlets, and during their undergraduate

---

[58] The date is September 8, 1926, little more than two months later. *Collected Letters, II*, 669.

[59] "A gap much to be deplored." This is a quotation from Lord Chesterfield in his *Letters, Vol. II*, No. 101 (1774).

[60] The date of this letter is March 21, 1930. *Collected Letters, I*, 887.

[61] Ibid.

[62] The date is January 11, 1939.

[63] Lewis writes to Jenkin, "You'll probably be the only atheist present, by the way, but we will respect your susceptibilities." *Collected Letters, II*, 241.

studies. Lewis's diary and letters to Jenkin did not discuss literature very much because they had other venues in which to talk about literature. Many other occasions could be added to the few that appear here, such as the times that Lewis showed *Dymer* to Jenkin, [64] but they overlap with meetings that have been described above.

In the spring of 1921, Lewis spent part of the morning in the Union, where "little Jenkin," as Lewis calls him (in a letter to Warren, since Jenkin was apparently short) appeared after lunch and invited Lewis on a bike ride. Needing a break from his work, Lewis accepted, and they stopped at Garsington for a drink. They saw Sidney Groves of Univ., investigated an old windmill near Wheatley, and rode over Shotover Hill past English barns and haystacks. They also came near the house where the first Mrs. John Milton once lived, and Lewis wrote that Milton courted her when she lived there, adding sarcastically (because this bike ride took place during Lewis's atheistic years), "God help her!" [65]

A year later, after taking the train to Reading to interview for a faculty position, Lewis left University College at two o'clock and cycled to Bradfield College to see Sophocles' *Antigone* performed in Greek. Lewis met Edward Watling and Jenkin outside the theater. The *Antigone* was performed with largely inaudible voices and in the rain, so after the play Lewis, Watling, and Jenkin left early to find a marquee to have tea together. As they left, Jenkin kept shaking the water off his hat and stating again and again, "Oh, it was a tragedy!"[66]

CORNWALL, OXFORD, AND IRELAND

As far as we know, the last letter Lewis ever wrote to Jenkin was sent on May 31, 1947, eight years after the most recent letter. [67] Lewis wrote to Jenkin about Ulster as his "ain countrie," [68] clearly as proud of his Irish heritage as Jenkin was of Cornwall. Perhaps it is most appropriate that appreciation for one's home formed a major theme of this last letter.

---

[64] For example, on June 6, 1922, and November 30, 1922. See *All My Road Before Me*, 45, 146.

[65] The date is May 11, 1921. *Collected Letters, I*, 545f.

[66] The date is June 24, 1922. *All My Road Before Me*, 55f.

[67] We do not know if Jenkin kept all his letters from C. S. Lewis, so there could have been other letters.

[68] His "own country." Colin Duriez, *Tolkien and C. S. Lewis: The Gift of Friendship*, Mahwah, NJ: HiddenSpring (Paulist), 2003, 136.

No Ordinary People

Lewis and Jenkin met during their undergraduate years in Oxford, the friendship began with the Martlets and literature, continued with a love of being in the moment, but cooled after Jenkin returned to Cornwall to establish his reputation. Marriage, divorce, and World War II probably added to the distance between them, possibly even leading to Jenkin's atheism. Jenkin was "all things Cornwall," but Lewis had a wider perspective on literature, life, and writing. Lewis, on the other hand, was "all things Christ," as he once wrote, "I believe in Christianity as I believe that the Sun has risen, not only because I see it, but because by it I see everything else." [69]

---

[69] C. S. Lewis, "Is Theology Poetry?" *The Weight of Glory and Other Addresses*, 106.

Twenty-One Friendships of C.S. Lewis

SECTION II

OPPONENTS, BUT FRIENDS

Arthur C Clarke in his home office in Sri Lanka
Photo courtesy of Amy Marash, 2008
All rights and permissions are granted, with attribution

Chapter 10
ARTHUR C. CLARKE
Clark, Lewis, and Science Fiction

C. S. Lewis, the sub-creator[1] of sorns and pfifltriggi, Tor and Tinidril, Elwin Ransom and the revived Merlin, both read and wrote science fiction. One of the science fiction writers with whom Lewis corresponded was Arthur C. Clarke. Clarke, one of the three most well-known science fiction writers[2] of the twentieth century, was known both for his science fiction writing and his popularization of science and space travel, all of which earned him the title "Prophet of the Space Age."[3] Lewis wrote eight letters to Clarke over a twelve-year period, at Clarke's initiative, mostly about science fiction writing.[4] As a result, Clarke became a better writer.

---

[1] The word "sub-creation" comes from J. R. R. Tolkien, who described human creativity, even in writing, as derived from the original creative actions of God. See "On Fairy Stories," *Essays Presented to Charles Williams*. Grand Rapids: Eerdmans, 1966, 51. This idea can be traced back further to S. T. Coleridge who wrote "The imagination I consider either as primary, or secondary. The primary imagination I hold to be the living Power and prime Agent of all human Perception, and as a repetition in the finite mind of the eternal act of creation in the infinite I AM. The secondary I consider as an echo of the former" (*The Biographia Literaria*, 1817). Later, George Macdonald explained the same thing this way: "... man may, if he pleases, invent a little world of his own, with its own laws; for there is that in him which delights in calling up new forms--which is the nearest, perhaps, he can come to creation. When such forms are new embodiments of old truths, we call them products of the Imagination." ("The Fantastic Imagination" (1893)

[2] At least according to some, along with Robert Heinlein and Ray Bradbury.

[3] See, for example, an article in *The Sydney Morning Herald*, dated March 20, 2008. http://www.smh.com.au/articles/2008/03/19/1205602429117.html

[4] The dates of the eight letters are Dec. 7, 1943, Sept. 24, 1946, Oct. 2, 1946, Jan. 2, 1947, Feb. 14, 1953, Jan. 20, 1954 (twice on the same day), and Jan. 26, 1954. That correspondence between Clarke and Lewis was the subject of a book published in 2003. See *From Narnia to A Space Odyssey: The War of Ideas Between Arthur C. Clarke and C. S. Lewis*, edited and with an Introduction by Ryder W. Miller. New York: ibooks, distributed by Simon & Schuster, 2003. The book includes three essays written by Lewis and seven by Clarke.

No Ordinary People

Arthur C. Clarke

Arthur Charles Clarke was born to Charles and Nora Clarke on December 16, 1917, in Minehead, Somerset, England, a half-mile from the sea.[5] He was educated at Huish Grammar school, an all-boys' school in Taunton. When Arthur was thirteen years old, his father died of complications from the inhalation of poison gas and the harsh conditions of trench warfare during World War I.[6]

In his early years, Arthur was interested in space travel and built his own telescopes to scan the night sky and think about what might be out there. He also made his own fireworks and small rockets.[7] In 1928, he became enthralled with the stories in the science fiction magazine *Amazing Stories* and, later, in *Astounding Stories of Super-Science*, reading the latter magazine from cover to cover.[8] At age sixteen, Clarke joined the Junior Astronomical Association and the British Interplanetary Society (BIS). Clarke eventually served two terms as chairman of the BIS.[9] One of the science fiction books that Clarke read in the 1930s was Olaf Stapledon's *Last and First Men*.[10] Clarke states that "no book before or since ever had such an impact on my imagination."[11] He eventually began collecting science fiction magazines and writing science fiction stories himself. His collection continued to grow until he entered the Royal Air Force during the early years of World War II.[12]

In 1936 Clarke moved to London to take a civil service job with the Exchequer and Audit Department where, in his off hours, he pursued his interest in space travel, science fiction, and writing.[13] Two

---

[5] Andy Sawyer, "Clarke, Sir Arthur Charles (1917-2008)," *Oxford Dictionary of National Biography*, Oxford University Press, January 2012, online edition May 2012.

[6] Neil McAleer, *Visionary: The Odyssey of Sir Arthur C. Clarke*. Baltimore, MD: The Clarke Project, 2010, 6.

[7] Neil McAleer, *Visionary*, 9f.

[8] Neil McAleer, *Visionary*, 12f. That issue was published in March 1930.

[9] He was Chairman in 1946-47 and again in 1951-53.

[10] Clarke read this book in 1930. C. S. Lewis also read this book. See Lewis's letter to Roger Lancelyn Green on Dec. 28, 1938. *C. S. Lewis: Collected Letters, II. Books, Broadcasts and War 1931-1949*. Edited by Walter Hooper. London: HarperCollinsPublishers, 2004, 236.

[11] Neil McAleer, *Visionary*, 15.

[12] Neil McAleer, *Visionary*, 14.

[13] Neil McAleer, *Visionary*, 17, 19, 22. See also "Arthur C. Clarke," *Wikipedia*.

years into World War II, Clarke joined the Royal Air Force as a radio wireless aircraftsman, working in radar[14] and assisting in Britain's early-warning radar defense system.[15] During the war, Clarke thought about what it would take to send a crew to the moon and back. After World War II and his demobilization, Clarke attended King's College, London, where he earned a first-class degree in mathematics and physics.[16] Probably at some point in these early years, Clarke adopted atheism, although the precise date remains uncertain.[17]

In 1945, the young writer Clarke sold his first science fiction piece, a short story called "Rescue Party."[18] That same year, in an article entitled "Extra-Terrestrial Relays," Clarke laid out the principles for satellites to become telecommunications relays, thirteen years before the US launched its first satellite. This article became his most famous non-fiction article and earned him recognition as the father of communication satellites.[19] In Clarke's honor, the International Astronomical Union calls the geostationary orbit 22,000 miles above the equator The Clarke Orbit.[20]

In 1953, Clarke married Marilyn Torgenson, an American divorcee, but the couple separated after a few months.[21] The marriage had been hastily entered into and was also exited hastily. He never married again.

During the 1940s and 1950s, Clarke became a space travel and science fiction sensation, including in his credits *Prelude to Space*

---

[14] Neil McAleer, *Visionary*, 33. McAleer describes his position as "an aircraft hand radio wireless mechanic/aircraftsman class II." The *Wikipedia* article calls him a "radar specialist."

[15] On March 18, 1941.

[16] In 1948.

[17] Andy Sawyer, "Clarke, Sir Arthur Charles (1917-2008)," *Oxford Dictionary of National Biography*, Oxford University Press, January 2012, online edition May 2012.

[18] Neil McAleer, *Visionary*, 40. He sold it to the periodical *Astounding Science Fiction*.

[19] Neil McAleer, *Visionary*, 41. The article was written for the British periodical *Wireless World*. It is reprinted in Clarke's book, *Voices from the Sky: Previews of the Coming Space Age*, New York: Harper & Row, 1965, pages 233-241.

[20] https://web.archive.org/web/20110725175711/http://www.clarkefoundation.org/acc/biography.php

[21] Andy Sawyer, "Clarke, Sir Arthur Charles (1917-2008)," *Oxford Dictionary of National Biography*, Oxford University Press, January 2012, online edition May 2012. They married on June 15. The divorce was not formalized until 1964.

(1947), *Interplanetary Flight* (1950), *The Exploration of Space* (1951), and *Childhood's End* (1953).[22] As a result, Clarke was invited to be the guest of honor at the annual World Science Fiction Convention, held in New York City in 1956. He was the first non-American guest of honor, and he gave one of the keynote addresses, as did Isaac Asimov,[23] Robert Bloch,[24] and others. This convention provided one of the hundreds of podiums from which Clarke lectured over the next decades. He became widely known and respected as "the philosopher of spaceflight,"[25] lecturing on science fiction, science, space flight, satellites, satellite communication, and even UFOs. He was both astonished and disturbed by the level of interest in that last topic, and he soon formulated his rule for UFO observers: "It's not a spaceship unless you can read the Mars registration plate."[26]

Clarke teamed up with director Stanley Kubrick to produce the screenplay for the film *2001: A Space Odyssey*, coordinating the production of the film with writing a novel of the same name. Clarke was the almost exclusive writer of the novel, while Kubrick was the almost exclusive writer of the screenplay.[27] After hundreds of hours of discussion, Kubrick and Clarke decided to base the novel on seven of Arthur's short stories, laying out the entire plot before taking their movie proposal to Metro-Goldwyn-Mayer. With more than fifty printings, the book has sold more than three million copies since its original publication.[28] Later George Lucas would draw inspiration

---

[22] Considered by some to be one of his most important books. McAleer, *Visionary*, 65. See reviews in *The New York Times*, the *LA Times* (by Don Guzman), and by William DuBois references in the article on Wikipedia, "Childhood's End." The book was nominated for a retroactive Hugo Award for Best Novel for 1954.

[23] Isaac Asimov (1920-1992) was a Russian-born writer of science fiction and popular science who taught biochemistry at Boston University and who was considered, along with writers Arthur C. Clarke and Robert Heinlein, one of the "Big Three" science fiction writers.

[24] Robert Bloch (1917-1994) was an American writer of crime, horror, fantasy, and science fiction who came from Milwaukee, Wisconsin. He wrote the script for the Alfred Hitchcock film, *Psycho*.

[25] Neil McAleer, *Visionary*, 105. This comes from a letter by Clarke to Val Cleaver written on Feb. 23, 1959.

[26] Neil McAleer, *Visionary*, 106f.

[27] The film was released in 1968. Clarke also wrote three Odyssey sequels: *2010: Odyssey Two*, McAleer, *Visionary*, 236; *2061: Odyssey Three*, McAleer, 261; and *3001: The Final Odyssey*, McAleer, 298.

[28] Neil McAleer, *Visionary*, 140.

from *2001* for the *Star Wars* movies,[29] while Carl Sagan and Gene Roddenberry acknowledged Clarke's important influence on the public toward space exploration.[30] Clarke wrote more than a hundred books and many essays about science, science fiction, and space travel.

On July 20, 1969, Clarke appeared on CBS with Walter Cronkite, Eric Severeid, and former astronaut Wally Schirra as a commentator for the Apollo 11 moon landing.[31] Eight years after President John F. Kennedy set the vision for a moon-landing, they watched the *Saturn V* rocket launch from Cape Canaveral, the touchdown on the surface of the moon nearly 103 hours later, and the walk on the lunar surface. Clarke stated that it was "one of the most thrilling things I've ever seen."[32] When Neil Armstrong and Buzz Aldrin stepped onto the surface of the moon, Clarke was in the CBS studio. When Neil Armstrong stated, "The *Eagle* has landed," and uttered his immortal words, "That's one small step for man; one giant leap for mankind," Clarke said he felt as though time had stopped.[33]

Clarke anticipated the Space Shuttle program when he stated, "We've got to have spaceships that we can use over and over again as often as we use a conventional airliner. The reusable space transporter is the next thing which we have got to get."[34] Years later, Clarke, a strong advocate for joint space exploration, joined Cronkite and Neil Armstrong for the launch and rendezvous of Russia's *Soyuz 19* and the US's *Apollo 18*.[35]

---

[29] Neil McAleer, *Visionary*, 166.

[30] Gerald Jonas, "Arthur C. Clarke, Author Who Saw Science Fiction Become Real, Dies at 90," New York Times Obituaries, March 19, 2008, http://www.nytimes.com/2008/03/19/books/19clarke.html. Roddenberry wrote, "Arthur literally made my Star Trek idea possible, including the television series, the films, and the association and learning it has made possible for me." Back cover of Neil McAleer, Visionary. Sagan wrote about Clarke's first non-fiction book, Interplanetary Flight, that the book was "a modest-looking book, beautifully written, its stirring last two paragraphs still of great relevance today." McAleer, *Visionary*, 51. During the 1980s, Clarke hosted the television programs *Arthur C. Clarke's Mysterious World*, *Arthur C. Clarke's World of Strange Powers*, and *Arthur C. Clarke's Mysterious Universe*.

[31] Walter Cronkite wrote a Foreword for *Visionary: The Odyssey of Arthur C. Clarke*.

[32] Neil McAleer, *Visionary*, 174.

[33] Neil McAleer, *Visionary*, 177.

[34] Neil McAleer, *Visionary*, 175.

[35] Neil McAleer, *Visionary*, 208. Clarke witnessed the launch of the *Apollo 18*, but not the launch of the *Soyuz 19*. He was in the CBS studio

No Ordinary People

Clarke emigrated to Sri Lanka in 1956, where he continued to write, but he also enjoyed table tennis, skin-diving, scuba diving, and underwater photography. These last three activities made their way into additional writing projects, which once included a collaboration with Jacques Cousteau.[36] Apart from trips to the United States and other countries for lecture tours and meetings with publishers, he lived in Sri Lanka for the rest of his life. In 1962, Clarke contracted polio, which affected him in later years. Post-polio syndrome normally affects polio survivors years after the initial case of polio.[37] As a result, he spent the last years of his life in a wheelchair.[38]

Additional honors were awarded him. He was designated Commander of the British Empire (CBE) by Queen Elizabeth II in 1989[39] and was knighted by Linda Duffield, England's High Commissioner to Sri Lanka, in 2000. He received many other honors,[40] including a nomination for a Nobel Peace Prize,[41] the designation of Grand Master from the Science Fiction Writers of America, the NASA Distinguished Public Service Medal,[42] the Charles A. Lindbergh Award,[43] and the Kalinga Prize for science

---

with Walter Cronkite when the linkup took place in orbit on July 17. This took place in July 1975.

[36] Neil McAleer, *Visionary*, 119. This took place in 1962.

[37] In 1988, he was diagnosed with post-polio syndrome. Post-polio syndrome results in the weakening of the muscles that were originally affected by the disease, fatigue, and decrease in the size of muscles. See https://www.ninds.nih.gov/Disorders/Patient-Caregiver-Education/Fact-Sheets/Post-Polio-Syndrome-Fact-Sheet

38 Andy Sawyer, "Clarke, Sir Arthur Charles (1917-2008)," *Oxford Dictionary of National Biography*, Oxford University Press, January 2012, online edition May 2012.

[39] Neil McAleer, *Visionary*, 283.

[40] Including the Nebula, Hugo, Campbell and *Locus* magazine awards. The honorary degrees included the D.Litt. from Bath, Liverpool, and Baptist University, Hong Kong. Andy Sawyer, "Clarke, Sir Arthur Charles (1917-2008)," *Oxford Dictionary of National Biography*, Oxford University Press, January 2012, online edition May 2012.

[41] In 1994. See Miller, *From Narnia to A Space Odyssey*, 31.

[42] This happened in 1995. See Miller, *From Narnia to A Space Odyssey*, 31.

[43] Neil McAleer, *Visionary*, 275. In 1987, he was the tenth recipient of this award, given for contributions toward Lindbergh's concept of balancing technology and nature. See http://lindberghfoundation.org/lindbergh-award.

writing.⁴⁴ He was also awarded three honorary degrees. Since 2005, the British Interplanetary Society gives out annual Sir Arthur Clarke awards. Clarke died in Sri Lanka on March 19, 2008 at the age of ninety.

C. S. Lewis and Science Fiction

C. S. Lewis enjoyed the science fiction writings of H. G. Wells—he read and reread *Time Machine, First Men in the Moon, The Door in the Wall and Other Stories, The Sleeper Awakes, God the Invisible King, A Modern Utopia, The Invisible Man, The Country of the Blind*, and others.⁴⁵ Wells seems to have been a major cause of Lewis's original interest in science fiction. Lewis read Wells at least as early as 1909,⁴⁶ and he maintained his interest in science fiction for the rest of his life. In *Surprised by Joy*, Lewis states about his time at Wynyard School, "what I took to at the same time, is the work of Rider Haggard; and also the 'scientifiction' of H. G. Wells."⁴⁷ Later, the works of Olaf Stapledon, author of *Last and First Men*, and David Lindsay, author of *A Voyage to Arcturus*, also intrigued him.

In 1955, Lewis read the essay, "On Science Fiction,"⁴⁸ to the Cambridge University English Club. In the opening paragraph he mentions that about twenty years ago, an era in which science fiction writing flourished like never before, many science fiction stories were being written and entire magazines were devoted to science fiction. The quality of such stories in that era, he lamented, was poor despite the increased quantity. But these statements demonstrate that the interest of Lewis in science fiction grew significantly in the mid-1930s.

---

⁴⁴ Neil McAleer, *Visionary*, 128. This award is administered by UNESCO.

⁴⁵ See, for example, *Collected Letters*, *I*, 11, for a reference to Lewis reading *First Men in the Moon*; *Collected Letters*, *I*, 329, for a reference to *God the Invisible King*; *Collected Letters*, *I*, 335, which mentions Wells' *A Modern Utopia*; and *Collected Letters*, *I*, 852, which contains a reference to Wells' 1927 novel *Meanwhile*. See also *The Lewis Papers*, Vol. 3, 173f. for a reference to Lewis reading *First Men in the Moon* in 1909. Many more examples could be included. The first three citations in this footnote are all referring to reading Wells in 1917.

⁴⁶ See "Chronologically Lewis" for the date February 21, 1909. http://www.joelheck.com/chronologically-lewis.php

⁴⁷ *Surprised by Joy*, 35.

⁴⁸ On November 24. "On Science Fiction," *Of Other Worlds: Essays and Stories*, C. S. Lewis, edited by Walter Hooper, New York: Harcourt Brace & Company, 1966, 59-73.

Soon thereafter, he ventured into science fiction writing himself with *Out of the Silent Planet*, partly in response to the poor quality he was seeing in print.

Stapledon's writing was part of Lewis's motivation to write science fiction. Writing to Roger Lancelyn Green in 1938, the year that Lewis's *Out of the Silent Planet* was released, Lewis states, "What immediately spurred me to write was Olaf Stapledon's *Last and First Men* ... and an essay in J. B. S. Haldane's *Possible Worlds* both of wh. seemed to take the idea of such travel seriously and to have the desperately immoral outlook wh. I try to pillory in Weston."[49] Years later, Lewis praised Clarke's *Childhood's End* to Joy Davidman, comparing it to the writings of Lindsay and Wells, "It is quite out of range of the common space-and-time writers; away up near Lindsay's *A Voyage to Arcturus* and Wells's *First Men in the Moon*. It is better than any of Stapledon's. It hasn't got Ray Bradbury's delicacy, but then it has ten times his emotional power, and far more mythopoeia."[50]

THE CORRESPONDENCE OF CLARKE AND LEWIS

Lewis's Space Trilogy, or Ransom Trilogy, starting with *Out of the Silent Planet* (1938) and *Perelandra* (1943),[51] led to his correspondence with Arthur C. Clarke. The second volume of that science fiction trilogy, *Perelandra*, the story of the temptation of the first "Adam" and "Eve" on Venus, was published by the Bodley Head in 1943.[52] Later that year, Clarke wrote to Lewis, objecting to some ideas Lewis expressed in *Perelandra*. Clarke had previously read *Out of the Silent Planet*, with some concern, and had now finished *Perelandra*.[53] Clarke began his letter by stating, "I wish to disagree, somewhat violently, with you."[54] Clarke then calls Lewis's characterization of the scientist Weston "an outburst of unreasoning and emotional panic."[55] Then he

---

[49] Weston is a character in Lewis's Space Trilogy. *Collected Letters*, II, 236.

[50] *Collected Letters*, III, 390. The letter is dated Dec. 22, 1953.

[51] The third volume, *That Hideous Strength*, was published in 1945.

[52] On April 20.

[53] Miller, *From Narnia to A Space Odyssey*, 36-39. The complete letter appears in this collection of Clarke and Lewis correspondence, along with introductory essays by Ryder W. Miller, a poet, journalist, and science fiction writer, and a Preface by Clarke himself.

[54] Neil McAleer, *Visionary*, 48.

[55] Ibid.

states, "I have never encountered a single science fiction enthusiast of mature age who regarded the idea of the conquest of other races with anything but disgust."[56] Although Clarke never mentioned it in his letter, one suspects that Clarke was especially incensed with Lewis's comment in *Perelandra*, which spoke disparagingly of "little Interplanetary Societies and Rocketry Clubs,"[57] an oblique reference to Clarke's British Interplanetary Society.

After the initial outburst against Lewis, Clarke goes on to describe spaceflight that had the potential to help mankind in many ways in the future and, just two years later, he suggested this when he wrote about a global network of telecommunications satellites. As Clarke biographer Neil McAleer writes, "Clarke's words ceased to blaze and became cordial, then friendly and Lewis responded in kind."[58]

Despite his disagreements with Lewis, Clarke once described Lewis as spaceflight's "earliest and most brilliant critic."[59] He also complimented Lewis for rejecting the idea that anything alien is likely to be ugly and horrible—as was the case with the writings of H. G. Wells. He appreciated Lewis's portrayal of something alien, and good, in *Perelandra*. The alien need not be horrific, and Lewis had described a creature on Venus as "something strange, not hideous at all,"[60] just different.

Lewis subsequently wrote to Clarke in defense of *Perelandra*, particularly concerned with the moral assumptions in popular fiction. He cited Olaf Stapledon's *Star Gazer* (which ends in devil worship), J. B. S. Haldane's *Possible Worlds*, and C. H. Waddington's *Science and Ethics* as examples of the type of ethics displayed by Weston in *Perelandra*.[61] Weston, Lewis wrote, was anxious to increase his own

---

[56] Ibid.

[57] *Perelandra*, New York: Macmillan, 1944, 81.

[58] Ibid.

[59] Ibid., 47. McAleer writes, "The assessment was made, in respect and admiration, from personal experience." See the 1953 hardcover reissue of *Prelude to Space*, the 1947 novel where Clarke made this retrospective comment about Lewis.

[60] Arthur C. Clarke, "H. G. Wells and Science Fiction," *Voices from the Sky: Previews of the Coming Space Age*, New York: Harper & Row, Publishers, 216.

[61] *Collected Letters, II*, 594. The date of this letter was December 7, 1943. Waddington later spoke at a meeting of the Socratic Club, an undergraduate club devoted to the discussion and debate of issues related to the Christian faith, on Feb. 11, 1946. Lewis was the faculty advisor to

power and that of the human race through technology and was willing to set aside ethics.⁶² Lewis defends *Perelandra*'s implications about ethics, even while agreeing that science fiction as a genre is merely on the level of cowboy stories. Lewis concludes that the increase of power by technology with indifference to ethics appears to be a cancer in the universe. "Certainly, if he goes on his present course much further man can *not* be trusted with knowledge."⁶³ This concern coincides with the lectures Lewis gave that same year at the University of Durham, later published as *The Abolition of Man*.⁶⁴ Whether or not Clarke agreed with Lewis is unknown.

Lewis adopted a different opinion of Stapledon's book *Last and First Men* than Clarke had. While Clarke liked the book, Lewis did not, disagreeing with Stapledon's views about man's ultimate destiny. Lewis wrote, "Mr. Stapledon is so rich in invention ... I admire his invention (though not his philosophy) ...."⁶⁵ His disagreement with Stapledon's worldview did not diminish his praise, calling Stapledon "a corking good writer."⁶⁶ Lewis put Stapledon and Clarke in the same writing category, once stating about their science fiction writings, "This kind gives an imaginative vehicle to speculations about the ultimate destiny of our species. Examples⁶⁷ are Wells's *Time Machine*, Olaf Stapledon's *Last and First Men*, or Arthur Clarke's *Childhood's End*."⁶⁸ Lewis feared that humanity would either destroy itself or in

---

the club. The topic was "Can Science Provide a Basis for Ethics?"

⁶² *Collected Letters, II*, 594. The date of the letter is December 7, 1943.

⁶³ Ibid.

⁶⁴ In *The Abolition of Man or Reflections on education with special reference to the teaching of English in the upper forms of schools*. New York: Simon & Schuster, 1996, 37, Lewis famously wrote the failure to produce just sentiments in our schools, "We make men without chests and expect of them virtue and enterprise. We laugh at honor and are shocked to find traitors in our midst. We castrate and bid the geldings be fruitful."

⁶⁵ The Preface to *That Hideous Strength*, New York: Macmillan, 1946, 6f.

⁶⁶ *Collected Letters, III*, 71. In a Dec. 14, 1950 letter to Sheldon Vanauken.

⁶⁷ That is, these writings are examples of speculation about the ultimate destiny of mankind, Lewis writes. He does not specify further. *Of Other Worlds: Essays and Stories*, C. S. Lewis, edited by Walter Hooper, New York: Harcourt Brace & Company, 1966, 65f.

⁶⁸ C. S. Lewis, "On Science Fiction," *Of Other Worlds: Essays and Stories*, C. S. Lewis, edited by Walter Hooper, New York: Harcourt Brace & Company, 1966, 65f. The essay was read to the Cambridge University English Club on Nov. 24, 1954. Clarke's *Childhood's End* was

attempting to preserve itself, destroy other species.

In 1946, Clarke gave a lecture in London on interplanetary matters, probably his inaugural lecture as Chairman of the British Interplanetary Society, and he invited Lewis to attend. Lewis had to send his regrets,[69] so Clarke sent Lewis a copy of his lecture. A few days later, Lewis wrote a letter of thanks.[70] The following January, Lewis wrote another short note of thanks for an additional lecture Clarke had sent.[71]

Although they differed greatly on theological matters (Clarke's secular and atheistic perspective explains the major reason),[72] Clarke invited Lewis to write or speak to his society because of their mutual love for science fiction,[73] warning him, good-naturedly, "that your position might be somewhat analogous to that of a Christian martyr in the arena."[74] Lewis suggested that the invitation might only be "a plan for kidnapping me and marooning me on an asteroid."[75] Clarke's invitation came at a time when Lewis's heavy schedule of teaching, writing, and speaking engagements made it difficult to accept many such invitations.

---

published in 1953. It deals with a group of aliens who arrive on Earth, hovering over the planet's major cities. With vast powers to prevent space travel and violence among people on Earth, the Overlords and the leader, Karellen, preside over Earth for 150 years in relative peace and harmony among nations and between mankind and the Overlords, until the last generation of children is born. At that time, that last generation of children is taken over by an Overmind, to which the Overlords were subject. The Overmind is undefined power in the universe that controls Karellen and the Overlords. The children seemingly merge with the Overmind in one vast intelligence. At the end of the novel, Earth vanishes in a flash of light while Karellen watches from his spaceship.

[69] In a letter of September 24, 1946. *Collected Letters, II*, 741. The lecture took place on September 23.

[70] The date of the Lewis letter is October 2, 1946. *Collected Letters, II*, 742.

[71] January 2, 1947. *Collected Letters, II*, 752.

[72] Andy Sawyer, "Clarke, Sir Arthur Charles (1917-2008)," *Oxford Dictionary of National Biography*, Oxford University Press, January 2012, online edition May 2012.

[73] On February 14, 1953, Lewis wrote to Arthur C. Clarke, thanking him for an invitation to speak or write for his society. *Collected Letters, III*, 292f.

[74] McAleer, *Visionary*, 48.

[75] This letter has apparently not survived, but is cited in McAleer, *Visionary*, 48.

Joy Davidman first recommended Clarke's *Childhood's End* to Lewis,[76] giving him a first edition of the book as a Christmas gift in 1953. When Lewis read the book, he expressed himself as having been "thoroughly bowled over" and describing the book as "an absolute corker."[77] Lewis describes it as "harmony piling up on harmony, grandeur on grandeur, pity on pity."[78] Neil McAleer states that the letter came from "a distinguished academician and writer" and that it "acknowledged that Clarke's work ... deserved serious recognition."[79] McAleer adds, "Lewis's assessment could not help but have a profound impact on Clarke's view of himself as a novelist."[80]

Just a month later, Clarke wrote to Lewis, requesting permission to quote from that letter for the upcoming British edition.[81] Later that year, a portion of Lewis's letter was printed on the dust cover of Clarke's *Childhood's End*,[82] and McAleer describes Lewis's praise as "a boon to Clarke's literary career."[83] Clarke was only thirty-six years old, his writing career still largely in front of him.

LEWIS AND CLARKE MEET

In early 1954, Joy Davidman met Clarke and British author Marie Stopes at an Oxford pub.[84] Lewis was apparently not present for that meeting, but Davidman's meeting provided the opening for Clarke and Lewis to meet. The two men did, in fact, meet at the Eastgate Hotel in Oxford. For that meeting, Val Cleaver, a space

---

[76] Abigail Santamaria, *Joy: Poet, Seeker, and the Woman Who Captivated C. S. Lewis*, Kindle edition. Chapter 13, "November 1953-April 1954." See also McAleer, *Visionary*, 74.

[77] *Collected Letters*, III, 390, 392. The letter's date is Dec. 22, 1953.

[78] Ibid., 391.

[79] McAleer, *Visionary*, 75.

[80] McAleer, *Visionary*, 75.

[81] McAleer, *Visionary*, 75.

[82] *Light on C. S. Lewis*, 147. The letter is the one Lewis wrote to Joy Davidman on December 22, 1953. The dust jacket quotes three sections from this letter of Lewis, beginning with the phrase "It is quite out of range" to the phrase "his emotional power," then from "It's rather like the effect" to "pity on pity" and, finally, from "The first climax" to "a higher claim on humanity than its own 'survival'." *Collected Letters*, III, 390f.

[83] McAleer, *Visionary*, 77.

[84] The date is January 7, 1954. Don W. King, ed. *Out of My Bone: The Letters of Joy Davidman*, Grand Rapids: Eerdmans, 2009, 169. Lewis seems to have been in Oxford, but we don't know why he was unable to attend.

buff, joined Clarke, and J. R. R. Tolkien accompanied Lewis. The conversation most likely centered around science fiction, space travel, and the books Clarke and Lewis were writing. As they parted, Lewis stated, tongue-in-check, "I'm sure you're very wicked people—but how dull it would be if everyone was good."[85] After this meeting, Clarke and Lewis continued to write to one another. Through Joy Davidman, who frequently attended the White Horse tavern in London, where science fiction writers, editors, and publishers regularly met, they had additional indirect communication. Clarke was usually in that group.[86]

Also in 1954, Lewis wrote to Clarke three times in one week. The first letter, written on January 20,[87] expressed the hope that Clarke might visit him in Oxford and thanked Clarke for sending a copy of Clarke's book *Expedition to Earth*. He also writes about a request from Clarke's publisher, since Lewis wanted to know which portion of his letter would be used on the book jacket of *Childhood's End*. Quoting him would be fine, Lewis writes, if the selection fairly represents what he has written.

In addition, Lewis also writes about the type of science fiction that he most appreciates. He wants to see where Clarke will go in his future writing. "Not, I devoutly hope, into the kind where we leap forward to a date at wh. space-travel has become as common & dull as tramways and *within* that framework we get an ordinary spy-story, or wreck-story, or love-story wh. might as well, or better, be located in present-day Hampstead."[88] A space travel story must have its own unique space-travel nature, just as a story about the old American West must have a uniquely Western flavor.[89] Each type of story must

---

[85] McAleer, *Visionary*, 75-76. Although the precise date of that meeting is not known, McAleer concludes that they met in August or September 1954.

[86] McAleer, *Visionary*, 73. See also Miller, *From Narnia to A Space Odyssey*, 24.

[87] *C. S. Lewis: Collected Letters, III. Narnia, Cambridge and Joy 1950-1963*. Edited by Walter Hooper. London: HarperCollinsPublishers, 2006, 410f.

[88] *Collected Letters, III*, 411. The letter was written on Jan. 20, 1954.

[89] C. S. Lewis, "On Stories," *Of Other Worlds: Essays and Stories*, C. S. Lewis, edited by Walter Hooper, New York: Harcourt Brace & Company, 1966, 4. In this essay, Lewis writes, "For though I had never read Fenimore Cooper I had enjoyed other books about 'Red Indians.' And I knew that what I wanted from them was not simply 'excitement.' Dangers, of course, there must be: how else can you keep a story going?

make effective use of its setting.

Lewis again wrote to Clarke a few hours later. He had just read Clarke's short story, "Jupiter Five."[90] Lewis liked the story but gave Clarke some advice on how to make the unique nature of an interplanetary story a central feature rather than something that hovers on the fringes,[91] just as he had just written in his previous letter.

Such advice undoubtedly helped Clarke become a better writer. In fact, Ryder W. Miller writes favorably of Lewis's influence, "One can see Lewis's influence in Clarke's non-fiction piece 'The Moon and Mr. Farnsworth.'"[92] Lewis was an established author, professor of English, and a master of language, but Clarke was only thirty-six years old and still a novice. Lewis gives Kris Neville's *She knew He Was Coming* as an example of a poorly written story with the same fault that Clarke had in "Jupiter Five." However, Mark Clifton's *The Kenzie Report* and Richard Stockham's *Circle of Flight* were examples of stories done right. The Stockham book, writes Lewis, "tho' not at all well executed, is the real thing: i.e. the thing he professes to be doing is the thing he is *really* doing."[93]

Six days later, Lewis writes to Clarke about science fiction writing and escapism. Clarke had replied to the two previous letters of Lewis, had tried to make his case, and now Lewis replies with some additional advice. Clarke had apparently pleaded his case by appealing to the importance of human interest. Lewis replies that human interest is important in writing, but human interest is not unique to science fiction.[94] It needs to be present in every kind of writing. In addition, he writes, don't allow anyone to criticize you for writing science fiction as though it were escapism. Only those "people who want to keep the world in some ideological prison" will make the charge of escapism.[95]

But they must (in the mood which led one to such a book) be Redskin dangers. The 'Redskinnery' was what really mattered."

[90] It had appeared in the May 1953 issue of *IF: Worlds of Science Fiction*. IF apparently stood for Interplanetary Flight.

[91] *Collected Letters, III,* 411f. The letter is dated Jan. 20, 1954.

[92] Miller, *From Narnia to A Space Odyssey,* 7.

[93] *Collected Letters, III,* 411f. The date of letter is Jan. 20, 1954.

[94] One suspects that Clarke had defended his space stories by appealing to human interest as adequate to his task.

[95] *Collected Letters, III,* 418. The date is January 26, 1954.

Twenty-One Friendships of C.S. Lewis

SOME FINAL NOTES

Lewis's appreciation of Clarke's writing did not decline in subsequent years. He liked good writing, whether it came from someone who shared his worldview or from someone, like Clarke, who did not. Shortly after his last letter to Clarke,[96] Lewis wrote to Katharine Farrer about the pluses and minuses of a book she had written, and, in a short sentence at the end of his letter, recommended Clarke's *Childhood's End*.[97]

Lewis's essay, "On Science Fiction,"[98] mentioned earlier, was read to the Cambridge University English Club in November 1955. His exchange of letters with Clarke earlier that year provided some of the motivation for this essay. The essay opens with a brief history of science fiction.[99] Lewis argues that one must not write about a genre that one detests.[100] Since he enjoys science fiction, he implies, he is qualified to write about it. Nor must one group all kinds of science fiction together, as though every reader of science fiction is the same as every other reader.[101] He then discusses the various types of science fiction, ranging from speculative science fiction to prophetic writing about an imaginary future and stories about geographically distant locations.

Lewis contends that, in science fiction, characterization must be light rather than deep,[102] that the Eschatological type of story gives "speculations about the ultimate destiny of our species" (Clarke's *Childhood's End* is one example he cites),[103] and he challenges those who level a charge of escapism against the writer of science fiction.[104] In this essay, Lewis uses the same answer about escapism which he had used in his reply to Clarke: those people who are "most preoccupied with, and most hostile to, the idea of escape" are jailers, i.e., those who want to keep others in a mental or intellectual prison.[105] In that

---

[96] *Collected Letters, III*, 423. On February 3, 1954.

[97] *Collected Letters, III*, 423f. She had written *The Cretan Counterfeit*.

[98] "On Science Fiction," *Of Other Worlds: Essays and Stories*, C. S. Lewis, edited by Walter Hooper, New York: Harcourt Brace & Company, 1966, 59-73.

[99] Lewis, "On Science Fiction," 59.

[100] Lewis, "On Science Fiction," 60.

[101] Ibid., 61.

[102] Ibid., 64f.

[103] Ibid., 65f.

[104] Ibid., 67.

[105] *Collected Letters, III*, 418. The actual date of the letter is Jan. 26,

answer, Lewis himself was indebted to Tolkien, who had made the same point earlier.[106]

A few years later, Lewis writes to Vice Principal Robin Anstey[107] about science fiction and the quotation of part of Lewis's letter in Arthur C. Clarke's book *Childhood's End*. He commends science fiction as "the chief vehicle for 'thoughts that wander up and down eternity.'"[108] Too many modern novelists address trivial matters, but Lewis sees science fiction as a way of awakening the concern of the typical reader for eternal matters,[109] including the science fiction writings of Arthur C. Clarke.

Nor did Clarke fail to return his appreciation for Lewis. When Alice Turner, then at *Publishers Weekly*, interviewed Clarke in 1973, they talked about his recently released novel *Rendezvous with Rama* and Clarke's love of science fiction. Clarke commented on the common criticism that science fiction is escapism. Lewis didn't think so, claimed Clarke. "C. S. Lewis, who wrote it himself, said, 'The only people who think there's something wrong with escapism are jailers.'"[110]

Conclusion

Arthur C. Clarke was one of the most well-known people with whom Lewis corresponded during his lifetime. He made his reputation by writing science fiction, a reputation that was solidified by his role in the movie *2001: A Space Odyssey*. More than Clarke's notoriety, however, Lewis carried on a sustained correspondence—after a feisty beginning—with Clarke, exchanged invitations to visit, met Clarke on at least one occasion, wrote words of endorsement for one of Clarke's books, and offered advice on writing science fiction. All of this took place after an initial antagonism expressed in Clarke's first letter, which later resulted in a friendship between the two men. In the process C. S. Lewis helped Clarke become a better writer.

1954; "On Science Fiction," 67.

[106] C. S. Lewis, "On Science Fiction," *Of Other Worlds: Essays and Stories*, C. S. Lewis, edited by Walter Hooper, New York: Harcourt Brace & Company, 1966, 67.

107 On November 2, 1960. At this time, the Rev. Christopher Robin Anstey was serving as Vice-Principal of Chichester Theological College. See *Collected Letters, III*, 1205, n. 178.

[108] *Collected Letters, III*, 1206.

[109] Ibid.

[110] McAleer, *Visionary*, 194.

Twenty-One Friendships of C.S. Lewis

Lewis still does that for anyone who reads him.

T. D. Weldon
By kind permission of the
President and Fellows, Magdalen College Oxford

Chapter 11

HARRY WELDON
and the Resurrection

"Rum thing. It almost looks as if it had really happened once."[1] So spoke Thomas Dewar Weldon in one of the most well-known comments ever made to C. S. Lewis, one that has enshrined Weldon forever on the pages of Lewisian history. Weldon was talking about the resurrection of Jesus Christ, which had surprisingly strong evidence behind it. Lewis himself tells the story of that conversation in his autobiography:

> Early in 1926 the hardest boiled of all the atheists I ever knew ... remarked that the evidence for the historicity of the Gospels was really surprisingly good. "Rum thing ... All that stuff of Frazer's about the Dying God. Rum thing. It almost looks as if it had really happened once." To understand the shattering impact of it, you would need to know the man .... If he, the cynic of cynics, the toughest of the toughs, were not—as I would still have put it—"safe," where could I turn? Was there then no escape?[2]

Even more surprising is the fact that Weldon was a confirmed atheist at the time, at least according to Lewis. Evidence from a hostile source is better evidence than that from a friendly source. According to Lewis, Weldon was a card-carrying atheist, as was Lewis himself at that time.[3] In 1926, they had a great deal in common, both of them Fellows of Magdalen College, both of them bachelors, both great conversationalists, and both keeping barrels of beer in their rooms to entertain undergraduates![4] Lewis taught English Language and

---

[1] *Surprised by Joy*, 223f.

[2] Ibid. The phrase "rum thing" appears three times in Lewis's autobiography on pages 223, 224, and 235. This quotation is from 223f.

[3] I have argued elsewhere, in my book *From Atheism to Christianity: The Story of C. S. Lewis*, that Lewis had become an Idealist by 1924, but this date is not completely certain. Atheism was still his creed, even if he was an Idealist, until he admitted that God was God in the Trinity term of 1930. And, in fact, Lewis took to Idealism because it "enabled one to get all the conveniences of Theism, without believing in God." *Surprised by Joy*, 209.

[4] R. W. Johnson, *Look Back in Laughter: Oxford's Postwar Golden Age*. Newbury Berks, UK: Threshold Press, 2015, 49.

Literature and an occasional philosophy student, while Weldon taught philosophy.

Commenting on that unexpected comment about the resurrection, Lewis writes:

> The real clue had been put into my hand by that hard-boiled Atheist .... The question was no longer to find the one simply true religion among a thousand religions simply false. It was rather, "Where has religion reached its true maturity? Where, if anywhere, have the hints of all Paganism been fulfilled?" ... Where was the thing full grown? ... There were really only two answers possible: either in Hinduism or in Christianity. Everything else was either a preparation for, or else (in the French sense) a *vulgarization* of, these.[5]

In *Surprised by Joy*, Lewis does not identify "that hard-boiled Atheist,"[6] but the identity of that atheist is almost certainly Weldon.[7] In his diary, Lewis states that Weldon came into his room on one particular night (Weldon always lived in college), and they discussed the historical truth of the Gospels.[8] The date in Lewis's diary fits the "rum thing" comment, the diary identifies Weldon by name, and the topic was the historical truth of the Gospels.[9]

This is how it happened. On April 27, 1926, Lewis settled down to read Skeat's introduction[10] in the larger sitting room of his private rooms at Magdalen College[11] when Weldon came in.[12] They drank whiskey and talked late into the evening. Among other topics, they discussed the historical truth of the Gospels. Lewis states it this way:

---

[5] *Surprised by Joy*, 235.

[6] *Surprised by Joy*, 235.

[7] The compendium "Chronologically Lewis" does not give evidence of any other person during the first four months of 1926 who might be called a "hard-boiled Atheist." See http://www.joelheck.com/chronologically-lewis.php.

[8] *All My Road Before Me*, 379.

[9] Lewis writes, "We somehow got on the historical truth of the Gospels, and agreed that there was a lot that could not be explained away." Ibid.

[10] He was probably reading Walter William Skeat, *An Etymological Dictionary of the English Language*, revised and enlarged, Courier Dover Publications, 1910.

[11] Oxford faculty typically have rooms in which the faculty member can meet students, conduct tutorials, hold social gatherings, and function in other ways, including overnight stays.

[12] *All My Road Before Me*, 379.

Twenty-One Friendships of C.S. Lewis

> ... Weldon came in. This meant whiskey and talk till 11.30 .... We somehow got on the historical truth of the Gospels and agreed that there was a lot that could not be explained away. He believes in the Hegelian doctrine of the Trinity and said the whole thing fitted in: in fact he is a Christian "of a sort." I should never have suspected it.[13]

Weldon claimed to be a Christian "of a sort,"[14] which makes it difficult to understand exactly what Weldon believed about God. During his lifetime Hegel insisted that he was a Christian, and his doctrine of the Trinity emphasized the three persons within the single Godhead.[15] But Hegel was also elusive, almost mystical, attempting to describe God in new and creative ways, and Weldon's position on "the Hegelian doctrine of the Trinity" is likewise elusive.

While Weldon's talk does not implicate him, his conversation about murderers, sodomy, and laying traps for Bishops (according

---

[13] *All My Road Before Me*, 379.

[14] This Hegelian doctrine of the Trinity is very unlike the Christian teaching from Scripture. Peter Leithart writes that Hegel's logic defines God as Absolute Spirit, "as he is in his eternal essence before the creation of Nature and of a Finite Spirit." Hegel does not think of God as "a being or a particular self-conscious personality. God is not actual apart from the world." Also, in Jesus "God has again passed out of universality and entered into the realm of particular being." "God's life is the concept, manifested in the three moments of universality, particularity, and individuality." The particularity of God is seen in the Incarnation of Jesus, and the individuality of God appears in the Spirit, which is "the Christian community's reconciled union with God." so the universality of God must be the near equivalent of God the Father. http://www.patheos.com/blogs/leithart/2007/11/hegels-trinity/ Other sources seem to identify Hegel's teaching as a statement in philosophical terms what theologians state in religious terms, and, therefore, orthodox. https://www.sunypress.edu/pdf/62561.pdf, which describes Hegel's God as "a triadically structured inclusive infinite, God inclusive of the world."

[15] For the content of this footnote and some of the text above, I am indebted to Ryan Haecker, Ph.D. student in the faculty of divinity at the University of Cambridge. Peter Benson, "Hegel and the Trinity," *Philosophy Now*, Issue 42, online edition at https://philosophynow.org/issues/42/Hegel_and_the_Trinity For Hegel, the Spirit was the relation of love between the Father and the Son. See also Robert Wallace, "Hegel's God," *Philosophy Now*, June/July 2015, online edition. If as Dale M. Schlitt writes, Hegel thought of Spirit as "the structured movement of integrating reason," he is not using any Trinitarian terms in their biblical sense and can hardly be considered orthodox in any sense, or, most likely, Christian. Dale M. Schlitt, "Trinity and Spirit," *American Catholic Philosophical Quarterly*, 42:4 (1990):468.

to Lewis's diary) does not suggest a Christian ethical foundation.[16] Weldon also made his famous "rum thing" comment about death and resurrection, the comment that Lewis cites in *Surprised by Joy*.[17] If Weldon thought that it almost looked as if it had really happened once, Weldon didn't really think that Jesus had risen from the dead. But more to the point, was Lewis correct in assuming Weldon to be "that hard-boiled Atheist," if indeed he was that open to the resurrection account in the New Testament Gospels?

Martin Moynihan did not think so. Moynihan studied with both Weldon and Lewis and concluded two things. First, although Weldon was certainly non-Christian, he rarely offered his own views about Christianity. Second, various comments by Weldon and some of his writings in his book on Kant,[18] sounded to Moynihan very much like the argument Lewis made in *Mere Christianity*.[19] While he couldn't be certain, he concludes that Weldon "in the last resort did" believe in the existence of God,[20] that he could have been an agnostic or an agnostic deist, but not an atheist.[21]

Why, then, did Lewis conclude that Weldon was a "hard-boiled Atheist"? The two men met when Lewis was an atheist, but at the time Lewis's atheism was wavering. One suspects that Lewis heard comments from Weldon that undergirded Lewis's own position, but misread Weldon in the process. Writing about Weldon twenty-five to thirty years later, Lewis could easily have remembered some aspects of that relationship incorrectly, but the interaction between Lewis and Weldon that led to the "Rum thing" comment was undoubtedly firmly planted in Lewis's mind. He likely remembered Weldon accurately. He more likely imputed to Weldon the position that he himself held at the time and chose not to inquire more deeply into what Weldon believed. As a result, he was simply mistaken about Weldon's atheism.

Lewis had read Chesterton's *The Everlasting Man* prior to this conversation with Weldon.[22] That reading had convinced Lewis that Chesterton's assessment of history—a history filled with purpose—

---

[16] *All My Road Before Me*, 435.

[17] *Surprised by Joy*, 223f.

[18] T. D. Weldon, *Introduction to Kant's Critique of Pure Reason*. Oxford University Press, 1945.

[19] Martin Moynihan, "C. S. Lewis and T. D. Weldon," *VII*, Volume 5 (1984), 105.

[20] Moynihan, 105.

[21] Moynihan, 101.

[22] *Surprised by Joy*, 223.

made more sense than H. G. Wells' popular *Outline of History*. Chesterton's understanding of history may well have made Weldon's comment more influential with Lewis, motivating him to take a closer look at the New Testament Gospels. That Lewis later became a theist and then a Christian owes a great deal to this verbal exchange between Weldon and Lewis.

Who was Harry Weldon?

Thomas Dewar Weldon, the son of Thomas Weldon and Amelia Ellen, *née* Dewar, was born on Dec. 5, 1896. After attending Tonbridge School,[23] an independent boys school in Kent, he matriculated to Magdalen College, Oxford, in 1919. He had won a scholarship to read *Literae Humaniores*, or Greats, a course of study in ancient history and classical philosophy. He began his study at Oxford University probably at the very same time that Lewis did, graduating with a First Class degree in 1921. The next year, he was named a Lecturer at Magdalen and then a Fellow of Magdalen College and Tutor in Philosophy in 1923. He became known to students and colleagues as "Harry," because of the similarity of his name to a famous vaudeville comedian, Harry Weldon.[24]

T. D. Weldon
By kind permission of the
President and Fellows,
Magdalen College Oxford

During World War I, Weldon served as an officer in the Royal Field Artillery beginning in 1915, serving in France and Belgium, winning the Military Cross and Bar for acts of gallantry, and eventually achieving the rank of acting captain.[25] This war service delayed his arrival at Magdalen College to begin undergraduate studies. During World War II, he was a temporary civil servant in

---

[23] Mark J. Schofield, "Weldon, Thomas Dewar (1896-1958)," *Oxford Dictionary of National Biography*, Oxford University Press, 2004, accessed Oct. 5, 2017.

[24] Sebastian Faulks, *The Fatal Englishman: Three Short Lives*, New York: Vintage, 2002, 212.

[25] Mark J. Schofield, "Weldon, Thomas Dewar (1896-1958)," *Oxford Dictionary of National Biography*, Oxford University Press, 2004, accessed Oct. 5, 2017.

London for the first three years of the war, and then he became the Personal Staff Officer to "Bomber Harris," Sir Arthur Harris in H.Q. Bomber Command at High Wycombe (1942-1945). Along with William Temple, Archbishop of Canterbury, and others, he believed that the bombing was necessary for the conduct of the war to achieve victory. As the Personal Assistant of Harris, Weldon was invited by Harris to speak on the bombing. At High Wycombe, Weldon praised the work of the Bomber Command, concluding that the bombing was strategically justified, even if it killed non-combatants, because it shortened the war and reduced the loss of life.[26]

Weldon has been described as "the most influential Fellow in the College ... who fought hardest to raise Magdalen's academic standards."[27] Weldon demanded "higher standards and greater meritocracy" especially for his own subject, PPE, i.e., Politics, Philosophy and Economics.[28] His specialty in philosophy was the German philosopher Immanuel Kant, which in itself created a higher standard. He published three works, *Introduction to Kant's 'Critique of Pure Reason'* (1945; 2nd ed., 1958), *States and Morals* (1946), and *The Vocabulary of Politics* (1953).

Weldon had a volatile temper, a love for argumentation, and a good deal of insolence. Lewis wrote of him, "He is insolent by custom to servants and to old men, yet capable of kindliness ...."[29] Though not appreciative of some of Lewis's writings, Weldon nevertheless appreciated Lewis. He once offered a left-handed compliment about Lewis when speaking to an undergraduate, stating, "The man is not as bad as his books."[30] One of those bad books, apparently, was *The Pilgrim's Regress*, which Weldon thought should not have been written.[31] Seeing through something is a prominent idea in *The Pilgrim's Regress*, suggesting that some people whom Lewis knew, Weldon among them, believed they could understand things that others couldn't.[32] C. S. Lewis once said of Weldon, "He believes that

---

[26] "Black, White and Grey": Wartime Arguments for and against the Strategic Bomber Offensive," David Ian Hall. www.wlu.ca/~wwwmsds/vol7n1hallbomber.

[27] Email correspondence from Dr. Robin Darwall-Smith, Magdalen College, Oxford, Archivist, June 26, 2002.

[28] R. W. Johnson, *Look Back in Laughter*, 47.

[29] *All My Road Before Me*, 482.

[30] Sayer, *Jack*, 286.

[31] Ibid.

[32] See C. S. Lewis, *The Pilgrim's Regress: an allegorical apology for*

he has seen through everything and lives at rock bottom."[33] Weldon had an intelligent mind, which probably led to an overconfidence in his ability to see things more clearly than other people did. And, in fact, he probably did at times, but he probably also saw himself in *Regress*, as was Lewis's intent.

Some have also seen in Weldon the character of Devine, aka Lord Feverstone, one of the villains in the Ransom Trilogy, given the similarity between Devine's ego and that of Weldon, the insolence of both men, their penchant for alcohol,[34] and because Ransom and Devine had been at the same school just as Lewis and Weldon were both at the same College of Oxford University. The comparison is not exact, since Lewis's fictional characters were always composites.

T. D. Weldon died on May 13, 1958 from a brain hemorrhage.[35]

Whiskey, Words, and Weldon

Lewis and Weldon crossed paths on at least fifteen occasions over a period of two months in early 1926 for conversation, recreation, and alcoholic drinks.[36] Lewis also frequently mentioned Weldon in his diary, *All My Road Before Me*, especially in the years before Lewis came to believe in God.

The frequent late-night conversations between the two men indicate that they enjoyed one another's company. Since both men had rooms in New Building and were colleagues on the same faculty, it was not unusual for them to meet. They even had some of the same students. However, for Lewis to record so many meetings in his diary means that the meetings were more than mere coincidences, demonstrating a bond of friendship between the two men in Lewis's early years as a Fellow of Magdalen. In fact, about half of the references to Weldon in Lewis's diary refer to this two-month period.

Christianity, Reason, and Romanticism. Grand Rapids: William B. Eerdmans, 1958, for example on page 123, where the giant sees through.

[33] *All My Road Before Me*, 483.

[34] See Lewis, *Out of the Silent Planet*, New York: Macmillan, 1965, 143, for Devine's delight in discovering that the creatures of Malacandra had an alcoholic drink. In general, see https://praymont.blogspot.com/2015/12/timothy-dewar-harry-weldon.html and Kathleen Burk, *Troublemaker: The Life and History of A.J.P. Taylor.* New Haven: Yale University Press, 2002, 436.

[35] R. W. Johnson, *Look Back in Laughter*, 49.

[36] The fifteen dates are April 27, May 6, 7, 9, 10, 12, 18, 26, 27, June 2, 6, 10, 14, 25, and 28. See Joel D. Heck, "Chronologically Lewis," on each of these dates in 1926.

The "hard-boiled Atheist" Weldon occasionally showed interest in religion, even discussing whether the virtuous heathen were capable of salvation[37] or whether or not God can understand His own necessity.[38] Weldon probably only showed such interest because of his profession as a philosopher; but he clearly had enough interest not to shut down all religious talk. Moynihan was probably right—and Lewis wrong—Weldon was some sort of a deist or agnostic.

The friendship continued, along with the whiskey and late-night talks,[39] especially during the years leading to the conversion of Lewis to theism. Lewis even referred to Harry Weldon as the "one honest man" at Magdalen College, who preaches what he practices, who tells Lewis that he (Lewis) is "an incurable romantic," who "drinks a great deal without getting drunk," and is the "best of our younger fellows."[40]

In a letter to his father a few months later, however, Lewis mentions "those philosophy pupils whom I share with Weldon and whom he regards as his if they turn out well and mine if they turn out ill—I am now heartily sick of the whole business."[41] While Lewis was clearly bothered by the necessity of teaching philosophy students— and only those whom Weldon assigned to him—his impatience with Weldon points to another conclusion: the friendship was nearing the end.

THE END OF A FRIENDSHIP

Having once referred in his diary to Weldon's "cynical demeanor,"[42] and at another time to Weldon as "the cynic of cynics, the toughest of the toughs,"[43] Lewis knew both the strong points and the weak points of Harry Weldon. Lewis even wrote of Weldon, "Contempt is his ruling passion: courage his chief virtue."[44] A few years later,[45] in 1929, Lewis wrote to his father about a variety of topics, including the

---

[37] *All My Road Before Me*, 448. Feb. 8, 1927.

[38] *All My Road Before Me*, 450. Feb. 10, 1927.

[39] See *All My Road Before Me*, 453, for Feb. 22, 1927.

[40] *Collected Letters, I*, 763. The date of this recollection is May 27, 1928.

[41] *Collected Letters, I*, 777. The date of this letter is November 3, 1928.

[42] *All My Road Before Me*, 392. The date of this diary entry is May 10, 1926.

[43] *Surprised by Joy*, 224.

[44] *All My Road Before Me*, 483.

[45] *Surprised by Joy*, 224.

good news that Harry Weldon's "sinister presence" would be gone for two terms.[46] This indicates that the relationship between Weldon and Lewis was no longer as friendly as it had been. Weldon and Lewis continued to have contact with one another because they taught at the same College, but Lewis's Christian outlook may have put him at odds with Weldon in later years.

R. W. Johnson tells a story that took place in October 1945. Lewis and Weldon frequently carried on Magdalen College battles, Johnson tells us, with Weldon usually winning. The main exception, however, came when Weldon wanted his friend and bridge partner David Hunt to be named Dean and got President Sir Henry Tizard to support his proposal. At a meeting where this was to be decided, Lewis stood up and spoke about "plum" jobs with such eloquence that the support disappeared and Hunt was never made Dean. One of those present told Johnson about Lewis's use of the word "plum":

> Lewis let it roll off his tongue and with each repetition of the word 'plum' you could just feel support for the proposal ebbing away. By the time he finished speaking it was a hopelessly lost cause. Weldon, sensitive to this and keen not to suffer public defeat, quickly changed sides, said he agreed entirely—it was all nonsense—and left President Tizard to go down with the ship.[47]

Weldon was a complex figure, both kind and talented on the one hand and dismissive on the other hand. Johnson writes, "Whatever his angularities, Weldon was widely liked and admired. His former pupils always talked of him with awe and affection."[48] Lewis wrote of him that he was "powerful in dialectic" and a man of "great abilities."[49] On the other hand, he could be cruel. One night a guest appeared at High Table in Magdalen College for the dinner hour. He passed a notepad to Weldon, which read, "My name is John Smith. I am deaf and dumb and have to communicate with this notebook." Weldon wrote on the pad, "I can neither read nor write," and then passed it back to the guest.[50] But did the relationship between Weldon and Lewis end?

---

[46] *Collected Letters, I*, 801. The date is July 7, 1929, less than a year before his conversion to theism.

[47] R. W. Johnson, *Look Back in Laughter*, 50.

[48] R. W. Johnson, *Look Back in Laughter*, 51.

[49] *All My Road Before Me*, 482.

[50] R. W. Johnson, *Look Back in Laughter*, 51.

Certainly, Lewis and Weldon were no longer close in the decades after Lewis's conversion to Christianity, but they continued to work together on College matters. Warren Lewis's friendly conversation with Weldon at a dinner at Magdalen in 1947, which honored Arthur Dixon on his eightieth birthday,[51] indicates that there probably was no animosity between Lewis and Weldon, or at least that their animosity was submerged and that they treated one another cordially. Furthermore, the next year Weldon was twice invited to speak at the Socratic Club, while Lewis was the President of the club,[52] invitations not likely if there were any personal animosity.

Conclusion

Throughout their professional relationship Lewis remained on cordial terms with Weldon; they were, after all, Magdalen College colleagues who worked together as part of the same faculty. But after Lewis abandoned atheism for the Christian faith their relationship cooled. Weldon was committed to philosophical and linguistic clarity and truth; Lewis was committed to linguistic clarity and truth as well, especially the revealed truth in Scripture. The whiskey thing brought Weldon and Lewis together, but the rum thing helped to create a major turning point in the life of C. S. Lewis.

---

[51] *Collected Letters, I*, 416. The date of the dinner was November 27, 1947.

[52] Weldon spoke on Jan. 26, 1948, at St. Hilda's College on the topic "Political Faiths" and on April 26, 1948, again at St. Hilda's on "Our Political Predicament Theologically Considered."

Twenty-One Friendships of C.S. Lewis

London: Thomas Nelson & Sons, Ltd. 1940.

Chapter 12

C. E. M. JOAD
Agnostic, Intellectual Scallywag, & Convert

He spoke often on BBC radio, appeared at the Oxford Socratic Club, had a background in philosophy, and thought highly of reason. He left the church in his youth and returned to the Christian faith later in life. He disliked the automobile and thought that cigarette ashes were good for the carpet. He valued the Golden Rule, and he had a longing for another world. He loved Oxford University and argued for the so-called Free Will Defense. He rated friendship as one of life's greatest pleasures, and he enjoyed walking tours in the countryside.

While most people familiar with C. S. Lewis would recognize this as an accurate portrayal of the English scholar and author, it also describes one of Lewis's contemporaries, the philosopher C. E. M. Joad. Joad's and Lewis's interest in philosophy and the world of ideas, their reading of one another's work and the mutual respect that emerged from this, their published debate over the justice of God in 1941,[1] their lively debate over the merits of Christianity at the Socratic Club in 1944, and their exchange over the troubling issue of animal pain in 1950, comprise the central events of an occasional relationship that eventually witnessed Joad's return to the Christian faith.

CYRIL EDWIN MITCHINSON JOAD

Cyril Edwin Mitchinson Joad was born on August 12, 1891.[2] He attended Balliol College, Oxford (1910–1914), earning his degree three years prior to Lewis's arrival at University College, Oxford. While at Oxford, Joad read the plays of George Bernard Shaw and the novels of H. G. Wells,[3] both of whom belonged to the socialist Fabian

---

[1] C. E. M. Joad's article, "Evil and God," appears in *The Spectator* on January 31, 1941. Lewis's reply, "Evil and God," a response to Joad's article of January 31, appears one week later in the February 7 issue of *The Spectator*. See C. S. Lewis, "Evil and God," *God in the Dock*, Grand Rapids: Eerdmans, 1970, 21-24.

[2] Jason Tomes, "Joad, Cyril Edwin Mitchinson (1891-1953)," *Oxford Dictionary of National Biography*, Oxford University Press, 2004; online edition May 2007, accessed Oct. 5, 2017.

[3] Cyril Joad, *The Recovery of Belief: A Restatement of Christian Philosophy*

Society, which Joad then joined. "In those four years at Oxford," he wrote, "I became an ardent Socialist."[4]

During his Oxford years, Joad abandoned the Christian faith.[5] He once described Christianity as a dying religion. Organized Christianity, he predicted, "will disappear within the next hundred years."[6] While he could still express admiration for the church, he also stated, "I know too much of its record."[7] The world needed more rational thinking, not redemption. No creed was worth dying for; in fact, "to hold any belief with fervor is illogical."[8] Reason now became his guiding philosophy.[9]

Joad's reliance on reason led him to support a series of radical (for the time) if not bizarre political and social reforms, including the legalization of abortion and sterilization, military disarmament, and less frequent bathing.[10] His irascible nature came to the surface when describing his approach to country walks, "Whenever I can, I trespass."[11] His dislike of cars was well known but he disliked almost all machines, branding them noisy products of the Industrial Revolution, and arguing that the contemporary worship of the machine was both the symbol and the cause of mistaking the means for the end.[12]

Joad's flirtation with marriage proved short-lived.[13] His early, rationalistic views of women explain why: "What I fell in love with was not a woman but the aura of fictitious qualities with which my

---

(London: Faber & Faber, 1951), 59. In *The Book of Joad*, he called Shaw and Wells "the gods of my generation" and says they "were like men opening the windows of a rather stuffy room, letting in air and light and laughter." He also considered Shaw "the greatest English writer of all time," Cyril Joad, *The Book of Joad*. (London, 1932), 12-14.

[4] Joad, *The Book of Joad*, 11.

[5] Joad, *God and Evil*. (London, 1942), 13.

[6] Joad, *The Testament of Joad* (London, 1937), 211.

[7] Joad, *The Testament of Joad*, 207.

[8] Joad, *The Testament of Joad*, 25.

[9] G. K. Chesterton described his book, *Return to Philosophy*, as "a rattling good book," but also "a faith in reason." See the book review by G. K. Chesterton in "Back to Reason," The Listener XIII, 319+ (February 20, 1935):338.

[10] *Oxford DNB*. See especially Joad's "Charter for Rationalists" in *The Book of Joad*, 68.

[11] Joad, *The Testament of Joad*, 46.

[12] Joad, *The Testament of Joad*, 108, 112.

[13] Joad married Mary White in 1915 and left her in 1921. During a portion of that time, he lived away from home avoiding conscription.

sentimentality invested her."[14] After leaving his wife, he moved to Hampstead with Marjorie Thomson, a student teacher, the first of many mistresses. Some years later, while reflecting on his early life, Joad made no attempt to conceal his serial promiscuity: "I have liked women too much to pay them the poor compliment of cold shouldering all for the sake of one."[15] In 1925 he was expelled from the Fabian Society for sexual misbehavior during the society's summer school. So unconventional was Joad's behavior that even a free-thinker and fellow-philanderer like Leonard Woolf could condemn him as "high-minded, loose-living, loose-thinking … a selfish, quick-witted, amusing intellectual scallywag."[16] A repentant Joad was permitted to rejoin the Fabian Society in 1943.

Joad and Lewis shared a number of interests and, perhaps, these paved the way for the opening of their occasional relationship. Joad enjoyed walking the countryside. He read with pleasure the works of George Eliot, Mrs. Gaskell, Jane Austen, Thomas Hardy, and Anthony Trollope. He lamented the fact that the composition of good poetry was a dying art.[17] Philosophy was his life and his first love, and he liked to "rub [his] brains against those of [his] fellows in argument and discussion."[18] He did not share Lewis's humility, however, as he described himself: "In the world of ideas … I feel at home; I take to them so readily, I am so quickly and so easily their master that I can be at play with them."[19]

After taking his degree from Oxford, Joad worked as a civil servant at the Board of Trade.[20] In 1930, he left the civil service to become Head of the Philosophy Department at Birkbeck College, London.[21] He was a gifted teacher and writer; he raised considerably the public profile of philosophy, making it accessible to a wide range of the reading public. In 1936, he received a D.Litt.; in 1945, he was promoted to Reader in the department. In spite of his personal

---

[14] Joad, *The Book of Joad*, 35.

[15] Joad, *The Testament of Joad*, 20-21.

[16] Leonard Woolf, *Downhill All the Way: An Autobiography of the Years 1919-1939*, London, 1967, 81, cited in Martin Ceadel, "The 'King and Country' Debate, 1933: Student Politics, Pacifism and the Dictators," in *The Historical Journal*, 1979, 401.

[17] Joad, *The Testament of Joad*, 160.

[18] Joad, *The Testament of Joad*, 133.

[19] Joad, *The Testament of Joad*, 135.

[20] www.spartacus.schoolnet.co.uk/Jjoad.htm. See also Joad, *Book*, 45.

[21] *Oxford DNB*.

behavior, he believed that ethics and aesthetics were objective,[22] a trait that inclined him towards the Natural Law that Lewis articulated. He also felt that existentialism and logical positivism were leading the country to an unhealthy relativism.[23] For Joad, the ultimate values were goodness, truth, and beauty.[24]

While a student at Oxford, Joad had been active in the debates at Oxford Union Society,[25] so he was capable of returning to the same venue years later. In February 1933, he participated in the most famous debate in the history of the Union, which discussed the motion: "That this House will in no circumstances fight for its King and Country." At the time, many in Oxford and England were growing uneasy over the prospects of another European war. Adolph Hitler had recently been elected Chancellor of Germany. The Weimar Republic, Germany's brief experiment in democracy, had proved a dismal failure. Emotions were running high, and not just at the university. Joad was the principal speaker in favor of the motion, and was opposed by Quintin Hogg, the future Lord Hailsham and Chancellor of the Exchequer. The motion passed by a vote of 275 to 153, with many (including Winston Churchill) believing at the time of its passage that it did irreparable damage to prospects of averting another war with Germany. Joad's speech was described as "well-organized and well-received," and may have tipped the balance in favor of the motion.[26] While he was quick to return to London, others were left with the task of repairing the Union's tattered reputation. Churchill now refused to participate in debates at the Union until it acquired "a sense of responsibility," and others were similarly upset. As tensions in Europe increased, however,

---

[22] For example, Joad wrote, "...many people still subscribe to the subjectivist fallacy of supposing that the merit of a work of art depends upon its effects." Joad, *The Book of Joad*, 167.

[23] See Joad, *A Critique of Logical Positivism*, University of Chicago Press, 1950, originally published in England by Jarrold and Sons, Limited, Norwich.

[24] Joad, *God and Evil*, 229.

[25] The Oxford Union Society is a debating society in Oxford, England, founded in 1823, whose membership is drawn primarily from the University of Oxford.

[26] Ceadel, "The 'King and Country' Debate," 404. Joad later wrote articles about the debate, as did the creator of Winnie-the-Pooh, A. A. Milne. Joad's articles appeared in the *Daily Herald* on Feb. 20, 1933, and the *Sunday Referee*, March 5, 1933. They were reprinted in the pamphlet *The fight—for peace* and in *The Oxford resolution*, respectively. He also wrote an article for the *Sunday Dispatch* on Feb. 19, 1933. See Ceadel, 408, n. 43.

attitudes at Oxford began to change. Pacifism was becoming less fashionable. In 1938, less than a year before the outbreak of hostilities with Germany, the Union debated a very different motion, "That war between nations can sometimes be justified." Despite Joad's opposition, the motion carried by a vote of 176 to 145.[27]

Joad believed that the First World War was due, in part, to the use of jargon by the government and the popular press, which cajoled young people into fighting for their country. We fight wars, he wrote, "because we mistake words and phrases for realities."[28] The "King and Country" debate was thus essentially about patriotism and duty. Those who supported its passage objected to the jingoism and false patriotism of the popular press of 1914, the persecution of conscientious objectors, and the suggestion that it was a privilege to die for one's country.[29] When war in Europe broke out in 1914, the government made extensive use of the expression, "Your King and Country Need You," words that appeared daily in *The Times* beginning on August 5. Lord Kitchener used the same language in a full-page appeal six days later, urging 100,000 men to sign up for the duration of the war.[30] Many people felt duped by the language. Some even described the war as a spiritual conflict, while others glamorized the fighting and created a false sense of optimism.[31]

Like many intellectuals of the day, Joad's pacifism did not endure the harsh realities of the Second World War. The horrors of Nazi death camps challenged his commitment to agnosticism, while the election of a Labour government in 1945 under Clement Atlee diminished his enthusiasm for socialism.[32] Various events eventually led Joad to return to Christianity shortly before his death, a momentous change described in his book, *The Recovery of Belief: A Restatement of Christian Philosophy*. There were a number of preludes to this, however. Joad wrote of Beethoven's compositions in transcendent terms, for example, describing the last four sonatas, the ninth symphony, and the posthumous quartets as conveying

---

[27] Ceadel, "The 'King and Country' Debate," 419.

[28] Joad, *The Testament of Joad*, 193.

[29] J. M. Winter, "Oxford and the First World War," Chapter 1 in *The History of the University of Oxford*, 8 vols. Vol. VIII: The Twentieth Century (Oxford, 1994), 24–5.

[30] This was published on August 11, 1914. Ceadel, "The 'King and Country' Debate," 418, n. 77.

[31] Doris Myers, *C. S. Lewis in Context* (Kent, Ohio, 1994), 2, 27.

[32] *Oxford DNB*; Joad, *God and Evil*, 15.

unearthly tranquility which to my mind can only receive adequate interpretation on mystical lines. There is another world, it seems, static, permanent and perfect, in a sense in which ours is fluctuating, transitory and faulty, of which we may catch fleeting intimations in this last-period music.[33]

Around the same time, he wrote in a similar fashion about the nature of art. "That all great art has this power of suggesting a world beyond is undeniable."[34] He might better have written about longings, expressed in music, art, and nature, that demonstrated a human desire for God, a God he did not yet believe in. Here, he would have paralleled Lewis's desire, or *Sehnsucht*, or Joy, which eventually led to the latter's conversion.[35] But Joad remained an agnostic, unconvinced by the aesthetical qualities of music and art. As he wrote, such longings, however transcendent in quality, did not "mean that the universe is good, that life has a purpose, that God is in heaven."[36]

During the Second World War, Joad was asked to become one of the initial panelists for a new BBC radio program, the *Brains Trust*, to be launched on January 1, 1941. Listeners submitted questions on a wide range of topics. The questions selected to be read out on a given program were chosen in order to spark off debate and discussion by the three panelists. *Brains Trust* proved enormously successful. His favorite expression, "It depends on what you mean by…," spoken with his usual careful distinction between words, became widely known, and frequently repeated.[37] Julian Huxley (biologist) and Commander A. B. Campbell (retired naval officer), appeared alongside Joad on the initial programs.[38] Over time other panelists were added, including Noel Annan (writer), A. J. Ayer (philosopher), Isaiah Berlin (philosopher and historian), Sir Malcolm Sargent (conductor and composer), Robert Boothby, M.P.,[39] Malcolm Muggeridge, and Barbara Ward (economist).

---

[33] Joad, *The Book of Joad*, 164. Joad said much the same of Bach on the same page, even stating that a part of Bach "quite obviously lived in heaven."

[34] Joad, *The Book of Joad*, 218.

[35] See C. S. Lewis, *Surprised by Joy: The Shape of My Early Life* (San Diego, 1955), 7, 16, 72, 155, 166, 169, 175, 177, 203, and especially 217.

[36] He wrote these words in 1932. Joad, *The Book of Joad*, 218f.

[37] See www.spartacus.schoolnet.co.uk/Jjoad.htm.

[38] *Oxford DNB*.

[39] See https://www.bbc.com/historyofthebbc/anniversaries/january/the-brains-trust

Twenty-One Friendships of C.S. Lewis

Extracts from a program aired on December 31, 1945 provide a flavor of the discussion and Joad's contribution to it. The Question Master was Donald McCullough, and the panelists included (in addition to Joad, Huxley, and Ward) Mrs. H. A. Hamilton and Prof. J. M. Mackintosh.[40] To the question, "Should there be international control over discoveries affecting methods of warfare?," Joad replied that international control was the only alternative to destruction, though it was impractical; he then forecast various scientific discoveries, including atomic warfare. The only feasible solution—international government—seemed to him an impossible achievement. Huxley argued that control would check both scientific discovery and the wrongful use of discoveries. Mackintosh agreed with Joad that international control would not be practical and that anti-war publicity was the only answer. Joad was then permitted to give a "short parable" about the last survivors of the human race.[41]

After having boasted in print that "I cheat the railway company whenever I can,"[42] Joad was caught traveling on a Waterloo-Exeter train in April 1948 without a ticket. He was later convicted of the offence and fined £2.[43] News of his conviction was featured on the front pages of the newspapers. As a result, he was dropped from *The Brains Trust*; moreover, despite his enormous popularity as a philosopher and radio celebrity (he was a frequent after-dinner speaker, he was asked to open bazaars, and he even lent his name to popular advertisements), his chances of gaining a hoped-for peerage vanished.

The humiliation of his arrest and conviction brought on both depression and ill health. During this unsettled period, he published *The Recovery of Belief*. He died of cancer at the age of 61 at his home in Hampstead on April 9, 1953. Among his more than seventy-five books were *Modern Philosophy* (1924), *Matter, Life and Value* (the book that provided an academic foundation for creative evolution, 1929), *The Present and Future of Religion* (a work critical of the religious view, 1930), *The Book of Joad* (subtitled "a belligerent autobiography," 1932), *Guide to Modern Thought* (1933), *Guide to Philosophy* (1936), *The Testament of Joad* (1937), *God and Evil* (1942), *Teach Yourself Philosophy* (1944), *The English Counties* (1948), and *The Recovery of Belief* (1951),

---

[40] Professor of Public Health at the University of London.

[41] http://www.spokenword.ac.uk/record_view.php?pbd=gcu-a0a0d7-b.

[42] Joad, *The Testament of Joad*, 54.

[43] http://www.spartacus.schoolnet.co.uk/Jjoad.htm

his last publication. His *Guide to Modern Thought* and *Guide to Philosophy* contributed to him becoming a national figure. The popularity of his writing suggests both their value and, in the main, the trustworthiness of his insights. As his final book makes clear, his return to faith did not require the abandonment of his considerable intelligence.

JOAD AND LEWIS

In spite of some significant differences, Lewis and Joad held many things in common.[44] Joad came to share Lewis's belief in the free will defense as made in *Mere Christianity*, that the creation of beings who could do no wrong would be the creation of robots rather than human beings capable of choice.[45] In emphasizing free will, both men rejected determinism. Joad and Lewis also held reason in high regard. When, for instance, the devilish Screwtape wrote to Wormwood about the temptation of his patient, he advocated strategies that were aimed at preventing the patient from engaging in rational argument.[46]

Joad's views about psychology reflected Lewis's critique of Naturalism: "If the conclusions of this psychology are correct, there is no reason to think them true."[47] That is, if behaviorist psychology is true and behavior merely follows the laws of physics and does not reflect free will or a capable reason, then even the positions held by behaviorists about human behavior are determined by the laws of physics and we can have no assurance of their validity. Almost a decade before Lewis, Joad criticized the practice Lewis came to call "Bulverism;"[48] that is, he expressed dismay that objective truth is not what concerns people most, but "the reasons which lead people to formulate their particular brands of error."[49] Similarly, in 1941, Lewis complained:

> ... you must show *that* a man is wrong before you start explaining *why* he is wrong. The modern method is to assume without discussion *that* he is wrong and then distract his

---

[44] See Joad, *The Testament of Joad*, 170.

[45] See Joad, *The Recovery of Belief*, 221.

[46] C. S. Lewis, *The Screwtape Letters* (New York, 1996), 2. See Letter I, paragraph two, in several other places in the letters, and elsewhere in the writings of Lewis; on Joad, see above on the elevation of reason about Christianity. *The Book of Joad*, 15f.

[47] Joad, *The Book of Joad*, 99.

[48] See C. S. Lewis, "'Bulverism' or, The Foundation of 20th Century Thought," in C. S. Lewis, *God in the Dock*, ed. by Walter Hooper (Grand Rapids, 1970), 273.

[49] Joad, *The Book of Joad*, 103.

attention from this (the only real issue) by busily explaining how he became so silly. In the course of the last fifteen years I have found this vice so common that I have had to invent a name for it. I call it Bulverism. Someday I am going to write the biography of its imaginary inventor, Ezekiel Bulver ... "Assume that your opponent is wrong, and then explain his error, and the world will be at your feet. Attempt to prove that he is wrong or (worse still) try to find out whether he is wrong or right, and the national dynamism of our age will thrust you to the wall."[50]

Both men also thought a great deal about the precise meanings of words, as we find expressed repeatedly in both their written work and their verbal comments.

Joad and Lewis also expressed similar admiration for the physicist Sir Arthur Eddington, whose observations of a solar eclipse had confirmed Einstein's theory of relativity. Joad wrote, "There is a celebrated passage in Eddington's writing in which he describes how the physicist, when he wishes to establish contact with his world, is required to divest himself one by one of his sense-organs."[51] Here, he was probably referring to Eddington's *Science and the Unseen World*, in which Eddington stated that science could not discover the meaning of the world and that such meaning must be sought in spiritual reality. Since Eddington, a devout Quaker, believed there was more to the physical world than meets the eye, he concluded that physics does not deal with the actuality of real things, but only with "a set of abstracted appearances and the relations between them."[52] For Eddington, "Mind is the first and most direct thing in our experience; all else is remote inference."[53] Eddington also understood the limitations of science and natural law: "Dismiss the idea that natural law can swallow up religion; it cannot even tackle the multiplication table single-handed."[54] Lewis, who had read Eddington's *The Nature of the Physical World*, cited Eddington in favorable terms on more than a dozen occasions.[55]

---

[50] C. S. Lewis, "Bulverism," in *God in the Dock* (Grand Rapids, 1970), 273.

[51] Joad, *The Recovery of Belief*, 116.

[52] Joad, *The Recovery of Belief*, 124.

[53] Eddington, cited in Joad, *The Recovery of Belief*, 125.

[54] Eddington, cited in Joad, *The Recovery of Belief*, 144.

[55] See especially C. S. Lewis, *Mere Christianity* (New York, 2001), 55, and *Miracles: A Preliminary Study* (New York, 1996), 138, 199.

Joad's return to Christianity prompted personal reflection on his own moral shortcomings. On the Golden Rule, for example, he wrote: "...the adoption of the Christian view of the world ... has complicated the problem of conduct...."[56] One of those complications is the fact that "I do not do unto others as I would be done by." Forgiveness thus becomes a necessity. Here, again, Joad's views agreed with those of Lewis, as we can see in Lewis's formulation of the Golden Rule.[57]

Joad could not easily identify the influences that led to the development of his views and opinions. No doubt, the sources were many and various, but at least some credit—especially in terms of Joad's eventual return to the Christian faith—must be ascribed to at least two of Lewis's books, *The Problem of Pain* (1940) and *The Abolition of Man* (1943). Joad gave major credit to Lewis's book, *The Abolition of Man*, for the change in his thinking that led to his conversion.[58] Joad must have found Lewis a formidable intellectual sparring partner; no doubt, Lewis held a similar view of Joad. Curiously, in all of Lewis's voluminous correspondence, there is no evidence of any written exchange between the two men; even as Joad moved closer to Christianity, it appears that their relationship remained professional and distant.[59] This perhaps seems strange, especially given their mutual interests and similarities, six of which seem particularly obvious.

First, both men were brought up in the Church of England, and both resolutely rejected Christianity during adolescence.[60] Both also returned to the faith during adulthood, but only after first passing through a theistic phase. Additionally, both proved to be reluctant converts.[61] *Second*, for both men a longing for something else, something beyond themselves and their own immediate experiences, influenced their conversion. Joad once wrote about a different world in

---

[56] Joad, *The Recovery of Belief* 15.

[57] Joad, *The Recovery of Belief*, 16. Lewis said, "Do as you would be done by." C. S. Lewis, *The Abolition of Man or Reflections on education with special reference to the teaching of English in the upper forms of schools*. (New York, 1996), 52 and 57.

[58] Joad, *The Recovery of Belief*, 81.

[59] Although compare Tolkien's comments on the wide-ranging discussion with Joad in Lewis's rooms at Magdalen on Tuesday, October 26, 1943, in J. R. R. Tolkien, *The Letters of J. R. R. Tolkien*, ed. by Humphrey Carpenter (Boston, 2000), 63.

[60] "I had been brought up in the Church. All my childhood I had regularly attended, once every Sunday morning, the country church of a Midland village." Joad, *The Testament of Joad*, 209.

[61] Joad, *The Recovery of Belief*, 21; *Joy*, 228f.

language reminiscent of Lewis's moving descriptions of Northernness and "shadowlands": "One never quite got to this world; but the sense of its nearness..." was like one "sitting chained under the shadow of a hill on the other side of which was a great light....he knew for a certainty that the lighted place was there," but he could not see it directly.[62] *Third*, both men became popular radio personalities over the BBC during the 1940s, even beginning their radio "careers" in the same year—Joad with *Brains Trust* and Lewis with *Broadcast Talks*, which were later incorporated into *Mere Christianity*. *Fourth*, the two men valued friendship highly. Joad described friendship as that which "springs up between those whose interests and enthusiasms are centered upon something else,"[63] while Lewis described it as "Friends, side by side, absorbed in some common interest."[64] *Fifth*, both enjoyed intellectual argument. In a manner reminiscent of Lewis, Joad lamented the nature of modern Western man, who "still conceives of himself as the center of the universe; often, indeed, he behaves as if the only function of the universe is to put him in its center."[65]

Finally, in his essays "Religion and Rocketry" (1958) and "The Seeing Eye" (1963), Lewis referred critically to the views of the Cambridge astronomer, Professor Fred B. Hoyle (1915-2001). Hoyle was a naturalist who claimed to be unable to conceive of immortality, except as a mind animated by some sort of a body.[66] In "The Seeing Eye," Lewis took issue with Hoyle's claims. Hoyle had argued that life must have originated in many times and places, given the vast size of the universe.[67] Lewis countered by arguing that the enlargement of the universe did not reduce the importance of mankind or lead to the elimination of a Creator. Lewis thought it unlikely that life existed anywhere else in our solar system, but that it was at least possible elsewhere in the galaxy. Moreover, "those who do not find Him on earth are unlikely to find Him in space."[68] Thus, science is

---

[62] Joad, *The Testament of Joad*, 215.

[63] Joad, *The Book of Joad*, 17.

[64] C. S. Lewis, *The Four Loves*, (New York, 1988), 61.

[65] Joad, *The Testament of Joad*, 228.

[66] Hoyle cited in Joad, *The Recovery of Belief*, 188.

[67] Lewis was referring to a series of broadcast talks that Hoyle had given during the summer of 1950 and published as *The Nature of the Universe*, where he argued in favor of the steady state theory, and against a Christian view of cosmic origins and the uniqueness of the Christian faith.

[68] C. S. Lewis, "The Seeing Eye," in *Christian Reflections*. (Grand

not equipped to do theology and evaluate arguments for the existence of God; nor would the discovery of life in other parts of the universe have any adverse effect upon Christianity. Joad had previously made a similar claim. He argued that the size of the universe, or the span of time in which it formed, had no "*necessary* bearing upon our views as to the nature of the universe as a whole, more particularly as regards its origin, purpose, destiny and end."[69] Moreover, the enlargement of the scale of the universe did not reduce the importance of mankind.[70] In fact, "vastness and majesty are, surely, precisely what we should expect to find as characteristics of God's creation."[71] Lewis made a similar argument in his essay, "Religion and Rocketry":

> Each new discovery, even every new theory, is held at first to have the most wide-reaching theological and philosophical consequences. It is seized by unbelievers as the basis for a new attack on Christianity; it is often, and more embarrassingly, seized by injudicious believers as the basis for a new defense.
>
> But usually, when the popular hubbub has subsided and the novelty has been chewed over by real theologians, real scientists and real philosophers, both sides find themselves pretty much where they were before.[72]

However, Lewis and Joad also failed to see eye-to-eye on numerous points, a quality that Lewis (and perhaps Joad) greatly appreciated in a number of his many friendships. They differed, for example, in their opinions of certain writers, including David Hume, Edward Gibbon, William Makepeace Thackeray, William Wordsworth, Samuel Taylor Coleridge, and Dr. Johnson. Lewis loved poetry; Joad less so, even admitting on one occasion, "I have little use for poetry."[73] Lewis saw much value in Romance, while Joad, the rationalist, did not. Lewis loved the music of Wagner, while Joad did not. Agreement on a few issues does not require agreement on every issue.

Rapids, 1967), 171.

[69] Joad, *The Recovery of Belief*, 32, 109.

[70] Joad, *The Recovery of Belief*, 33.

[71] Joad, *The Recovery of Belief*, 110.

[72] C. S. Lewis, "Religion and Rocketry." *Fern-Seed and Elephants and other essays on Christianity* (Glasgow, 1975), 86f.

[73] Joad, *The Book of Joad*, 77.

The Reconversion of Joad

Joad's return to Christianity was not a sudden affair, brought on exclusively by the humiliation of his arrest and subsequent dismissal from the BBC. As we have seen, he was, for a time, highly antagonistic to Christianity, even rejoicing in his prediction that the clergy would be extinct by 1960.[74] So, what lay behind Joad's conversion? Details are sketchy, but a number of steps in his spiritual development surface. One arose as a consequence of the evil connected with the Second World War, as documented by an exchange between Joad and Lewis in *The Spectator*. Joad's article, "Evil and God," appeared on January 31, 1941, and Lewis's article (with the same title) appeared a week later.[75] By this stage in his spiritual development, Joad had come to question many of his previous opinions. Both mechanism and Henri Bergson's notion of emergent evolution were now to be set aside. In their place, Joad advocated either a form of monotheism or a form of dualism. Lewis concurred with Joad's rejection of mechanism, which, "like all materialist systems, breaks down at the problem of knowledge."[76] Likewise, the two were on the same page in rejecting emergent evolution, Lewis writing:

> If things can improve, this means that there must be some absolute standard of good above and outside the cosmic process to which that process can approximate. There is no sense in talking of 'becoming better' if better means simply 'what we are becoming'—it is like congratulating yourself on reaching your destination and defining destination as 'the place you have reached'. Mellontolatry, or the worship the future, is a *fuddled* religion.[77]

Lewis was less sympathetic toward Joad's consideration of dualism, or "two equal, uncreated, antagonistic Powers, one good and the other bad."[78] Anticipating some of the arguments he would include in his second series of BBC *Broadcast Talks*, Lewis argued that the difficulty with dualism is twofold: one metaphysical, the other moral. The metaphysical problem is that the two Powers, good

---

[74] *Oxford DNB*.

[75] Cyril Joad, "Evil and God," in *The Spectator* (31 January 1941),112–13, reprinted in *God and the Dock* (Grand Rapids: 1970), 161-66. C. S. Lewis, "Evil and God," in *God in the Dock* (Grand Rapids: 1970), 21–4. The exact date of Lewis's article is February 7, 1941.

[76] Lewis, "Evil and God," 21.

[77] Lewis, "Evil and God," 21.

[78] Lewis, "Evil and God," 22.

and evil, do not explain each other; thus neither can claim to be the Ultimate. How do they exist? Where do they come from? Why are they together? Dualism is thus "a truncated metaphysic."[79] In regard to the other, Lewis wrote:

> The moral difficulty is that Dualism gives evil a positive, substantive, self-consistent nature, like that of good. If this were true, if Ahriman existed in his own right no less than Ormuzd, what could we mean by calling Ormuzd good except that we happened to prefer *him*. In what sense can the one party be said to be right and the other wrong? If evil has the same kind of reality as good, the same autonomy and completeness, our allegiance to good becomes the arbitrarily chosen loyalty of a partisan.[80]

Just days before Joad's review of *The Screwtape Letters* appeared in *New Statesman and Nation*, the *Brains Trust* met.[81] Donald McCullough served as Master of Ceremonies, or Question Master, while Julian Huxley, A. B. Campbell, Mary Hamilton, and both Joad and Lewis joined in. Together, the panel answered questions from listeners, such as "What would be *The Brains Trust*'s conception of a man in his last stages of evolution in mind and body?" "Does *The Brains Trust* consider that religious teaching should be included in the school curriculum?" and "How can I find out for myself whether or not there is a God?" In answer to this last question, Lewis recommended books by Berkeley, Jeans, Eddington, and Chesterton. Joad commented that he had been going through the same struggle—trying to determine whether or not there is a God—and had read Friedrich von Hügel's *Essays and Addresses in the Philosophy of Religion* and Edwyn Bevan's *Christianity*, authors and books Lewis read and may well have recommended to Joad.[82] Joad's review demonstrates an awakening of Joad's conscience when he writes, "One may suspect that one's resentment at the censoriousness of the Letters is due to the fact that they touch off known failings of one's own. One is, after all, a miserable sinner, and it is inevitable that many of Mr. Lewis's shots should, however obliquely, strike home."[83]

---

[79] Lewis, "Evil and God," 22.

[80] Lewis, "Evil and God," 22-23.

[81] On May 7, 1942.

[82] Bruce R. Johnson, "C. S. Lewis and the BBC's *Brains Trust*: A Study in Resiliency," *VII*, Volume 30 (2013):67, 68, 69f., 71.

[83] C. E. M. Joad, "Mr. Lewis's Devil," Review of C. S. Lewis, *The Screwtape Letters*, *New Statesman and Nation*, Vol. 23 (May 16, 1942):324.

Charles Williams' review of Joad's book, *God and Evil*, indicates further that Joad's conscience had by this time been awakened. Williams writes, "But part of the evidence in this matter of Almighty God is 'a sense of sin,' and it is the rise of this in him which (if I understand him right) has stirred Dr. Joad to a reexamination of all the evidence and to a different conclusion from that which (without the sense of sin) he originally held."[84]

Another step in Joad's spiritual transformation can be traced to his encounter with Lewis in January 1944, where the motion, "On Being Reviewed by Christians," was debated at the Oxford Socratic Club. More than two hundred and fifty students, the largest number ever to attend a Socratic Club meeting, crowded into a room at Lady Margaret Hall.[85] Joad's name recognition was high, because of the 1933 debate at the Oxford Union Society, the *Brains Trust*, his books, his position at Birkbeck College, and his various controversial viewpoints.

At the Socratic, Joad presented a defense of his book, *God and Evil* (1942), a book that mentioned Lewis by name fifty-three times. He revealed that previously, he had contracted with himself not to think about religion for the next thirty years, but that time had now passed. His book discussed the arguments in favor of theism, while the final chapter spelled out his reasons for rejecting Christianity. Following the claims in his book, it appears that Joad asserted that the balance of the logical argument seemed to be against the view that an omnipotent, benevolent God created the universe, although data from aesthetic and moral experience suggested a level of reality beyond pure logic. Mystics seemed to make direct contact with this level of reality. After rejecting subjectivism, creative evolution, emergent evolution, and impersonal consciousness, Joad offered a tentative conclusion that pointed toward the religious view, concluding that man's desire to accept the religious, but not Christian, hypothesis was evidence itself in favor of the hypothesis.

Joad then stated that he considered the reviews of his book—whether written by atheists or Christians—to have been disgraceful.[86] Given the intellectual and debating skills of both Joad and Lewis,

---

[84] Charles Williams, "Dr. Joad and Sin," *Time and Tide* 24 (March 13, 1943):211.

[85] Roger Green and Walter Hooper, *C. S. Lewis: A Biography*, 2d edition (San Diego, 1994), 216.

[86] Minutes of the Oxford Socratic Club, 24 January 1944, reported in an email from Christopher Mitchell on 11 February 2008.

the evening must have been lively and stimulating. The novelist John Wain later described the atmosphere as "positively gladiatorial."[87] The minutes record only a single comment: "Mr. Lewis opened the discussion. He agreed with Dr. Joad that the standard of reviewing today was disgraceful, and that the Christian's refusal to take agnosticism seriously was perturbing. Dr. Joad had, however, not admitted the possibility that the Christian hypothesis might be true."[88] Joad apparently presented arguments against Christianity, while Lewis took the opposite side of the debate. Walter Hooper mentions the warmth of the debate (influenced perhaps by the temperature of the crowded room), despite the freezing temperatures outside. Both men were so energetic in advancing their views that, at the end, they were "dripping with perspiration." Joad wanted to remove his jacket and Lewis was invited to follow suit but declined, informing the moderator that he couldn't because of a large hole in his shirt.[89]

Additional details of the debate appear in a paper entitled "The Churches," which Joad had presented at a symposium some months prior to the Socratic Club debate. Here he expressed dismay over the nature of the reviews of *God and Evil*.[90] He objected equally to rationalists, who deplored his favorable view of theism, and to Christians, who deplored his rejection of Christianity. Those produced by Christians, he complained, were patronizing. As one Christian reviewer wrote, "Mr. Joad travels well-worn ground without perhaps much originality." Of the evidence for the existence of God, another claimed that Joad had come to the obvious conclusion that God did, in fact, exist.[91] Other Christians offered condolence: "It is unlikely that this is Mr. Joad's last word. So honest a searcher after truth who has already traveled so far is bound to travel further." "The pilgrim is half way home." "When honest searchers after truth" have gone this far, "it is best to leave them to their own journeying and not to press them indiscreetly."[92] The Jesuit priest and historian, James Brodrick, provocatively dismissed Joad's arguments as evidence that he had been

---

[87] John Wain, *Sprightly Running* (New York: 1963), 141.

[88] Unprocessed Stella Aldwinckle Archive, "Socratic Minutes," The Marion E. Wade Center, Wheaton College, Wheaton Illinois, 24 January 1944.

[89] Hooper, "Oxford's Bonny Fighters," 145.

[90] Cyril Joad, "The Churches—Diagnosis and Recipe." *In Search of Faith: A Symposium* (London, 1943).

[91] Joad, "The Churches," 61.

[92] Joad, "The Churches," 62.

"educated on Tit-bits[93] and/or the *Reader's Digest*," implying that only practicing Christians were qualified to offer coherent arguments on the claims and counter-claims of Christianity. This drew a heated counterattack from Joad. Referring to Brodrick, he wrote:

> ... his anger is only one more proof of the inability of a Christian to put himself into the shoes of an enquirer who is not yet convinced of the truth of Christianity, the consequence being that, lacking charity and supplying its place with presumption, he proceeds to denounce the enquirer for his lack of conviction.[94]

Some reviewers questioned Joad's claim that most churches were nearly empty, while others questioned his judgment for suggesting that Christians had been crueler toward others than the members of any creed or cause. Joad also drew criticism for taking issue with the exclusive claims found in the Athanasian Creed: "which faith except everyone do keep whole and undefiled: without doubt he shall perish everlastingly."[95] Still others complained that Joad had not read carefully, or widely enough, in Christian texts, or that he failed to understand the history or the Gospels set in their historical context.[96]

Taking the offensive in his paper, Joad asked a series of challenging questions. Why had his reviewers failed to ask him to read both sides? Why had the churches failed to live up to the faith which they claim to believe? Why do the churches claim an exclusive corner on the truth? Why did his critics belittle reason?[97] He then offered his own advice to the clergy, suggesting that they avoid the subjects of geography and the history of man, and avoid speaking in unnatural voices.[98] A portion of Joad's paper likely found its way into his talk before the Socratic Club.

The American literary scholar Clyde Kilby (founder of and first curator at the Wade Center in Wheaton, Illinois) met Lewis for the first time in 1953. He later described the substance of their initial conversation:

---

[93] *Tit-bits* was the name of a weekly magazine founded in 1881 by George Newnes. Its full title was Tit-*Bits from all the interesting Books, Periodicals, and Newspapers of the World.*

[94] Joad, "The Churches," 63.

[95] Joad, "The Churches," 63, 65. This is the so-called *Quicunque vult.* See, for example, https://st-takla.org/books/en/ecf/007/0070399.html

[96] Joad, "The Churches," 67.

[97] Joad, "The Churches," 68–71.

[98] Joad, "The Churches," 76.

No Ordinary People

We talked of C. E. M. Joad, Professor of Philosophy at the University of London who had died a few weeks earlier. Lewis said he and Joad had talked on two different occasions until far into the night and that in light of these experiences he had changed his mind about him. He had found him sincere—vain but unconscious of his vanity and fundamentally honest in his thinking. He had respect, he said, for Joad's turn to Christianity and was sure he was no charlatan.[99]

The evening following the Socratic Club debate very likely served as one of those occasions, since it was not uncommon for Lewis to arrange for a guest room at Magdalen for those traveling from outside Oxford. Lewis greatly enjoyed conversation and heated debate, even with those with whom he disagreed, and these lengthy talks between himself and Joad—combined with Lewis's considerable conviviality—may have played a further role in Joad's gradual return to the Christian faith.

By the time of Joad's appearance before the Socratic Club, he may have already progressed considerably toward his return to Christianity. The fifty-three references to Lewis in *God and Evil* indicate the considerable extent of Lewis's influence on his thinking. Although the precise date of Joad's return to faith is not known, it must have occurred between his appearance before the Socratic Club in 1944 and his writing of *The Recovery of Belief* in 1950-1951. Did his arrest and conviction in 1948 play a role in this? Perhaps his recognition of the need for forgiveness was connected to his return to Christianity. The Law must do its work before one sees the need for the Gospel.

Six years after their debate before the Socratic Club, Joad and Lewis engaged in a written exchange, with both statements appearing in the same edition of the British periodical *The Month* and reprinted, four months later, in *The Atlantic Monthly*.[100] Although he had once believed that there was "no fundamental and incurable wickedness in human beings"[101] and that "calamity and suffering have no purpose

---

[99] Clyde S. Kilby, "The Creative Logician Speaking" in *C. S. Lewis: Speaker and Teacher*, ed. by Carolyn Keefe (Grand Rapids, 1971), 16.

[100] C. E. M. Joad, "The Pain of Animals: A Problem in Theology," *God in the Dock* (Grand Rapids: 1970), 161–66, and C. S. Lewis, "The Reply," 166–71.

[101] Joad, *The Testament of Joad*, 13. See also Joad, *The Book of Joad*, 88, where he wrote, "It is not because men are bad at heart, but because they are weak in the head that they so harry and torment one another and make their world a hell." The book was published in 1937.

whatever,"[102] he later came to regard Shaw's expression of human evil as "intolerably shallow."[103] With the conviction, drawn from his observation of the Second World War, that mankind is evil, came the conviction that evil resided also in himself.[104] That eventually led to the conclusion that taking the facts of moral experience seriously required a supernatural view of life.[105] Moreover, Joad began to notice that others possessed a quality that he lacked.[106] As he put it, "I would like to cultivate virtue and to be a better man, but I simply do not know how to do it."[107] But none of this came quickly, or easily. As Joad later wrote, "I was for years baffled by the problem of pain and evil; in fact, it was this problem that for years denied belief in the Christian religion."[108] Of course, Joad's reference to "the problem of pain" echoes the title of Lewis's book and further suggests Lewis's strong influence on Joad's thinking.

Early in the essay, Joad provides clear evidence that he had, by now, returned to some form of belief in theism, if not Christianity itself, including the doctrine of original sin:

> I have come to accept the Christian view of pain as not incompatible with the Christian concept of the Creator and of the world that He has made. That view I take to be briefly as follows: It was of no interest to God to create a species consisting of virtuous automata, for the 'virtue' of automata who can do no other than they do is a courtesy title only; it is analogous to the 'virtue' of the stone that rolls downhill or of the water that freezes at 32°. To what end, it may be asked, should God create such creatures? That He might be praised by them? But automatic praise is a mere succession of noises. That He might love them? But they are essentially unlovable; you cannot love puppets. And so God gave man free will that he might increase in virtue by his own efforts and become, as a free moral being, a worthy object of God's love. Freedom entails freedom to go wrong: man did, in fact, go wrong, misusing God's gift and doing evil. Pain is a by-product of evil; and so pain came into the world as a result of

---

[102] Joad, *The Testament of Joad*, 68.

[103] Joad, *The Recovery of Belief*, 63.

[104] Joad, *The Recovery of Belief*, 64, 76. He does not tie this conviction to any event or series of events.

[105] Joad, *The Recovery of Belief*, 78.

[106] Joad, *The Testament of Joad*, 89.

[107] Joad, *The Testament of Joad*, 102.

[108] Joad, *The Recovery of Belief*, 23.

man's misuse of God's gift of free will.[109]

Joad accepted the existence of evil, and its cause in man's abuse of free will. His problem now lay elsewhere, specifically with the difficulty of animal pain. Nothing in Lewis's extensive treatment of the subject in *The Problem of Pain* had solved this problem. In fact, Joad challenged Lewis's suggestion that animals have sentience but not consciousness, that domestic animals may achieve immortality "as members of a corporate society of which the head is man,"[110] and that Satan might have tempted monkeys. He went on to argue that animals appear to remember pain, as evidenced by their cringing at the sight of a whip by which it had previously been beaten, suggesting both sentience *and* consciousness. He concluded by stating:

> ... either animals have souls or they have no souls. If they have none, pain is felt for which there can be no moral responsibility, and for which no misuse of God's gift of moral freedom can be invoked as an excuse. If they have souls, we can give no plausible account (a) of their immortality—how draw the line between animals with souls and men with souls?—or (b) of their moral corruption, which would enable Christian apologists to place them in respect of their pain under the same heading of explanation as that which is proposed and which I am prepared to accept for man?[111]

Lewis's rather tentative reply supplied little beyond the already unsatisfactory answers found in the ninth chapter of *The Problem of Pain*. As he reminded readers, these earlier answers had been "confessedly speculative," and he reiterated that God has provided us with very little information about animal pain:

> We know neither what they are nor why they are. All we can say for certain is that if God is good (and I think we have certain grounds for saying that He is) then the appearance of divine cruelty in the animal world must be false appearance.[112]

After responding at greater length to several of Joad's specific inquiries, Lewis concludes:

> We do not know the answer: these speculations were guesses at what it might possibly be. What really matters is the argument that there must be an answer: the argument that if, in our

---

[109] Joad, "The Pains of Animals," 162.
[110] Joad, "The Pains of Animals," 164.
[111] Joad, "The Pains of Animals," 166.
[112] Lewis, "The Reply," 167-168.

own lives, where alone (if at all) we know Him, we come to recognize the *pulchritudo tam antiqua et tam nova*,[113] then, in other realms where we cannot know Him (*connâitre*), though we may know (*savoir*) some few things about Him—then, despite appearances to the contrary, He cannot be a power of darkness. For there were appearances to the contrary in our own realm too; yet, for Dr. Joad as for me, they have somehow been got over.[114]

We do not know to what extent Joad was satisfied by Lewis's remarks. Sometime later, when he published an account of his path to spiritual restoration, he returned briefly to the topic of pain in the animal world by pointing out that Lewis's proposal that the fall affected all of life included animal life, but he went no further.[115] Shortly after their exchange over animal pain, Joad wrote in the *New Statesmen and Nation*[116] a favorable review of Lewis's *Screwtape Letters*, which had just been published. His comments reveal nothing specific about his own spiritual position, but they provide some suggestion of the nature of its trajectory, as well as expressing his respect for Lewis's views: "Mr. Lewis possesses the rare gift of being able to make righteousness readable, and has produced a pretty piece of homily lit by flashes of insight."[117]

Joad stated of *The Recovery of Belief*, "The following book is an account of some of the reasons which have converted me to the religious view of the universe in its Christian version."[118] He acknowledged the influence of Lewis's *The Abolition of Man* in helping to bring about his return to faith,[119] quoting from its third chapter, which addresses the potential for tyranny in a world which has discarded objective truth and forgotten the wisdom of earlier ages:

> For the wise men of old the cardinal problem had been how to conform the soul to reality, and the solution had been knowledge, self-discipline, and virtue. For magic and applied

---

[113] St. Augustine, *Confessions*, bk. X, ch. 27. 'Beauty so ancient and so new'.

[114] Lewis, "The Reply," 170.

[115] Joad, *The Recovery of Belief*, 24.

[116] See the book review by C. E. M. Joad, "Mr. Lewis's Devil," *New Statesman and Nation*, Vol. 23 (May 16, 1942):324f.

[117] Cited in Hooper, Walter. *C. S. Lewis: A Companion & Guide* (New York, 1996), 276.

[118] C. E. M. Joad, *The Recovery of Belief: A Restatement of Christian Philosophy*, 13.

[119] Joad, *The Recovery of Belief*, 81.

science alike the problem is how to subdue reality to the wishes of men: the solution is a technique; and both, in the practice of this technique, are ready to do things hitherto regarded as disgusting and impious—such as digging up and mutilating the dead.[120]

Christianity had thus tempered Joad's idealism and given him a discipline which could teach him to conform his wishes to the world, rather than the other way around. Moreover, he now concluded that optimism about human nature had been a mistaken viewpoint. Finally, from the Appendix in The *Abolition of Man*, Joad had gained an understanding of how many of Christ's ethical precepts appear in the teachings of other religions, even in the Greek philosophers.[121]

Joad acknowledged—characteristically—that "belief in religion comes with a quite special degree of difficulty to persons of my training and equipment."[122] In fact, "the findings of the contemporary intellect tell heavily against religion…the climate of the time is hostile to it." Consequently, "for most of my life I have been not only an agnostic but a vocal and militant agnostic."[123] An even greater influence on his return to faith was what he termed "The Significance of Evil."[124] Having earlier fallen under the influence of Shaw and Bergson, Joad now believed that the attempt to make man the master of his fate had achieved nothing but death and destruction. Shaw and Bergson, and many others, including the English philosopher Herbert Spencer, all believed in modernist theories of progress—that human perfection was achievable,[125] that evolution was moving mankind inexorably toward biological, moral, cultural, and social improvement, without the assistance of God. They held the idea that all imperfections are the consequence of external conditions that can be remedied by further progress in science, eugenics, and education.[126] If, as the great intellectuals assert, Joad concluded, the future of the world lies in our hands, then we have made a great mess of it and the optimism of the age is ill-founded. He framed the Christian alternative to this modernist imperative in personal terms:

---

[120] C. S. Lewis, *The Abolition of Man*, 83f., cited in Joad, *The Recovery of Belief*, 81.

[121] Joad, *The Recovery of Belief*, 164.

[122] Joad, *The Recovery of Belief*, 20.

[123] Joad, *The Recovery of Belief*, 21.

[124] The title of Chapter III in *The Recovery of Belief*.

[125] Joad, *The Recovery of Belief*, 49f.

[126] Joad, *The Recovery of Belief*, 56f.

Christianity, moreover, tells me that He will not only assist me personally by the bestowal of grace, but that He has assisted mankind as a whole by sending His Son into the world to win for men by His suffering and death the chance of eternal life and to provide them with an example of right living, by following which they may come to deserve it.[127]

Like Lewis, Joad began attending worship services at his parish church long before his return to the Christian faith. During this time, he came to appreciate the Church of England, which he attended faithfully for the rest of his life.[128] He concluded that the history of Christianity, including the changed lives of the disciples, was impossible to explain without reference to supernatural causes. Moreover, Christianity did, in fact, work in practice.[129] At the same time, Joad did not always find religious faith easy to grasp. Like Lewis, he admitted to "doubts and reservations," even wondering from time to time if the historical accounts of the events surrounding the life of Jesus could be trusted.[130]

The Victorian age was a time of peace and prosperity, with little sense of urgency arising out of great worldwide evil and suffering. Its philosophers, whom Lewis described as "the favored members of the happiest class in the happiest country in the world at the world's happiest period,"[131] perhaps naturally interpreted the events of their age as undisputed proof of material and human progress that would continue. Joad's age, by contrast, was far less tranquil and prosperous. Two World Wars inflicted evil and suffering of unimagined brutality on tens of millions, the staggering consequences of which could not be ignored. Of course, to many people the evil and suffering brought about by the two wars either affirmed their atheistic convictions or caused them to abandon faith in God. Many now asked how a loving, powerful, and just God could allow evil and suffering to occur on such an unprecedented scale. By 1942, Joad was referring to a "new urgency" that demanded a response.[132] Lewis, however, preferred to take a longer view of the current situation:

---

[127] Joad, *The Recovery of Belief*, 174f.

[128] Joad, *The Recovery of Belief*, 242.

[129] Joad, *The Recovery of Belief*, 243, 248.

[130] Joad, *The Recovery of Belief*, 248. See Lewis, *Mere Christianity*, Book 3, Chapter 11, 140.

[131] Lewis, "Good and Evil," in Lewis, *God in the Dock*, 22.

[132] Quoted in Lewis, "Evil and God," 22.

No Ordinary People

> But *what* new urgency? Evil may seem more urgent to us than it did to the Victorian philosophers …. But it is no more urgent for us than for the great majority of monotheists all down the ages. The classic expositions of the doctrine that the world's miseries are compatible with its creation and guidance by a wholly good Being come from Boethius waiting in prison to be beaten to death and from St. Augustine meditating on the sack of Rome. The present state of the world is normal; it was the last century that was the abnormality.[133]

During the next decade, as Joad continued to reflect on these two opposing views, he adopted a position on evil and suffering similar to that held by Lewis. Ironically, these sharply contrasting circumstances—the irenic nature of the Victorian age and its confident (if misplaced) philosophical speculations, and the violent and unsettled nature of his own age and the pessimism that it produced—contributed directly both to Joad's abandonment of Christianity prior to the First World War, and to his return to it after the Second.

Joad was one of the most prominent philosophers of his generation, best known for his numerous writings, for appearing on *The Brains Trust* and at the famous Oxford Union debate of 1933, and for his success at popularizing philosophy. It was perhaps inevitable that he and Lewis would cross paths at various times, given their mutual interest in philosophy and its many offshoots, the remarkable similarity of their personal views and character traits, and the relative intimacy of English intellectual life during the 1940s and early 50s. Ultimately, these two men, so much alike and yet, in so many ways, so different, came to dwell under the same life-transforming banner. This spiritual dimension, worked out in an age of great evil, suffering, and uncertainty, remains the lasting legacy of their commonality.

---

[133] Lewis, "Evil and God," 22.

Twenty-One Friendships of C.S. Lewis

What I Require from Life: Writings on Science from J. B. S. Haldane

Includes a Preface written by the late Sir Arthur C. Clarke, who provides a personal perspective on Haldane's unique place in 20th century science.

Chapter 13

J. B. S. HALDANE
AKA Edward Rolles Weston

When Elwin Ransom hurled a stone into the face of the Un-man,[1] Edward Rolles Weston, on Perelandra, C. S. Lewis was metaphorically driving a fist into the face of scientism, i.e., "the belief that the supreme moral end is the perpetuation of our own species, and that this is to be pursued even if, in the process of being fitted for survival, our species has to be stripped of all those things for which we value it—of pity, of happiness, and of freedom."[2] Those words did not sound the death knell of scientism, or Lewis's definition of scientism, but they did express his concern for an over-confident faith in the findings of some scientists.

J. B. S. Haldane was the model C. S. Lewis used for the physicist Weston in the Ransom Trilogy.[3] Although the two men had opposing points of view, they were similar in many ways.[4] Both had been atheists, Lewis for a number of years in his youth and Haldane for most of his life. Both were intelligent men with an excellent memory,[5] both were precocious in their early years, and both carried

---

[1] C. S. Lewis, *Perelandra*. New York: Macmillan, 1944, 181.

[2] C. S. Lewis, "A Reply to Professor Haldane," *Of Other Worlds: Essays and Stories*, 76f.

[3] The Ransom Trilogy, also known as the Space Trilogy, consists of *Out of the Silent Planet* (1938), *Perelandra* (1943), and *That Hideous Strength* (1945). Weston appears in the first two books, in the first book as a scientist who has discovered how to do space travel. In that book Weston takes his university friend Devine to Mars (Malacandra), a sinless world, mistakes the intentions of the creatures there, and seeks to bring Cambridge philologist Elwin Ransom to Malacandra as a human sacrifice. In *Perelandra*, Weston journeys to Venus (Perelandra), tries to tempt the Eve of that world to sin, particularly after Satan enters his body, and is subsequently attacked and killed by Ransom. Lewis does not try to state that all scientists, nor all university faculty, are evil, but he does demonstrate his opposition to those who might use either science or academia for selfish purposes.

[4] This chapter is especially indebted to a book by Ronald Clark, *JBS: The Life and Work of J. B. S. Haldane*, Oxford: Oxford University Press, 1984.

[5] Sir Peter Medawar, the Oxford professor who wrote the Preface to *JBS: The Life and Work of J. B. S. Haldane*, called Haldane "the cleverest man I ever knew"; Medawar was Lewis's colleague at Magdalen College,

the nickname Jack. Both studied Greats at Oxford,[6] and both earned First Class Honours in their studies. Both men joined the Oxford University Officers' Training Corps early in the twentieth century and fought in World War I. Haldane received his commission in the Third Battalion of the Black Watch, while Lewis served in the 3rd Battalion of the Somerset Light Infantry.[7]

Born on Guy Fawkes Day,[8] November 5, 1892, to John Scott Haldane and Louisa Kathleen Trotter, John Burdon Sanderson Haldane had a scientist for a father and future writer Naomi Mitchison for a younger sister.[9] After six years at Eton, he enrolled at New College in 1911 on a mathematical scholarship. After Eton, biographer Ronald Clark wrote, "Haldane was against—against authority and against the Government, any authority and any Government; if possible in the cause of reason, if not as a matter of principle."[10] Although he earned his reputation in mathematics and biology, Haldane never earned a degree in any field of science.[11]

In January 1915, Haldane entered war service in France as the Bombing Officer of the First Battalion.[12] He took to the task with such enthusiasm that he was nicknamed Bombo. Later in the war he ran the Nigg Bombing School so effectively that the school had no serious accident or fatal casualty. His largely self-taught background in science enabled him to provide advice on defensive measures against a gas attack and to do initial study of the effects of chlorine gas on the soldier with or without a respirator. His service throughout the war demonstrated an outspoken showmanship and fearlessness that characterized his entire life. He even conducted many of

---

Oxford from 1938 to 1944 and Haldane's colleague at University College, London from 1951 to 1957. See also Ronald Clark, *JBS*, 19.

[6] Greats is a course of study in ancient history and classical philosophy.

[7] V. M. Quirke, "Haldane, John Burdon Sanderson (1892-1964)," *Oxford Dictionary of National Biography*, Oxford University Press, 2004, accessed Oct. 5, 2017.

[8] In British history, November 5 is the day in 1605 that Guy Fawkes attempted, unsuccessfully, to blow up the House of Lords, and that act of insurrection is now celebrated in England every year. The day was previously known as the Gunpowder Treason Day. The day was originally celebrated as a day of thanksgiving for the failure of the plot, but today it is celebrated by some as a day of tongue-in-cheek rebellion against the British government. This writer remembers a Guy Fawkes celebration in 1995 in Hampstead Heath, London, that involved a band and fireworks, including a replica of the House of Lords going up in fireworks.

[9] V. M. Quirke, "Haldane."

[10] Ronald Clark, *JBS*, 23.

[11] Haldane did, however, attend various lectures, including those of E. S. Goodrich in zoology and that of A. D. Darbishire on the genetic work of Gregor Mendel. Ronald Clark, *JBS*, 29.

[12] He completed his war service in January 1919.

his scientific experiments on himself. Throughout his life Haldane's showmanship would turn into rudeness and a hot temper at times, but it also demonstrated a sense of humor, wit, and originality.

Before the war was over, Haldane had accepted a Fellowship at New College, Oxford, where he would teach physiology, even without the appropriate academic training. In 1923, he left Oxford to accept a Readership in Biochemistry at Trinity College, Cambridge. During his nine years at Cambridge with Gowland Hopkins,[13] Haldane worked on enzymes and genetics, particularly the mathematical side of genetics. After he developed Haldane's Law, a mathematical calculation on how genetic characteristics are passed on to the next generation,[14] he wrote what many have considered his most important work, ten papers on "Mathematical Contributions to the Theory of Natural Selection." These papers were published between 1924 and 1934 in the *Proceedings* and *Transactions* of the Cambridge Philosophical Society. During the teens and twenties, Haldane wrote many popular essays on science that were eventually collected and published in a volume entitled *Possible Worlds*. Lewis referred to that work several times in his writings and correspondence. Lewis's opposition to eugenics, including the views of Haldane, derives especially from a comment by Haldane in *Possible Worlds* about certain people, "It is on the whole undesirable that they should beget their like."[15]

In 1924, Haldane met Charlotte Burghes, a young reporter for the *Daily Express*. Burghes was working on a novel, had read Haldane's *Daedalus*, and therefore sought out an interview with Haldane. As a result of their meeting, Charlotte eventually divorced her husband and married Haldane a year later. Haldane was dismissed from his Readership in Biochemistry in 1925 due to charges of adultery,

---

[13] Hopkins was the Sir William Dunn Professor, that is, the Senior Professorship in Biochemistry at Cambridge University. This Chair was established in 1914 by banker and philanthropist Sir William Dunn, who left money in his will for this position.

[14] This includes what is known as Haldane's Dilemma, which states that it takes a minimum of three hundred generations for a new genetic characteristic to be distributed throughout a species.

[15] Haldane, "Eugenics and Social Reform," *Possible Worlds*, 191. *Possible Worlds* was published in 1927. Other publications by Haldane included *Daedalus, or Science and the Future*, a booklet of scientific prediction of the future that Lewis called "a diabolical little book," books such as *Callinicus: A Defense of Chemical Warfare*; *Biology in Everyday Life*; *The Inequality of Man*; *The Causes of Evolution*; *The Man with Two Memories*; and hundreds of articles.

apparently because of his relationship with Charlotte, but, after Haldane's appeal, was reinstated in 1926.[16]

In 1930 he became Professor of Physiology at the Royal Institution's Fullerian, from this time on focusing on genetics. He left Cambridge in August 1932, resigning his Readership at Trinity College.[17] In the spring of 1933 Haldane took up the post of Professor of Genetics at University College, London. He administered the department, taught, and conducted research.[18] Four years later he became the first Weldon Professor of Biometry at University College, London.[19] Then, in 1937, Haldane became a Marxist and an open supporter of the Communist Party.[20] He joined the Party in 1942 and became a member of their Executive Committee two years later, involving himself in British-Soviet rallies. Several visits to Spain during the thirties confirmed Haldane in his belief that the Communists were the only ones who would stand up to dictators.[21]

By 1937, Haldane had become the science correspondent for the *Daily Worker*, the official publication of the Communist Party in England,[22] and in 1940 Haldane became the Chair of its Editorial Board. He wrote nearly three hundred and fifty articles for the publication. When the *Daily Worker* became pro-Moscow in 1939, it gathered the attention of Herbert Morrison, the Home Secretary. In early 1941, the paper was suppressed by police action because its articles hindered the cooperation of the public in the national war effort,[23] and ceased to publish. The paper received permission to start publication again less than a year later after Haldane wrote to the Home Secretary, claiming that the paper had been misunderstood.[24]

Haldane continued to support his country, including campaigning for adequate air raid protection and assisting in the war effort. Shortly after the start of World War II, he was working for

---

[16] Ronald Clark, *JBS*, 75-77. V. M. Quirke, "Haldane."

[17] Ronald Clark, *JBS*, 91.

[18] Ronald Clark, *JBS*, 93.

[19] Ronald Clark, *JBS*, 101. Biometry is the application of statistical analysis to biological research data, resulting in a combination of two of Haldane's strengths—mathematics and biology.

[20] Ronald Clark, *JBS*, 115.

[21] Ronald Clark, *JBS*, 119f.

[22] Ronald Clark, *JBS*, 125.

[23] Ronald Clark, *JBS*, 164. On January 21, 1941.

[24] Ibid.

the Directorate of Home Publicity at the Ministry of Information.[25] Various experiments on oxygen deprivation, exposure to excess carbon dioxide, and related issues helped him write reports about the use of miniature submarines and submarine escape. He and his future spouse Helen Spurway also did statistical investigations for the R.A.F., the Army, and the Ministry of Aircraft Production to determine which tactics offered the best chances of shooting down enemy planes.[26] His wife Charlotte defected to the Soviet Union as a war correspondent, and in spring of 1945, she divorced him. Haldane then quietly married Helen Spurway.

In the late 1940s, Haldane's Marxist beliefs led him to support the Ukrainian scientist Trofim Lysenko, who believed that acquired characteristics could be inherited.[27] While cautious about this position, since he had not seen the documented research, Haldane supported Lysenko. This would change, however, by the end of 1949 because of the way in which the Russian government was controlling science and limiting free scientific research. As late as 1962, he would describe Joseph Stalin as "a very great man who did a very good job."[28]

In the 1930s and 1940s, Haldane became well known around the world for his research and writing. In 1932, Haldane was elected a Fellow of the Royal Society. He gave many speeches over the decades, including the Princeton Centennial in the United States and the Herbert Spencer lecture at Oxford, and he also spoke at various international Congresses. In 1952, he received the Darwin Medal from the Royal Society. In 1956, he was awarded the Huxley Memorial Medal of the Royal Anthropological Institute. He received the Feltrinelli Prize, an Honorary Doctorate in science, an Honorary Fellowship at New College, and the Kimber Award from the U.S. National Academy of Sciences.

Unhappiness with British authorities eventually led Haldane to emigrate to India. While he claimed his emigration was the result of Anglo-French aggression in Suez, he was also attracted by the Hindu non-violent philosophy of life, pessimistic about what he perceived as the increasingly anti-socialistic tendencies of Europe, and unhappy with working conditions at University College. He and Helen left England for India in the summer of 1957, and he spent the rest of his

---

[25] Ronald Clark, *JBS*, 131. By the end of September 1939.

[26] Ronald Clark, *JBS*, 151.

[27] This position, since discarded, gave hope to the evolutionary explanation for the wide-ranging development of species.

[28] Clark, *JBS*, 248.

life there.

In India, Haldane held positions at the Indian Statistical Institute in Calcutta, at a Genetics and Biometry Research Unit in Calcutta, and at a Genetics and Biometry Laboratory in Bhubaneswar. He died of cancer on December 1, 1964. Over his career he popularized science; contributed to physiology, biochemistry, and genetics; and was best known for hihe s work on the mathematical theory of natural selection.

C. S. Lewis and J. B. S. Haldane

Haldane's scientific views influenced Lewis's writings. In *Possible Worlds*, for example, Haldane wrote about "the silence of interstellar space," the very opposite of what Lewis proposed in his book, *Out of the Silent Planet*.[29] For Lewis, Earth was the silent planet, but the rest of the universe was teeming with life and sound. In *Possible Worlds*, Haldane also expressed his anti-Christian sentiment, writing, "On a planet more than a thousand million years old it is hard to believe—as do Christians, Jews, Mohammedans, and Buddhists—that the most important event [i.e., the Incarnation] has occurred within the last few thousand years."[30] In 1943, Lewis wrote,

> If we discovered no objects in this infinite space except those which are of use to man (our own sun and moon), then this vast emptiness would certainly be used as a strong argument against the existence of God. If we discover other bodies, they must be habitable or uninhabitable: and the odd thing is that both these hypotheses are used as grounds for rejecting Christianity. If the universe is teeming with life, this, we are told, reduces to absurdity the Christian claim—or what is thought to be the Christian claim—that man is unique, and the Christian doctrine that to this one planet God came down and was incarnate for us men and our salvation. If, on the other hand, the earth is really unique, then that proves that life is only an accidental by-product in the universe, and so again disproves our religion. Really, we are hard to please. We treat God as the police treat a man when he is arrested; whatever He does will be used in evidence against Him.[31]

Lewis was referring to Haldane, whose understanding of the vastness of the universe led him to conclude that the Incarnation

---

[29] Haldane, "On Scales," *Possible Worlds*, 1.

[30] Haldane, "Some Dates," *Possible Worlds*, 17.

[31] Lewis, "Dogma and the Universe," *God in the Dock*, 40.

could not be true.

In 1938, shortly after the publication of *Out of the Silent Planet*, Lewis wrote, "What immediately spurred me to write was Olaf Stapledon's *Last and First Men* . . . and an essay in J. B. S. Haldane's *Possible Worlds* both of wh. seemed to take the idea of such [space] travel seriously and to have the desperately immoral outlook wh. I try to pillory in Weston. I like the whole interplanetary idea as a *mythology* and simply wished to conquer for my own (Christian) pt. of view what has always hitherto been used by the opposite side."[32]

A few months later, Lewis described Haldane's writings as silly nonsense, writing, "Please tell my youthful critics that tho' Weston is a caricature, Weston*ism* is v. nearly as silly as I have made out. The crowning idiocy on p. 224 ('It is enough for me that there is a Beyond') is the last words of Lilith in Shaw's *Back to Methuselah*. Most of the other nonsense derives from the last essay in J. B. S. Haldane's 'Possible Worlds.'"[33]

Haldane was one of those, along with Olaf Stapledon, C. K. Ogden, I. A. Richards, and H. G. Wells, whom Lewis accused of scientism. *Out of the Silent Planet*, *Perelandra*, and *That Hideous Strength*, provide the novelistic embodiment of Lewis's views of a society where science had attained an influential position, where ethics were relative, and where the secular aims of society and science were more important than truth. Lewis's *Abolition of Man* summarizes much of his opposition to positions held by Haldane.

Shortly after the third book of the Ransom Trilogy appeared, Haldane sarcastically criticized the trilogy in an article entitled "Auld Hornie, F.R.S."[34] Auld Hornie was the pet name given to the devil by the Scots, and F.R.S. stood for "Fellow of the Royal Society," an honorific title given to those elected to the Royal Society. In the article, Haldane contends that Lewis's science is wrong, that Lewis casts scientists in an unfavorable light, and that Lewis considers scientific planning as a road to hell.

Lewis's response, "A Reply to Professor Haldane," demonstrates Haldane's misunderstandings. Lewis shows that he does not intend

---

[32] Lewis, *Collected Letters*, II, 236.

[33] Lewis, *Collected Letters*, II, 255f. The last essay is entitled "The Last Judgment," 287–312. In "On Science Fiction," *Of Other Worlds*, 66, Lewis called it "brilliant, though to my mind depraved, paper." The date is March 21, 1939.

[34] This essay was published in the Autumn 1946 issue of *The Modern Quarterly*.

for all his science to be totally accurate; after all, he was writing a romance. Then he indicates that he was attacking scientism, not scientists, by challenging the view that the supreme goal of our species is to perpetuate itself at any expense. Haldane had written in such a way that he could be accused of scientism, even though in another essay Lewis referred to Haldane as "a real scientist."[35] Lewis offers Shaw's *Back to Methuselah*, Olaf Stapledon's *Last and First Men*, and Haldane's own "Last Judgment" in *Possible Worlds* as examples of scientism. As to the suggestion that he was attacking science, Lewis once said, "Nothing I can say will prevent some people from describing this lecture as an attack on science. I deny the charge."[36] Lewis actually casts science in a good light by putting an ethical scientist in *That Hideous Strength* and by stating that the sciences were "good and innocent in themselves."[37] Finally, he states in his reply to Haldane that he does not think of scientific planning as a road to hell, but the very opposite: that an invitation to hell would likely appear dressed up as scientific planning.

In *That Hideous Strength*, Professor Frost, a psychologist who is one of the two leaders of the National Institute of Coordinated Experiments (N.I.C.E.), is the mouthpiece of the ethical theories of Professor Conrad Waddington. Waddington once published a genetics paper with Haldane and taught that "an examination of the direction of evolution could provide us with the criteria from which we could judge whether any ethical system was fulfilling its function."[38] In *The Abolition of Man*, published just two years before *That Hideous Strength*, Lewis expressed his view that the triumphs of science might have come too quickly and have been purchased at too high a price. Increase in knowledge was running ahead of ethical developments that could provide the knowledge, self-discipline, and virtue that science needed.[39]

---

[35] Lewis, "The Funeral of a Great Myth," *Christian Reflections*, 85.

[36] Lewis, *The Abolition of Man*, Chapter 3, 82. The charge that Lewis was attacking science seems strange in view of the fact that as an Oxford student Haldane attacked religion. V. M. Quirke, "Haldane, John Burdon Sanderson (1892-1964)," *Oxford Dictionary of National Biography*, Oxford University Press, 2004, accessed Oct. 5, 2017.

[37] The character's name is William Hingest. Lewis, *That Hideous Strength*, 203.

[38] Robertson, "Waddington, Conrad Hal (1905–1975)," rev. L. Wolpert, *Oxford Dictionary of National Biography*, Oxford University Press, 2004 [http://www.oxforddnb.com/view/article/31790, accessed 4 June 2005].

[39] Lewis, *The Abolition of Man*, Chapter 3, 84f.

Twenty-One Friendships of C.S. Lewis

J.B.S. Haldane
in front of a propaganda poster of the Spanish Republican 5th Regiment
Permissions: The Creative Commons Universal Public Domain, circa 1937

The only face-to-face meetings that occurred between Lewis and Haldane took place at the Socratic Club, the first time on November 15, 1948. That evening the topic was "Atheism" with Haldane and Ian M. Crombie, philosophy tutor at Wadham College, as speakers. Haldane timed his last words to coincide with his exit.[40] One can imagine Haldane disliking the possibility of locking horns with Lewis or Crombie on this topic, especially knowing that Lewis had once been an atheist and had discarded that conviction. Haldane and Lewis could have met again at the Socratic Club four years later, when the topic was "Ethics and Instinct" with speaker Prof. Conrad Lorenz, from the Max Planck Institute, and Lewis as respondent. No record remains of any direct discussion between Lewis and Haldane, although Haldane and his wife Helen Spurway are listed in the attendance records.[41]

Lewis sometimes agreed with Haldane. In one instance, he quoted Haldane in favor of his argument that Naturalism is self-

---

[40] Green and Hooper, 217.

[41] The exact date is February 9, 1953. The Stella Aldwinckle Papers, the Wade Center, 8-365, attendance list book for Socratic Club meetings. Also 8-391.

contradictory.⁴² Haldane had written, "If my mental processes are determined wholly by the motions of atoms in my brain, I have no reason to suppose that my beliefs are true . . . and hence I have no reason for supposing my brain to be composed of atoms."⁴³ In other instances, in opposition to the myth of progress or improvement, he cited Haldane's comment that degeneration, not progress, is the rule in evolution.⁴⁴

Haldane and Lewis also agreed on vivisection, i.e., experimentation on animals in the interests of science. Early in his life Haldane defended vivisection, stating, "All others who demand the prohibition of experiments on anaesthetized animals are quite definitely hypocrites."⁴⁵ While Haldane later modified his views, early in his career he was opposed to those who wanted to eliminate all use of animals in scientific experimentation. In 1927, for example, he offered £100 to the National Canine Defense League if they could produce the name of any demonstrator who had performed "a painful experiment on a dog before a class of students in Great Britain and Ireland within the last ten years."⁴⁶ He further claimed that he had never seen an experiment that caused pain to an animal or one that he would not have performed on himself.

Lewis wrote an essay on the topic for the New England Anti-Vivisection Society, included a chapter on animal pain in his book *The Problem of Pain*, and showed the triumph of the anti-vivisectionists at the end of *That Hideous Strength* when all the animals were released from their experimentation cages. In his article, "Vivisection," Lewis deplores the worst aspect about modern vivisection, i.e., the slippery slope which could lead to the preferring of one human race over another. He fears that the mistreatment of animals could lead to the mistreatment of humans, especially since some considered human beings merely a more highly developed animal. He states that experiments had already begun on people, that the Nazis had done so, and that British scientists may do so also. *That Hideous Strength* described the imprisonment of Ivy Maggs' husband and the intent of the N.I.C.E. to use him for their experiments, an image that illustrates

---

⁴² See the original title of chapter three in *Miracles: A Preliminary Study*, London & Glasgow: Collins/Fontana, 1947.

⁴³ Haldane, *Possible Worlds*, 209, cited in *Collected Letters, II*, 715.

⁴⁴ Lewis, "De Futilitate" and "The Funeral of a Great Myth," *Christian Reflections*, 58, 85.

⁴⁵ Haldane, "Some Enemies of Science," *Possible Worlds*, 251.

⁴⁶ Clark, *JBS*, 88.

Lewis's concern. His greatest concern, however, was the additional experimentation to which vivisection could lead.

Conclusion

These two talented men had much in common and agreed on several points, including their opposition to vivisection, but their attitude toward what Lewis called the Tao, Lewis's term for the Natural Law or traditional morality, led them in opposite directions. Haldane was the main reason for Lewis's portrayal of Westonism in the Ransom Trilogy. Although Haldane criticized Lewis for being opposed to science, Lewis supported science and opposed scientism, a point of view that placed science as the highest arbiter of goodness, truth, and beauty. That position, Lewis believed, belonged only to God.

Scenes from a Cherical Life
Alec Vidler's 1977 autobiography

Chapter 14

ALEC VIDLER
C. S. Lewis Was His Permanent Opposition

Alexander Roper "Alec" Vidler was born on December 27, 1899, a little more than a year after C. S. Lewis.[1] His career encompassed that of an Anglican priest, theologian, and historian. In 1939, he became the third editor of the monthly journal *Theology*,[2] and he began to recruit both subscribers and authors who could help him energize the periodical,[3] one of the latter being C. S. Lewis. Lewis replied to Vidler,[4] enclosing the names of potential subscribers to *Theology* and expressing a willingness to write some book reviews for the journal. Lewis joined T. S. Eliot and Charles Williams, among others, as recruits.[5]

The two men continued to write to one another for a time, but then, about nine years after the start of their communication, the correspondence ceased. Was there some animosity between them? Did Lewis think Vidler too liberal, or did Vidler think Lewis too conservative? Did Lewis sour on Vidler because of *Windsor Sermons*, a book of Vidler's sermons which Lewis later criticized? Were other letters lost, or destroyed? Or did the two men simply turn their energies in other directions? This chapter will explore the relationship between C. S. Lewis and Alec Vidler, their views on theology and related writings, and attempt to answer these questions, arguing that even people with profound disagreements can work together.

---

[1] He died on July 25, 1991 at the age of ninety-one.

[2] The journal began publication in 1920. Vidler would remain as editor until the 1960s. In his autobiography, *Scenes from a Clerical Life*, he states that he was editor of *Theology* for twenty-five years, which would mean until 1964. Alec R. Vidler, *Scenes from a Clerical Life*. London: William Collins Sons & Co., Ltd., 1977, 174.

[3] Besides the theologians, other authors, or collaborators, included laymen Montgomery Belgion, T. S. R. Boase, T. S. Eliot, J. Middleton Murry, Joseph Needham, and Charles Williams. Vidler, *Scenes*, 112.

[4] Lewis answered quickly, i.e., on January 17, 1939. C. S. Lewis, *Collected Letters, Volume 2. Books, Broadcasts and War 1931-1949*. Edited by Walter Hooper. London: HarperCollinsPublishers, 2004, 243.

[5] Editorial, *Theology*, Vol. LXVIII, January 1965, No. 353, 1.

No Ordinary People

LEWIS AND VIDLER

Lewis and Vidler had many similar interests and characteristics, some of them literary and others theological. After the brief war service by the two men, they both returned to their universities—Lewis to University College in Oxford and Vidler to Selwyn College in Cambridge—for the term that began on January 14, 1919.

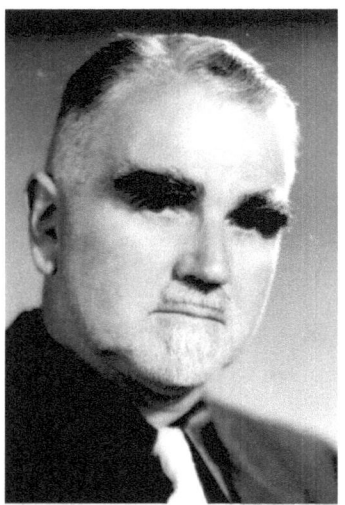

Photo used by permission of King's College, Cambridge

They had other commonalities. Both men were single, Lewis for most of his life and Vidler for his entire life. Early in life both Vidler and Lewis accepted the conclusions of the critical study of the Bible,[6] which "quickly became of absorbing and rewarding interest"[7] for Vidler. Much later, Vidler's acceptance of higher criticism became a point of contention since Lewis did not agree.

Both men were concerned about communicating the biblical message in fresh and relevant ways to the public,[8] but they chose different routes for this communication. Vidler wrote,

> My own sympathies, then and later, were especially with a group of liberal Roman Catholics, known as 'the Catholic Modernists,' who struck me as, in the best sense, both more catholic and more liberal than their more cautious, moderate and dull Anglican counterparts.[9]

Paul Crook agrees, stating that "Vidler imbibed leftist sympathies."[10] When Vidler became the Dean of King's College,

---

[6] The higher critical study of the Bible approaches the Bible as it would any other book, denying any special inspiration and including a bias against the supernatural, accounts of miracles, statements alleging to come directly from God, and the like.

[7] *Scenes*, 27.

[8] See "God in the Dock," 184 (Grand Rapids: Eerdmans, 1970), where Lewis calls his task that of a translator.

[9] *Scenes*, 47.

[10] Paul Crook. "Alec Vidler." https://dpcrook.wordpress.

Cambridge, in 1956, Crook tells us, King's had a reputation for intellectual unbelief.[11] Two years later, Vidler started meeting with a network of radical theologians in Cambridge who would produce several significant theological works that argued for changes in Christian theology in the face of great difficulties in theology and society.[12] In a Pentecost sermon Vidler once stated that "we were not to suppose that on the day of Pentecost the apostles were miraculously endowed with a knowledge of foreign languages...."[13] Lewis would have disagreed.[14] Paul Tillich was one of Vidler's favorite theologians,[15] and Lewis once wrote to Mary Van Deusen, describing Tillich as a "temptation against faith" and "one of those sincere semi-Christians who are now a greater danger to the Faith than the open unbeliever."[16]

Vidler's alignment with the Labour Party and the socialist movement would not have found a kindred spirit in Lewis.[17] Furthermore, by 1941, "Vidler was not optimistic about Christianity's chances of survival. Theology had badly neglected important social issues."[18] Vidler was interested in translating theology into the language of the people as a way of addressing social concerns, but in the process he was willing to set aside many traditional teachings.[19]

com/2013/05/17/alec-vidler (May 17, 2013). According to Crook, Vidler liked the writings of Reinhold Niebuhr, Paul Tillich, Will Spens, Baron Friedrich von Hügel, F. D. Maurice, Alfred Loisy (whom Vidler met twice), and George Tyrrell. Much of his views is represented in Vidler's book, *The Modernist Movement in the Roman Church: Its Origins and Outcome*, Cambridge University Press, 1934. Neo-orthodoxy was a movement in theology that, among other positions, denied the plenary inspiration of Scripture.

[11] Crook, "Alec Vidler."

[12] Crook, "Alec Vidler."

[13] *Scenes*, 71.

[14] See Lewis's essay "Transposition," *The Weight of Glory and Other Addresses*. New York: Simon & Schuster, 1980, 72.

[15] Vidler also valued George Tyrrell quite highly, describing Tyrrell as meaning "more to me than any of the others and I return to him most often...." *Scenes*, 184.

[16] *Collected Letters, Volume III. Narnia, Cambridge and Joy 1950-1963*. Edited by Walter Hooper. London: HarperCollinsPublishers, 2006, 1011f., The date is January 16, 1959.

[17] See especially *Scenes*, 51f. See also Lewis, *Collected Letters, II*, 1076, for reference to Vidler's alignment with the Labour Party.

[18] Crook, Essay No 9, "Alec Vidler."

[19] Lewis wrote of Vidler, "He wants—I think he wants very

During the 1930s he had urged that theology must change as the times changed,[20] while Lewis usually favored traditional positions even while offering innovative ways of expressing those positions—a change in the opposite direction.

VIDLER AND *THEOLOGY*

In 1938, Alec Vidler became the Warden of St Deiniol's Library (pictured below) and took up residence in Hawarden, Flintshire, Wales, at the beginning of October 1938. He wanted to serve as editor of *Theology* from that study center.[21] St Deiniol's Library, the only residential library[22] in the United Kingdom, had started as the result of a generous endowment by former Prime Minister William Gladstone. The library originally contained much of Gladstone's 32,000-volume personal library and grew from there, becoming a place for retreat and for personal study.

Image used with the permission of Gladstone's Library

---

earnestly—to retain some Christian doctrines. But he is prepared to scrap a good deal. 'Traditional doctrines' are to be tested." *Letters to Malcolm: Chiefly on Prayer*, London: HarperCollins Publishers, 1977, 32.

[20] Crook, "Alec Vidler."

[21] *Scenes*, 96f.

[22] A library, now known as Gladstone's Library, with accommodations that allow visitors to spend several days studying or retreating. At the time of Vidler, it was the only residential library in the UK. See https://www.gladstoneslibrary.org/.

Twenty-One Friendships of C.S. Lewis

Interior of Gladstone's Library
Courtesy of John McNeill

Although *Theology* had originally been conceived as "an organ of English liberal Catholicism," Vidler intended to broaden the periodical to include a lay readership, not just a clergy readership.[23] Since circulation of the periodical had been declining, this broadening helped to save the periodical.[24] Vidler's first editorial, published in January 1939, stated his three purposes: (1) to offer the best in contemporary theology to a wide readership, (2) to serve as an organ for Anglican theology, and (3) to provide a liaison between theological thought and contemporary literature, art, and political philosophy in the Christian tradition.[25] In this latter category, Vidler would attempt to bridge the gap between Christianity and society.

Lewis's Contributions to *Theology*: Permanent Opposition

In his first contribution for *Theology* Lewis reviewed Charles Williams' complex poem *Taliessin through Logres*, a review which he sent to Vidler in early 1939 for publication.[26] The review was published

---

[23] *Scenes*, 111f. See also *Theology* 38, no. 223 (1939), 2.

[24] *Scenes*, 89. Circulation had been between 1,700 and 1,800, but it quickly expanded by one-third and then eventually surpassed 5,000. *Scenes*, 113.

[25] *Scenes*, 112f.

[26] *C. S. Lewis: Collected Letters, Volume 2*, 247. The date is Feb. 1, 1939.

later that year as "A Sacred Poem." Lewis thought highly of Williams' poetry, describing this poem as having enough quality to outweigh the problem of its difficult content.

Then, on February 27, 1939, Lewis wrote to Vidler about E. L. Mascall's six conditions for a just war. The January issue of *Theology* had contained Mascall's essay "The Christian and the Next War." In his letter, Lewis challenged Mascall's conditions, particularly Condition 4, which stated that "it must be morally certain that the losses, to the belligerents, the world, and religion, will not outweigh the advantages of winning"; and Condition 6, which insisted that "there must be a considerable probability of winning." Since sincere people can disagree over those two conditions, Lewis felt that the decision whether to wage war must fall to the appropriate people, i.e., the governing authorities. To give the private citizen the same voice as the government, he writes, is absurd, just as it is absurd to expect the hangman to determine the guilt or innocence of the condemned man. The private citizen, however, engaged in war, can refuse some commander who expects him to sin, since "a man is much more certain that he ought not to murder prisoners or bomb civilians than he ever can be about the justice of a war."[27] A paragraph on chivalry and pacifism suggests that Lewis, a World War I veteran, considered the conditions for a just war as much a veiled pacifism as an ethical exercise in Christian thought: "I doubt whether chivalry has such an unbroken record of failure as pacifism."[28]

Continuing the literary conversation two weeks later, Lewis wrote to Vidler with a corrected proof of his review of Williams' *Taliessin* poem, comments about the letter on just war he had written (the letter of February 27), and his role as permanent opposition. He writes, "At the same time I ought to warn you that each number makes it clear to me that my only use to you in literary matters can be that of permanent opposition ...." He dislikes some of the content of *Theology* and, therefore, states that he is willing to be ejected from the stable of regular contributors, if Vidler feels the need, with no personal animosity over the removal.[29]

Less than a week later, Lewis wrote to Vidler about contributing an occasional article to *Theology*, beyond the occasional book review, and then, days later, another letter, telling Vidler not to worry who

---

This is the second of twelve letters that Lewis wrote to Vidler.

[27] *Collected Letters, II*, 251.
[28] *Collected Letters, II*, 252.
[29] *Collected Letters, II*, 253.

peer-reviews things he writes for *Theology*.[30] Lewis did not have a thin skin, and he rather enjoyed the thrust and parry of academic debate. Therefore, he could appreciate anyone who dismissed his position, especially when his opponent offered clear and compelling reasons.

Two months later, Lewis wrote to Vidler again about his letter against the just-war position of Mascall, adding that his schedule forced him to decline an invitation for the evening of June 10 because of a prior commitment.[31] The event to which Lewis was invited was undoubtedly the gathering of "literary collaborators," to which Lewis had referred in his earlier letter.[32] Vidler had wanted to host a social evening, and Lewis wanted to attend but could not. Despite theological disagreements, the relationship between them was warm and respectful.

Then, Lewis's review of A.C. Bouquet's *A Lectionary of Christian Prose from the Second Century to the Twentieth Century*, appeared in the December 1939 issue of *Theology*. In that review, Lewis described this collection of extra-biblical writings for private reading, worship services, and school prayers from both Christian and non-Christian writers. He questioned the inclusion of the non-Christian writers, as well as excerpts from the philosopher Berkeley and one from Chaucer. He also would have liked more Chesterton and von Hügel and less Robertson and Jowett; he would like to have seen Boethius and George MacDonald as well. Ultimately Lewis commended Bouquet for this book.

Eight months later, Lewis sent Vidler a copy of his article "Christianity and Culture."[33] The article illustrates what Lewis meant by "permanent opposition." The essay dealt with articles by British historian and theologian Br. George Every, and writer and literary scholar S. L. Bethell. In an article for *Theology* the previous year,[34] George Every had, according to Lewis, implied that "'sensitivity' or good taste were among the *notes* of the true Church, or that coarse, unimaginative people were less likely to be saved than refined and

---

[30] *Collected Letters*, II, 255. The date is March 23, 1939.

[31] *Collected Letters*, II, 259. The date is May 10, 1939.

[32] *Collected Letters*, II, 253. The date of the letter is March 11, 1939.

[33] *Collected Letters*, II, 332. The date of Lewis's letter is January 25, 1940. The article was published in *Theology* in March 1940.

[34] *The Necessity of Scrutiny*, Vol. XXXVIII, Issue 225 (March 1939):176-186. Every also wrote for *Theology* in September 1940. See C. S. Lewis, *Christian Reflections*, 28.

poetic people."³⁵ Bethell's article that started the exchange, "Poetry and Belief,"³⁶ supported Every. This led Lewis to explore the New Testament and various authors to determine their perspective on culture. The New Testament, Aristotle, Plato, St Augustine, Thomas Aquinas, Jerome, the Church Fathers, and Thomas à Kempis all seemed to warn about culture. On the other hand, Pope Gregory and John Milton seemed to support a positive appraisal of culture. Some aspects of culture are neutral, Lewis concluded, and others contain abuses that need to be confronted. In addition, however, some aspects of culture bring pleasure, and pleasure is one of God's gifts. Lewis here describes his own pre-Christian longing as "spilled religion"³⁷ and aspects of culture as potential schoolmasters³⁸ and roads into Jerusalem,³⁹ so Lewis doesn't oppose all aspects of culture. Nevertheless, Lewis calls the view of Bethell and Every an "inordinate esteem of culture by the cultured ...."⁴⁰ Although he finds value in spending time in "the suburbs of Jerusalem," those very same echoes of Christian truth point to God.⁴¹ Good taste or sensitivity is not one of the notes of the true Church; unimaginative people are *not* less likely to be Christian than refined and poetic people.⁴²

Edgar F. Carritt, a man whom Lewis greatly respected, had been Lewis's philosophy tutor during his undergraduate years at University College (1920-1922). Carritt was a Realist philosopher, who held to a materialistic view of the universe.⁴³ "Popular realism," which Lewis

---

[35] C. S. Lewis, "Christianity and Culture," *Christian Reflections*, Grand Rapids: Eerdmans, 1967, 13.

[36] *Theology*, July 1939.

[37] A phrase he borrowed from T. E. Hulme and also used in his 1943 Preface for *The Pilgrim's Regress*. C. S. Lewis, "Christianity and Culture," 23, n. 1.

[38] See Gal. 3:24-26 in the King James Version.

[39] "Christianity and Culture," 22.

[40] "Christianity and Culture," 12.

[41] "Christianity and Culture," 24. Or, Lewis concludes, "culture has a distinct part to play in bringing certain souls to Christ. Not all souls—there is a shorter, and safer, way which has always been followed by thousands of simple affectional natures who begin, where we hope to end, with devotion to the person of Christ." 24.

[42] "Christianity and Culture," 13.

[43] C. S. Lewis, *Surprised by Joy*, 212. In *C. S. Lewis & Philosophy as a Way of Life*, Adam Barkman goes into more detail than Lewis himself does, describing Lewis as holding Lucretian Materialism between 1912 (or even earlier) and 1917 (23ff.), then Pseudo-Manichean Dualism between 1917 and 1919 (30ff.), then Stoical Materialism from 1919 to

held at the time, refers to his belief that the world experienced through the five senses is the only reality.[44] The May 1940 issue of *Theology* contained a reply from both E. F. Carritt and S. L. Bethell. Bethell, "encouraged by the candour and charity of Mr Lewis's exposition,"[45] disagrees with Lewis's definition of culture, finding both Aquinas and Augustine in support of the notion of Christian culture. He also argues implausibly, that Lewis's position implies that there is nothing of value in culture. He disagrees with Lewis's position that salvation is an individual matter rather than a church matter, and he maintains that Lewis needs to consider the unconscious materialism that exists in the church.[46]

Carritt's reply shows his disdain for what he calls Lewis's "puritanical tradition" of "text-hunting in the Gospels."[47] Carritt claims that Lewis obscured the main argument, which is a moral one and what Carritt defines as the question of whether a creature who is heading to heaven or hell can afford to spend any time on the study of literature. That was not the issue. Carritt misunderstood. Lewis had merely objected to the suggestion that refined taste was a mark of the Christian.

Carritt states that Lewis felt that the values of European literature could be instructive and helpful in bringing people to Christ. Second,

---

1924 (35), Absolute Idealism from 1924 to 1925 (42), Subjective Idealism between 1925 and 1926 (47), then back to Absolute Idealism in 1926 until 1928 (47), and finally Subjective Idealism again from 1928 until his conversion to theism in 1930 (49). Although a generalization, Lewis's materialist phase lasted from 1912 until 1924 and fits more consistently with his atheism. His Idealist phase, then, ran from 1924 until his adoption of theism in 1930 and is more akin to agnosticism than atheism. The reader who wishes to pursue the nature and extent of those stages is referred to Barkman's book. Allentown, PA: Zossima Press, 2009.

[44] David C. Downing, *The Most Reluctant Convert*, 123. Adam Barkman defines popular realism as "metaphysical realism," which holds to "the existence of real, spatiotemporal objects that exist separately of people's knowledge of them and which have properties and enter into relations independently of the concepts with which people understand them." *C. S. Lewis & Philosophy as a Way of Life*, Allenton, PA: Zossima Press, 2009, 22.

[45] S. L. Bethell, "Christianity and Culture: Replies to Mr. Lewis," *Theology*, 356.

[46] S. L. Bethell, "Christianity and Culture: Replies to Mr. Lewis," *Theology*, 356-362.

[47] E. F. Carritt, "Christianity and Culture: Replies to Mr. Lewis," *Theology*, 362.

he claims that Lewis argues that culture can have value in the life of the believer, especially in leisure hours. Carritt does not like the idea of spending leisure time with Shakespeare or Dante in order to move a person from self-centeredness to a God-centered perspective. He does not like Lewis's two options: on the one hand, the salvation of souls and the glory of God (supernature), and, on the other hand, nature, which Carritt calls "the crux of the matter."[48] Nor does he like the suggestion from Lewis that when aspects of culture conflict with our service to God, we should set aside those parts of culture. Carritt's inability to understand what Lewis means by "the salvation of human souls" results in a conclusion that misses the point, stating, "I can best, and indeed only, glorify God by doing my duty, which would include, if that is possible, helping others to do theirs."[49]

On April 28, 1940, Lewis wrote to his brother Warren about Carritt's attack, expressing unhappiness with both his former tutor Carritt and Vidler. Carritt wrote as a non-Christian, which surprised and annoyed Lewis, because *Theology* was committed to Christian theology. Why did Vidler publish such an attack from a non-Christian writer in a Christian periodical? In his letter, Lewis compares his own position to Warren writing an article for a military journal and the article being attacked by a pacifist.

About a week after his letter to Warren, Lewis wrote to Alec Vidler about publishing a letter in *Theology*. Lewis wanted to address the reply of E. F. Carritt against Lewis's "Christianity and Culture."[50] He suggested to Vidler that if articles in *Theology* must be prepared for criticism by unbelievers, then the character of *Theology* will change significantly. While he didn't complain, nor did he ever respond to Carritt's attack (although he did reply to Bethell), he was unhappy that Vidler allowed Carritt's reply.

Lewis's review of "Denis de Rougemont, Poetry and Society and Claude Chavasse, The Bride of Christ," appeared in *Theology* in June 1940. He questioned de Rougemont's historical conclusions that the earliest medieval literature of Courtly Love was not an expression of sexual passion, but the symbolic expression of a wish for death and

---

[48] Ibid., 364.

[49] Ibid., 366.

[50] *Collected Letters, II*, 412. The date of the letter is May 8, 1940. Then, in January 1941, Charles Williams' untitled review of *The Problem of Pain* appeared in Alec Vidler's *Theology*. Lewis's letter was later reprinted as part II of the three-part text reprinted under the single title "Christianity and Culture" in *Christian Reflections*.

pain, but he agreed with his ethical conclusions. He also agreed with de Rougemont's thesis that marriage need not have "falling in love" as its efficient cause, nor world "happiness" as its final cause. Lewis writes, "Eros ceases to be a demon only when he ceases to be a god."[51]

PERMANENT OPPOSITION OR CONFLICT?

In November 1940, Lewis's letter, "The Conflict in Anglican Theology," appeared in *Theology*, responding favorably to Oliver C. Quick's letter of the previous month.[52] Quick was at that time Regius Professor of Divinity at Oxford University and Canon of Christ Church (in July 1943, he was to suggest that Oxford University grant Lewis an honorary doctorate in theology.)[53] In responding to a recent article over whether Christianity is subject to human judgment or criticism,[54] Quick had affirmed that the only way to forgiveness was through the Cross, dying and rising with Christ. He had also stated that Moderns of every kind—whether ultra-orthodox Catholics, disciples of Karl Barth or John Macmurray,[55] Communists, or Fascists—have in common the fact that they hate liberalism. Lewis wrote that it might be equally true simply to say that Moderns hate, i.e., that Moderns are known for their attitude of hate rather than anything they oppose.[56]

In the December 1940 issue of *Theology*, Lewis presented "Peace Proposals for Brother Every and Mr. Bethell." In this extended letter, Lewis claims that there is very little disagreement between him and the two men. He does not respond to E. F. Carritt, who did not operate with the same Christian premises, although he states that he regards Carritt "with all the respect and affection I feel for my old tutor and friend."[57] The position Lewis adopts in the March 1940 issue of *Theology*, he states, is that "culture, though not in itself meritorious, was innocent and pleasant, might be a vocation for some, was helpful in bringing certain souls to Christ and could be pursued to the glory

---

[51] *Image and Imagination: Essays and Reviews by C. S. Lewis*. Edited by Walter Hooper. Cambridge: Cambridge University Press, 2013, 62.

[52] *Theology*, October 1940, 234-237.

[53] Alistair McGrath, *C. S. Lewis—A Life: Eccentric Genius, Reluctant Prophet*, Carol Stream, IL: Tyndale House, 2013, 217.

[54] The article, written by Michael Bruce, appeared in *Theology*.

[55] John Macmurray was a Scottish philosopher and Christian.

[56] *God in the Dock*. Edited by Walter Hooper, Grand Rapids: Eerdmans, 1970, 327.

[57] C. S. Lewis, *Christian Reflections*, 27.

of God."⁵⁸ Both Bethel and Every thought that the beliefs of the writer were often implicit in their writings, and Lewis agrees, still affirming that he does not want excellence in reading and writing to be elevated to the level of a spiritual value. This letter concluded the exchange between Lewis and the two men.

Lewis's eighth contribution to *Theology*, a favorable review of Dorothy L. Sayers' new book, was published in October 1941 as "Dorothy L. Sayers, *The Mind of the Maker*."⁵⁹ He describes every sentence as intelligible and every page as advancing the argument.⁶⁰

On August 17, 1941, Lewis writes to Vidler, undoubtedly in response to Vidler's request to publish his famous sermon, "The Weight of Glory." The sermon was delivered in Oxford at St. Mary two months earlier, and he also writes about the time commitment caused by his RAF talks,⁶¹ which include travel and prevent him from doing a book review for *Theology*.⁶² This is the last piece from Lewis published in *Theology* (see the appendix on page 285 for a list of Lewis's ten contributions to *Theology*). In fact, the 1940s were such a busy decade of speaking and writing for Lewis that it is perhaps surprising that he made time to write for Vidler, especially if his primary role was that of opposition.

On July 27, 1948, Lewis writes to Vidler in Vidler's capacity as the editor of *Theology*, about a reviewer's comments on *Essays Presented to Charles Williams*, inviting real criticism of his work rather than vague innuendo, such as "guesses about the feelings of the dead or the bereaved family which are demonstrably wrong."⁶³ He then writes a second letter to Vidler, asking that the first letter from this "permanent opposition" not be published because it is uncharitable.⁶⁴ Neither letter was published. Lewis seems to have expressed his annoyance and then withdrawn his letter. Might this explain why Lewis ceased writing to Vidler?

---

⁵⁸ C. S. Lewis, *Christian Reflections*, 28.

⁵⁹ *Image and Imagination*, 167.

⁶⁰ *Image and Imagination*, 169.

⁶¹ His last RAF talk seems to have taken place in July 1945, so these talks continued for another four years. Bruce R. Johnson, "Scripture, Setting and Audience" *Journal of Inklings Studies*, 2014, 90.

⁶² *Collected Letters, II*, 490.

⁶³ *Collected Letters, II*, 867.

⁶⁴ William Griffin, *Clive Staples Lewis*, 284. The date is May 8, 1940.

"Modern Theology and Biblical Criticism"

C. S. Lewis's best-known public engagement with Alec Vidler's writings took place in 1959 at Westcott House in Cambridge. Two years after being named Dean of King's College, Vidler had published a book called *Windsor Sermons*,[65] sermons written during Vidler's time as a Canon of St. George's Chapel, Windsor (i.e. the chapel at Windsor Castle, one of the principal residences of Queen Elizabeth II). Then, on May 11, 1959, at the invitation of the Principal, Rev. Kenneth Carey, Lewis delivered the talk "Modern Theology and Biblical Criticism"[66] at Westcott House,[67] Cambridge, in response to one of the sermons, "The Sign at Cana," published in *Windsor Sermons*.

Lewis delivered the talk in the Common Room of Westcott House.[68] His first paragraph describes the circumstances under which he was invited to deliver this address, some of the surface reasons for the address, and his concern for the outsider, i.e., the non-theologian, of which Lewis himself was one:

> This paper arose out of a conversation I had with the Principal one night last term. A book of Alec Vidler's happened to be lying on the table and I expressed my reaction to the sort of theology it contained.... One thing led to another and before we were done I was saying a good deal more than I had meant about the type of thought which, so far as I could gather, is now dominant in many theological colleges. He then said, "I wish you would come and say all this to my young men." ... I think his idea was that you ought to know how a certain sort of theology strikes the outsider. Though I may have nothing but misunderstandings to lay before you, you ought to know that such misunderstandings exist. That sort of thing is easy to overlook inside one's own circle. The minds you daily meet have been conditioned by the same studies and prevalent

---

[65] Alec R. Vidler, *Windsor Sermons*. London: SCM Press Ltd, 1958.

[66] The article was later entitled "Fern-seed and Elephants" and is published in *Fern-Seed and Elephants and other essays on Christianity*, edited by Walter Hooper, Glasgow, Great Britain: William Collins Sons & Co. Ltd., 1975, 104-125.

[67] Westcott House is one of the theological colleges (seminaries) of the Church of England.

[68] For a thorough exposition of the theology addressed in this essay and an evaluation of the Cambridge theology faculty that was included in Lewis's address, see my online article, "Modern Theology and Biblical Criticism in Context," located at:http://www.wheaton.edu/wadecenter/Journal-VII/Contents/Online-Articles

opinions as your own. That may mislead you. For of course as priests it is the outsiders you will have to cope with. You exist in the long run for no other purpose. The proper study of shepherds is sheep, not ... other shepherds.... I am a sheep, telling shepherds what only a sheep can tell them. And now I start my bleating.[69]

In an email, retired Cambridge Professor of Modern Church History David Thompson told me, "Ken Carey was a relatively conservative figure as Principal of Westcott ... and I do not find it difficult to imagine him warming to the idea that Lewis might share his ideas with his students."[70] Alister McGrath added in another email that Lewis's concern for the liberal positions held in Cambridge probably motivated him to accept the invitation.[71] Consequently, in his 1959 essay, we find Lewis bringing a conservative biblical perspective, but speaking as a scholar of English literature as well as an experienced writer and an astute thinker.

THE ADDRESS

During the talk, Lewis laid out his four major concerns about the New Testament theology being taught at that time in Cambridge. Those points, briefly summarized, are as follows:

(1) Some biblical critics lack literary judgment (this is Lewis's forte; some critics don't understand extra-biblical literary genres, e.g., incorrectly reading John's Gospel as a romance when, in fact, it is history);

(2) Some wrongly claim that the real teaching of Christ came rapidly to be misunderstood and has only been recovered by modern scholars (Vidler is an example of one of those modern scholars);

(3) Some wrongly claim that miracles don't occur (given the earlier mentioned comments of Vidler about Pentecost, Vidler seems at least to be sympathetic to this viewpoint);

(4) Attempts to recover the origin of a text often

---

[69] C. S. Lewis, "Fern-seed and Elephants," *Fern-Seed and Elephants and other essays on Christianity*, edited by Walter Hooper, Glasgow, Great Britain: William Collins Sons & Co. Ltd., 1975, 104f.

[70] David Thompson. Email correspondence, January 25 and 26, 2013.

[71] Alister McGrath. Email correspondence March 2013.

err (as has happened in the past among academics with some of Plato's and Shakespeare's works and in Lewis's experience with his own writings, which were often attributed to causes which he knew to be non-existent).

Lewis encouraged the Westcott House students to think that one can entertain serious doubts about the conclusions of modern critics who theorize about how a biblical text originated.

VIDLER'S THEOLOGY (NOT VIDLER'S *THEOLOGY*)

Lewis apparently thought highly of the journal *Theology* when it began, but did he sour on the publication? Why would he write ten pieces for *Theology* (see Appendix I) during the first three years of Vidler's editorship, but none thereafter? While some of Vidler's theological commitments have been stated earlier, Vidler continued to develop as a theologian throughout his life, probably moving even further to the left.

In 1962, Vidler edited a book entitled *Soundings: Essays Concerning Christian Understanding*.[72] Contributors included Cambridge theologians H. W. Montefiore and J. N. Sanders, the former a Dean at Gonville and Caius College and lecturer in Divinity and the latter a New Testament scholar from Peterhouse, and H. A. Williams, Dean of Trinity College, who contributed "Theology and Self-Awareness." In his *Soundings* chapter, Montefiore affirms Jesus as God and man "in the same Person." However, he also claims that the author of the Fourth Gospel mingled his own experience with the words and works of Jesus "in such a way that the critic cannot distinguish the two."[73] Later he states that Jesus "seems explicitly to have denied" His deity, with his affirmation of God as "My Father," which is something other than that he was "of one substance with the Father."[74] For Montefiore, Jesus made functional or relational statements about Himself rather

---

[72] Vidler, A. R., ed. *Soundings: Essays Concerning Christian Understanding*, Cambridge University Press, first edition 1962. Vidler's chapter was entitled "Religion and the National Church," 239-63. This chapter and all other chapters in *Soundings* were accessed at the Marion E. Wade Center, Wheaton, Illinois. This copy of *Soundings* was Lewis's copy, which contains Lewis's notes on various pages.

[73] Montefiore, Hugh W. "Towards a Christology for Today." *Soundings: Essays Concerning Christian Understanding*. Cambridge: At the University Press, 1966, 150.

[74] Montefiore, "Towards a Christology for Today," 158.

than statements about His nature.⁷⁵ Montefiore seems to be trying to write about God as person without suggesting that human personhood was the model for God. However, Montefiore shows his support for the theology expressed by Bishop J. A. T. Robinson, Dean of Clare College,⁷⁶ and J. S. Bezzant, Dean of St. John's, when he states, "The old theology starts with the divinity of Christ and tries to explain how God became man. The new theology starts with the only indisputable fact—that Christ was man—and tries to show how God acted through Him uniquely."⁷⁷ Montefiore states that the death of Jesus "enabled man to accept himself and thereby to enter into a right relationship with God and with his fellow men, and so to fulfill the purpose for which he was created."⁷⁸ This falls far short of stating the purpose of the death of Jesus. Nor does Montefiore clearly hold to the physical resurrection of Jesus from the dead, as indicated from his statement, "The Resurrection appearances are not dissimilar in form from other paranormal phenomena of the same general kind."⁷⁹

Sanders' chapter was a historical study of nineteenth century views of the authority of the New Testament. He suggests that apparent discrepancies in matters of doctrine are "smoothed over by nice distinctions and more or less ingenious special pleading."⁸⁰ Like Montefiore, Sanders was willing to set aside the doctrinal statements of the past which he thought inadequate for the twentieth cenury, largely for the sake of "freeing of the interpretation of the New Testament from dogmatic control."⁸¹

In "Theology and Self-Awareness," H. A. Williams writes, "This, to begin with, was the basis of Christ's quarrel with the Pharisees. Modern research has shown that the typical Pharisee was not a pious

---

⁷⁵ Montefiore, "Towards a Christology for Today," 159.

⁷⁶ Robinson was later the author of the best-selling book, *Honest to God*, which was considered by many to deny the existence of a personal God.

⁷⁷ Wren, Christopher S. "An American Bishop's Search for a Space-Age God." *Look* February 22, 1966 (Vol. 30, No. 4):29.

⁷⁸ Montefiore, "Towards a Christology for Today" 167.

⁷⁹ Montefiore, "Towards a Christology for Today" 170.

⁸⁰ Sanders, Joseph N. "The Meaning and Authority of the New Testament." *Soundings: Essays Concerning Christian Understanding.* Cambridge: At the University Press, 1966, 125.

⁸¹ Sanders, "The Meaning and Authority," 127. He cites the Council of Chalcedon (451 A.D.) as adequate for the fifth century but not for the twentieth century. Sanders also rejects Bultmann, but he commends higher criticism. Sanders, "The Meaning and Authority," 130, 139.

fraud. He was upright, conscientious and God-fearing, and certainly not given to conscious hypocrisy."[82] In the margin of his personal copy of *Soundings*, next to Williams' chapter, Lewis writes, next to the word "hypocrisy," "Our Lord was singularly misinformed? He had not the advantage of modern research."[83] Lewis was unhappy with Williams here and with other conclusions in *Soundings*. Other notes indicate that he was pleased with some of the insights of the authors, so we need not conclude that he was merely acting out his role as permanent opposition.

In 1963, Alec Vidler co-edited with J. S. Bezzant and two other Cambridge Fellows a book entitled *Objections to Christian Belief*.[84] The book was the result of a series of lectures in Cambridge attended by about 1,500 people each week. The book dealt with whether the Christian faith depended upon the historical truthfulness of Christ's life, crucifixion, and resurrection.

In his chapter, "Intellectual Objections," Vidler contributed the most radical of the four essays. He writes of the "striking inconsistencies" in the New Testament writers. His opinion that the descendants of Adam and Eve were intended to replace those angels who had rebelled against God sounds strange at best. Describing the early Christian message as "free imaginative composition" reflects a non-historical understanding of the New Testament. Vidler wonders whether "Christians then live and die for what they must allow to be not certainly, but only probably, the case."[85] Bezzant cites Rudolf Bultmann favorably when Bultmann considered the resurrection a matter of faith only, not a historical confirmation of the crucifixion and the power of Christ over death, and he also states that "we cannot be sure that we have the actual words of Jesus."[86] One reviewer was especially unhappy with the book, writing, "In effect it is like seeing

---

[82] H. A. Williams, "Theology and Self-Awareness." *Soundings*, 91. See https://vufind.carli.illinois.edu/vf-whe/Record/whe_196050/Description

[83] H. A. Williams, "Theology and Self-Awareness," *Soundings: Essays Concerning Christian Understanding*. Cambridge: At the University Press, 1966, 91.

[84] MacKinnon, D. M.; Vidler, A. R.; Williams, H. A.; Bezzant, J. S. *Objections to Christian Belief*. Middlesex, England: Penguin Books, 1963. D. M. Mackinnon was The Regius Professor of Moral Philosophy at the University of Aberdeen (1947-1960) and later the Norris-Hulse Professor of Divinity at the University of Cambridge (1960-1978).

[85] *Objections*, 65.

[86] MacKinnon, *Objections*, et al. 83.

the resident firemen of Christianity acting as incendiaries, cutting their own hoses, in order to demonstrate how well they understand the human condition of arson."[87]

These modernist perspectives—especially those of Vidler, Bezzant, Montefiore, Williams, and Robinson—were unacceptable to Lewis. On one occasion, Lewis writes, "Mere 'modernism' I reject at once."[88]

VIDLER ELSEWHERE IN LEWIS'S WRITINGS

Lewis and Vidler had other interactions. In 1942, probably because of their association through the publication of *Theology*, Lewis published a letter in the *Christian News-Letter*,[89] a newsletter started by Dr. J. H. Oldham and assisted by Alec Vidler. The newsletter addressed current theological issues from a Christian point of view. The editorial board of the *Christian News-Letter* included Vidler, poet T. S. Eliot, Lord Hambleden, and writer Philip Mairet.[90] In that 290-word letter, Lewis wrote about dealing with Germans captured by the British during World War II, and how they might read English while imprisoned and be examined by university examiners. The request originally came from the German prisoners and led to a meeting between Lewis and Miss Ethel Herdman,[91] Secretary, and later Director, of the Educational Books Section of the Joint War Organisation's Prisoners of War Department. She oversaw meeting some of the needs of the German prisoners of war and housed them in the New Bodleian. This apparently led to contacts between her and Lewis, who helped to develop recommended readings in English literature (by steps Lewis does not enumerate; the prisoners

---

[87] *Scenes*, 181f., citing a review of June 27, 1963 in *The Listener*.

[88] *C. S. Lewis: Collected Letters, Volume 2. Books, Broadcasts and War 1931-1949.* Edited by Walter Hooper. London: HarperCollinsPublishers, 2004, 646. The date of the letter is May 8, 1945.

[89] On February 4, 1942.

[90] Vidler, *Scenes*, 120.

[91] Miss Herdman is not elsewhere mentioned in the writings of Lewis. In *The Irish Times*, Sarah Franklin writes that it was not uncommon for German POWs to become friends with many British citizens, to be paid wages for work at various jobs, and even to be invited into British homes for Christmas lunch. https://www.irishtimes.com/culture/books/the-untold-story-of-britain-s-pow-camps-1.3169823. *Light on C. S. Lewis*, 145. Dr. J. H. Oldham, publisher, *The Christian News-Letter*, No. 119, 21 Northmoor Road, Oxford, Feb. 4, 1942. See also Bruce R. Johnson, "The Efforts of C. S. Lewis to Aid British Prisoners of War during World War II," *Sehnsucht*, Volume 12, 2018.

were allowed to study many different subjects, including medicine, agriculture, aviation, accounting, and other disciplines) and a non-degree course of study. The intent was that such studies would enable these POWs find employment after the war, once their captivity had ended.[92]

In his autobiography, Vidler also wrote about spending a night with Lewis in Magdalen College at a time when the office of the *Christian News-Letter* had been moved during the war to Manchester College, Oxford.[93] Such a move might have facilitated the publication of this letter by Lewis, but it also suggests they were on friendly terms.

Lewis wrote rather favorably of Vidler in *Letters to Malcolm*,[94] mentioning Vidler by name nine times in the book. He writes, "About Vidler. I never heard the program which created all that scandal, and naturally one wouldn't condemn a dog on newspaper extracts. But I have now read his essay in *Soundings* and I believe I go a good deal further with him than you[95] would. Much of what he quotes from F. D. Maurice and Bonhoeffer seems to me very good; and so, I think, are his own arguments for the Establishment."[96] Vidler wrote about Maurice, who rejected religion in the sense of rejecting beliefs and practices devised by men which separate people from one another, and about Dietrich Bonhoeffer, who talked about "religionless Christianity."[97] Lewis tells Malcolm that he agrees with the quotations from Maurice and Bonhoeffer, particularly when religion refers to the practices of humans, while theology refers to revelation from God.[98] When Vidler called for less religion, Lewis writes, people misunderstood him to mean that the church should remove what little belief system that liberalism had left. He also commends Vidler's ideas about delight in religious organization while acknowledging the danger of that organization leading to legalism.[99]

---

[92] Dr. J. H. Oldham, publisher, *The Christian News-Letter*, No. 119, 21 Northmoor Road, Oxford, Feb. 4, 1942.

[93] Vidler, *Scenes*, 121.

[94] C. S. Lewis, *Letters to Malcolm: Chiefly on Prayer*. London: HarperCollins Publishers, 1977, 30. *Letters to Malcolm* was originally published in January 1964, two months after Lewis's death.

[95] The fictional Malcolm, recipient of these letters.

[96] Lewis, *Letters to Malcolm*, 29f.

[97] *Soundings*, 241-44.

[98] Lewis, *Letters to Malcolm*, 29f.

[99] Lewis, *Letters to Malcolm*, 30. See *Soundings*, 252.

Lewis also states of Vidler in that same work, "He wants ... to retain some Christian doctrines. But he is prepared to scrap a good deal. 'Traditional doctrines' are to be tested."[100] Later in *Letters to Malcolm* he writes, "Shall we then proceed on Vidler's principles and scrap the embarrassing promises as 'venerable archaisms' which have to be 'outgrown'?"[101] Lewis was opposed to this approach, which is reflected in Vidler's comment,

> All traditional doctrines and institutions must be subject to this test,[102] and there is no obligation on Christians to promote or to preserve what does not survive it.... Many of the religious elements in historic Christianity and much that has gone under the name of religion may thus be outgrown, or survive chiefly as venerable archaisms or as fairy stories for children, and we cannot tell in advance how they will be replaced or which of them will need to be replaced.[103]

Vidler was prepared to set aside whatever religion had outgrown, including many of the fundamental biblical truths that have stood the test of time and that have strong historical and biblical foundation.

Some might interpret the diminishing correspondence between Lewis and Vidler in later years as a cooling of their relationship, but this would probably be a mistake, not only because some correspondence might not have been preserved, but also because of the favorable comments about Vidler in *Letters to Malcolm*. In fact, for the weekend of March 17-20, 1945, Ridley Hall[104] hosted a weekend conference on "Christian Faith," organized by Stella Aldwinckle primarily for members of the Oxford University Socratic Club. Lewis, Dr. L. W. Grensted,[105] and Baptist minister Rev. F. C. Bryan were scheduled to speak, with each person delivering two talks. All of them had spoken at a similar conference in 1943. At the last minute, Dr. Grensted got the flu and could not attend, so Stella Aldwinckle invited Alec Vidler to replace him. Vidler was unable to accept the invitation,

---

[100] Lewis, *Letters to Malcolm*, 32.

[101] *Letters to Malcolm*, 59, citing Vidler in *Soundings*, 254.

[102] The fruit of the Spirit test.

[103] *Soundings*, 254.

[104] A theological college (seminary) of the Church of England in Cambridge.

[105] Oriel Professor of the Philosophy of the Christian Religion.

Twenty-One Friendships of C.S. Lewis

but the invitation suggests a still cordial relationship with Lewis in 1945.

Finally, what did Vidler himself say about Lewis when he wrote a review of Lewis's *The Discarded Image* for the *New York Herald Tribune* in 1964? In this review, which was far more an article full of praise for Lewis than a book review, Vidler writes, "Lewis was an exceedingly gifted and versatile man with great strength of personality and charm of manner."[106] Vidler compliments Lewis for his skill as a Christian apologist, skill that he finds "comparable with, but superior to, and more varied than, those of G. K. Chesterton in the previous generation."[107] He concludes his review by stating, "More alluring and more effective, however, than his argumentative or expository essays were his oblique or indirect presentations of Christian faith in his allegories, his novels and his tales for children. Here the extraordinary fertility of his imagination found full scope, and could delight readers who did not at first, or perhaps ever, perceive the point of his parables."[108] Those are not the words of a man at odds with Lewis, nor did Lewis feel himself at odds with Vidler. While they had theological disagreements, they still appreciated the talents of one another.

Lyle W. Dorsett once interviewed Vidler and asked him about Lewis. Dorsett writes, "Vidler said without hesitation that Lewis was one of the brightest, if not the most brilliant man in England in this century. Vidler showed obvious respect and admiration for Lewis. He never said an unfavorable word about his old colleague."[109]

Conclusion

During the years of their correspondence, Lewis contributed ten written pieces for publication in *Theology* under Vidler's editorship. The best interpretation of this interaction, which ended just three

---

[106] Alec Vidler, "Unapologetic Apologist," *New York Herald Tribune*, July 26, 1964, Book Week section, 3.

[107] Ibid.

[108] Ibid.

[109] Oral history interview excerpt with Alexander R. Vidler, June 4, 1986. Used by permission. Later, when asked by Malcolm Muggeridge about Lewis's essay "Modern Theology and Biblical Criticism," Vidler stated (this is a paraphrase, rather than a direct quotation, based on the recollection of Lyle Dorsett) "that he never did really enjoy Lewis's company because the Oxonian was abrasive, argumentative and quite dogmatic. In brief, he was never wrong."

years later, is that Lewis saw a need to help *Theology* establish itself under Vidler's editorship and that, though he disagreed with Vidler on some points of theology, he chose to channel his energies in other directions after 1941, a decade during which Lewis was especially prolific as an author. That choice was probably based, not on theological disagreements, but on the press of Lewis's many duties, the heavy schedule of teaching, speaking, and writing and, perhaps, on his interest in supporting other worthy publications. With the beginning of his BBC broadcasts in 1941 and the serializing of *The Screwtape Letters* in 1941 and their publication in 1942, Lewis was becoming much more widely known and in far greater demand as a speaker and writer. Furthermore, Lewis had only offered to write book reviews for Vidler, and the occasional article was something over and above his original offer.

Lewis himself loved the exchange of views, whether friendly or hostile, and it is doubtful that he was offended by the theology of Vidler to the point that he withdrew from writing for *Theology*. Some might have advised Vidler no longer to publish anything by Lewis, since their theological disagreements were clear, but Lewis did not withdraw from Vidler. Several connections between Lewis and Vidler, as well as between Lewis and some of Vidler's friends, after those ten pieces of writing, indicate that they remained friends even while their careers moved in different directions. That Lewis had favorable comments on Vidler in his last book, *Letters to Malcolm*, provides further confirmation. Lewis may have offered to be "permanent opposition," but he was certainly not permanently opposed to everything that Vidler had to offer.

Appendix: C. S. Lewis's Publications in *Theology*

C. S. Lewis was published ten times in *Theology*: two articles, four book reviews, and four letters. In the following list, they appear in chronological order.

1) Review: "A sacred poem: Charles Williams, *Taliessin Through Logres*," *Theology*, Vol. XXXVIII, Issue 226 (April 1939): 268-276. DOI: 10.1177/0040571X3903822605

2) Letter: "The Conditions for a Just War," *Theology*, Vol. XXXVIII, Issue 227 (May 1939): 373-374. DOI: 10.1177/0040571X3903822709

3) Review: *"A Lectionary of Christian Prose from the Second Century to the Twentieth Century*, ed. A. C. Bouquet, *Theology*, Vol. XXXIX, Issue 234 (December 1939): 467-468. DOI: 10.1177/0040571X3903923417

4) Article: "Christianity and Culture," *Theology*, Vol. XL, Issue 237 (March 1940): 166-179. DOI: 10.1177/0040571X4004023702

5) Letter: "Christianity and Culture," *Theology*, Vol. XL, Issue 240 (June 1940): 475-477. DOI: 10.1177/0040571X4004024027

6) Review: "Denis de Rougemont, Poetry and Society and Claude Chavasse, The Bride of Christ," *Theology*, Vol. XL, Issue 240 (June 1940): 459-461. DOI: 10.1177/0040571X4004024014

7) Letter: "The Conflict in Anglican Theology," *Theology*, Vol. LXI, Issue 245 (November 1940): 304. DOI: 10.1177/0040571X4004124513

8) Extended Letter: "Peace Proposals for Brother Every and Mr Bethell," *Theology*, Vol. XLI, Issue 246 (December 1940): 339-348. DOI: 10.1177/0040571X4004124604

9) Review: "Dorothy L. Sayers, *The Mind of the Maker*," *Theology*, Vol. XLIII, Issue 256 (October 1941): 248-249. DOI: 10.1177/0040571X4104325618

10) Article: "The Weight of Glory," *Theology*, Vol. XLIII, Issue 257 (November 1941): 263-274. DOI: 10.1177/0040571X4104325702

SECTION III

CO-WORKERS AND FELLOW PILGRIMS

Christ's Shadow in Plato's Cave: A Meditation on the Substance of Love
Oxford: Amate Press 1990, 83 pages. Limited Edition 76 copies.

Chapter 15

STELLA ALDWINCKLE,
Atheists, and Agnostics

Stella Aldwinckle invited "atheists, agnostics, and those who are disillusioned about religion or think they are" to discuss the positions they had adopted against Christianity. Unafraid to hear arguments from the other side, Aldwinckle modeled the openness for which C. S. Lewis was well-known. She had confidence in her faith and the biblical foundation on which it was based, and the Oxford University Socratic Club provided the venue for those face-to-face discussions.

Best known as the founder of the Oxford University Socratic Club, Aldwinckle served as the Club's Chairman during the twelve years that C. S. Lewis was President. The two worked side by side, planning and conducting one of the most popular undergraduate societies at the university. The Socratic's many guest speakers over the years showcased a star-studded lineup of English intellectuals whose reputations often spanned the globe—people like atheists Antony Flew and J. B. S. Haldane, philosophers Isaiah Berlin and Gilbert Ryle and Michael Dummett, writer Dorothy L. Sayers, and philosophers C. E. M. Joad and Gabriel Marcel[1]—many of them supporters of the Christian faith but many of them opponents. Aldwinckle and Lewis planned to bring the best people they could find to present a view that challenged the Christian faith to see if Christianity could stand its ground. This essay deals with the organizer of those Socratic Club meetings rather than the challenges between two opposing points of view, although it is to her lasting credit that she was able to recruit such an impressive list of speakers.

"ALL ATHEISTS AND AGNOSTICS"

After five years of teaching theology in other parts of England, Elia Estelle "Stella" Aldwinckle returned to Oxford in 1941, late in the Michaelmas Term.[2] The idea for the Socratic Club surfaced at a

---

[1] Jim Stockton, "Chaplain Stella Aldwinckle: A Biographical Sketch of the Spiritual Foundation of the Oxford University Socratic Club," *Inklings Forever* 8 (2012), 2.

[2] Stella Aldwinckle, "Socrates Was a Realist," *Socratic Digest* No. 1, 1942-43, 10.

"fresher's tea,"³ which Aldwinckle hosted in the rectory of St. Aldate's Church to discuss ministry hopes for the term. There undergraduate Monica Shorten⁴ complained that there was no forum to discuss important matters about the Christian faith. She stated, "The sermons and the religious clubs just take the real difficulties as solved—things like the existence of God, the divinity of Christ, and so on."⁵ They determined that they needed a place to discuss "the intellectual difficulties connected with religion and with Christianity in particular." Soon thereafter, Aldwinckle posted an invitation for "all atheists, agnostics, and those who are disillusioned about religion or think they are" to meet in the Junior Common Room of Somerville College. Two informal meetings were held during the Michaelmas Term, the first with female students at Somerville College only and the second with these students and their boyfriends to standing room only, again in the Junior Common Room of the college.⁶ These two meetings paved the way for the start of the Socratic Club.

Monica Shorten
With permission of Principal and Fellows of Somerville

Since the club was required to have a senior member of the University as its President, they invited Lewis. Lewis had recently completed his second series of talks over the BBC, his *Screwtape Letters* were being serialized in *The Guardian*, and his three Ballard

---

³ That is, tea and cakes for incoming university freshmen.

⁴ It is my guess that this 'fresher's tea" is the time and place where Monica Shorten voiced this opinion. Monica Shorten attended Somerville College, 1941-1943, in a Shortened Honours program due to the war, studied Zoology, earning a BA degree in Natural Science in 1944 and the MA in 1948. She worked as a Research Assistant at the Bureau of Animal Population in Oxford from 1943 to 1948; as a Scientific Officer with Infestation Control, which was part of the Ministry of Agriculture; and then Senior Scientific Officer until 1958. She wrote for *Nature, New Naturalist, Proceedings of the Zoological Society of London*, and other publications. Email from Kate O'Donnell, Assistant Archivist, December 3, 2019.

⁵ Ibid.

⁶ Stella Aldwinckle, "Oral History Interview with Lyle W. Dorsett," July 26, 1985, 5. Call no.: OH / SR-1, The Marion E. Wade Center, Wheaton College, Wheaton, IL. Used by permission. The size of these rooms meant that they might have up to seventy-five students in attendance.

Mathews lectures on *Paradise Lost* were about to be delivered at University College of North Wales, Bangor. Furthermore, his best-known sermon, "The Weight of Glory," had been delivered to a packed house at the University church a few months earlier and was on its way to publication.[7] Lewis was a rising star on the Oxonian landscape, clearly the best choice for President.

Although it is unclear when they met, Lewis and Aldwinckle probably met soon after that "fresher's tea." When Aldwinckle invited Lewis to be president of the Socratic Club, the club was well under way, having already held two unofficial meetings during Michaelmas Term in 1941.[8] Soon after Christmas, the Oxford University Socratic Club was fully established with Aldwinckle as Chairman and Lewis as President.[9] For the next twelve years, Aldwinckle worked closely with Lewis to set the schedule of speakers, book meeting space, publicize the meetings, and conduct the meetings of the Club.

THE SOCRATIC CLUB BEGINS

The first official meeting of the Socratic Club took place on Monday evening, January 26, 1942, at Somerville College.[10] Guest speaker Robert Emlyn Havard, the Lewis family physician and an Inkling, spoke on the topic, "Won't Mankind Outgrow Christianity in the Face of the Advance of Science and of Modern Ideologies?" Havard, a devout Catholic, undoubtedly answered the question with a resounding "No!"[11]

Socratic Club, Somerville College
Left window at corner, first floor
Author photo

---

[7] June 8, 1941, St. Mary the Virgin Church, Oxford.

[8] Jim Stockton, unpublished essay, *The Oxford University Socratic Club 1942—1972: A Life*.

[9] Walter Hooper, *C. S. Lewis: Companion & Guide*, New York: HarperCollins Publishers, 1996, 617f.

[10] The location of the meeting is shown in the photograph, taken by the author in the Somerville quad. It was determined when the author visited Somerville College while on sabbatical in 2004 and inquired about that meeting at the Porter's Lodge.

[11] Meetings normally started at 8:15 p.m. and usually lasted until

No Ordinary People

The first issue of the *Socratic Digest* explains the origin of the Socratic Club in an essay entitled "Socrates Was a Realist." In that essay, Aldwinckle contends that realists, not escapists, are welcome because Socrates was a realist. The Club is for those who ask ultimate questions, and who desire to live an unselfish life. Two main questions were to be entertained at the Socratic: "First, is existence significant at all?" Secondly, is there any way out of the bondage to self-centeredness?[12]

In the second issue of the *Socratic Digest*, Aldwinckle's editorial explains that this issue of the *Digest* was concerned with truth, how we know that something was true, what we mean by words such as *knowledge* and *truth*, and to what extent our convictions are based on rational grounds. Often a person's attitude is neither rational nor scientific. She writes, "With such considerations at the back of our minds, Reason is here discussed, and also Faith, as *practical* issues."[13]

In a later issue of the *Socratic Digest*,[14] Aldwinckle argues that philosophy in Oxford is too often used to confuse rather than to clarify, and Austin Farrer's essay "On Credulity"[15] provides an antidote. Farrer invites us to ask important questions, such as those about the existence of God, rather than trivial ones. Not only do such questions "keep philosophical fashion in perspective …," they help us to find "a bridge between scientific and personal knowledge, between 'reason' and 'faith.'" Furthermore, such questions …

> … may be fundamentally of a piece with the childlikeness which Christ teaches us can open the Kingdom of God to a man, and it is also possible that the fragmentary and more than untidy intellectual answers to our untidy questions may remove misunderstanding and ignorance and so prepare the way … to another kind of answer—that spiritual discovery which sets the questions in a new frame of reference, and so gives them an intelligibility in which scientific and personal knowledge both find their due place.[16]

For Aldwinckle, faith and reason work together.

10:30 p.m. Green and Hooper, 215.

[12] *Socratic Digest*, No. 1, 10f.

[13] Editorial, *Socratic Digest*, No. 2, June 1944.

[14] Issue No. 4, 1947-48.

[15] Austin Farrer, "On Credulity," *Illuminatio* 1 (1947):3-9. See also the Preface of Stella Aldwinckle in *Socratic Digest*, Number 4, page 5.

[16] Stella Aldwinckle, Preface, *Socratic Digest*, No. 4, 102.

Twenty-One Friendships of C.S. Lewis

In the second meeting, speakers Dr. William Stevenson[17] and C. S. Lewis addressed a Freudian claim, "Is God a Wish Fulfillment?" Freud had claimed that belief in God arose out of a wish for an omnipotent Father: "When a human being has himself grown up… he is in possession of greater strength, but his insight into the perils of life has also grown greater…he still remains just as helpless and unprotected as he was in his childhood … .Even now, therefore, he cannot do without the protection which he enjoyed as a child."[18] Religious ideas, Freud stated, owe their origin neither to reason nor experience but to a need to overcome fear: "[they] are not precipitates of experience or end results of thinking: they are illusions, fulfilments of the oldest, strongest and most urgent wishes of mankind. The secret of their strength lies in the strength of those wishes."[19]

Aldwinckle spoke at the third meeting of the Socratic Club. The remaining speakers during this first term included W. B. Merchant, Lord Elton,[20] Charles Williams, and L. W. Grensted, Oriel Professor of the Philosophy of the Christian Religion. That Lewis spoke at the second meeting surprises no one. Aldwinckle once wrote, "C. S. Lewis himself always came. He came to every meeting, eight meetings a term, unless he was actually ill or had to attend something in London. His support was simply wonderful."[21]

Subsequent terms at Oxford University featured an impressive array of speakers, and Lewis himself often provided the first response to a speaker who was challenging Christianity. Aldwinckle states about Lewis, "In meetings, he was never ever dogmatic or domineering. He would listen sympathetically to the other person's point of view and

---

[17] Stevenson was Assistant Director of the Institute of Experimental Psychology and, presumably, represented the Freudian point of view. See the *Socratic Digest*, No. 1, 1942-43, reprint edition, Joel D. Heck, editor, 3.

[18] Freud, "The Question of a Weltanschauung," in *The Standard Edition of the Complete Psychological Works of Sigmund Freud*, vol. XXII, James Strachey, editor, London: The Hogarth Press and the Institute of Psycho-Analysis, 1974, 163.

[19] Sigmund Freud, *The Future of an Illusion*, New York: W. W. Norton, 1961, 30.

[20] Possibly Godfrey Elton, British historian, 1st Baron Elton (1892-1973), Fellow of Queen's College, Oxford, 1919-1939, and secretary of the Rhodes Trust,1939-1959. He would have been living in Oxford at the time.

[21] Stella Aldwinckle, "Memories of the Socratic Club," *C. S. Lewis and His Circle: Essays and Memoirs from the Oxford C. S. Lewis Society*, Roger White, Judith Wolfe, and Brendan Wolfe, eds., 193.

would comment helpfully, not antagonistically. Because, you see, we weren't debating. In a debating society you are out to score points and to win the votes. But we were Socratic, that is, we wanted to get to the truth of things, and to follow the argument in good faith and good temper wherever it went."[22]

The typical Socratic Club meeting featured a major paper, sometimes a formal response by another speaker and then questions from the audience. Aldwinckle would sit in the chair, the speakers would join her on the stage, and students would sit on the floor.[23] So valuable were the various meetings of the Socratic, Aldwinckle notes, that students frequently "used to go on talking under the streetlamps until two or three in the morning."[24] The first term of meetings took place in Somerville College, but subsequent meetings met in other colleges of the University, such as the Junior Common Room of St. Hilda's College or St. John's College or Oriel College. Attendance varied from a high of 250 on January 24, 1944—when C. E. M. Joad spoke to a standing room only crowd about his controversial views on atheism and theism—to a couple of dozen.[25] Throughout the years of the Socratic Club's existence, Stella Aldwinckle guided the club through 414 meetings with 306 scholars and guest speakers, many of them the most famous names of their day in England.

Socratic Teas, Weekends, and a Socratic Farm

To advance the mission of the Socratic Club, Aldwinckle held regular Socratic teas and experimented with Socratic Weekends. Three of the Socratic teas took place in the Michaelmas Term of 1949. Presumably, there were many others in every year, especially during the Michaelmas Term—the first term of the new school year. In 1949, as the Michaelmas term was beginning, Stella Aldwinckle held a Socratic Tea with several students to discuss Socratic Club policy.[26]

---

[22] Ibid.

[23] Stella Aldwinckle, "Memories of the Socratic Club," *C. S. Lewis and His Circle: Essays and Memoirs from the Oxford C. S. Lewis Society*, Roger White, Judith Wolfe, and Brendan Wolfe, eds., 192.

[24] Stella Aldwinckle, "Memories of the Socratic Club," *C. S. Lewis and His Circle: Essays and Memoirs from the Oxford C. S. Lewis Society*, Roger White, Judith Wolfe, and Brendan Wolfe, eds., 192.

[25] During its heyday in 1944, the Socratic Club had 164 student members.

[26] Notebook of Stella Aldwinckle, The Stella Aldwinckle Papers, Box 8, Folder 386. The Marion E. Wade Center, Wheaton College, Wheaton,

One week later, she held another afternoon Socratic Tea, where they discussed the type of paper that should be read at the Socratic Club.[27] Then, in November, she held a high tea Socratic Meeting, discussing topics, getting college representatives, and gathering volunteers to sell the *Socratic Digest* between academic terms. Since students served the Socratic Club as secretaries and treasurers, they undoubtedly attended such meetings, serving as an executive committee to advance the aims of the Socratic Club and promote the Christian faith.

In the early years of the Socratic, weekend retreats offered teaching on important biblical concepts, but no retreats were held after 1945. Apparently, a good idea was tried and found to be unable to fit into the schedules of busy university students. Unfortunately, the 1945 conference was held during the last week of term, a time when students were preoccupied with completing assignments and preparing for exams, so this may have been the death knell of the Socratic weekends.

In 1943,[28] a weekend Socratics' Conference on "Christian Faith" was held at the Old Jordans Hostel, Beaconsfield, about halfway between Oxford and London. A second Socratics' Conference was held with the same theme in Cambridge in 1945.[29] The broad theme of the conferences allowed for a wide range of topics in the lectures. The speakers at these two conferences included Lewis, Dr. L. W. Grensted, Dr. R. W. Kosterlitz of New College,[30] Rev. F. C. Bryan, and Rev. Eric Fenn.[31] Stella Aldwinckle was the driving force behind this conference, as she was for most Socratic activities. In attendance were many students from the colleges of Oxford University. At these

---

IL. Used by Permission. Notebook. Paul Piehler of Magdalen, P. B. Topham of Somerville, I. L. Lee of Magdalen, and six others were in attendance. The date is October 13.

[27] The Stella Aldwinckle Papers, Box 8, Folder 386. The Marion E. Wade Center, Wheaton College, Wheaton, IL. Used by Permission. Notebook. Those in attendance including Hare, Aldwinckle, Alvarez of Christ Church, and E. Thompson of Balliol.

[28] On March 13-16.

[29] On March 17-20, 1945 at Ridley Hall, Cambridge.

[30] Kosterlitz spoke at the Socratic Club on five different occasions—June 2, 1942, June 26, 1942, March 11, 1946, October 25, 1948, and January 28, 1952.

[31] Eric Fenn, a Presbyterian minister, worked for the BBC as assistant head of religious broadcasting. He replaced Grensted at the 1945 conference, speaking on "Faith in Christ" and "Prayer – before or after faith?"

conferences, Grensted spoke on "Prayer—Before or After Faith?", "The Nature of Faith," and "The Consequences of Faith.", and Lewis spoke on "Presuppositions of Faith" and "The Church."[32]

The topics of the weekend conferences indicate Aldwinckle's interest in providing basic instruction in the Christian faith and helping students to understand how to defend their faith during the impressionable college years. Difficult topics—eschatology, sacramental theology, denominational differences, and the like—were not on the docket; rather, the weekends aimed at what Lewis later called mere Christianity. His four series of BBC talks on the Christian faith may actually have led Aldwinckle to select topics that reflected what he had taught over the radio. These weekend conferences were no longer held after 1945, perhaps because the war had ended, the soldiers had returned, and everyone's schedules became much busier.

The Socratic Farm never got off the ground. In the Editor's Notes to the second issue of the *Socratic Digest*, Aldwinckle writes,

> We have in mind the possibility of beginning a 'Socratic Farm' after the war, immediately outside Oxford, combining a 'Socratic' Library and Guest House for extra-Oxford and gone-down Socratics on holidays, with a Club House for undergraduate Socratics during term. Here Socratic conferences could be held in vacation. We would welcome the considered views of readers and their friends on whether such facilities would be welcomed (also any donations towards the Library, now in embryo!), and the names of any who would like to combine a country holiday with a Socratic Conference in the summer of 1945.[33]

---

[32] Weekend Conference Programme. 1943 Conference on Christian Faith. Stella Aldwinckle Papers. Box 8, Folder 367. The Marion E. Wade Center, Wheaton College, Wheaton, IL. It was apparently Stella Aldwinckle (possibly someone else) who took handwritten notes (still extant at the Wade Center) on the talks by the various speakers, including those by C. S. Lewis. Her prayer, written on the bottom of a follow-up letter after the 1943 conference, shows something about her faith: "O God, the God of all goodness and of all grace, who art worthy of a greater love than we can either give or understand, pour into our hearts, we beseech Thee, such love toward Thee, that nothing may seem too hard for us to do or to suffer in obedience to Thy will; and grant that, thus loving Thee, we may become daily more like unto Thee, through Jesus Christ our Lord." Stella Aldwinckle letter, March 30, 1943. Ibid. See the chapter on F. C. Bryan for more information about the weekend conference. The conference began on Saturday evening and continued all day on Sunday and Monday.

[33] Future Developments, *Socratic Digest*, No. 2, June 1944, 30.

Twenty-One Friendships of C.S. Lewis

The funds apparently never materialized, and the Socratic Farm never saw the light of day.

THE LONDON SOCRATIC CLUB

Early in 1943, buoyed by the success of the Oxford Socratic, Stella Aldwinckle met with Mr. M. Kinchin-Smith[34] about establishing a Socratic Club in London. The Oxford Socratic Club was enjoying the popularity of its early years and the influence of Lewis, so its leaders wanted to extend the Socratic to other locations. They asked Dorothy L. Sayers to serve as Chairman (they had originally wanted her to lead the Oxford Socratic Club),[35] and Kinchin-Smith would serve as deputy chairman. The London Socratic Club would have two secretaries and a student's committee to represent various London colleges, among them King's, Bedford, University College, London School of Economics, and Westfield. The geographical distribution of students probably made a student committee much less efficient than in Oxford and may have contributed to the failure of the London Socratic Club.

The following year, Aldwinckle met with Dorothy L. Sayers and Rev. Gilbert Shaw once again to discuss the Socratic Club of London.[36] Some months later, Aldwinckle wrote to Sayers about the fall program for the London Socratic Club being cancelled and inviting her to come to address the Oxford Socratic Club.[37] Dorothy L. Sayers was certainly as capable as C. S. Lewis to serve as a leader and advisor of a Socratic Club. One can surmise that her heart really was not in this proposal and that her reticence to take up this task was the major reason why a London Socratic Club never got off the ground.

Although the London Socratic Club did not materialize, one did start at Cambridge University, probably beginning with the 1945 weekend conference in Cambridge mentioned earlier. Little is known about it, but in the summer of 1951, D. M. Walsh, Secretary of the

---

[34] Probably David Michael Alexander Kinchin-Smith, the author of *Forward from Victory*, Faber, London, 1943, a book dealing with the problems of post-war reconstruction from a conservative point of view. The exact date of the meeting was February 1.

[35] Aldwinckle, "Interview," 8, cited in Jim Stockton's unpublished essay, *The Oxford University Socratic Club 1942—1972: A Life*.

[36] The Stella Aldwinckle Papers, 8-373. The date was March 13, 1944.

[37] The Stella Aldwinckle Papers, 8-374. The date of the letter was August 14, 1944.

No Ordinary People

Cambridge University Socratic Club, wrote to Aldwinckle about the possibility of the two Socratic Clubs meeting for a weekend party.[38]

HEART AND SOUL

Stella Aldwinckle founded, organized, and served as the driving force for the Socratic Club. She planned the schedule of speakers,[39] determined who would introduce each speaker,[40] and did the publicity. While Lewis was the prominent name behind the Socratic Club, Aldwinckle was its heart and soul. She attended nearly every meeting, took notes, participated in the discussion,[41] and edited those

---

[38] The Stella Aldwinckle Papers, 8-376. The letter was dated August 14.

[39] We only get a glimpse of the work behind the scenes when we read that on October 18, 1943, Cyril E. M. Joad wrote to Stella Aldwinckle, agreeing to speak on January 24, 1944, provided that they provide a room for him, pay his fare, provide dinner, and accept his title. In other words, Stella handled the day-to-day arrangements for recruiting speakers and handling arrangements associated with them coming to speak to the Socratic Club. Letter from C. E. M. Joad to Stella Aldwinckle, October 18, 1943. The Stella Aldwinckle Papers, Box 8, Folder 372. The Marion E. Wade Center, Wheaton College, Wheaton, IL. Then on November 18, 1943, Lewis received a letter from writer and critic Joyce Pyddoke of London, about the possibility of speaking at the Socratic Club, and he passed it on to Stella Aldwinckle. Letter from Joyce Pyddoke to C. S. Lewis, November 18, 1943. The Stella Aldwinckle Papers, Box 8, Folder 369, The Marion E. Wade Center, Wheaton College, Wheaton, IL. Used by permission. On September 25, 1945, Lewis forwarded a letter from Shaw Desmond, who had offered to speak at the Socratic Club, to Stella Aldwinckle. Letter from Shaw Desmond, September 25, 1945. The Stella Aldwinckle Papers, Box 8, Folder 369, The Marion E. Wade Center, Wheaton College, Wheaton, IL. Used by permission. On June 12, 1950, Lewis wrote to Stella Aldwinckle about the next term's program for the Socratic Club, especially encouraging an invitation to G. E. M. Anscombe to speak on the topic "Why I believe in God."

[40] On October 14, 1944, Lewis wrote to Stella Aldwinckle about his introduction on October 22.

[41] For example, on March 5, 1945, the Socratic Club heard Rev. Douglas Reginald Vicary, Chaplain of Hereford College and Tutor and Chaplain of Wycliffe Hall, speak on the topic "It and Thou (Scientific Knowledge and Personal Knowledge)." During the discussion period, Stella Aldwinckle spoke about three other options: "It-it" (scientific knowledge relating to scientific knowledge) being present in all intelligent perception, "I-it" (first person personal knowledge relating to scientific knowledge) and "I-thou" (first person personal knowledge relating to second person personal knowledge) knowledge. Notes by

notes and the presenters' papers for publication in the *Socratic Digest*. She oversaw the editing and proofreading of the *Socratic Digest* for publication, worked with a local printer, publicized the *Digest*, and filled orders, although she undoubtedly had help from students. She also tended to the needs of the speakers as they traveled, were housed and fed, and presented their papers.

Aldwinckle also spoke at the Socratic Club. On February 9, 1942, the third meeting in the Socratic's history, when the Socratic Club was so new that speakers were not easily lined up, Aldwinckle spoke on the topic "Was Christ Really Any More Than a Great Teacher and Prophet?" She spoke on a similar topic two years later,[42] probably a paper developed from her initial presentation in 1942, given the similarity of the two titles. That second paper was published in the second issue of the *Socratic Digest* under the title "Concerning the Question: 'Jesus, Prophet or Son of God?'"

In her published essay, she writes about how we can have certainty of what we know, and why different people arrive at different conclusions.[43] To what extent, she asks, can unbiased reason come to reasonable conclusions, particularly regarding the deity of Christ, "The judgment concerning the 'metahistorical' fact of Christ's deity ... uniquely invites the danger of a vicious subjectivity, since if it be fact it must drive a man ... from the last strongholds of his egocentricity— his right to himself and his self-esteem."[44] A couple of years earlier, Lewis had stated on BBC radio, "You can shut Him up for a fool, you can spit at Him and kill Him as a demon; or you can fall at His feet and call Him Lord and God. But let us not come with any patronizing nonsense about His being a great human teacher. He has not left that open to us. He did not intend to."[45] Aldwinckle and Lewis were of the same mind.

In that same paper, Aldwinckle also presents the basic facts

Stella Aldwinckle, March 5, 1945, The Stella Aldwinckle Papers, Box 8, Folder 384. The Marion E. Wade Center, Wheaton College, Wheaton, IL. There are also numerous other records of her participation in the discussion.

[42] On May 22, 1944.

[43] All of the issues of the *Socratic Digest* have been reprinted, with permission, in one volume by the author and are available online at www.Lulu.com.

[44] Stella Aldwinckle, "Concerning the Question: 'Jesus, Prophet or Son of God?'" *Socratic Digest*, No. 2 (June 1954):54.

[45] *Mere Christianity*, New York: HarperCollinsPublishers. Copyright 1980, 52. The date of the BBC broadcast was February 1, 1942.

which affirm Christ's deity:

(1) the changed lives of the apostles,
(2) belief in Christ's deity among monotheistic Jews (a belief which the Jews would ordinarily have resisted),
(3) the persistence of the Church through the ages,
(4) the impact of a living faith in Christ, and
(5) the character and claims of Christ Himself.

Then she asks what role faith plays in perceiving these facts about Christ correctly. She answers that faith "involves both intellectual assent and a continued act of trust by unconditional surrender of the will to God," but it also includes an awareness of sin and an admission of guilt. She concludes, "Faith gives the kind of *certain* knowledge beside which all other certainty seems empty and insecure, and all other knowledge mere tentative description. It is by such spiritual cognition that we come to *know* that our existence has meaning and purpose."[46]

The central activity of the Socratic Club, of course, was the meetings themselves. The most well-known meeting is the Anscombe-Lewis debate in 1948 that dealt with a chapter in Lewis's book *Miracles*. The most well attended meeting in the history of the Socratic Club, however, took place in the third year of the Socratic. On January 24, 1944, the Socratic Club met in the dining hall at St. Hilda's College to a standing-room only crowd of 250 people, which Aldwinckle called "the most amusing, and the most moving" meeting of the Socratic Club.[47] John Wain, former student of Lewis, later described the atmosphere as "positively gladiatorial."[48] At a time when he was seriously considering a return to the Christian faith, popular philosopher and radio personality C. E. M. Joad spoke on the topic "On Being Reviewed by Christians." He gave a defense of his book, *God and Evil*, which had been released fourteen months earlier. In this meeting, Aldwinckle invited Lewis to remove his jacket because of the heat (even though it was January), after Joad had removed his. Lewis declined because his shirt was patched![49] Joad later rejoined the

---

[46] *Socratic Digest*, No. 2, June 1944, 31ff.

[47] Stella Aldwinckle, "Oral History Interview with Lyle W. Dorsett," July 26, 1985, 5. Call no.: OH / SR-1, The Marion E. Wade Center, Wheaton College, Wheaton, IL. Used by permission. Page 29.

[48] Walter Hooper, "Oxford's Bonny Fighter," in *C. S. Lewis at the Breakfast Table*, 145.

[49] Oral history interview excerpt with Stella Aldwinckle, January 24, 1984. The Stella Aldwinckle Papers, CSL-Y, SR-276, The Marion E.

Twenty-One Friendships of C.S. Lewis

Church of England and wrote about his spiritual journey back to the Christian faith in his last book, *The Recovery of Belief,* published in 1951 shortly before his death in 1953.[50] He gave some credit to the influence of C. S. Lewis.[51]

STELLA ALDWINCKLE

Stella Aldwinckle was born on Dec. 16, 1907, in Johannesburg, South Africa. Her family moved to South America in 1911[52] and to England in 1915. Because World War I was underway, her father wanted to contribute to the war effort, so the family returned to England. The return trip faced danger when their ship was chased by a German submarine for nine days.[53] In England, Stella attended Westcliff School in Weston-super-Mare, near Bristol. Stella's aunt operated this private school, located in southwestern England with a view of the Bristol Channel.[54] The family returned to Brits, South Africa, in 1925, where Stella engaged in tobacco farming with her younger brother.[55] While in South Africa, a country and continent she grew to love, Stella decided to devote her life to pointing people to the Christian faith. That goal later fit well with her leadership of the Socratic Club. Aldwinckle was raised in a "conventional Anglican middle-class family—church was regularly attended, the Lord's Prayer formed a focal point and was frequently recited, and her father's advice to the family was that the greatest book ever written was St.

Wade Center, Wheaton College, Wheaton, IL. Used by permission. See also Stella Aldwinckle, "Memories of the Socratic Club," *C. S. Lewis and His Circle: Essays and Memoirs from the Oxford C. S. Lewis Society*, Roger White, Judith Wolfe, and Brendan Wolfe, eds., 192.

[50] *The Recovery of Belief: A Restatement of Christian Philosophy*, London: Faber & Faber, 1951. For a more complete description of this evening and Joad's spiritual journey, see Joel D. Heck, "From Vocal Agnostic to Reluctant Convert: The Influence of C.S. Lewis on the Conversion C.E.M. Joad," *Sehnsucht* Vol. 3 (2009).

[51] See Joad's *God and Evil*, 298.

[52] They moved to South America because her father hoped he could find work there in his capacity as an architect. Walter Hooper, *C. S. Lewis: Companion & Guide*, New York: HarperCollins Publishers, Inc., 1996, 617.

[53] Stella Aldwinckle, "Oral History Interview with Lyle W. Dorsett," July 26, 1985, 5. Call no.: OH / SR-1, The Marion E. Wade Center, Wheaton College, Wheaton, IL. Used by permission.

[54] Ibid.

[55] Ibid.

John's Gospel."[56] The influence of the Gospel on Stella was clearly felt during her formative years.

In 1928, Aldwinckle returned to England, where she worked as a nursemaid for a Baptist in North London.[57] Before enrolling in the university, she taught herself Greek by correspondence to improve her chances of acceptance into Oxford University.[58] In 1932, Stella attended St. Anne's College in Oxford to study Theology. Austin Farrer, who became a lifelong friend, was one of her tutors.[59] She earned a BA in 1936 and the MA in 1941.

After completing her studies at Oxford, she taught Divinity in Yorkshire for three years, where she also pursued her love of horseback riding, and then she served as Tutor of Old and New Testament at St. Christopher's College in Blackheath, a London suburb near Greenwich.[60]

In 1941, Aldwinckle joined the Oxford Pastorate, a team of workers attached to St. Aldate's Church, serving the undergraduates of Oxford University.[61] She held the position of Chaplain to Women Students from 1941 until her retirement in 1966, working primarily among "the members of the four women's colleges—Somerville, Lady Margaret Hall, St. Hugh's and St. Hilda's—as well as amongst the large number of Home Students."[62] During her time in Oxford, her

---

[56] Richard Leachman, "Biographical Postscript." *Christ's Shadow in Plato's Cave: A Meditation on the Substance of Love.* By Stella Aldwinckle. Oxford: Amate, 1990. Cited in Jim Stockton, "Chaplain Stella Aldwinckle: A Biographical Sketch of the Spiritual Foundation of the Oxford University Socratic Club," *Inklings Forever* 8 (2012), 3.

[57] Jim Stockton, "Chaplain Stella Aldwinckle: A Biographical Sketch of the Spiritual Foundation of the Oxford University Socratic Club," *Inklings Forever: Published Colloquium Proceedings 1997-2016*: Vol. 8, Article 26.

[58] Stella Aldwinckle, "Oral History Interview with Lyle W. Dorsett," July 26, 1985, 5. Call no.: OH / SR-1, The Marion E. Wade Center, Wheaton College, Wheaton, IL. Used by permission.

[59] Stella Aldwinckle, "Oral History Interview with Lyle W. Dorsett," July 26, 1985, 5. Call no.: OH / SR-1, The Marion E. Wade Center, Wheaton College, Wheaton, IL. Used by permission.

[60] Jim Stockton, unpublished essay, *The Oxford University Socratic Club 1942—1972: A Life,* drawing on Stella Aldwinckle, "Oral History Interview with Lyle W. Dorsett," July 26, 1985, 5. Call no.: OH / SR-1, The Marion E. Wade Center, Wheaton College, Wheaton, IL. Used by permission):7.

[61] Leachman, Ibid., 4.

[62] Vicar G. Foster-Carter, "A Pastor for Women Students," *The*

two most important ministries were working as an advisor to the students at Somerville College and her work with the Socratic Club. In 1958, she founded the Oxford University Horsemanship Club, served with the ecumenical Christian community at Lee Abbey in Devon, and founded SCARS, an interdenominational prayer and fellowship group.[63]

After retiring, Aldwinckle worked on a philosophical treatise that had interested her for a long time with some help from her former tutor, Austin Farrer.[64] This treatise eventually developed into the poem *Christ's Shadow in Plato's Cave: A Meditation on the Substance of Love*,[65] for which Iris Murdoch wrote the Foreword. Jean Iris Murdoch, a Fellow of St. Anne's College, was one of Aldwinckle's close friends "who would eventually become recognized as one of the twentieth century's leading intellectuals and novelists."[66] In fact, Plato was one of three authors Aldwinckle was reading when, in 1985, Lyle and Mary Dorsett visited her for an in-person interview. The other two authors were Percy Bysshe Shelley and C. S. Lewis.[67] In retirement, Aldwinckle continued to attend meetings of the Socratic Club. She

Stella on horseback
Used by permission of the
Marion E. Wade Center,
Wheaton College, Wheaton, IL.

Oxford Pastorate Forty-fifth Report: July 1940—June1941 (Oxford: Oxford Pastorate, 1941), 10, cited in Jim Stockton, unpublished essay, *The Oxford University Socratic Club 1942—1972: A Life*.

[63] https://archon.wheaton.edu/index.php?p=creators/creator&id=241 The first two letters, SC, undoubtedly stand for Socratic Club. She also grew to love lions, decorating her home with drawings and pictures of lions. See Stella Aldwinckle, "Oral History Interview with Lyle W. Dorsett," July 26, 1985, 5. Call no.: OH / SR-1, The Marion E. Wade Center, Wheaton College, Wheaton, IL. Used by permission.

[64] Stella Aldwinckle, "Oral History Interview with Lyle W. Dorsett," July 26, 1985, 5. Call no.: OH / SR-1, The Marion E. Wade Center, Wheaton College, Wheaton, IL. Used by permission.

[65] Hooper, *Companion & Guide*, 618.

[66] Jim Stockton, "Chaplain Stella Aldwinckle: A Biographical Sketch of the Spiritual Foundation of the Oxford University Socratic Club," *Inklings Forever* 8 (2012), 4.

[67] Stella Aldwinckle, "Oral History Interview with Lyle W. Dorsett," July 26, 1985, 5. Call no.: OH / SR-1, The Marion E. Wade Center, Wheaton College, Wheaton, IL. Used by permission.

died on Dec. 28, 1989, and the poem was published in 1990.

Conclusion

Outside of the Inklings and his Oxford colleagues, Lewis worked more closely with Stella Aldwinckle than with anyone else. His reliance upon her leadership in the Socratic Club demonstrates his trust in her. The success of the Socratic Club had as much to do with the untiring work of Stella Aldwinckle as it did with the reputation and the brilliant repartee of Lewis.

One major reason for this close cooperation was their similar theological views. This similarity may have led to their cooperation in the Socratic Club, but some examples further affirm them as kindred spirits. One can hear Screwtape in the background railing against the Socratic Club's approach, "By the very act of arguing, you awake the patient's reason; and once it is awake, who can foresee the result?"[68] Echoing Aldwinckle's emphasis on reason, we hear Lewis telling his BBC listeners that God "lends us a little of His reasoning powers and that is how we think: He puts a little of His love into us and that is how we love one another. When you teach a child writing, you hold its hand while it forms the letters: that is, it forms the letters because you are forming them. We love and reason because God loves and reasons and holds our hand while we do it."[69] He also writes, "It is not reason that is taking away my faith: on the contrary, my faith is based on reason."[70]

In his last letter to Aldwinckle, Lewis gives his opinion of her. Nearly a dozen other letters merely address the lineup of speakers, his ability or inability to attend the Socratic Club, or possible speakers and their arrangements,[71] but Lewis's letter of resignation in early 1954 marks the shift from a Lewis presidency of the Socratic Club to another president, Keble College philosopher Basil Mitchell. Lewis had heard of the establishment of a Professorship of Medieval and Renaissance English at Cambridge University, which would begin later that year, and he probably knew he was the most likely candidate. His complimentary words serve as a fitting conclusion to this chapter:

---

[68] C. S. Lewis, *The Screwtape Letters*, New York: HarperCollins, 1996, 2.

[69] C. S. Lewis, *Mere Christianity*, New York: HarperCollinsPublishers. Copyright 1980, 57.

[70] C. S. Lewis, *Mere Christianity*, 139.

[71] Because they met frequently before, during, and after the meetings of the Socratic Club, Aldwinckle and Lewis could make many necessary decisions at those times.

Twenty-One Friendships of C.S. Lewis

The moment seems a good one for saying how very much I have admired the great work you have been doing in Oxford all these years; a work which, I expect, no one else could have done, and v. few others *would* have done. I have worked with some who had your energy and with some who had your good temper, but I am not sure that I have worked with any who had both. It has been a great privilege and I have at all times appreciated it more than (I fear) my behavior showed. May you long continue the work. *Oremus pro invicem.*[72]

---

[72] *Collected Letters, III*, 400f. The date of the letter is January 1, 1954. The Latin means, "Let us pray for one another."

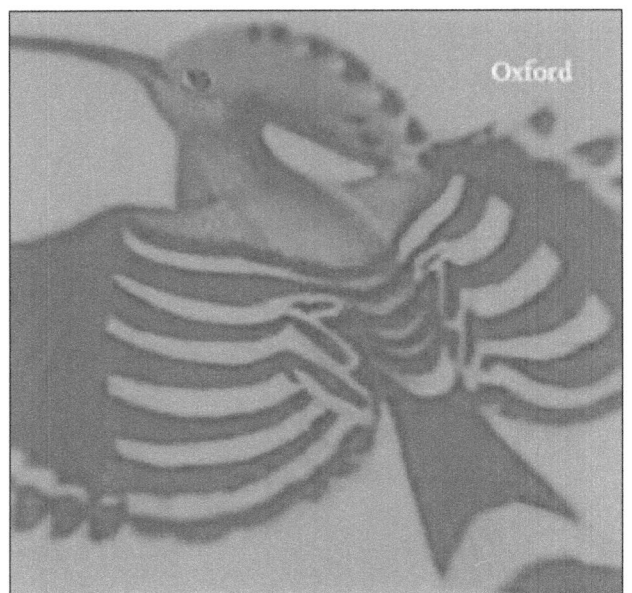

Chapter 16

NAN DUNBAR,
Statius, and C. S. Lewis

Nan Vance Dunbar was teaching Classics[1] at Girton College, Cambridge, her alma mater, when C. S. Lewis first met her. He had just arrived for his first year of teaching at Magdalene College.[2] She had much in common with Lewis: a love for the Classics, three First Class Honours in examinations, expecting the very best effort from undergraduates in their studies, a Christian commitment, and a congenial spirit. Dunbar's interest in the Classics, however, was her primary life's work rather than a side interest; it was only a side interest for Lewis. For that reason, their relationship was friendly, but Dunbar was the expert in the Classics and Lewis skilled but not expert.

Nan Dunbar
Used with permission of
Somerville College

How did these two get along? Lewis was the world-renowned scholar, thirty years Dunbar's senior. He had only recently filled the Chair of Medieval and Renaissance English that had been especially created for him. He had achieved international recognition for his *Chronicles of Narnia*, *Mere Christianity*, and *The Screwtape Letters*, among many other writings. Her major academic achievement was many years in the future, and yet, although she was only twenty-seven years of age, he treated her with scholarly respect and deferred to her expertise.

---

[1] I.e., Greek and Latin languages and literature.

[2] Most readers will know that he came to Cambridge on January 1, 1955 after twenty-nine years at Magdalen College, Oxford.

No Ordinary People

THE LIFE AND CAREER OF NAN DUNBAR

Nan Dunbar was born in Glasgow, Scotland, on July 18, 1928, one of four children of John Dunbar.[3] Dunbar excelled in Latin and Greek at Hutcheson's Girls' School in Glasgow, which she attended from 1943 to 1946. She earned a First at Glasgow University, and she earned two additional Firsts in both parts of the Classics Tripos[4] at Girton College, Cambridge, which she attended from 1949 to 1952. In 1952, she was appointed to a lectureship in Greek at Edinburgh University, where she taught for three years, while retaining a bye-fellowship[5] at Girton.

At age twenty-seven, she returned to Girton College as a research Fellow and Lecturer in Classics in 1955, the same year that Lewis began to teach at Cambridge University. She left Girton in 1957 to become a Lecturer at St Andrews University,[6] and then in 1965 she moved to Somerville College, Oxford, as a Fellow, where she remained for the rest of her academic career. Dunbar married one of her former tutors, D. Mervyn Jones, on July 1, 1972. She became Somerville's first Tutor for Admissions, later Vice-Principal,[7] then, upon her retirement, was named Emeritus Fellow of Somerville from 1995 until her death in 2005.[8]

Nan Dunbar was an inspiring teacher, a committed Christian, and a strong supporter of St. Columba's United Reformed Church in Oxford. She was a sociable woman who loved entertaining, which helps to explain her friendship with Lewis.[9] In her last years, she

---

[3] "Dunbar, Nan Vance," in "Biographical Appendix," *Collected Letters, III*, 1658. For some unexplained reason all the obituaries and biographical notes omit the name of her mother.

[4] Tripos are exams named for the three-legged stools on which candidates sat when examined orally by Fellows of the university. See C. S. Lewis, *Collected Letters, III*, 963.

[5] She was not a Fellow of the College, but still was associated with Girton.

[6] One wonders if she was related to William Dunbar, the Scottish poet (1460-ca. 1522), who earned his bachelor's degree from St Andrews.

[7] Nigel Wilson, "Nan Dunbar," *The Independent* (April 21, 2005), 42, cited in *Collected Letters, III*, 1661.

[8] *Collected Letters, III*, 1661.

[9] http://www.telegraph.co.uk/news/obituaries/1490597/Nan-Dunbar.html, which states that she was "a sociable woman who loved entertaining ..." See also http://www.independent.co.uk/news/obituaries/nan-dunbar-495769.html, which concludes, "Anyone who

Twenty-One Friendships of C.S. Lewis

published the definitive edition of Greek playwright Aristophanes' comedy *The Birds*; her edition is considered the finest edition of the play ever published.[10] The play is known for its many species of birds about which any student of the play must become an expert. She died on April 3, 2005 at the age of seventy-six.

Dunbar and Lewis in Cambridge

During her years at Girton College, Dunbar crossed paths with Lewis through their common interest in the Classics, particularly through a writer named Statius. Statius, a Roman poet of the first century, appears as a guide in the *Purgatory* section of Dante's *Divine Comedy* and is especially known for his poetry.[11] Lewis wrote significant pieces about Statius in both *The Allegory of Love* and *The Discarded Image*. Nineteen hundred years after his death, Statius helped to bring Dunbar and Lewis together.

In Michaelmas Term 1955,[12] Dunbar attended one of Lewis's lectures in Cambridge.[13] A few days later, Lewis wrote to Dunbar for the first time, thanking her for her critique about a passage in Statius.[14] She had probably written to him in response to some things he had stated in that lecture. Most of the specific points of his letter depend upon what Dunbar had written, and we do not have her letter. Lewis's customary practice was to destroy letters he received after

---

met her could not fail to be struck by her energy and gift for lively conversation, punctuated frequently by hearty chuckles and laughter."

[10] Nan Dunbar, ed., *Aristophanes: Birds*, Oxford: Clarendon Press, 1995. Reviewer John Gilbert called it "a rich store of information and sure to be long-lasting." He also writes, "The first mention of each species of bird occasions a precise ornithological identification (or as precise as possible), often accompanied by lengthy further observations on habitat, migratory behavior, habits, diet and, where applicable, poetic, iconographic, and culinary associations. There is much to marvel at in this assortment of knowledge." See the online review at http://bmcr.brynmawr.edu/1996/96.05.04.html.

[11] That is, the *Thebaid*, the *Silvae*, and the *Achilleid*, the completion of the latter cut short by his death. He lived in Naples, Italy ca. 45–ca. 96 A.D.

[12] Either October 4 or 11. See "Chronologically Lewis" for the dates of his lectures in Michaelmas Term in Cambridge. http://www.joelheck.com/chronologically-lewis.php

[13] The lecture was on "Some Major Texts: Latin and Continental Vernaculars."

[14] Whether this was initiated by Lewis or Dunbar, we do not know. The date is October 14. *Collected Letters, III*, 658f.

responding to them, so we will never know precisely what she wrote.

During the 1990s while writing his doctoral dissertation, Andrew Cuneo interviewed Dunbar about her letters to Lewis.[15] From Lewis's letter we can tell that she had offered both some kind words about his writings and some critique of his Latin and Greek translations. The mention of Dido in his letter tells us he was writing primarily about Virgil's *Aeneid*, but the mention of Ismene indicates that he was also writing about Sophocles, either Sophocles' *Oedipus Rex*, *Oedipus at Colonus*, or *Antigone*. Dunbar told Cuneo that Lewis (and Statius, in Lewis's view) "had an attitude to the sexual life which Dante would not easily have found in any other ancient text."[16] Statius' virgins demonstrated, Lewis thought, "a degree of modesty uncommon to the classical world of that period."[17] For Lewis, the virgins about which Statius wrote were especially modest; for Dunbar, not so much.

Lewis's follow-up letter to Dunbar acknowledged her expertise. He writes, "And now we differ on translating wh. is rash of me, for you're a real classic and it's years since I was."[18] He was aware of her strengths and his limitations. The mention of Lavinia, a character from Shakespeare's *Titus Andronicus*, indicates that they are ranging far and wide in literature. Later that month, Lewis continues his discussion with Nan Dunbar. He agrees that the meaning of words is based on their usage in context.[19] And he writes, *vicisti*, i.e., "you have conquered."[20] Andrew Cuneo concludes, "The cross-fire of texts, references, and authors display[s] two minds arguing with a fairness and honesty which leads them, in the end, to a qualified acceptance of the other's position."[21] Two more letters over the next week concluded this exchange.

Lewis next wrote to Dunbar, thanking her for a document from Justin Martyr and asking her for the location of a quotation in Thomas

---

[15] Andrew Cuneo, "Selected Literary Letters of C. S. Lewis," Bodleian Library, MS. D.Phil. Merton College 2001. c. 16354.

[16] Ibid., 84.

[17] Ibid., 84f.

[18] *Collected Letters*, *III*, 660. The date is October 17, 1955.

[19] *Collected Letters*, *III*, 663, 665. The dates of the two letters are October 20 and October 24, 1955.

[20] *Collected Letters*, *III*, 665. In 1957, Lewis had an article published about Statius, "Dante's Statius," in *Medium Aevum*, Vol. XXV, No. 3, 1957. The article was later incorporated into *Studies in Medieval and Renaissance Literature*, viii. He did not cite Dunbar anywhere in the article.

[21] Andrew Cuneo, "Selected Literary Letters of C. S. Lewis," Bodleian Library, MS. D.Phil. Merton College 2001. c. 16354, 87.

Hobbes' *Leviathan*.[22] From this point on, Lewis sees Nan Dunbar as a congenial person with whom he can share ideas and a person to consult because of her expertise on the Classics. Later that year, in response to a note of praise from Dunbar for a lecture he had given, he wrote to her with high praise for Herodotus and Tacitus, whom they were discussing in their letters, but also for Froissart, Snorri, Joinville and Pitscottie. He states that Shakespeare scholar Miss Muriel Bradbrook says that he makes books better than they are.[23] Apparently, Dunbar has become his "go-to" person for Greek and Latin.

The playful humor of Lewis also appears in his letters. Early the next year, Lewis met Dunbar for the very first time at a dinner at Girton College. On meeting her, he states, "Ah! Miss Dunbar! I'm glad to find you actually exist—I'd thought perhaps you were only the personification of my conscience!"[24] According to Cuneo, Lewis enjoyed her company and they talked about Scottish and Irish writers. Dunbar remembers discussing the Scottish writer William McGonagall, sometimes described as the world's worst poet, and Lewis introduced her to the writings of the Irish novelist Amanda McKittrick Ros, who was sometimes described as the world's worst novelist.[25] The next day, he wrote to Dunbar in Latin about Virgil, Aristotle, and Virtue in response to a note from Dunbar herself. He entitles his letter (translated here from the Latin), "C. S. Lewis to the most learned Nan Dunbar, Doctor of Sacred Theology,"[26] accepting her explanation of a passage in Virgil but disputing her views of a passage from Aristotle.[27] The Aristotle passage combined a picture of Virtue as both a mistress and a task; apparently Dunbar thought that only one of the two was in view. About three months later,[28] Lewis wrote to Dunbar about Sappho and some Greek word meanings, enclosing a poem to her that he had written in Latin. The friendly and

---

[22] The topics were the Scottish word *kerfuffle* and the Waverley novels. *Collected Letters, III*, 668 and 669. The dates of the letters are October 27 and November 1, 1955. His letter of November 1 was a rather irrelevant letter.

[23] *Collected Letters, III*, 1680. The date is December 7.

[24] *Collected Letters, III*, 1659. This took place on January 25, 1956.

[25] Andrew Cuneo, "Selected Literary Letters of C. S. Lewis," Bodleian Library, MS. D.Phil. c. 16354, 88n.

[26] This is the Latin: "C. S. Lewis Doctissimae Annae Dunbar, S[acrae]. T[heologiae]. D[octor]." *Collected Letters, III*, 696. The was January 26, 1956.

[27] Perhaps Aristotle's *Economics*, Book 1, 1344a.

[28] On April 20, 1956.

jocular Lewis is reflected in this poem, which begins with the phrase, "Nan is more learned than all the girls...."[29]

During the remaining years of Lewis's life, numerous other letters passed between the two, mostly about various scholarly matters,[30] including her specialty, Aristophanes and his play *The Birds*.[31] During her two years at Girton College in the mid-1950s, Lewis wrote fifteen letters to her, and he probably met her at a variety of social events hosted by the university.

A HANDFUL OF SOCIAL OCCASIONS

On at least two occasions, Lewis and Dunbar enjoyed a meal together. In 1956, Lewis dined at Girton College with Muriel Bradbrook and Dunbar,[32] the event described above when they first met. Lewis was undoubtedly a guest of both Dunbar and Bradbrook. Poet and William Blake scholar Kathleen Raine,[33] a colleague of Dunbar's at Girton, was present and later described Jack as "a man of great learning" and someone with "a kind of boyish greatness."[34] Lewis impressed Raine, who seems to have been invited in order for her to meet Lewis.

Dunbar with Somerville students at her retirement
Used with permission of Somerville College

---

[29] Again, the Latin: *"Nan est doctor omnibus puellis," Collected Letters, III*, 740.

[30] *Collected Letters, III*, 718, 761, 840, 852, 854, 1466, 1468, 1483. The dates are March 7, and June 7, 1956; March 15, May 16, and May 21, 1957; October 18 and November 21, 1963.

[31] *Collected Letters, III*, 840.

[32] *Collected Letters, III*, 695. This is the event of January 25, 1956.

[33] 1908-2003.

[34] *Light on C. S. Lewis*, 102.

A few months later,[35] Lewis met Dunbar for a college dinner, presumably at Girton College. On another social occasion in Cambridge Dunbar visited Jack[36] to discuss *Beowulf* and Aristophanes' comedy *The Birds*. One wonders if that visit to see Lewis was a kind of farewell, since she left Girton for her lectureship at St. Andrews University shortly thereafter.

POST-GIRTON CONTACTS

Lewis wrote three letters to Nan Dunbar after she left Girton College, all three of them in the last year of his life. In the autumn of 1963, Lewis wrote to Dunbar about their past discussions, inviting her to visit him in his retirement.[37] After all, they were both living in Oxford at the time. Three days later, he wrote to Dunbar about welcoming a visit from her and, in reply to her request for follow-up reading to the Narnia series, about Edith Nesbit.[38] The last letter that Lewis ever wrote to Nan Dunbar was written on November 21, 1963. In this brief letter, Lewis wrote to Dunbar with directions for her coming to see him; she had accepted his invitation to visit. Since he died on November 22, that meeting never took place.

One cannot assume that letters were the only means by which Lewis and Dunbar encountered one another. Some social occasions, university-sponsored dinners and meetings, some chapel services, and other special occasions may have allowed them to cross paths. What stands out, however, is the respect Lewis had for Nan Dunbar, as evidenced by his rather frequent correspondence, i.e., eighteen letters in all, and the nature of those letters. He honored her scholarship and her personality. Throughout their epistolary exchange, Lewis addressed her with respect and bowed to her greater expertise in the Classics. As Andrew Cuneo has written about Lewis's correspondence with Nan Dunbar, Muriel Bradbrook, and Kathleen Raine, "Far from disparaging the female intellect, Lewis engaged it. Far from being dishonest and arguing only to win, he would hold to a scholar's honor and recant publicly should he not be able to prove his position—even

---

[35] The date is May 4, 1956.

[36] The date is May 22, 1957. See Lewis's letter of May 21, 1957. *Collected Letters, III*, 854.

[37] *Collected Letters, III*, 1466f. The date is October 18.

[38] Andrew Cuneo, "Selected Literary Letters of C. S. Lewis," Bodleian Library, MS. D.Phil. Merton College 2001. c. 16354, 111. See *Collected Letters, III*, 1468.

to a 'completely unknown young woman.'"[39]

---

[39] Andrew Cuneo, "Selected Literary Letters of C. S. Lewis," Bodleian Library, MS. D.Phil. Merton College 2001. c. 16354, 103, n. 243. The phrase "completely unknown young woman" was used by Dunbar to describe herself.

Twenty-One Friendships of C.S. Lewis

Appendix

The following is a complete list of contacts and correspondence between Nan Dunbar and C. S. Lewis:

Date	Occasion
October 14, 1955	Letter from Lewis to Dunbar
October 17, 1955	Letter from Lewis to Dunbar
October 20, 1955	Letter from Lewis to Dunbar
October 24, 1955	Letter from Lewis to Dunbar
October 27, 1955	Letter from Lewis to Dunbar
November 1, 1955	Letter from Lewis to Dunbar
December 7, 1955	Letter from Lewis to Dunbar
January 24, 1956	Lewis has dinner with Nan Dunbar and Muriel Bradbrook in Cambridge
January 26, 1956	Letter from Lewis to Dunbar
March 7, 1956	Letter from Lewis to Dunbar
April 20, 1956	Letter from Lewis to Dunbar
April 23, 1956	Letter from Lewis to Dunbar
May 4, 1956	A college dinner in Cambridge
June 7, 1956	Letter from Lewis to Dunbar
March 15, 1957	Letter from Lewis to Dunbar
May 16, 1957	Letter from Lewis to Dunbar
May 21, 1957	Letter from Lewis to Dunbar
May 22, 1957	A visit from Dunbar to Lewis
October 18, 1963	Letter from Lewis to Dunbar
October 21, 1963	Letter from Lewis to Dunbar
November 21, 1963	Letter from Lewis to Dunbar

Chapter 17

MURIEL BRADBROOK, C. S. Lewis, and Shakespeare

C. S. Lewis knew English literature, especially "English literature in the sixteenth century excluding drama," and particularly Edmund Spenser's *Fairie Queene*, but when it came to Shakespeare, he ceded the ground to those with more expertise, among them Muriel Bradbrook. Lewis wrote very rarely on Shakespeare (although he knew his Shakespeare).[1] His contact with Cambridge Shakespeare scholar Muriel Bradbrook was mostly confined to his years teaching at Cambridge University, i.e., 1955 to 1963, although he undoubtedly knew about her before those years and had probably met her during the many times he was in Cambridge for summer examining. The first record in Lewis' correspondence to Bradbrook comes from a passing reference to her in a letter he wrote to Nan Dunbar about literary topics, including Bradbrook, in late 1955.[2]

C. S. Lewis and Muriel Bradbrook

During Lewis's second year of teaching in Cambridge, Dr. Bradbrook, Fellow of Girton College and University Lecturer, invited Lewis to dinner at Girton College along with Nan Dunbar, very likely at the initiation of Dunbar.[3] His acceptance, which had been lost in the mail, was followed by another letter which included a quotation from Chaucer. He stated lightheartedly that he would be there unless "I be sickle outher in prisoun," i.e., unless "I am sick or in prison."[4] Poet and William Blake scholar Kathleen Raine, long a friend of Bradbrook, was also present and later described Lewis as "a man of great

---

[1] In the chapter on Hugo Dyson, see, for example, the lecture series on Shakespeare in which he participated with Hugo Dyson, Lascelles Abercrombie, Miss Ethel Seaton, Nevill Coghill, and others.

[2] December 7, 1955. *Collected Letters, III*, 680.

[3] This happened in January 1956. *Collected Letters, III*, 693. This letter, which included mention of his previous acceptance by post, is dated January 20, 1956. Lewis had written to Dunbar the previous October about a passage in the first century Roman poet Statius.

[4] Ibid. This letter, which included mention of his previous acceptance by post, is dated Jan. 20, 1956. As far as we know, it would be the second letter of Lewis to Bradbrook, and the lost letter would be the first.

learning" and someone with "a kind of boyish greatness."⁵

That dinner seems to have established the relationship between Lewis and Bradbrook as a friendship rather than mere acquaintance. Three months later, Lewis felt comfortable enough to write Bradbrook about a request he had received that dealt with Shakespearian tragedy. Since Lewis knew that Bradbrook was primarily a Shakespeare specialist, he asked if she would respond to the letter he had received, enclosing the letter for her to consider.⁶ That he would write to her with this request indicates that they were on more than speaking terms, but it says a great deal more. He trusted her judgment on literary tmatters, concluding that she was better equipped to address the concerns of that letter than he was. It also marked an advance in their friendship since one is less likely to make such a request of a stranger or a mere acquaintance. Since she, like Lewis, was both a medievalist and a Renaisance scholar, Lewis also wrote to her a year later, addressing her as Muriel, inviting her to call him Jack, and requesting her critique of a paper he had written on Chaucer.⁷ Clearly, she agreed to communicating on a first-name basis, since he called her Muriel in later letters. Lewis had frequently lectured on "Textual Criticism: Chaucer, Troilus and Criseyde," so this request may have been related to that Chaucerian poem.⁸

The scholarly exchange of ideas went in both directions. In 1958, Lewis replied to Bradbrook about the meanings of words such as "simple meal," whose meaning we always know, the nuances of the word "slow," and the various meanings of "sad."⁹ A few years later, he wrote to Bradbrook about some translations of modern Greek poetry she sent him and about William Empson's book *Milton's God*. He knows that he has a sympathetic reader in Bradbrook when he states, "We must congratulate him [Empson] on making it quite clear that

---

⁵ *Light on C. S. Lewis*, 102.

⁶ We don't know the nature of the letter, only that he had to do with Shakespearian tragedy. The date of the letter was April 4, 1956.

⁷ The date was March 1, 1957. We don't know what paper that was, but it certainly was not "What Chaucer Really Did to *Il Filostrato*," a paper he had published in 1932.

⁸ He also lectured at Cambridge University on Chaucer in 1958 and 1959, under the titles "Romance" and "Epilogue."

⁹ Since Lewis did not keep letters sent to him for reasons of confidentiality, we don't know the exact nature of Bradbrook's letter. *Collected Letters, III*, 937. The date was April 18.

what he objects to is M's[10] theology, not his art."[11]

Lewis's letter was replying to a letter from Bradbrook. Bradbrook had written to Lewis, probably empathizing with him because of his poor health in addition to addressing other topics. The Michaelmas Term had begun on October 1, and Lewis had been scheduled to give a lecture series on "English Literature 1300-1500." In his letter, Lewis expressed his hope to return to teaching in January. He did not return, however, due to illness, beginning again only in April for the Trinity Term. Upon his return, Lewis wrote to Bradbrook about the possibility of her visiting him one weekday evening and drinking a glass of sherry with him at The Kilns.[12]

That fall, the friendship was renewed with a dinner, apparently at Magdalene College, attended by Bradbrook, J. A. W. Bennett, and Bennett's wife. By the following summer Lewis had resigned his position at Cambridge University, and then, just four days before his death, Lewis wrote to Bradbrook about his recent retirement and the possibility of their meeting in December.[13] He longed for the renewal of some of the friendships he had made in Cambridge, and hers was one of them. But, sadly, it was not to be. Although they respected one another to the end, this friendship had to be renewed in eternity.

C. S. Lewis had great respect for Muriel Bradbrook as a Shakespeare scholar, academic colleague, a fellow Christian, and friend. The respect was reciprocated by Bradbrook, whose accomplishments in the field of Shakespeare studies (but also medieval literature) rivaled that of Lewis in sixteenth-century medieval and renaissance literature. Although they would have known about one another prior to Lewis' move to Cambridge, their acquaintance appears to have originated through fellow Girton scholar Nan Dunbar and to have become one of the many reasons Robert E. Havard later wrote, "He was happier in his new surroundings."[14]

---

[10] That is, Milton's.
[11] The date is October 15, 1961. *Collected Letters, III*, 1286.
[12] The date is May 7, 1962. *Collected Letters, III*, 1337.
[13] *Collected Letters, III*, 1482. The date is November 18, 1963.
[14] Robert E. Havard, "Philia: Jack at Ease," in James T. Como, ed., *C. S. Lewis at the Breakfast Table and Other Reminiscences*, New York: Macmillan, 1979, 224.

No Ordinary People

MURIEL BRADBROOK, SHAKESPEARE SCHOLAR

Muriel Clara Bradbrook was born on April 27, 1909 in greater Liverpool.[15] She was the daughter of Samuel Bradbrook, Superintendent of H. M. Waterguard,[16] and Annie Wilson Harvey. Bradbrook's early years near the sea led to a lifelong love of the sea, which explains her decision to learn Norwegian and later to dedicate her book *Ibsen the Norwegian* to members of the Kongelige Norske Marine.[17] She studied at Hutcheson's Girls' School, Glasgow, the same school Nan Dunbar attended, and then at Oldershaw School, Wallasey.[18] She matriculated to Girton College, Cambridge, as an undergraduate in 1927, where she studied medieval literature under Hilda Murray. She earned a Double First in English in 1930,[19] and she earned the Charity Reeves Prize[20] in English in 1929 and 1930. Her education in medieval literature made her a kindred spirit with C. S. Lewis, who considered himself a medievalist, an old Western man, and a dinosaur.[21] Bradbrook came to Girton College as an agnostic, but later, like Lewis, she became a Christian and made Great St Mary's, the University church across the street from King's College chapel, her church home. This made her, like Lewis, an Anglican.

Muriel Bradbrook
Used by permission of the National Portrait Gallery

---

[15] More specifically, Wallasey, Cheshire.

[16] The Waterguard was a division of Her Majesty's Customs and Excise, similar to the U.S. Coast Guard and later Her Majesty's Revenue and Customs. The Waterguard was responsible for the control of vessels, aircraft, vehicles, and persons entering and leaving the United Kingdom.

[17] Radinowicz, Mary Ann, "Muriel Clara Bradbrook," *Girton College Newsletter* (Cambridge: Piggott Printers Ltd, 1993), 63f. Archive reference: Girton College Archive: GCCP 3/1.

[18] *Collected Letters, III*, 1652.

[19] Ibid. She earned First Class Honours in English Tripos in Part I in 1929 and First Class Honours in English Tripos in Part II in 1930.

[20] The prize was founded in 1910 by Miss Mary Gurney (1836-1917), a member of Girton College from 1894 until her death in 1917. The prize is still given annually.

[21] C. S. Lewis, "De Descriptione Temporum," *Selected Literary Essays*, 14.

After her Double First, she became an Ottilie Hancock Research Fellow at Girton College, earning both the MA and Ph.D. in 1933[22] and the Litt.D. in 1955.[23] Her distinguished career included additional honorary degrees from Liverpool, Sussex, London, Gothenburg, and, in the United States, from both Smith College and Kenyon College, Ohio.[24] She became an Official Fellow at Girton in 1935, Director of Studies in 1952, Vice-Mistress in 1962, Professorial Fellow from 1965 to 1968, Mistress in 1968, and then Life Fellow from 1976 until her death in 1993. Bradbrook was named University Lecturer at Cambridge University in 1945, Reader in 1962, the first woman Professor of English in 1965,[25] and then Honorary Professor of the Graduate School of Renaissance Studies at Warwick University, 1987-90. She became a Fellow of the Royal Society of Literature in 1947,[26] and she taught as a Visiting Professor in Santa Cruz, California (1966), Kuwait (1969), Tokyo (1975), Kenyon College (1977), and Rhodes University, South Africa (1979).[27] Bradbrook was an honorary member of the Modern Language Association of America.[28] She was affectionately known to her colleagues and former students as Brad, but to her friends outside of the Cambridge circle as Mollie.[29] She

---

[22] Girton College, *Girton College Register, 1869-1946*, edited by K. T. Butler and H. I. McMorran (Cambridge: privately printed by Cambridge University Press for Girton College, 1948), 678. Archive reference: Girton College Archive: GCCP 2/1/1.

[23] Radinowicz, Mary Ann, "Muriel Clara Bradbrook," *Girton College Newsletter* (Cambridge: Piggott Printers Ltd, 1993), 63. Archive reference: Girton College Archive: GCCP 3/1.

[24] Ibid.

[25] In her inaugural lecture as first woman Professor of English at Cambridge, she stated about Shakespeare's play *Timon of Athens*: "Life begins on the other side of despair—the maxim of Sartre would not have seemed unfamiliar to the 17th century, for something like it was found in the writings of Luther." After quoting Bradbrook, Dusinberre comments on Bradbrook's insight, "The combination of the big statement, the authority for it, and its precise application remains her unique hallmark as a scholar." See http://www.independent.co.uk/news/people/obituary-professor-muriel-bradbrook-1492586.html.

[26] Girton College, *Girton College Register, 1844-1969, Volume II*, edited by A. Duke (Cambridge: privately printed for Girton College, 1991), 412. Archive reference: Girton College Archive: GCCP 2/1/2.

[27] Ibid.

[28] "M. C. Bradbrook, 84, Shakespeare Scholar," https://www.nytimes.com/1993/06/21/obituaries/m-c-bradbrook-84-shakespeare-scholar.html.

[29] Eric Salmon, "Bradbrook, Muriel Clara (1909-1993)," *Oxford*

died in Cambridge on June 11, 1993.

In 1968, Bradbrook delivered the Clark Lectures in English Literature[30] at Trinity College in Cambridge, later turning them into a book, *Shakespeare the Craftsman*. She wrote *That Infidel Place*, a history of Girton College, for its centenary in 1969. In 1992, she received the prestigious Pragnell Award from the Shakespeare Birthday Celebration Committee for "outstanding achievement in extending the appreciation and enjoyment of the works of William Shakespeare." Juliet Dusinberre wrote of Bradbrook that her "name is a household word amongst scholars, teachers, theatregoers, and students at all levels."[31] Bradbrook published frequently on a wide range of literary subjects, including the Arthurian writer Sir Thomas Malory, the Norwegian playwright Henrik Ibsen, and the English poet and novelist Malcolm Lowry, but her chief interest was Shakespeare and the Elizabethans. Her approach to teaching, learning, and writing featured the study of primary texts and manuscripts, an approach that would also have appealed to Lewis. She believed that Shakespeare's drama was the product of the economic, social, and theatrical pressures of the day, a conviction about which she wrote in two of her books, *The Rise of the Common Player* and the earlier mentioned *Shakespeare the Craftsman*.[32]

Bradbrook was best known for her contributions to Elizabethan and Shakespearian studies, which are appreciated for their detailed knowledge of the social and cultural contexts of the period. Her major works include *Themes and Conventions of Elizabethan Tragedy* (1934), *Shakespeare and Elizabethan Poetry* (1951), *The Growth and Structure of Elizabethan Comedy* (1955), *The Rise of the Common Player* (1962), *Shakespeare the Craftsman* (1969), and *The Living Monument* (1976). Her other publications include *The School of Night* (1936), *Ibsen the Norwegian* (1946), and *Malcolm Lowry: His*

Dictionary of National Biography, Oxford University Press, 2004, online edition, May 2009, accessed October 2017.

[30] Lewis delivered the Clark Lectures at Trinity College in 1944.

[31] Bradbrook was an avid theatergoer. Juliet Dusinberre. "Obituary: Professor Muriel Bradbrook." June 19, 1993, *Independent*. http://www.independent.co.uk/news/people/obituary-professor-muriel-bradbrook-1492586.html.

[32] http://www.independent.co.uk/news/people/obituary-professor-muriel-bradbrook-1492586.html

Twenty-One Friendships of C.S. Lewis

Art and Early Life (1974).[33] The first-named six volumes[34] were later published together in 1979. In addition to her books, she contributed essays to *Theology* and *Christian Drama*, and she wrote on the religious imagination in W. B. Yeats, T. S. Eliot, George Herbert, and others.[35]

In Retrospect

In retrospect, this little-known (although not in Lewis's day) Shakespeare scholar was a friend and colleague of C. S. Lewis, highly respected by students, university colleagues, and the reading public. Lewis had met Nan Dunbar prior to his association with Bradbrook, and Dunbar likely introduced these two to one another. Bradbrook's expertise and her proximity in Cambridge made her the friend that Lewis most often consulted and most highly respected in Shakespeare studies. While their friendship was mostly limited to occasional dinners and meetings of the English faculty, Lewis enjoyed her company on a few occasions and would have enjoyed her company more frequently with the passing years had he lived beyond 1963.

---

[33] http://www.jrank.org/literature/pages/3421/Muriel-Bradbrook-(Muriel-Clara-Bradbrook).html

[34] That is, *Themes and Conventions of Elizabethan Tragedy, Shakespeare and Elizabethan Poetry, The Growth and Structure of Elizabethan Comedy, The Rise of the Common Player, Shakespeare the Craftsman,* and *The Living Monument.*

[35] Radinowicz, Mary Ann, "Muriel Clara Bradbrook," *Girton College Newsletter* (Cambridge: Piggott Printers Ltd, 1993), 63. Archive reference: Girton College Archive: GCCP 3/1.

Chapter 18

DEREK STANLEY BREWER
and C. S. Lewis

Over the decades, C. S. Lewis had many students who later rose to prominence in their fields, i.e., in English language and literature, but few rose higher than Derek Brewer. Brewer became Tutor, Fellow, and eventually Master of Emanuel College, Cambridge. The correspondence (approximately seven letters apiece) and social interaction between the two began as Brewer was preparing for entrance to Oxford University and continued to within a month-and-a-half of Lewis's death in 1963. Brewer is little known for one of the more important connections with Lewis—his involvement in an editorial committee that, in 1955, invited C. S. Lewis to be the General Editor for *Nelson's Medieval and Renaissance Library*, a series of medieval writings that had been largely neglected by the publishers. Although Eric Stanley wrote the letter of invitation, Brewer's experience with Lewis and his then-current work in medieval literature probably favorably disposed Lewis to accept.

DEREK STANLEY BREWER

Derek Stanley Brewer (July 13, 1923-October 23, 2008) was born in Cardiff, Wales, to a clerk who worked for General Electric. After attending the Crypt School in Gloucester, his education at Magdalen College, Oxford, was interrupted by World War II. Between 1942 and 1945, he served as an infantry officer in Italy with the Worcestershire Regiment and the 1st Battalion of the Royal Fusiliers during the war before returning to Oxford. While at Magdalen College, he won the Matthew Arnold Essay Prize, named after the nineteenth-century English poet and critic. In December 1947, Brewer completed

Derek Brewer
By courtesy of The Master and Fellows of Emmanuel College, Cambridge

Schools (the final examination for the BA) along with a few other ex-servicemen who had been granted a six-month extension in their studies because of war service.[1] He married his wife Elisabeth Hoole, the daughter of an Anglican clergyman,[2] in 1951. Elisabeth became a Lecturer at Homerton College, one of the constituent colleges of Cambridge University, and a specialist in medieval and Victorian literature, joining her husband in endowing a college prize for a 1st in Part I of the English Tripos.[3] They had three sons and two daughters.[4]

After Oxford University, Brewer was appointed assistant lecturer at the University of Birmingham in 1949, and while there he teamed up with Geoffrey Shepherd and Eric Stanley to invite C. S. Lewis to serve as the General Editor of the series of medieval writings that were eventually published by Thomas Nelson and Sons. From 1956 to 1958, Brewer taught for two years at the International Christian University of Tokyo, Japan, at a time when English literature was not part of the curriculum, and then he returned to the University of Birmingham.

In 1964, he took the position of lecturer in English at Cambridge University, becoming a Fellow of Emmanuel College. A readership in Medieval English followed in 1976 and he became Master of Emmanuel a year later. In 1983, he was elected to a university chair in English. He remained Master of Emmanuel until 1990 when he retired. At that time, he was appointed as a Life Fellow of Emmanuel College. During his career Brewer received several honorary doctorates from other institutions, including Keio University in Japan, Williams College, Williamstown, Massachusetts, and the Sorbonne, University of Paris. He was also an accomplished poet, winning the university's Seatonian Prize in poetry seven times and receiving the

---

[1] Derek Brewer, "The Tutor: A Portrait," in *C. S. Lewis at the Breakfast Table*, San Diego: Harcourt Brace & Company, second edition, 59f. The reference in the third edition of Como's book (*Remembering C. S. Lewis: Recollections of Those Who Knew Him*, San Francisco: Ignatius Press, 2005) is page 141, but since the essay by Brewer is the same in both editions, the page numbers from the second edition will be used.

[2] For this insight, I am indebted to Barry Windeatt, Fellow of Emmanuel College and former student of Brewer who delivered the memorial address "Derek Brewer (1923-2008)" on 7 February 2009 at the memorial service for Derek Brewer.

[3] https://www.walesonline.co.uk/news/wales-news/academic-died-just-month-after-2141733.

[4] https://www.walesonline.co.uk/news/wales-news/academic-died-just-month-after-2141733.

honor on several other occasions jointly with others. A collection of his poetry, *Seatonian Exercises and Other Verses*, was published in 2000.

Because of the difficulty in finding a publisher that would publish some specialized works, in 1972 Brewer and his wife Elisabeth founded an academic press named for him, D. S. Brewer, later combined with Richard Barber's Boydell Press in 1978 to become Boydell & Brewer.[5] He edited the Cambridge Review from 1981 to 1986 and served two terms as the president of the English Association.

Brewer was especially known for scholarship on Geoffrey Chaucer, so that it could be said that "his influence on modern study of both Chaucer and Malory is so fundamental and pervasive that it has become the mainstream."[6] He wrote *Chaucer*, *An Introduction to Chaucer* (1953), *Chaucer and His World* (1978) and *English Gothic Literature* (1983). Brewer wrote more than a dozen books and edited more than a dozen. His edited works include *Studies in Medieval English Romances: Some New Approaches* (1988), *Geoffrey Chaucer: The Writer and His Background* (1990), and *Medieval Comic Tales* (1996).

He died in Cambridge, England, on October 23, 2008, one month after the death of his wife Elisabeth. Most people spoke highly of his love of medieval literature and his academic profession, his help in getting less known medieval works published, his business skills, and his amiable character and friendliness. Barry Windeatt notes, appropriately, "People often commented that it was the moral concerns of English medieval literature with courtesy, honour, loyalty and integrity that they observed to be lived out in Derek's life."[7] He was a devout Anglican with a deep love for the Book of Common Prayer and served for many years as vice-president of the Church of England Record Society.[8]

Brewer at Oxford University

The first time that Derek Brewer had contact with C. S. Lewis took place in March 1941. On that occasion, several Oxford dons, led by Lewis, examined Brewer for a scholarship, known as a Demyship,

---

[5] "Derek Brewer (1923-2008)." Barry Windeatt, Fellow and Keeper of Rare Books, Emmanuel College. See also https://www.encyclopedia.com/arts/educational-magazines/brewer-derek-1923-2008-ds-brewer-derek-stanley-brewer.

[6] Ibid.

[7] Ibid.

[8] https://www.walesonline.co.uk/news/wales-news/academic-died-just-month-after-2141733.

at Magdalen College.[9] He was successful obtaining the Demyship. After his acceptance to the university, Brewer made plans to enroll and wrote to his future tutor for advice on how to prepare for his university education. One month after the examination, Lewis wrote back, recommending various books to read for his preparation.[10] That fall, Derek Brewer came up to Magdalen College for Michaelmas Term with Lewis as his tutor for English literature, a relationship that Brewer called his "good fortune."[11]

Since Brewer was studying in Lewis's field, the two of them found a certain camaraderie between them, even though, as Eric Stanley has stated, Brewer "never felt at ease with his tutor," and "had always remained in awe of him."[12] This led to an occasional social event during which the two met. Brewer himself stated that Lewis "held a few evening gatherings for undergraduates, where he shone with his most characteristic light."[13] A Socratic Club meeting in 1942, featuring Charles Williams as the speaker, was the first such recorded situation. Williams' topic "Are There Any *Valid* Objections to Free Love?," to no one's surprise, drew hundreds of interested university students.[14] After the meeting Lewis invited Brewer and others to meet Charles Williams in his college rooms and have a drink.[15] Talking to college students about sex drew a huge crowd.

After Williams' speech ended, Lewis took the chair to facilitate the discussion. When numerous comments from the floor danced around the key issue, Lewis told the students that they must now make up their minds whether they "wished to discuss the habits of

---

[9] Derek Brewer, "The Tutor: A Portrait," in *C. S. Lewis at the Breakfast Table*, 43f.

[10] The date was April 8, 1941. *Collected Letters, III*, 1540f.

[11] Derek Brewer, "The Tutor: A Portrait." *C. S. Lewis at the Breakfast Table*, 41, 45.

[12] Eric Stanley, "C. S. Lewis and J. R. R. Tolkien as I knew them (never well)," *Journal of Inklings Studies*, Vol. 4, No. 1 (April 2014):126, 129.

[13] Derek Brewer, "The Tutor: A Portrait." *C. S. Lewis at the Breakfast Table*, 57.

[14] The date was March 2, 1942. Erik Routley claims that they met in the Magdalen College dining hall. Routley, "A Prophet," in *C. S. Lewis at the Breakfast Table*, 35. William Griffin claims that they met at Somerville College. *Clive Staples Lewis*, 203.

[15] Colin Duriez, *C. S. Lewis: A Biography of Friendship*, Chapter 12, Kindle edition. See also Derek Brewer, "The Tutor: A Portrait," in *C. S. Lewis at the Breakfast Table*, 57.

bees or those of human beings."[16] Brewer was among those fortunate undergraduates who were invited to Lewis's rooms for beer and conversation and a chance to meet Charles Williams.[17] "After the lecture and discussion," writes Brewer, Lewis asked me and two or three others up to his room to meet Williams and have a drink."[18] In Lewis's rooms those half-dozen continued to discuss the topic, and the impossibility of avoiding either pleasure or pain. Brewer concluded, "It was a wonderful evening."[19]

On May 21, 1946, Lewis invited some undergraduates to drink beer in his room, "and I am sorry to say," Brewer writes, "we kept him up till 1:30 with a long and complicated argument on a hypothetical legal question."[20] Just a month later, Brewer was one of only four undergraduates to meet and dine at Magdalen College, something that the four of them did with C. S. Lewis and Hugo Dyson once a term for three or four terms.[21] Since both of them were war veterans—Lewis from the first World War and Brewer from the second—they had additional things in common.

Lest it be thought that Brewer was a Lewis devotee, Brewer offered fair criticism as well as notable praise, for example, when he described *The Allegory of Love* as "remarkable and splendid, though misleading."[22] He wrote about a tutorial on medieval drama, "we had a dull tutorial," hastening to add that "this was most unusual."[23] He also

---

[16] Derek Brewer, "The Tutor: A Portrait," in *C. S. Lewis at the Breakfast Table*, 57.

[17] For example, on May 21, 1946, Lewis invited a group of undergraduates, including Derek Brewer, to his room to drink beer, and they talk about a hypothetical legal situation. They must have enjoyed the evening because they stayed until 1:30 a.m. Derek Brewer, "The Tutor: A Portrait," in *C. S. Lewis at the Breakfast Table*, 57.

[18] Colin Duriez, *C. S. Lewis: A Biography of Friendship*, Chapter 12, Kindle edition. See also Derek Brewer, "The Tutor: A Portrait," in *C. S. Lewis at the Breakfast Table*, 57.

[19] Ibid., 57.

[20] Ibid., 57.

[21] The date is June 30, 1946. The same event took place on February 4, 1948. Derek Brewer, "The Tutor: A Portrait," in *C. S. Lewis at the Breakfast Table*, 58. See also Peter Bayley, "From Master to Colleague," in *C. S. Lewis at the Breakfast Table*, 79. See also Peter Bayley, "From Master to Colleague," in *C. S. Lewis at the Breakfast Table*, 79.

[22] Derek Brewer, "The Tutor: A Portrait," in *C. S. Lewis at the Breakfast Table*, 47.

[23] Derek Brewer, "The Tutor: A Portrait," in *C. S. Lewis at the Breakfast Table*, 48.

claimed that Lewis displayed a lack of theory and an unawareness of his own presuppositions,[24] although Lewis himself would undoubtedly have challenged those claims.

During the first half of the war, Brewer did not see action. Then he became an infantry officer with the Worcestershire Regiment and served in the Royal Fusiliers from 1942 to 1945. After the war, he returned to Oxford University to resume his studies. On September 19, 1945, Lewis wrote to Brewer about what he should read as he planned his return to the University. Lewis recommended reading as widely as he could among the major English writers and resurrecting his Old English.[25]

Brewer engaged in all the usual academic experiences—attendance at lectures, tutorials with his tutor, etc. On February 16, 1946, Lewis lectured on "Prolegomena to the Study of Medieval Poetry" at noon at Magdalen. Derek Brewer was in attendance and heard some remarks that were anti-feminist.[26] On March 1, 1946, Derek Brewer had a tutorial with Lewis on medieval drama, one of a series of tutorials that term.[27]

Since Brewer completed his degree in December 1947, Lewis wrote to Brewer about an area of research Brewer might attempt, namely Gower, at a time when Brewer was looking into additional studies. He also encouraged Brewer about his chances for a Fellowship by Examination that Magdalen College held every year, but for which Brewer was unsuccessful.[28] In addition, Brewer writes, Lewis wrote many letters in support of Brewer as he applied for various teaching positions.[29]

After Oxford

In 1949, Brewer was appointed to an assistant lectureship in English at the University of Birmingham.[30] Lewis wrote him a

---

[24] Ibid., 51.

[25] *Collected Letters* III, 1561.

[26] Derek Brewer, "The Tutor: A Portrait," in *C. S. Lewis at the Breakfast Table*, 55.

[27] Ibid., 48.

[28] The date is December 21, 1947. Derek Brewer, "The Tutor: A Portrait," 60.

[29] The date is December 21, 1947. Derek Brewer, "The Tutor: A Portrait," 59.

[30] *Collected Letters, III*, 1589.

congratulatory letter upon that appointment, but the friendship was not especially close, and they did not correspond regularly. The two men did not write to one another for nearly a decade until a professional relationship began under the initiative of Brewer and two other Birmingham English Fellows—Geoffrey Shepherd and Eric Stanley. In 1955, the three men invited Lewis to serve as the General Editor for a series of medieval texts that they convinced Thomas Nelson to publish. Since the three men at the University of Birmingham were relatively young, they needed a recognizable name to serve as General Editor of the series and to lend his reputation and expertise to the project.

In 1958, while Lewis was serving as General Editor for *Nelson's Medieval and Renaissance Library*, Lewis wrote to Brewer about a draft of Brewer's introduction to Chaucer, including a reference to a delightful reunion between the two of them at Jack Bennett's home. Lewis included in that letter a critique of Brewer's introduction to Geoffrey Chaucer, *The Parlement of Fowlys*.[31] Chaucer's story was one of the documents that were to be published in *Nelson's Medieval and Renaissance Library*.[32] Brewer's edition of this work by Chaucer was published in 1960, and Lewis offered positive, but also critical, comments. He also wrote in a jocular, but mildly critical, fashion when he stated, "I rather got the impression—let's mix our metaphors well—that you are skating on thin ice over various hornets' nests that might at any moment burst into flame."[33] A spoonful of humor helps the medicine go down.

In the midst of Lewis serving as General Editor, he wrote to Brewer on November 16, 1959 about their recent meeting, apparently a meeting of Lewis with the Editorial Committee (Shepherd, Brewer, and Stanley, perhaps with one of the editors of Thomas Nelson) related to the Nelson project, and Lewis's inability to edit. He writes, "Lor' bless you, I can't edit any more than I can audit. I'm not accurate. Sorry."[34]

---

[31] The date is August 30, 1958. Derek Brewer, "The Tutor: A Portrait," 61f.

[32] He starts his letter with a quotation from this work of Chaucer: "Trusteth wel I am not textual." *Collected Letters, Vol. III*, 969.

[33] *Collected Letters, Vol. III*, 969. In *Remembering C. S. Lewis: Recollections of Those Who Knew Him* (2005), James Como says that he has a long list of notes from Lewis about this book by Chaucer. The list, Como writes, "testifies to the sharpness and care with which he performed this valuable but tedious chore."

[34] This letter does not appear in *Collected Letters*. Derek Brewer, "The

No Ordinary People

The last correspondence from Lewis was written on a postcard in 1963, the last year of Lewis's life. Lewis writes briefly to Derek Brewer about having retired, nearly dying last July, and being quite comfortable and cheerful.[35] The younger Brewer was still early in his career, retiring almost thirty years later, but greatly encouraged and enriched for the rest of his life by the friendship between tutor and student.

Tutor: A Portrait," 62f.

[35] The date is October 8, 1963. Derek Brewer, "The Tutor: A Portrait," 67. This letter does not appear in Vol. III of *Collected Letters*. Lewis also apparently wrote a letter to Elisabeth Brewer, the wife of Derek Brewer, on October 26, 1960, declining a speaking engagement with regret. Since he wrote to "Miss Brewer," the letter could well have been a daughter of Derek Brewer or another person with the name Brewer. *Collected Letters, III*, 1202.

Twenty-One Friendships of C.S. Lewis

Rev. F. C. Bryan
by permission of Tyndale Baptist Church, Bristol

Chapter XX

F. C. BRYAN
and the Oxford Socratic Club

Good communicators have a way of finding one another. C. S. Lewis and F. C. Bryan were especially good at communicating with one audience they had in common—college students, Lewis as one of their professors and Bryan as a local pastor. When they met one another, they connected and began to team together to teach the truth of God to these young, impressionable students. The Oxford Socratic Club was started for the students of Oxford University, and to that club both Lewis and Bryan migrated, the former as its first president and the latter as one of its speakers.

Among the many names associated with the Oxford Socratic Club—its founder and Chair Stella Aldwinckle, Monica Shorten,[1] C. S. Lewis, Austin Farrer, C. E. M. Joad, Antony Flew, J. B. S. Haldane, and others—few people would include F. C. Bryan. But the Rev. F. C. Bryan had significant contacts with Lewis and the Socratic Club on at least three occasions.

We don't know how or precisely when F. C. Bryan and C. S. Lewis met, but Lewis may well have met Bryan because of other common acquaintances in Clifton, a southwestern suburb of Bristol, the city where Bryan was serving at the time the two men may have first met. Time spent in Bristol could easily have resulted in their friendship.

Lewis had at least three early life experiences in Bristol, the city where Janie Moore had lived with her children Paddy and Maureen. First, the teenage Lewis, having met Paddy Moore because of the Oxford University Officers' Training Corps, spent time with the family in Bristol before being deployed to the war in France.[2] Secondly, Lewis convalesced in Bristol for several months in 1918 after being wounded in the war, and, thirdly, he vacationed there in

---

[1] She was the Oxford student who expressed a need for an undergraduate club where intellectual difficulties related to the Christian faith could be discussed.

[2] Lewis was in Bristol from September 29 to October 11, 1917, *The Lewis Papers* V: 233, and on November 15, 1917, George Sayer, *Jack*, 129, from June 25 to September 3, 1918 or later, September 12 to October 4, 1918, and late March 1919, Green and Hooper, 62.

1924.

Other members of the Moore family lived in Bristol, including Janie Moore's brother Dr. Rob Askins and his wife, Molly, and another brother, Dr. John Askins,[3] along with his wife Mary and daughter Peony. Janie's daughter Maureen Moore spent time in Bristol studying music with Miss Kathleen Whitty.[4] In addition, Lewis once spoke at the University of Bristol,[5] delivering the Skemp Memorial Lecture on the English essayist Joseph Addison,[6] and Lewis's article, "The Trouble with 'X' ...," was later published by the *Bristol Diocesan Gazette*, a Church of England publication, very possibly another result of Lewis's contacts in Bristol.[7]

FRANK COLIN BRYAN

Frank Colin Bryan was born in Bluntisham, Cambridgeshire, England, on March 22, 1891. He was the son of a minister, the Rev. W. C. Bryan. He attended Christ's Hospital School in Horsham, West Sussex, and then entered Jesus College, Oxford, in 1910, to read mathematics. From 1914-17 he attended Mansfield College, a Non-Conformist Theological College (seminary), under Dr. W. B. Selbie, Principal.[8] After Mansfield College, Bryan held pastorates at Hope Baptist Church, Cardiff, Wales (1917-20); Herne Bay Baptist Church (1920-28), Herne Bay being a seaside town in Kent; the Clapton Downs Baptist Church, Clapton (1928-33); and Tyndale Baptist Church, Bristol (1933-50). During his service in Bristol, he was working in the same community as a curate named John Robinson, who later became Bishop of Woolwich, author of the controversial *Honest to God*, and subsequently Dean of Trinity College, Cambridge.

---

[3] This is the Doc Askins who experienced mental problems between February 21, 1923 and April 6, 1923, the day the Doc died. *All My Road Before Me*, 201. Another brother, William James Askins, was the clergyman brother of Mrs. Moore, who served a church in from Cavan County, Ireland at this time in 1923.

[4] In April and May 1922. See "Chronologically Lewis" at http://www.joelheck.com/chronologically-lewis.php.

[5] October 7, 1943.

[6] This lecture survives as "Addison," *Selected Literary Essays*, Edited by Walter Hooper. Cambridge: Cambridge University Press, 1969, 154-168.

[7] The article was published in 1948. Jocelyn Gibb, *Light on C. S. Lewis*, Harcourt, 1966, 132.

[8] http://www.thecrimson.com/article/1930/1/22/w-b-selbie-will-be-noble/

Bryan left Bristol for Cambridge when the Baptist churches appointed him Superintendent for the Eastern Area of England, a position he held for eight years.[9]

In September 1931, the World Alliance for International Friendship through the Churches, one of the precursors to the World Council of Churches, held its eighth International Conference in Cambridge. On behalf of the Cambridge Free Churches, Bryan gave the welcome address, which demonstrates both Bryan's interest in the interdenominational reach of the Christian church and the respect with which he was received.[10]

F C Bryan
©Tyndale Baptist Church

Bryan authored several books, including *Concerning the Way*, a book about the Christian faith as "the Way,"[11] *Concerning God*, and *The New Knowledge and the Old Gospel*, all of which addressed the intellectual and religious difficulties of the post-war generation.

The New Knowledge and the Old Gospel, with a Foreword by Dr. Selbie, consisted of sermons he delivered at the Downs, Clapton, and at a Summer School at Sandwich. The fact that many requested a reprint of his messages[12] suggests that he was an engaging speaker. This book of sermons attempted to address the "new knowledge" of

---

[9] Information about Bryan's work with Robinson and his appointment as Superintendent for the Eastern Area of England came to me in an email of July 25, 2017 by way of David T. Roberts, who drew this information from the church archives.

[10] Keith Clements, in an email to me dated 7/26/2017.

[11] SCM Press, 1946. Chapter 1, "The Nature of the Way"; Chapter 2, "The Rule of the Road," i.e., the law of love; Chapter 3, "Equipment for the Journey," i.e., faith and both Word and Sacrament; Chapter 4, "Springs by the Wayside," i.e., the interior life and the essence of prayer; Chapter 5, "Hill, Valley and Desert," the hill being self-denial, the valley of humiliation, and the desert of aridity; Chapter 6, "Encountering Enemies," i.e., hypocrisy, self-esteem, cynicism, and sentimentality; and Chapter 7, "The Ordering of the Journey," which deals with the practice of prayer, the use of time, and the use of money. The chapters were probably a sermon series.

[12] Introduction, *The New Knowledge and the Old Gospel*, London: The Kingsgate Press, 9.

modern physics and astronomy.[13] There he describes the challenge of Darwinism to the Christian faith and the challenge of Einstein to the Rationalist Press Association. He ends the first chapter with the statement that, because of the new scientific knowledge, five biblical teachings are now easier to accept: (1) the existence of God and the reality of the unseen world; (2) the original creation of the universe; (3) miracles and the providence of God; (4) the special revelation of God through His Son; and (5) the cosmic significance of Christ and the cross.[14]

In *The New Knowledge and the Old Gospel*, Bryan tells the story of an argument between Dr. Johnson and and his biographer Boswell. Boswell was claiming that the argument of Bishop Berkley, i.e., that matter is merely ideal rather than real, was impossible to refute. Byran writes, "Dr. Johnson kicked his foot with mighty force against a stone, crying, 'I refute it thus.'"[15] This story suggests some reasons that Lewis and Bryan got along well, since Lewis not only had a great sense of humor, but he also appreciated both Johnson and Berkeley. Bryan goes on to cite Eddington, who states, "The solid substance of things is an illusion,"[16] since atoms with their protons, electrons, and neutrons are what is real. In the same message, he cites Sir James Jeans, who, with Eddington, was also a familiar name to Lewis. "The fundamental nature of the material universe," writes Bryan, "is as much a mystery as is the appearance of life, or the manifestation of the mind."[17] Lewis once wrote favorably about Jeans and Eddington: "Two admittedly great physicists (Jeans and Eddington) have both arrived at a spiritual view of the universe."[18] Both Bryan and Lewis had great respect for science and scientists, but where science conflicted with Scripture either they looked for a legitimate compromise or they insisted on the supremacy of Scripture.

---

[13] Bryan, Introduction, *The New Knowledge and the Old Gospel*, 13.

[14] Bryan, *The New Knowledge and the Old Gospel*, 21f. Chapter titles: Chapter 1: "The Impact of Science on Religion," Chapter 2: "God and the Unseen World," Chapter 3: "The Creation and the End of the World," Chapter 4: "Providence, Freedom, and Miracles," Chapter 5: "Revelation," and Chapter 6: "The Cosmic Significance of Christ."

[15] Bryan, *The New Knowledge and the Old Gospel*, 24.

[16] Bryan, *The New Knowledge and the Old Gospel*, 25.

[17] Bryan, *The New Knowledge and the Old Gospel*, 25.

[18] Bryan, A letter to his brother Warren, *Collected Letters*, II, 407.

In the fourth chapter, Bryan writes about natural law and Sir Isaac Newton, and he discusses the implication of natural law for prayer, providence, and miracles. He cites Matthew Arnold, who said, "Miracles don't happen,"[19] but he insists that fixed laws cannot rule out the supernatural, and in this insistence anticipates, or follows, Lewis in his book *Miracles*. In other chapters, he discusses the possibility of other worlds, the unlikelihood of other forms of life in other worlds, the witness of special revelation in the Bible, the uniqueness of Christ, and the significance of the cross, all themes that Lewis addressed at different times.

Bryan's skill in writing and speaking can be seen, for example, in this excerpt from Chapter 5, "Revelation":

> Call mankind the mere froth and spume on the waves of a timeless, shoreless ocean, if so indeed it seems to you. But the living soul of man is, in fact, not a by-product, or an accident, but both the most amazing and the most significant product of it all, that which gives meaning and point to the whole cosmic process. Paul has it surely in one of his unerring, inspired intuitions—"The whole creation groaning and travailing in pain ... waiting for the revealing of sons of God."[20]

This style of writing—and, undoubtedly, his winsome smile—explain why Bryan was invited to speak at the Socratic Club and Socratic weekend conferences. It also explains why he played a considerable part in the young people's work of the Baptist Union and was much sought after as a speaker for Summer Schools and retreats. After his death, *The Baptist Times* described his tenure in Bristol as "exercising a wide influence over old and young, and not least over the swiftly changing generations of students."[21] While in Bristol he participated in several ecumenical ventures, one of which may have brought him into contact with Lewis.

In 1950, Bryan was elected Chair of the Baptist Missionary Society. On the Baptist Union Council, he was an advocate of Christian unity, and in 1960 he was elected chairman of the Baptist Ministers' Fellowship and President of the Baptist Union of Great Britain and Ireland. He was married to Greta, the daughter of the Rev. Charles Hobbs, the minister of Woodstock Road Baptist Church, Oxford.[22]

---

[19] Bryan, *The New Knowledge and the Old Gospel*, 47.

[20] Bryan, *The New Knowledge and the Old Gospel*, 64.

[21] A clipping from *The Baptist Times*, written by Baptist historian E A Payne, sent to me on July 25, 2017 by David T. Robert.

[22] Information about Woodstock Road Baptist Church, Oxford, came

Greta died in 1942. The couple had one daughter, Margaret, who married Rev. Leonard E. Addicott. Bryan died in Cambridge on May 4, 1972, at the age of 81, leaving a legacy of a sensitive and gracious personality, an engaging and effective preacher and speaker, and a man of faith who was rich in spiritual understanding.[23]

BRYAN AND LEWIS

The first known contact between Lewis and Bryan took place in January 1943. That evening the Socratic Club met to discuss "What Is Prayer?" with Bryan as guest speaker, but we know nothing about his talk apart from the title.[24]

On March 13-16, 1943, a weekend Socratics' Conference on "Christian Faith" was held at Jordans, Beaconsfield, Buckinghamshire, with speakers Dr. L. W. Grensted, Oriel Professor of the Philosophy of the Christian Religion, Lewis, and Bryan. In attendance were many students from the various colleges of Oxford University, as well as speakers and organizers R. W. Kosterlitz, Lewis, Grensted, Bryan, and Stella Aldwinckle. Grensted spoke on "Prayer—before or after faith?", and Lewis spoke on "Presuppositions of Faith" and "The Church."[25] No record of the content of Bryan's talks, or their titles, exists.

Two years later,[26] the Socratic Club held another weekend conference, again on "Christian Faith," organized by Stella Aldwinckle, this time at Ridley Hall, Cambridge. Lewis, Rev. Eric Fenn,[27] and Bryan each spoke twice. Lewis began the weekend with his talk on "Presuppositions of Faith" on Saturday evening, giving the same two talks that he had given two years previously. Eric Fenn, replacing Grensted, spoke on "Faith in Christ" and "Prayer – before or after faith?" while Bryan spoke on "The Nature of Faith" and "The

---

to me in an email of July 25, 2017 by way of David T. Roberts, who drew this information from the church archives.

[23] *Memoirs of Deceased Ministers and Missionaries*, 283f., sent to me by Ray Macpherson, Herne, England, UK.

[24] The *Socratic Digest* does not contain his speech or any notes on his talk. The date was January 25, 1943.

[25] Stella Aldwinckle Papers, Box 8, Folder 367. The Marion E. Wade Center, Wheaton College, Wheaton, IL. 1943 Conference on Christian Faith. Weekend Conference Programme.

[26] On March 17-20, 1945.

[27] Assistant Director of Religious Broadcasting for the BBC, well-known for his role in facilitating Lewis's BBC talks in the early 1940s.

Consequences of Faith," very possibly the same topics he had addressed in the previous conference.

On Sunday, March 18, Bryan spoke on "The Nature of Faith," and that afternoon Eric Fenn addressed "Faith in Christ," followed by "Questions & Discussion." On Monday morning, Eric Fenn spoke on "Prayer—before or after faith?" in the early morning, and later that morning Lewis spoke about "The Church." That evening Bryan talked about "The Consequences of Faith." Though predominantly Anglican,  the presence of a Presbyterian (Fenn) and a Baptist (Bryan) alongside Anglicans Lewis and Aldwinckle showed the interest of the conference's organizers in "mere Christianity," i.e., an ecumenical or inter-denominational spirit.

One sees that both Byran and Lewis had similar tastes in reading. Both men had read Irenaeus, whom Lewis cites in letters to Sister Penelope. Bryan cites Irenaeus, who states, "'Jesus became what we are that He might make us what He is'—sons, sharing 'by adoption' (in St. Paul's phrase) the Divine nature."[28] That passage echoes a similar passage in Mere Christianity, "The Son of God became a man to enable men to become the sons of God."[29] Bryan also writes, "This is not to imply that people who lived before Christ and people who have never known Christ have no hope of immortality."[30] This statement suggests the view that included Emeth, a character in Lewis' seventh Chronicle of Narnia, The Last Battle, in Aslan's kingdom.

Writing about World War II later in the same book, Bryan reflects the position that Lewis took in *The Abolition of Man*, stating, "Is this sort of thing, however, to be labelled as progress, when hatred seizes the fruits of man's ingenuity and turns it to his destruction? A little more of it and the only kind of progress apparent will be progress

---

[28] F. C. Bryan, *Concerning the Way*, London: SCM Press Ltd, 1946, 17. The Church Father Irenaeus lived in the second century A.D. in what is now France. *Collected Letters*, II, 451, 453.

[29] C. S. Lewis, *Mere Christianity*. New York: HarperCollinsPublishers. Copyright 1980, 178.

[30] Bryan, *Concerning the Way*, 15.

toward universal annihilation."[31] Bryan's occasional citing of Baron von Hügel,[32] Martin Buber, and H. G. Wells suggests other common interests.[33] His mention of practicing "the presence of God" is also a shared interest with Lewis.[34]

Bryan also writes, "Well, though we are told to love all men, we are not told, mercifully, that we have got to like all men ...."[35] For a BBC broadcast, Lewis once wrote about married couples, "They can have this love for each other even at those moments when they do not like each other; as you love yourself even when you do not like yourself."[36] Bryan writes that love for all men means "that we are to have goodwill towards all men; that we shall not injure them because we dislike them ... we shall not refuse to forgive them because we dislike them."[37] In his chapter on "Forgiveness" in *Mere Christianity*, Lewis writes, "we must try to feel about the enemy as we feel ourselves—to wish that he were not bad, to hope that he may, in this world or another, be cured: in fact, to wish his good."[38]

But similarity does not prove dependence in either direction, since both men could have written as they did because such ideas were commonly expressed in Christian circles in those days, making a coincidence out of some of these correlations. Still, these similarities demonstrate that both Bryan and Lewis shared a compatibility of Christian thought that made their friendship more likely and more rewarding. And the likelihood is that in some of these statements one of them influenced the other.

Although few people know the name Frank Colin Bryan, he exemplifies Lewis's ecumenical spirit. The two men had many common interests. Lewis, a member of the Church of England,

---

[31] Bryan, *Concerning the Way*, 27. *The Abolition of Man* was published in 1943.

[32] For example, although there are other such references, see F. C. Bryan *Concerning the Way*, London: SCM Press Ltd, 1946, 30, where Bryan cites von Hügel, who wrote, "Christianity taught us to care."

[33] Bryan *Concerning the Way*, 34f., 109. Bryan also mentions Evelyn Underhill, an author Lewis read and corresponded with. See *Concerning the Way*, 68. He also mentions St. Teresa (85), Thomas à Kempis (87), William Law (89), and Sir William Beveridge (93).

[34] Bryan, *Concerning the Way*, 107. See *Collected Letters, III*, 253., 752.

[35] Bryan, *Concerning the Way*, 33.

[36] C. S. Lewis, *Mere Christianity*, 109. This quotation comes from Chapter 6, "Christian Marriage" in Book III: Christian Behavior.

[37] Bryan, *Concerning the Way*, 33.

[38] C. S. Lewis, *Mere Christianity*, 120.

respected Bryan, a Baptist minister, as a capable and engaging speaker on the Christian faith, especially in speaking to young people, and he gratefully collaborated with Bryan in that mission.

Envelope addressed to Miss Shelley with the Magdalen crest on the flap
Inside letter is signed with initials C.S.L.
Postmarked 9th November, 1932
Not in the *Collected Letters*

Chapter 20

MARY SHELLEY
and Progressive Schools

In *The Silver Chair*, C. S. Lewis described the school attended by Jill Pole and Eustace Scrubb as a "mixed" school, that is, a school for boys and girls, but "some said it was not nearly so mixed as the minds of the people who ran it."[1] Mary Shelley taught at one of the schools that inspired Lewis's opinion about some schools of his day. She was also one of Lewis's students who, after some years as an atheist,[2] became a Christian, largely because of his influence. She studied English under Lewis at Oxford University, earned a Diploma in Education, and then began a teaching career at a school in Devon called Dartington Hall. Over the decades between 1929 and 1960, she corresponded several dozen times with Lewis, benefiting from his mentoring and spiritual guidance. She was the daughter of a distant branch of the family of the English poet Percy Bysshe Shelley, which makes her a distant relative of her namesake Mary Shelley, the author of *Frankenstein*.[3]

Mary Shelley Neylan

Mary Gwendolyn Shelley was born to Hugh and Maud Shelley in Watlington, Oxfordshire, on August 3, 1908. At the age of nine, she attended St. Katherine's School in Wantage, Oxfordshire, a school operated by The Community of St. Mary the Virgin, an Anglican religious order.[4]

---

[1] C. S. Lewis, *The Silver Chair*. New York: Macmillan Publishing Company, 1953, 1.

[2] Sarah Tisdall, "A Goddaughter's Memories," Chapter 14 in *C. S. Lewis Remembered Collected Reflections of Students, Friends & Colleagues*, Grand Rapids: Zondervan, 2006, 215. The obituary of Sarah Tisdall, written by her sister Elizabeth, appeared in *The Guardian* on August 25, 2017: https://www.theguardian.com/artanddesign/2017/aug/25/sarah-tisdall-obituary.

[3] Sarah Tisdall, "A Goddaughter's Memories," 213.

[4] The order was founded in 1848 by William John Butler. Sister Penelope (Ruth Penelope Lawson), a member of that same community whose story is told in chapter seven of this book, wrote several significant works and also corresponded with Lewis. These include *God Persists:*

No Ordinary People

After two years in Wantage, Shelley returned to Watlington and attended another boarding school where, she writes, she lost her faith.[5] She later enrolled at Reading University, where she became a student of Hugo Dyson. In 1929, she enrolled at St. Hugh's College, Oxford, to prepare for a teaching career, but she came to Magdalen College to take tutorials in English literature with Lewis because English was to become her teaching field. She took those tutorials during the years when Lewis adopted theism and then Christianity. She completed a BA in 1932 and a Diploma in Education in 1933.

Shelley began her teaching career at Dartington Hall, Devon, in 1933. Founded in 1926, Dartington Hall was a progressive coeducational boarding school which bragged about having "no corporal punishment, indeed no punishment at all; no prefects; no uniforms; no Officers' Training Corps; no segregation of the sexes; no compulsory games, compulsory religion or compulsory anything else ...; no competition; no jingoism."[6]

Shelley's future husband, Daniel Neylan, was managing investments in London when he heard about Dartington, visited, was given a tour of the place by Mary Shelley, and was appointed as classical master[7] at Dartington in 1934. The couple married a year later (photo, right[8]) on Aug.

Mary and Daniel Neylan
Used by permission

A Short Survey of World History in the Light of Christian Faith (1939), *Leaves from the Trees* (1937), *The Wood: An Outline of Christianity* (1936), *Scenes from the Psalms, Windows on Jerusalem: A Study in the Mystery of Redemption*, translator of Athanasius' *The Incarnation of the Word of God: being the treatise of Athanasius, De Incarnatione Verbi Dei* (1944), *They Shall be My People*, and *The Coming of the Lord: A Study in the Creed*.

[5] Mary Neylan, "My Friendship with C. S. Lewis," *The Chesterton Review*, Vol. XVII, No. 3-4 (August-November 1991), 405.

[6] *Wikipedia* article on Dartington Hall.

[7] Teaching the classical languages, Latin and Greek.

[8] This photo, the photo of Sarah looking at her grandfather, and the photo of the parents and daughters that appears later are used by kind permission of Mary Shelley's younger daughter, Elizabeth Neylan.

30, 1935⁹ and had two children, Sarah¹⁰ (b. Jan. 15, 1938) and Mary Elizabeth (b. 1946).

The Neylan family left Dartington in 1940,¹¹ moving to Headington, not far from the Lewis home in Oxford. Their daughter Elizabeth states that they left Dartington because of the war, choosing to join the war effort. They were unhappy with the Dartington attitude toward the war.¹²

Parenthood put life into a different focus for Mary,¹³ and one result was that she became a Christian in 1940.¹⁴ Lewis, by this time a good friend, became the godfather to Sarah when she was baptized two years later.¹⁵ Mary

Sarah (center) looks up at her grandfather
Used by permission

---

⁹ Sarah Tisdall, "A Goddaughter's Memories," Harry Lee Poe and Rebecca Whitten Poe, eds., *C. S. Lewis Remembered*, Grand Rapids: Zondervan, 2006, 216. Walter Hooper says that the date was Aug. 30, 1934. He probably gets the day and month correct, but the year wrong. If Mary Shelley met Daniel Neylan in 1934, it is likely that they married one year later rather than in the same year.

¹⁰ Sarah Tisdall, daughter of Mary Neylan, tells her story in Sarah Tisdall, "A Goddaughter's Memories," Harry Lee Poe and Rebecca Whitten Poe, eds., *C. S. Lewis Remembered*, Grand Rapids: Zondervan, 2006.

¹¹ https://archive.dartington.org/calmview/ Some think the reason for them leaving was that Daniel lost his job due to the dropping of Latin.

¹² Email from Elizabeth Neylan on April 28, 2018. The implication is that Dartington held to a pacifist position about war. Elizabeth further states that she does not think that her father lost his job because Dartington stopped offering Latin.

¹³ See Lewis's letter to his brother Warren in *Collected Letters, II*, 314, for documentation of this change of mind on her part.

¹⁴ Lewis writes to Griffiths on April 16, 1940, inviting Griffiths' prayers and stating that Mary Neylan is close to becoming a Christian, and on Jan. 4, 1941 he writes to Neylan about next steps. *Collected Letters, II*, 392.

¹⁵ Lewis was also the godfather of Lucy Barfield, daughter of Owen Barfield; Laurence Harwood, son of A. C. Harwood; and Richard Francis Dunbar, son of Maureen and Leonard Blake. Marjorie Lamp

Neylan had a breakdown in 1943, which resulted in sending the children to their grandparents for a year.[16] She had other health problems, especially depression. In 1944, Daniel got a job at the War Office, so the family moved to London.

According to her daughters, Mary was an accomplished violinist and a wonderful conversationalist. Her daughter Sarah adds, "She was also very strong intellectually, extraordinarily perceptive where other people were concerned, and an excellent artist."[17] Her husband Daniel died in 1969.[18] Mary died on Feb. 9, 1997 at the age of 88.[19]

MARY SHELLEY AND C. S. LEWIS

During the summer of 1931, Mary Shelley wrote to Lewis requesting a tutorial spot with him for the upcoming school year. Her tutor Hugo Dyson had told her that Lewis would accept her. Lewis turned her down because his schedule was full and because he was already saving a spot for another student. Later that month, Lewis wrote to Mary Shelley, stating that he hadn't realized that she was the very student for whom he was saving a spot, since Dyson had not mentioned her name to Lewis (nor had she mentioned Dyson to Lewis).[20] Consequently, Lewis accepted her and gave her a reading list to prepare for the coming term. She took tutorials from Lewis over the next two years.

Shelley graduated in 1933 with a Fourth Class degree and she was devastated by her poor exam performance. That summer, while she was applying for a teaching job, Lewis wrote her a letter of comfort. He told her that she had done good work on nineteenth

---

Mead, "Meeting children as equals," *Christian History*, No. 88 (Fall 2005) 36.

[16] Sarah Tisdall, "A Goddaughter's Memories," 218. The nature of this breakdown is not known.

[17] Sarah Tisdall, "A Goddaughter's Memories," 223. The sketch of C. S. Lewis was done by Mary. Its copyright is owned by Taylor University, Upland, Indiana. Used with permission.

[18] Mary Neylan, "My Friendship with C. S. Lewis," *The Chesterton Review*, Vol. XVII, No. 3-4 (August-November 1991), 406.

[19] Much of this brief biography is indebted to Walter Hooper's biography of Mary Neylan in his Biographical Appendix to the second volume of *Collected Letters*. *Collected Letters, II*, 1054f.

[20] Unpublished letter from Lewis to Shelley on June 18, 1931. Sarah Tisdall, "A Goddaughter's Memories," Harry Lee Poe and Rebecca Whitten Poe, eds., *C. S. Lewis Remembered*, Grand Rapids: Zondervan, 2006, 214.

century literature, but she had had difficulty with the language exam. He insisted that she did not have a fourth-class mind, and he concluded by accepting blame: "Try to forgive me both as an examiner and as a tutor."[21]

She applied for a position at Dartington Hall, Devon, and she asked Lewis for a reference. His recommendation was so good that she was hired ahead of the poet W. H. Auden.[22]

Lewis had a low regard for progressive schools, and Shelley eventually wrote to him with her concerns about Dartington Hall. Dartington probably provided some of the source material for his satirizing of such schools in *The Chronicles of Narnia*.[23]

Sketch of CSL by Mary Neylan
The Center for the Study of C.S. Lewis
& Friends, Taylor University
Used by Permission

Eventually Mary asked him, "Why do you think that Dartington is so much worse than anywhere else?"[24] When she visited him at Christmas in 1939, she did so "in order to discuss various issues with him." She writes, "I was beginning to doubt the educational theories of the School."[25]

At this time, Lewis wrote a letter to his brother Warren, then serving in the war effort in Le Havre, France, about that Christmas

---

[21] *Collected Letters, II*, 113. The date of the letter is July 21, 1933.

[22] Sarah Tisdall, "A Goddaughter's Memories," 216.

[23] While Alan Jacobs thinks that too much has been made of this, Lewis had to have some familiarity with such progressive schools or he would not have pilloried them in *The Silver Chair*. See Alan Jacobs, *The Narnian: The Life and Imagination of C. S. Lewis*, San Francisco: HarperSanFrancisco, 2005, 259. Still, George Sayer once told Lewis about a disciplinary incident at Malvern College, which suggests that Lewis probably did not have one particular progressive school in mind when he wrote *The Silver Chair*. See "Chronologically Lewis" for Aug. 13, 1947, which draws on the unpublished diary of Warren Lewis.

[24] Sarah Tisdall, "A Goddaughter's Memories," 219.

[25] Mary Neylan, "My Friendship with C. S. Lewis," *The Chesterton Review*, Vol. XVII, No. 3-4 (August-November 1991), 406.

visit from Mary Neylan, confirming her concerns about Dartington. He states,

> You remember her, she teaches at Dartington Hall, coeducation, no punishments and no obedience expected unless the *reason* for order can be made clear to the child. She now has a child of her own and finds it all won't work and is beginning to doubt the whole Dartington system, and what with that and the general stress of things, is just beginning to throw out a tentative feeler in the direction of Christianity ....[26]

Lewis's concern about scientism, or what he also called "scientific humanism," also influenced Neylan. In a letter written around the time that *Out of the Silent Planet* was published,[27] he wrote to her about the Ransom story and the "scientific humanism" shared by George Bernard Shaw, Olaf Stapledon, J. B. S. Haldane, and H. G. Wells.[28] Soon thereafter, Lewis wrote to her about Weston, the evil scientist in the first book in his trilogy who also appears in *Perelandra*, tempting the Green Lady of Perelandra, the "Eve" of that unfallen world, to sin. He describes Weston as a caricature and Westonism as very silly. He writes that most of the nonsense from the mouth of Weston comes from the last essay in J. B. S. Haldane's *Possible Worlds*.[29]

Despite her doubts about Dartington, Neylan enjoyed teaching. She wrote to Lewis, "The teaching I enjoyed enormously and succeeded in getting them [her students] to read and write for pleasure. I started play reading at home with the idea that a good tea and social atmosphere would be a good environment in which to learn; these play readings were very successful."[30] As she stated in a letter to Lewis,

> Dartington had never seemed to look more richly beautiful than the week we were down there packing up. ... Nor do I think the William Morris impression[31] I got when I first went there was altogether false. The family atmosphere, the real friendliness between staff and children and the business centering round the school farm, the pet shed and the

---

[26] *Collected Letters, II*, 314. The date of the letter is Dec. 31, 1939.

[27] *Out of the Silent Planet* was finished in September 1937 and released by The Bodley Head on September 1938.

[28] *Collected Letters, III*, 1534. The date is unclear, but the estimated date is sometime in 1938.

[29] *Collected Letters, II*, 254. The date is March 21, 1939.

[30] Sarah Tisdall, 219.

[31] Probably a reference to the adventurous novels of the nineteenth century British author William Morris whom Lewis very much enjoyed.

workshops, the amount of sun and fresh air and the healthiness of the children. The children are less silly and more courageous than other children.[32]

She left Dartington Hall at the end of the 1938-1939 school year.

At Dartington, Neylan taught Clement and Lucien Freud, grandsons of Sigmund Freud. Clement Freud later became the husband of Jill Flewett, who lived at The Kilns during the evacuation of school children from London during the war.[33] Atheist Bertrand Russell and Aldous Huxley sent their children to the school, and among other well-known names in the student population were future set designer Hein Heckroth,[34] sculptor Willi Soukop, and painter Cecil Collins.[35] Mary found a good friend in Heckroth, from whom she received a painting depicting the Spanish civil war, a painting which her daughter Elizabeth still cherishes.[36]

When Lewis's *Pilgrim's Regress* was published in 1933, Neylan immediately purchased it, stating, "It was a book which chimed in with my own experience and eventually influenced me to become a convert to Christianity."[37] While her tutorials with Lewis at Oxford probably mark the beginning of her spiritual journey, reading *The Pilgrim's Regress* provided additional impetus. Mary's daughter Sarah was not baptized until the age of four, which, Sarah writes, marked "the final conversion" of her parents.[38] About Lewis, Sarah writes, "He was enormously supportive of her and brought her into the Christian faith."[39]

---

[32] Sarah Tisdall, 219.

[33] Jill, or June, Flewett was one about a dozen young girls evacuated to The Kilns, the Lewis home, from London during World War II to protect them from bombing in London. This was an organized British plan which relocated more than three million people, most of them children.

[34] Hein Heckroth (1901-1970) was the set and costume designer for the first 1936 production of Mozart's *Don Giovanni* at the opera house in Glyndebourne in East Sussex (about an hour south of London) as well as designer for both *A Matter of Life and Death* (1946) and *The Red Shoes* (1948).

[35] Sarah Tisdall, "A Goddaughter's Memories," 216.

[36] Email from Elizabeth Neylan on April 28, 2018.

[37] Mary Neylan, "My Friendship with C. S. Lewis," *The Chesterton Review*, Vol. XVII, No. 3-4 (August-November 1991), 406.

[38] Sarah Tisdall, "A Goddaughter's Memories," 218. Sarah was baptized in 1942.

[39] Sarah Tisdall, "A Goddaughter's Memories," 223.

No Ordinary People

In 1956 for the first time, Lewis began a letter with the words "Dear Mary," their correspondence having reached the stage where they addressed one another on a first-name basis. As with several other letters, Lewis wrote about very personal topics, including Joy Gresham's illness[40] and his forthcoming marriage to her. Always the concerned godfather, he included the words "Love to Sarah."[41]

Years later during Lewis's Cambridge career, Neylan invited Lewis to an engagement party to meet their prospective son-in-law and his goddaughter Sarah. He declined the invitation because of a prior engagement, but he sent his congratulations.[42] When Lewis's wife was nearing the end of her earthly pilgrimage, he wrote to Neylan about several topics, including Joy's cancer.[43] Neylan later wrote a note of condolence after Joy's death, and Lewis wrote a brief note of thanks to Mary, inviting her continued prayers for him.[44]

Neylan's last association with Lewis was her attendance at Walter Hooper's "Friends of C. S. Lewis" party in the Univ. Senior Common Room on November 22, 1969, the sixth anniversary of Lewis's death and the same year that her husband died. Hooper held these events almost annually, and in 1969 she was able to attend and reminisce with others about their friend, Jack Lewis. Besides Mary, in attendance were Hugo Dyson, Colin Hardie, Chronicles of Narnia illustrator Pauline Baynes, the poet Ruth Pitter, Gervase Mathew, Roger Lancelyn Green, Jean Wakeman, Katharine Farrer, and Owen Barfield. That she was one of those invited to the gathering provides testimony to a sincere friendship with Lewis and appreciation for his spiritual mentoring.

C. S. Lewis as Godfather

While Lewis claimed he wasn't good with children,[45] he agreed to be Sarah's godfather and became a loving, thoughtful, and

---

[40] Joy Gresham is the American woman, former atheist, whom Lewis married in 1957. Joy died of cancer in 1960 after little more than three years of marriage.

[41] *Collected Letters, III*, 805. The date is November 14, 1956.

[42] *Collected Letters, III*, 1010. The date is January 8, 1959.

[43] *Collected Letters, III*, 1155. The date is May 30, 1960.

[44] *Collected Letters, III*, 1187. The date is September 23, 1960.

[45] *Collected Letters, II*, 517. This letter, agreeing to be Sarah's godfather, was written to Mary Neylan in April 1942.

supportive godfather. Sarah Neylan[46] later described the wonderful letters she received from her godfather.[47] Soon thereafter he wrote to Mary, stating that he would be present in Iffley for Sarah's baptism,[48] and, to the best of our knowledge, Lewis did attend.

One need not assume that letters were the only communication between Sarah and her godfather. Lewis visited the Neylan family from time to time, especially between 1939 and 1944 when they lived in Oxford, and the Neylans visited him. Some of the letters show us the caring concern of the godfather for his goddaughter. In one letter, for example, Lewis writes to Sarah about pictures she had sent and about making friends at Magdalen College with a rabbit, which he feeds and calls "Baron Rabbit." He sends her a poem he wrote about the rabbit:

Sarah, Daniel, Elizabeth, and Mary Neylan
Used by permission

> A funny old man had a habit
>
> of giving a leaf to a rabbit.
> At first it was shy
> But then, by and by,
> It got rude and would stand up to grab it.[49]

---

[46] Sarah was born on Jan. 15, 1938, which makes her four years old at the time of her baptism. https://archive.dartington.org/calmview/Record.aspx?src=CalmView.Catalog&id=T%2fPP%2fEST%2f1%2f021&pos=7 Sarah died in 2017 at the age of 79. https://www.theguardian.com/artanddesign/2017/aug/25/sarah-tisdall-obituary

[47] *C. S. Lewis: Letters to Children*. Edited by Lyle W. Dorsett and Marjorie Lamp Mead. New York: Macmillan, 1985.

[48] The baptism took place on Saturday, April 18, 1942. *Collected Letters, II*, 518. The letter is tentatively dated April 1942.

[49] *Letters to Children*, 21. See also *Collected Letters, II*, 619. The date of the letter is July 16, 1944.

A year later, Lewis writes a lengthy letter to seven-year-old Sarah, thanking her for a card she had sent him. He writes about her drawings of cats and dogs, and he includes some of his own drawings of an elephant and an owl. He also writes about Maureen Moore's[50] six-week-old baby, frozen winter pipes, the eight-year-old dog Bruce, cats, and other topics. He wonders how Sarah likes school and how she is getting on.[51] The letter is a model of how an adult should write to a child.

Several years later,[52] just six days before Sarah's confirmation, Lewis wrote to Mary Neylan and her daughter Sarah, including with his letter some sort of a financial gift for her. Lewis states that he prays daily for Sarah, but he is unable to attend the confirmation. Her confirmation day was the last day of Hilary Term at Oxford University, which may partly explain his absence, but Lewis himself mentions the poor health of Mrs. Moore as the reason.[53] The following January, he writes to Sarah about receiving from her a gift of "mats," apparently some sort of a decorative placemat or drawing.[54] We learn from the letter that he had paid for ballet lessons for her. He writes playfully about returning from Malvern, where he saw "one young pig cross the field with a great big bundle of hay in its mouth and deliberately lay it down at the feet of an old pig. I could hardly believe my eyes."[55]

Over the years Lewis wrote additional letters, often around the time of her birthday, sent her gifts at Christmas, thanked her for gifts she sent to him, and mentioned Sarah in letters to her parents. One December during the mid-1940s, Lewis sent her five pounds at Christmas.[56] In the early 1950s, Lewis writes to her about Rider Haggard's books, agreeing with her opinion about Haggard (without stating what her opinion, or his, was, but it was a positive one) and

---

[50] Maureen Moore was the daughter of Mrs. Janie Moore, Lewis's adopted "mother" who shared the household with the Lewis brothers in her childhood and teenage years. Maureen's older brother Paddy had been Lewis's friend and fellow soldier in the Officers' Training Corps. Paddy was killed in action during World War I.

[51] *Collected Letters, III*, 1557f. The date of the letter is February 11, 1945.

[52] The date is April 3, 1949. *Letters to Children*, 24.

[53] *Letters to Children*, 25.

[54] *Letters to Children*, 27. The date is January 9, 1950, and Sarah is eleven years old.

[55] *Letters to Children*, 28.

[56] Sarah Tisdall, "A Goddaughter's Memories," 220.

stating that *She* is the best of Haggard's books.[57] Sometimes Sarah initiated the exchanges between them. During Sarah's mid-teens, Lewis writes a letter to Mary Neylan about Sarah being old enough to talk to.[58] Then, one day after Sarah turned sixteen, Lewis writes to her about school, her pony, Jane Austen's *Pride and Prejudice*, the English writer Charles Lamb, the desire to learn a foreign language, and getting under his bath water like a hippo with only his nostrils above the water.[59] Partly because of his involvement in the Commission to Revise the Psalter,[60] but mostly because of the loss of his wife a few months previously, he was unable to attend Sarah's wedding, which took place on Dec. 31, 1960.[61]

C. S. LEWIS AS MENTOR

Before Lewis was a spiritual mentor, he was a teacher and literary mentor, making reading recommendations and assignments during tutorials with Neylan, as he did with every student, but the earliest letter with such recommendations after her graduation from Oxford University came in 1937. In that letter Lewis acknowledged some recommendations he had previously made, which she accepted.[62] He recommended some books on general tendencies of the seventeenth and eighteenth centuries, which Neylan had asked for.[63]

In October of 1941, Lewis made two more recommendations. On October 2, he recommended The Temple Classics or an Italian

---

[57] *Collected Letters, III*, 89. The letter is dated January 26, 1951.

[58] Sarah Tisdall, daughter of Mary Neylan, cited in Sarah Tisdall, "A Goddaughter's Memories," Harry Lee Poe and Rebecca Whitten Poe, eds., *C. S. Lewis Remembered*, Grand Rapids: Zondervan, 2006, 222. See also *Collected Letters, III*, 177.

[59] The date is January 16, 1954. *Collected Letters, III*, 407.

[60] On November 14, 1958, Lewis wrote to Archbishop Geoffrey Fisher of Canterbury, accepting appointment on a Commission to Revise the Psalter. Lewis's own book, *Reflections on the Psalms*, had been published just two months earlier, and Lewis's literary gifts, especially in the area of poetry, were deemed useful to this Commission.

[61] *Collected Letters, III*, 1210. The date of the letter is Nov. 21, 1960. Sarah's obituary, written by her sister, states that the wedding took place in 1961, probably 1960 is probably the correct year, given the date of Lewis's letter.

[62] Sarah Tisdall, "A Goddaughter's Memories," 217.

[63] Specifically, Herbert Grierson's *Milton and Wordsworth*, F. L. Lucas' *Decline and Fall of the Romantic Ideal*, and E. K. Chambers' *Sir Thomas Wyatt and Some Collected Studies*. *Collected Letters, II*, 211. The date is March 8, 1937.

version for reading Dante, and almost three weeks later, he wrote about two books he had recently read by E. L. Mascall.[64] In 1943, Lewis writes to Neylan about a number of topics, including some literary ones, describing the "horrid young men" in the writings of Charles Dickens and William Makepeace Thackeray, the excellence of Dickens' *David Copperfield* and Robert Browning's *The Ring and the Book*. He also names Jane Austen, Sir Walter Scott, and Anthony Trollope as his favorite authors to read when he is ill.[65] As stated earlier, both Lewis and Neylan enjoyed similar books and she relied on his many suggestions, not all of which are recorded in letters.[66] The tutor's role did not end with her Oxford education, and the two continued to stay in touch over the years.

Lewis's most important influence on Mary Neylan was spiritual. During the first week of April in 1939, as she was nearing the end of her work at Dartington, Neylan was considering both a change in her occupation—by leaving Dartington—and a change in her spiritual outlook—by becoming a Christian. She wrote to Lewis, expressing two opposite opinions,

> If I implied at Christmas that psychoanalysis was the only thing [that helped me] I was not honest. Your translation of Boethius & your books have meant as much more, and as I have been drawing secret refreshment from these Sources all along I feel it is time I came out into the open & remembered another lesson that I learned at the same time which was that I couldn't have it both ways. I should very much like to think how that is only your personality or your personal angle on literary criticism that I like so much but the suspicion has been growing on me that it is based on something else which I can't avoid indefinitely. And I should like to add here with some heat that I regard your books as just so much propaganda.[67]

She continued to think about these spiritual matters in 1940. In March 1940, Lewis writes her a lengthy letter, no doubt in response to her questions, about a variety of topics related to the Christian faith—when one ought to command, when one ought to obey, and

---

[64] The Mascall books were *Man, His Origins and Destiny* and *The God-Man*. The date of the letter is October 20. Email correspondence with Brenton Dickieson, August 17, 2015. One of the unpublished letters of Lewis.

[65] The date is January 31, 1943. *Collected Letters, II*, 550.

[66] Sarah Tisdall, "A Goddaughter's Memories," 217.

[67] https://apilgriminnarnia.com/2012/06/14/letters-to-an-oxonian-lady-c-s-lewis-relationship-with-mary-neylan/

when to teach a child to command or to obey. He also addresses humility as a good thing and an aid in obedience. Since Mary had undergone psychoanalysis, he explains his own hostility toward it and states that he has no quarrel with it as long as people "don't try to derive logic and values from it."[68] He also describes his early view of Jesus as influenced by nineteenth-century skeptics who denied the divinity of Jesus. Consequently, he recommends several books for her reading, books that would offer a more accurate picture of Jesus, among them G. K. Chesterton's *The Everlasting Man*, Mauriac's *Vie de Jésus*, Edwyn Bevan's *Symbolism and Belief*, George MacDonald's *Unspoken Sermons*, and the writings of both George Herbert and Thomas Traherne. Because Mary "got more out of him [MacDonald] than any else to whom I introduced his books,"[69] he dedicated his book *George MacDonald: An Anthology* to her. He encourages her to find someone with whom to discuss these matters, men like L. W. Grensted or O. C. Quick, both of whom lived in Oxford.[70]

Three days later Lewis writes to his brother Warren, describing Neylan as "trembling on the verge of Christianity."[71] He states that he feels "almost overwhelmed" by the responsibility he accepted when he replied to her questions, and he surmises that if God is in control, and He is, it will not matter what he writes, but that it is "a dangerous argument" to think that way.[72]

One of the major reasons for Mary's hesitation to adopt the Christian faith was the Christian view of marriage. Lewis wrote several letters to Neylan answering her questions about marriage. As both Mary and her husband considered the Christian faith, Lewis's first letter addressed marriage almost entirely. Lewis writes a second lengthy letter soon thereafter to Mary about the marriage service and the three main biblical reasons for marrying (having children, marriage as a sexual outlet, and partnership). He also describes the modern idea of "being in love" as a sufficient, but inadequate,

---

[68] The date of the letter is March 26, 1940. *Collected Letters*, II, 372f. Lewis expresses his position on psychoanalysis in *Mere Christianity*, "Morality and Psychoanalysis," Book 3, Chapter 4, 88-93. He accepts psychoanalysis as long as it does not spill over into morality.

[69] *Collected Letters*, II, 653. The date is May 20, 1945.

[70] *Collected Letters*, II, 371-376. Quick was Regius Professor of Divinity at Oxford University and Canon of Christ Church, and Grensted was Oriel Professor of the Philosophy of the Christian Religion.

[71] The letter was written on March 29, 1940. *Collected Letters*, II, 378.

[72] Ibid., 378f.

reason for marriage. He describes "being in love" as transitory and unrealistic as a perpetual state, marriages as "the fountains of History" by extending the human race for many generations, and the Christian view of sex as that of "one flesh" in a permanent marriage. He also writes about the difference in sexual appetite between males and females, the seriousness of sexual sin, and the Pauline teaching on marriage. He rejects Mary's term "slave-wife" as an expression of servile subordination, which was never what the biblical writers intended.[73] Lewis also invites Mary Neylan and her husband to lunch.[74] The primary topics for conversation during that lunch were undoubtedly the questions Mary had raised about marriage.[75]

The letter and lunch helped.[76] At some point late in 1940, Mary Neylan became a Christian. Soon thereafter, Lewis writes to Mary Neylan, suggesting next steps in her newfound faith, such as self-examination, partaking of the Lord's Supper, prayer, and daily reading. For the reading, he recommends Thomas à Kempis, the psalms, and the New Testament.[77] As Mary is making this change, Lewis serves as a spiritual mentor for her entry into the kingdom. Later that month, he writes to her about the importance of not relying on emotion in the spiritual life, but that does not mean that one should not rejoice at appropriate times. He cites John Donne, stating that one reward of conversion is the ability to see the point of much literature not previously seen.[78]

Mary Neylan is one of the reasons that Lewis wrote to Dom Bede Griffiths a few years later about the letters he got from recent converts, including his prayer list for the conversion of people to the Christian faith ("I have two lists of names in my prayers, those

---

[73] *Collected Letters*, II, 392-397. The date is April 18, 1940, less than a month after the previous letter.

[74] *Collected Letters*, II, 396. The lunch took place on April 27, 1940.

[75] One wonders whether Lewis invited both Neylans because of his concern that she may be infatuated with Lewis. Sarah Tisdall wrote that "during the agonies of her conversion, in her draft letters, she says once or twice, 'Perhaps it is not God that I desire but Mr Lewis.' Finally, I think she must have told him." Sarah Tisdall, "A Goddaughter's Memories," 224. Then, in an unpublished letter dated to that same year, 1940, and noted by Mary Neylan's daughter Sarah, Lewis wrote, "You have told me rather too much." Sarah Tisdall, "A Goddaughter's Memories," 224.

[76] *Collected Letters*, II, 375. This lengthy letter is dated March 26, 1940.

[77] *Collected Letters*, II, 459. On January 4, 1941.

[78] The date is January 29, 1941. *Collected Letters*, II, 467f.

for whose conversion I pray, and those for whose conversion I give thanks. The little trickle of *transferences* from List A to List B is a great comfort.").[79]

Because of their friendship, Neylan felt comfortable writing to Lewis about her problems, especially during the early years after her conversion. A few months later,[80] Lewis writes a lengthy letter on some of the problems Mary Neylan was experiencing—maternal jealousy when someone else provided care for her daughter Sarah, the value of God's approval ("Well done, thou good and faithful servant"), Hyoi's longing (Hyoi is one of the creatures in the first book of Lewis's space trilogy, *Out of the Silent Planet*)[81] as a longing for the past,[82] and confession of sins before God or in the presence of another human being.

A few days later, Lewis writes once again to Neylan about securing a confessor and about her husband's reaction to her recent conversion. He assures her that he is not bothered by her letters: "You may put out of your head any idea of 'not having a claim' on any help I can give. Every human being, still more every Christian, has an absolute claim on me for any service I can render them without neglecting other duties."[83] He recommends a confessor.[84] He also states that her husband Daniel, more reluctant than she to consider the Christian faith, may feel awkward about her searching and he

---

[79] The date of the letter is June 27, 1949. *Collected Letters, II*, 948.

[80] The date is April 26, 1941. *Collected Letters, II*, 480f.

[81] Hyoi is one of the hrossa, who specialize in fishing, farming, and poetry. The hrossa are one of three types of creatures on Malacandra, Lewis's word for the planet Mars.

[82] Mary Stewart Van Leeuwen surmises that Neylan was having her students read Lewis's space trilogy, and she cites evidence in *Collected Letters, II*, 480-81, 492 (probably here mistaking a reference to John's journey as an allusion to the space trilogy when it really refers to *The Pilgrim's Regress*), 254-55 as evidence, where Lewis mentions Meldilorn, Hyoi, and Weston. See Mary Stewart Van Leeuwen, *A Sword between the Sexes? C. S. Lewis and the Gender Debates*, Grand Rapids: Brazos Press, 2010, 119.

[83] *Collected Letters, II*, 482. The date of the letter is April 30, 1941. This quotation is one reason why many think, probably correctly, that Lewis answered every letter he ever received.

[84] He recommends either Dick Milford, the Vicar at St. Mary the Virgin, or Father Walter Adams. Father Walter Adams, the Society of St. John the Evangelist (SSJE), located on Marston Street, Cowley, Oxford. Lewis went to Father Adams for private confession and spiritual direction in the early 1940s.

hopes she understands her husband's position.[85]

The next month, Lewis writes to Neylan about Father Adams, who had invited her to contact him about an interview, preliminary to personal confession.[86] The note and interview must have gone well, since she went to him for confession for the next decade. In that same letter, Lewis compliments her, "When I suggested jealousy as one of the troubles—I never hope to see the human ship take a big wave in better style!"[87]

In a letter that June, Lewis continued his advice on marriage, advocating a focus on the objectivity of the traditional moral law and Christian custom rather than the subjectivity of inner thoughts and emotions.[88]

The following January, Lewis writes to Neylan about her being at a spiritual low point, just as he had been, the meaning of the word *believing*, proceeding to faith by acting as though we had faith just as one learns to swim in a similar way,[89] not making Christianity into a law, relaxing in prayer, and overcoming chronic temptations.[90] While Lewis had been a Christian for little more than a decade by this time, one suspects that the advice he gave to Mary Neylan bore a striking resemblance to the advice he had received from Father Walter Adams.

On each of these topics, Lewis provided valuable spiritual direction, mature advice, and his own personal experience as a guide. He had been a reluctant convert,[91] and she had been a free spirit who had been drawn to "no compulsory anything." Lewis is known for his pre-Christian desire for independence: "What mattered most of all was my deep-seated hatred of authority, my monstrous individualism, my lawlessness. No word in my vocabulary expressed deeper hatred than the word *Interference*."[92] He taught her that "His compulsion is

---

[85] *Collected Letters, II*, 481-483. The date is April 30, 1941.

[86] The date is May 9, 1941. See *Collected Letters, II*, 483. Mary Neylan benefited from the private confession she experienced with Father Walter Adams. After Adams' death on March 3, 1952, both parents and children went to the funeral and to Hugo Dyson's rooms afterwards.

[87] *Collected Letters, II*, 484. The date is May 9, 1941.

[88] Email correspondence with Brenton Dickieson, August 17, 2015. The letter is dated June 21, 1941, but it is not included in *Collected Letters, II* or III.

[89] One notes a similarity to the same idea in *Mere Christianity*, Book III, "Christian Behavior," Chapter 9, "Charity," 131.

[90] The date is January 20, 1942. *Collected Letters, II*, 506-508.

[91] C. S. Lewis, *Surprised by Joy*, 172.

[92] Ibid., 172.

our liberation."[93] He had helped her find the way to the Christian faith, and in the years after her conversion he had helped her along the way, having experienced many of the same challenges she had. In the process, tutor and student had become friends. The former atheist was able to provide much help to another former atheist. As Brenton Dickieson has written, "In truth, he was Lewis the spiritual director ... with a pastor's heart and a gift for literary friendship that emerges from these letters."[94]

---

[93] Ibid., 229.

[94] See "Letters to an Oxonian Lady: C.S. Lewis's Relationship with Mary Neylan," a Brenton Dickieson blog posting at https://apilgriminnarnia.com/2012/06/14/letters-to-an-oxonian-lady-c-s-lewis-relationship-with-mary-neylan/

Maureen Moore, 1971
©Douglas R. Gilbert

Chapter 21

MAUREEN MOORE,
Baronetess of Hempriggs

During the last year of his life, C. S. Lewis had a heart attack at the Acland Nursing Home in Oxford and went into a coma. Maureen Moore,[1] recently named the eighth Baronetess Dunbar, of Hempriggs, came to visit him. She had not seen him since she had been named Lady Dunbar earlier that year.[2] Others had come to see him earlier that day, but he had not recognized them. She came into his hospital room and said, "Jack,[3] it is Maureen." "No," he replied, "it's Lady Dunbar of Hempriggs." "Oh, Jack," she said, "How could you remember that?" "On the contrary," he replied, "How could *I* forget a fairy tale?"[4] While Maureen's story itself is almost a fairy tale, the greater lesson from this exchange is the warmth and pride that Lewis felt towards this woman whose life, for more than forty years, had been so wrapped up in his own.

Maureen Daisy Helen Moore was the only daughter of Janie and Courtenay Edward Moore and the sister of Paddy Moore, which means that she knew C. S. Lewis far more than most people, even more than many of his close friends. Maureen was born in Delgany, County Wicklow, Ireland,[5] on August 19, 1906. When her parents separated in 1908, she moved with her mother and brother to Bristol.

On May 7, 1917, Lewis began his training with the Oxford University Officers' Training Corps, and one month later, as part of his training, he took rooms at Keble College where he roomed with Paddy Moore, Maureen's brother. Soon thereafter, Maureen met Lewis because of the friendship between her brother and Lewis. When Lewis and Paddy made a pact to care for the other one's parent if only one of them survived World War I, Lewis, although only about eight years older than Maureen, became a surrogate father to Maureen.

Paddy was killed in action in the war, and Lewis followed through on his promise. After the war Maureen and her mother

---

[1] Her married name by this time was Blake, but I will refer to her throughout this chapter by her maiden name of Maureen Moore.
[2] Maureen visited Lewis at the Acland Nursing Home in July, 1963.
[3] Jack is the nickname by which C. S. Lewis was known to his friends.
[4] Hooper, *Companion*, 648.
[5] Hooper, *Companion*, 647.

returned to Oxford to be near Lewis,[6] and no later than September 12, 1918, he had written a letter from Mrs. Moore's home.[7] After his return to Oxford University in January 1919, he lived in the Radcliffe Quadrangle of University College. No later than August 1921, and probably much earlier, Lewis, Mrs. Moore, and Maureen were living in the same house.[8]

Maureen was educated at Headington School in Oxford. While she was attending Headington School, Lewis gave her tutorials in Latin and Greek to prepare her for the School Certificate,[9] and he tutored Miss Vida Mary Wiblin in Latin in exchange for her teaching music to Maureen.[10] Private tutoring was common, especially among friends. Lewis's friend A. K. Hamilton Jenkin also tutored Maureen, probably in English.[11] Sometimes Lewis taught Latin, English, and French to Maureen, but she also took French lessons with Mrs. Stevenson (in exchange for Lewis tutoring Mrs. Stevenson's daughter in Latin).[12] Not surprisingly, Maureen's interest in music also included dance[13] and theater.[14]

Mrs. Moore encouraged Maureen's interest in music. She had taken lessons in Bristol, and these continued in Oxford. After leaving

---

[6] Hooper, *Companion*, 647f.

[7] See Chronologically Lewis for this date.

[8] *Collected Letters*, Vol. 1, 570. In a letter to his brother Warren, C. S. Lewis describes how Pasley came to help him convince his father Albert that he wasn't living with Mrs. Moore. He had written to Warren on July 1, 1921, from 28 Warneford Road, the same address where Mrs. Moore and Maureen were living. *Collected Letters*, Vol. 1, 555.

[9] *All My Road Before Me*, 56. The date is June 26, 1922. This diary entry mentions the translation of Virgil.

[10] Ibid., 61. The date is July 1, 1922. See also *Collected Letters, I*, n. 3.

[11] Ibid., 149. The date is December 4, 1922. Since Jenkin worked with Maureen here, perhaps Lewis did also at other times.

[12] Ibid., 117. Lewis makes this comment about Mrs. Stevenson on October 10, 1922. For the teaching of Latin to Sydney Stevenson, see *All My Road Before Me*, 133.

[13] Ibid., 155, which indicates that Maureen took dance lessons. See also 429, 447.

[14] See, for example, *All My Road Before Me*, 452, where Lewis, Mrs. Moore, and Maureen attend a performance of the Oxford University Dramatic Society (OUDS) of Shakespeare's *King Lear*. See also *Collected Letters, I*, 596, where Lewis indicates that he will be going to see the play "Glorious England" with Maureen and Miss Wiblin. See *Brothers & Friends*, 169, which reports Minto, Maureen, Warren Lewis, and Mrs. Thomas going to see the OUDS performance of *Hamlet*.

Headington School Maureen went to the Royal College of Music, London, starting on September 17, 1928, and studying piano and violin.[15] Upon graduation she was awarded the ACRM, Associated of the Royal College of Music.[16] She left the Royal College of Music in December 1931. She taught music at Monmouth School for Girls, a boarding school in Wales from 1931 to 1934[17]; Oxford High School from 1935 to 1940; and Malvern College from 1957 to 1968.

Maureen Moore was a George MacDonald fan, since Lewis once borrowed from her MacDonald's *The Goblin and the Princess* and stated about her that she had "a well-stocked library of fairy tales."[18] Maureen was both clever and possessing a sense of humor, for it was she who once pointed out the absurdity of a statement Lewis had made, "We know there are no undiscovered islands."[19] She was also a typical child—in a letter to his brother Lewis wrote about the advantages and disadvantages of domestic life and included among the disadvantages both Maureen's practicing (the piano and the violin) and Maureen's sulks.[20] As Maureen grew and matured, Warren had complimentary words to say about her, writing, "Maureen's conduct throughout excited my warmest admiration."[21]

---

[15] Email dated May 30, 2019 from Maira Canzonieri, Assistant Librarian, Royal College of Music. The piano was her primary instrument.

[16] Email dated May 30, 2019 from Maira Canzonieri, Assistant Librarian, Royal College of Music.

[17] Lewis indicates in October 1931 that Maureen has accepted a job at Monmouth. *C. S. Lewis: Collected Letters, Volume 2. Books, Broadcasts and War 1931-1949*. Edited by Walter Hooper. London: HarperCollinsPublishers, 2004, 3.

[18] *C. S. Lewis: Collected Letters, I*. 1905-1930. Edited by Walter Hooper. London: HarperCollinsPublishers, 2000, 393. The date of the letter, written to Arthur Greeves, is August 7, 1918. Her literary interests also included *Jane Eyre*, and undoubtedly many other works of literature. *Collected Letters, II*, 706.

[19] *Collected Letters, I*, 777.

[20] *Collected Letters, I*, 870. The date is January 12, 1930.

[21] See the unpublished diary of Warren Lewis for August 7, 1934. See also June 17, 1933, when in response to Minto's criticism of her driving she said nothing. On December 21, 1933, Warren writes in his unpublished diary, "I now enjoy her society in the house and regret her departure, whereas in the old days it was exactly the reverse. I do not think however that the change can be entirely in me: I fancy that Maureen has improved a great deal since she took this job at Monmouth."

No Ordinary People

On August 27, 1940 she married Leonard James Blake, who was Director of Music at Worksop College, Nottinghamshire.[22] Oddly enough, Blake was born on the exact same date as Maureen, August 19, 1906.[23] Blake became Director of Music at Malvern College in 1945. Since her work at Oxford High School ended in 1940, and her next position began in 1957 at Malvern College, she apparently chose the role of homemaker and devoted her time to raising two children and supporting her husband. They had two children, Richard Francis Blake, Lewis's godson, and Eleanor Margaret Blake.[24] They also had four grandchildren,[25] including Emma Katherine Dunbar of Hemprigg and Fiona Blake, the daughters of Richard.[26]

The house that Maureen, her mother, Lewis, and his brother Warren purchased in 1930, The Kilns, was purchased with funds provided by the Lewis brothers and Janie Moore. Mrs. Moore's name was the only name on the deeds of the property, and the title allowed Jack and Warren a Right of Life tenancy, which permitted them to continue living there after Mrs. Moore's death. She died in 1951. The title to the house and estate then passed to Maureen when Warren Lewis died in 1973.

In later years, the Lewis brothers were occasional visitors in the Blakes' home in Malvern, where both had attended school. This allowed them to escape the difficult home situation with Mrs. Moore. On one occasion, Warren wrote, "Maureen came up from Malvern for a couple of nights after the crisis was past, and, to my astonishment, proved herself to be a diplomatist of the first order. Like everyone else, she is chronically indignant at the slavery in which M[27] keeps J[28], and

---

[22] He had held this position since 1935.

[23] http://www.thepeerage.com/p18045.htm

[24] The former was born on January 8, 1945 and the latter on November 16, 1949. Hooper, *Companion & Guide*, 648. According to thepeerage.com, Eleanor married David C. Eldridge in 1973. They divorced in 1987. Then she married Michael D. Constable and carried the name Dunbar-Constable.

[25] Michael Ward, "Lady Dunbar 1906-1997," *VII: An Anglo-American Literary Review*, Volume 14 (1997):7.

[26] "Dunbar (NS) 1706, of Hempriggs, Caithness-shire," *Debrett's Peerage & Baronetage 2008*. Patrick W. Montague-Smith, ed., 147th edition, London, UK: Debrett's Peerage Limited. In 1969, Richard married Elizabeth Margaret Jane Lister. *Who's Who 1994*, XXX 551.

[27] M stands for Minto, a nickname of Mrs. Moore.

[28] J is Warren's abbreviation for Jack, the lifelong nickname of C. S. Lewis.

had determined that J *must* have a holiday: which she accomplished by getting Dr. Radford and Nurse Figett to make M believe that *proprio motu* she herself had come to this decision."[29] Towards the end of her mother's life, Maureen would sometimes trade houses with Lewis, taking care of her mother while the Lewis brothers spent time in her home in Malvern.[30]

On February 4, 1963, Maureen became the 8th Baronetess Dunbar of Hempriggs and was recognized as such in 1965 by the Lyon Court.[31] She and her family began spending a month each summer at Ackergill Tower, not far from Wick, Caithness, on the northern coast of Scotland. While the inheritance did not bring wealth, she and her husband stewarded the tower with diligence.

When Maureen and Leonard retired from teaching at Malvern College in 1968, they declined to retire permanently in Scotland, where Ackergill Tower was located, preferring to settle in Cheltenham, a small village in Gloucestershire.[32] Maureen got a part-time job teaching music in nearby Winchcombe.[33] She died on February 15, 1997 at the age of ninety. On her death, the baronetcy returned to the male line, her son Richard.[34] She had been preceded in death by her husband Leonard, who died on August 1, 1989.

Maureen, Music, and the Lewis Brothers

In 1922, Maureen went to Bristol to study music, especially the piano, with Miss Kathleen Whitty. Miss Whitty had been Maureen's music teacher before she and her mother moved from Bristol to

---

[29] *Brothers & Friends*, 198. The date is March 17, 1947, about four years before Mrs. Moore's death. *Proprio motu* means "through her own initiative."

[30] For example, in 1947, Maureen came to The Kilns from April 4 to 15, while the Lewis brothers traveled the Malvern and stayed in her home. Leonard was at Rossall. *Brothers & Friends*, 199. They exchanged places again at Christmas time that same year and in April of the following year. They visited in August of the same year without changing places. Many more examples could be cited, but these few examples are sufficient to prove the point of the graciousness of Maureen and her husband Leonard.

[31] http://www.thepeerage.com/p18045.htm. A baronetcy is a hereditary knighthood.

[32] Hooper, *Companion & Guide*, 649.

[33] The unpublished diary of Warren Lewis for April 16, 1968.

[34] Michael Ward, "Lady Dunbar 1906-1997," *VII: An Anglo-American Literary Review*, Volume 14 (1997):7.

Oxford in 1917. Soon after her arrival in Bristol, Maureen wrote home to say that after an hour Miss Whitty had found Maureen's music "hopeless." A letter from Miss Whitty claimed that her technique had been neglected. Three days later, Mrs. Moore received another letter from Miss Whitty, stating that a musical career was out of the question for Maureen because of poor teaching and poor technique.[35] These opinions were clearly overstated, since Maureen later made a career out of music.

Unwilling to give up Maureen's hope for a musical career, Mrs. Moore sent Lewis to see Dr. Basil Allchin in Oxford about music lessons for Maureen. Maureen had her first meeting with Allchin a month after the "out of the question" letter, and she began to take lessons with him that October. Allchin did not have time in his schedule for her immediately, so Miss Vida Mary Wiblin taught Maureen until Dr. Allchin had room to teach another student.[36] In contrast to Kathleen Whitty, Dr. Allchin thought that Maureen "could be 'first rate' as a teacher …."[37]

Maureen had some musical talent, since we read about Lewis bringing Maureen home from the show at school where she had been playing her violin as part of the orchestra.[38] Occasionally Lewis tells us in his diary about the piano duets she played with Maureen's friend Helen Munro, and with Lewis's friends Arthur Greeves, Cecil Harwood, and Leo Baker.[39] Years later she took voice lessons.[40] Through the years, one or the other of the Lewis brothers enjoyed musical events with Maureen. For example, Lewis once wrote in his diary, "In the evening Maureen and I went to hear the carols in New College Chapel."[41] She attended the Lady's Musical on various occasions, often taking Jack or Warren with her.[42] They also helped

---

[35] *All My Road Before Me*, 26. The date is April 26, 1922.

[36] *All My Road Before Me*, 42. This took place on May 6, 1922.

[37] *All My Road Before Me*, 268.

[38] *All My Road Before Me*, 56. The date is June 24, 1922, just two months after her musical talent had been pronounced hopeless. We learn from *All My Road Before Me*, 68, that Maureen received a violin lesson from Miss Brayne on October 12. See *All My Road Before Me*, 21, where Lewis calls Miss Brayne her violin teacher.

[39] For example, *Brothers & Friends*, 77.

[40] The unpublished diary of Warren Lewis for April 14, 1933.

[41] *All My Road Before Me*, 154. The date is Dec. 17, 1922.

[42] *All My Road Before Me*, 304. The date is March 14, 1924. They also attended performances of the Oxford Bach Choir.

her in whatever ways they could. During the autumn term of 1922, for example, Maureen was studying the lives of famous composers. To assist her, Lewis checked out a life of Austrian composer Franz Schubert for Maureen.[43] A week later, he writes, "I then went to the Union where I took out the life of Beethoven for Maureen, ..."[44]

Warren especially became her musical friend, attending many a concert with her. Years later, he even took piano lessons from her.[45] In 1931, Maureen took Warren to Bournemouth to attend a concert of Grieg and Beethoven.[46] Just a month later, the two of them, along with Mrs. Moore and Jack, attended Vaughan Williams' opera *Sir John in Love*.[47] Many other examples could be cited. While teaching music in Monmouth, she invited Warren Lewis to visit her, see Monmouth School, and attend three choir festivals in the area that September.[48] Warren visited Maureen and her husband Leonard in Malvern for another Three Choirs Festival in 1947. The festival was an annual event, begun in 1709, that rotated between Hereford, Gloucester, and Worcester, three cathedral cities, and which featured the three choirs of those cathedrals. The choirs performed in nearby Gloucester, and Warren enjoyed Leonard's company during trips there and back again. Between concerts they were able to tour Gloucester Cathedral and enjoy its magnificent Norman and Perpendicular architecture.[49]

From Adolescence to Maturity

Despite early friction between Maureen and her mother, Maureen developed into a mature woman. In 1922, when she was 16, Jack notes in his diary that she could be a nuisance, noting that she teased Warren during an outing on the river.[50] However, by 1934, at the age of 28, she benefited from being more independent. Warren

---

[43] *All My Road Before Me*, 112. This diary entry is dated October 2, 1922.

[44] *All My Road Before Me*, 115. The date is October 9, 1922.

[45] The unpublished diary of Warren Lewis for June 2, 1933.

[46] The unpublished diary of Warren Lewis for April 19, 1931. See also, for example, the unpublished diary for February 10, 1933, and for March 5 and March 10, 1933.

[47] The unpublished diary of Warren Lewis for April 29, 1931.

[48] Warren did this on September 7 and 8, 1933. The unpublished diary of Warren Lewis.

[49] Warren's visit to the Blake's home took place September 6-13, 1947. The unpublished diary of Warren Lewis.

[50] *All My Road Before Me*, 85.

wrote, "I fancy that Maureen has improved a great deal since she took this job at Monmouth. Also, now that I come to think of it, I very rarely saw her alone in the old days, and she is always at her worst with Minto."[51] Having gone out on her own as an adult, she was able to take more control of her life.

While growing up, Maureen was quite athletic, participating in cricket, tennis, field hockey, lacrosse,[52] and golf. She was elected house captain of the cricket team for the day girls at Headington School,[53] and she played a great deal of field hockey.[54] She participated in family activities such as bike riding, badminton, croquet, and punting on the river.[55] She also learned how to play bridge.[56] She helped in various projects at The Kilns, which Warren liked to call their "public works," soon after the house had been purchased, working with Jack to clear the pond of reeds and with Warren to saw logs.[57]

The quarrels she had with her mother will surprise no one who is familiar with Janie Moore's story. Lewis once wrote, "I forgot to mention an absurd episode during lunch. Maureen had started saying she didn't mind which of two alternative sweets she had: and D, who is always worried by these indecisions, had begun to beg her to make up her mind in rather a weary voice."[58]

Warren also wrote about Maureen's spats with her mother in a way that made it clear that he thought Mrs. Moore primarily to blame:

> Here we are, with—comparatively speaking—plenty of money, a good home, and fair health, and yet life is apparently to be soiled for many years to come by this perpetual miserable trumpery quarreling about nothing. It is only fair to say that—when the scales have been given a surreptitious lift in

---

[51] The unpublished diary of Warren Lewis for December 21, 1933.

[52] The unpublished portion of *All My Road Before Me* for July 29, 1922.

[53] *All My Road Before Me*, 42. The date is May 30, 1922. See also *All My Road Before Me*, 80 and 224.

[54] *All My Road Before Me*, 271.

[55] For the latter, see, for example, *All My Road Before Me*, 85. In Lewis's diary entry for June 17, 1922, "Maureen had been on the river all day with the Rowells." *All My Road Before Me*, 51.

[56] The unpublished diary of Warren Lewis for August 17, 1922. She went golfing with her mother on March 25, 1923. *All My Road Before Me*, 224.

[57] The unpublished diary of Warren Lewis for November 16, 1930.

[58] *All My Road Before Me*, 111. The date is September 30, 1922,

Minto's favor—that 80% of the trouble is made by her, and 20% by Maureen. There are two things which stand out very brightly in Maureen's favor and make my heart warm to her: the first is that I have never heard her mention M in terms which would not have won the approval of a Victorian parent who had happened to overhear her: the second is that she is frequently and acutely conscious of what she and her mother owe to J.[59]

Maureen's generous spirit was apparent when she once gave both Warren and Jack a pipe as a gift.[60] She was generous with her time as well, helping the family during the frequent moves with painting, hauling boxes, and other tasks.[61] In later years, Warren wrote, "The more I study Maureen, the more I realize what a very delightful man the mythical Mr. Moore must have been!"[62] When Lewis's wife was hospitalized in 1957, Maureen helped care for her sons by having them stay with her in Malvern during the school holidays.[63] On other occasions, when Lewis was unable to travel, Warren would visit Malvern on his own, which enabled him to visit George and Moira Sayer as well as the Blakes.[64] Maureen and her husband Leonard were present at Lewis's funeral in 1963, and they probably attended Warren's funeral in 1973.

MAUREEN MOORE AND THE CHRISTIAN FAITH

Maureen apparently did not adopt her mother's atheism, going through confirmation, taking her first communion, and attending church at least occasionally.[65] Maureen convinced Jack to join her for worship at Highfield Church on Easter Sunday in 1922.[66] On December 14, 1922, Lewis, Mrs. Moore, and Maureen went to the

---

[59] The unpublished diary of Warren Lewis for August 9, 1934.

[60] The unpublished diary of Warren Lewis for August 22, 1922.

[61] *All My Road Before Me*, 231. The date is April 22, 1924.

[62] The unpublished diary of Warren Lewis for December 29, 1947.

[63] *Companion & Guide*, 647.

[64] The unpublished diary of Warren Lewis for August 9, 1960 indicates that Warren has just returned from a weekend in Malvern, probably because his brother was caring for his wife Joy. He visited George and Moira Sayer on this occasion, since George was teaching English at Malvern College.

[65] See, for example, an unpublished entry that belongs in *All My Road Before Me* for the date of July 1, 1923.

[66] *All My Road Before Me*, 21. The date was April 16, 1922.

cathedral to see the ceremony where Maureen, at age sixteen, was confirmed at Headington School.[67] Immediately after the service they met Mary and the Doc and invited them home for tea to celebrate the occasion. One month later, Maureen took her first communion.

Helen Munro, the daughter of the Rector at Lincoln, became a close friend of Maureen during her years at Headington School, and this daughter of a preacher was probably a positive influence on Maureen, the granddaughter of a preacher.[68] Years later, when Maureen had a weekend guest in Oxford, the Lewis brothers and Maureen brought her to church with them.[69] The same took place eight years after that and on numerous other occasions.[70]

On the other hand, Maureen once stated "that she thought religion quite a good thing provided you didn't let yourself take it up too seriously."[71] The influence of Lewis on Maureen's spiritual life must have been significant, even though her mother remained distant from the Christian church and the Christian faith until the end of her life.

DAME MAUREEN DUNBAR, 8TH BARONETESS OF HEMPRIGGS

After the seventh Baronet of Hempriggs died in 1963, Maureen became the eighth Baronetess, through her father's line, making her one of four baronetesses in British history.[72] Queen Anne originally created the baronetcy in 1706.[73] Sir George Duff-Sutherland-Dunbar had become the sixth Baronet upon his grandfather's death in 1897, but he took no part in the administration of the estate. He spent most of his life in India as an administrator, where he became

---

[67] *The Lewis Papers* VII: 300.

[68] *All My Road Before Me*, a portion of the unpublished part for the date of April 12, 1922.

[69] *Collected Letters*, II, 8. The date of the letter is October 24, 1931, but the church service was the following day.

[70] *Collected Letters*, II, 290. The date of the letter is November 19, 1939. And again on August 11, 1940, *Collected Letters*, II, 432. See also the unpublished diary of Warren Lewis for June 7, 1931, October 8, 1933, and November 5, 1933.

[71] *Brothers & Friends*, 164. The year is 1934.

[72] For much of this section, see the biographical information in Walter Hooper, C. S. Lewis: Companion & Guide, 647-649, and "Maureen Dunbar," Wikipedia. Last modified November 19, 2020.

[73] John Hayes, "C. S. Lewis and a Chronicle of the Moores," Irish University Review, Vol. 39, No. 1 [Spring-Summer 2009]:99.

well known as one of the country's greatest historians.

When Sir George Duff-Sutherland-Dunbar died, his son George, who had been a barrister in London, became the seventh Baronet. George died unmarried in 1963, leaving Maureen as the next in line. His first cousin and heir Capt. Kenneth Duff-Dunbar had died in World War II and his second cousin, Maureen, great granddaughter of Capt. Benjamin Duff, the only one of his daughters to leave descendants, became the eighth Baronetess of Hempriggs.

Maureen Dunbar was confirmed as Lady Dunbar of Hempriggs by the Lyon Court in 1965, and at that time she took the name of Dunbar in place of her married name of Blake. Sir Thomas Innes, the Lord Lyon King of Arms, ruled that Maureen would serve as the next Baronetess.

When Maureen became the Baronetess, she also acquired an estate, Ackergill Tower, near Wick, Caithness, Scotland. The tower is in the far northeast of Scotland and traces its origin to the fifteenth century. Maureen lived there in the summers and willingly opened the estate for tours. The Tower was sold in 1986, underwent renovation for two years, and now operates as a luxury hotel and conference center. The fifteenth-century legend of the beautiful Helen Gunn is an attempt to stoke the public's interest in this tower as a haunted venue.[74]

Conclusion

Reader of fairy tales and a fairy tale herself, Maureen Moore, or Dame Maureen Dunbar, 8th Baronetess of Hempriggs, grew up in the household of C. S. Lewis and his brother Warren. While her early years were fraught with friction with her mother, she developed into a fine musician while remaining a friend of the Lewis brothers until their dying day. Her care for her mother and her hospitality for the Lewis brothers—especially at her Malvern home—stand out among her chief characteristics. She teaches us that what we are is not necessarily what we will become, and that God refines us and by His Spirit shapes us so that we are more and more conformed to the image of His Son.

---

[74] https://www.hauntedrooms.co.uk/ackergill-tower-castle-wick-caithness-scotland

INDEX

A

A Grief Observed, 144, 144 n. 63, 161, 163

à Kempis, Thomas, 149, 270, 342 n. 33, 358

Abercrombie, Lascelles, 38

Abolition of Man, The, 204, 204 n. 64, 234, 234 n. 57, 245, 245 n. 120, 246, 257, 258, 258 n. 36, 258 n. 39, 341, 341 n. 31

Adams, Father Walter, 148, 359 n. 85, 360, 360 n. 87

Allchin, Basil, 368

Allegory of Love, The, 32, 32 n. 20, 309, 329

animal pain, 142 n. 49, 147, 225, 243, 244, 245, 260

Annan, Noel, 230

Anscombe, Elizabeth, 298 n. 39, 300

Anstey, Robin, 56, 210, 210 n. 107

Anthroposophy, 12, 12 n. 7, 24

Aristophanes, 309, 309 n. 10, 312, 313

Aristotle, 270, 311, 311 n. 27

Arnold, Matthew, 325, 338

Athanasian Creed, 241

Athanasius, 143, 143 n. 56, 146, 154, 157, 158, 159, 160, 163, 346 n. 4

Atlee, Clement, 229

Austen, Jane,

B

Ayer, A. J., 230

Bampton Lectures, 52

Barfield, Owen, 5, 12, 12 n. 6 and 7, 13, 14, 19, 24, 34, 35 n. 27, 43, 44, 44 n. 82, 45, 59, 60, 60 n. 81, 69, 79 n. 39, 100, 100 n. 70, 103, 123, 128, 172, 174 n. 55, 177, 180, 188, 347 n. 15, 352

Barfield, Lucy, 347 n. 15

Barth, Karl, 50, 273

Bayley, Peter, 43, 43 n. 80, 329 n. 21

BBC, 43 n. 76, 57, 126, 150, 159, 225, 230, 235, 236, 237, 238 n. 82, 284, 290, 295 n. 31, 296, 299, 299 n. 45, 304, 340 n. 27, 342

Beckett, Eric, 19

Benecke, Paul, 130

Bennett, J. A. W., 44, 172, 319, 331

Bennett, Stanley, 42

Beowulf, 77, 313

Bergson, Henri, 237, 246

Berkeley, George, 12, 12 n. 9, 13 n. 11, 238, 269, 338

Berlin, Isaiah, 230, 289

Bethel, S. L., 269-274, 271 n. 45 and 46, 285

Bevan, Edwyn, 238, 357

Birkbeck College, 227, 239

Blake, Leonard, 347 n. 13, 366, 367, 370 n. 52, 372

Blakiston, Herbert, 50

Bleiben, Thomas, 48

Blunden, Edmund, 38

Boehme, Jacob, 16

Boethius, 13, 142, 163, 247, 269, 356

Bonhoeffer, Dietrich, 281

Bosphorus, 121, 165, 171,

Bowra, Maurice, 44, 60

Brains Trust, 43, 230, 231, 235, 238, 238 n. 82, 239, 248

Brett-Smith, Herbert, 36

British Academy, 32, 38, 38 n. 50, 153

Broadcast Talks, 235, 235 n. 67, 237

Browning, Robert, 356

Brunner, Emil, 49, 50

Bryson, John, 38, 44

Buber, Martin, 142, 163, 342

Bulverism, 232, 232 n. 48, 233, 233 n. 50

Bunyan, John, 23, 85, 85 n. 80, 86

Butler, Joseph, 15, 16

C

Campbell College, 80, 81 n. 51

Carritt, Edgar F., 270-273, 271 n. 47

Cave, The, 36

Cecil, David, 40, 41, 44, 172

Chalcidius, 142, 163

Chaucer, Geoffrey, 269, 317, 318, 318 n. 6, 318 n. 7, 327, 331, 331 n. 32, 331 n. 33

Chesterton, G. K., 122, 127, 216, 217, 226 n. 9, 238, 269, 283, 357

Chronicles of Narnia, The, 50 n. 28, 52 n. 38, 95, 131, 140, 165, 307, 313, 341, 349, 352

Churchill, Winston, 115 n. 13, 117, 228

Clerk, N. W., 144, 161

Coghill, Nevill, 33, 37, 38, 38 n. 47, 44

Coleridge, Samuel Taylor, 195 n. 1, 236

Commission to Revise the Psalter, 151, 151 n. 115, 161, 355, 355 n. 61

communication, 161, 197, 198, 203, 207, 263, 264, 353

creative evolution, 231, 239

Crombie, Ian M., 47, 47 n. 6, 52 n. 40, 259

crucifixion, 62, 279

Cuddesdon Theological College, 49, 61, 62

Cuneo, Andrew, 310, 310 n. 15, 310 n. 21, 311, 311 n. 25, 313, 313 n. 38, 314 n. 39

D

Davidman, Joy, 5, 26, 66, 66 n. 118, 151, 161, 173, 173 n. 50, 173 n. 53, 202, 206, 206 n. 82, 206 n. 84, 207, 352, 352 n. 40

design, 25, 55, 55 n. 53

desire, 6, 23, 53, 64, 75 n. 9, 85, 86, 97, 108 n. 132, 230, 239, 292, 355, 358 n. 76, 360

determinism, 53, 53 n. 41, 232

Dickens, Charles, 22, 22 n. 65, 74, 125 n. 66, 180, 356

Dickieson, Brenton, 356 n. 65, 360 n. 89, 361, 361 n. 95

Discarded Image, The, 283, 309

Donne, John, 187

Dorsett, Lyle W., 23 n. 72, 40 n. 63, 151 n. 113, 168 n. 19, 283, 283 n. 109, 290 n. 6, 300 n. 47, 301 n. 53, 302 n. 58-60, 303, 303 n. 63, 303 n. 64, 303 n. 67, 353 n. 48

dualism, 237, 238, 270 n. 43

E

Eddington, Sir Arthur, 233, 233 n. 53, 233 n. 54, 238, 338

Einstein, Albert, 165, 233, 338

Eliot, George, 227

Eliot, T. S., 263, 263 n. 3, 280, 322

emergent evolution, 237, 239

Empson, William, 318

English Literature in the Sixteenth Century Excluding Drama, 38, 144, 161, 163, 317

Essays Presented to Charles Williams, 34 n. 25, 128, 195 n. 1, 274

eugenics, 185, 246, 253, 253 n. 15

Every, George, 269

Everlasting Man, The, 122, 216, 357

existentialism, 228

F

Fabian Society, 225, 227

Fenn, Eric, 295, 295 n. 31, 340, 341

Field, Walter, 43, 123

Finite and Infinite, 49, 53, 54 n. 50, 70

Firor, Warfield, 40, 41, 144 n. 60, 165, 170

Flewett, Jill, 160, 351, 351 n. 33

Fox, Adam, 41, 41 n. 66

free will, 53 n. 41, 159, 225, 232, 243

Free Will Defense, 225, 232

Freud, Clement, 351

Freud, Sigmund, 293, 293 n. 17-19, 351

G

Gaskell, Mrs., 227

Gifford Lectures, 47 n. 2, 52 n. 35, 53, 53 n. 41

Girton College, 307-309, 311-313, 317, 319, 320, 320 n. 16 & 19 & 21-22, 321, 321 n. 25, 322 n. 34

Glyer, Diana, 7, 31 n. 11, 31 n. 13-14, 32 n. 18, 39 n. 55, 127 n. 74, 128 n. 84, 129, 129 n. 85 & 88,

130, 130 n. 94, 167 n. 10 & 12, 170, 170 n. 27

Golden Rule, 225, 233, 234

Gower, John, 330

Great Divorce, The, 41, 144, 163

Great War, 12, 12 n. 7

Greats, 49, 50, 187, 217, 252, 252 n. 6

Green, Roger Lancelyn, 44, 44 n. 83, 66 n. 120, 169 n. 23, 173, 196 n. 10, 202, 352

Grensted, L. W., 282, 293, 295, 295 n. 31, 296, 340, 357, 357 n. 71

Gresham, Joy, see Joy Davidman

Guardian, The, 126, 290, 345 n. 2, 353 n. 47

H

Haggard, Rider, 74, 201, 354, 355

Hamlet, 38, 153, 364 n. 14

Hardie, Colin, 41, 44, 44 n. 83, 60, 62, 173, 352

Hardy, Thomas, 227

Harries, Richard, 47

Harwood, Cecil, 19, 43, 44 n. 83, 123, 177, 180, 185, 188, 347 n. 15, 369

Harwood, Laurence, 347 n. 15, 353 n. 46

Hawker, Robert, 179

Head, Ronald, 66, 66 n. 121, 105, 105 n. 111, 174

Henderson, Edward, 47

Herbert, George, 322, 357

Herdman, Ethel, 280, 280 n. 91

Hitler, Adolph, 171, 228

Hodgson, Leonard, 52

Holy Trinity, Headington Quarry, 48 n. 12, 66, 93, 123, 132, 173

Homer, 121 n. 40, 127, 142, 163

Honour Moderations, 11, 17, 48, 52

Houston, James, 30, 30 n. 8

Hoyle, Fred B., 235, 235 n. 66-67

Hume, David, 12 n. 9, 236

Huxley, Aldous, 351

Huxley, Julian, 230, 238

Ibsen, Henrik, 320

I

idealism (the general concept), 246

Idealism (the philosophical position), 12 n. 9-10, 14, 49, 49 n. 23, 77 n. 29, 213 n. 3, 271 n. 43

Incarnation, 61, 65, 106 n. 112, 143, 143 n. 56, 146, 154, 157-160, 163, 215 n. 14, 256, 346 n. 4

Inge, Dean, 15, 16

Inklings, 3, 5, 7, 29, 29 n. 4, 30 n. 9, 39, 39 n. 52-42, 39 n. 56, 39 n. 58, 40, 40 n. 59, 40 n. 63, 41, 41 n. 63, 42, 44, 44 n. 82, 58, 60, 60 n. 81, 79 n. 39, 122 n. 50, 125, 127, 129, 132, 165, 167-169, 169 n. 19,

169 n. 22, 170, 170 n. 26, 171, 171 n. 33, 172-174, 179, 304, 328 n. 12

Irenaeus, 341, 341 n. 28

J

argon, 229

Jeans, James, 238, 338

Julian of Norwich, 16

Johnson, Samuel, 105, 105 n. 110, 142, 163, 236, 338

K

Kant, Immanuel, 216, 216 n. 18, 218

Kilby, Clyde, 44, 60, 176, 241, 242 n. 99

Kilns, The, 37, 93, 97, 101, 103, 120 n. 35, 123-126, 132, 160, 167, 171, 181, 183, 319351, 351 n. 33, 366, 367 n. 33, 370

Kirk, Kenneth, 50, 52

Kirkpatrick, W. T., 75, 76 n. 17, 78, 114, 114 n. 9

Kolbitár, 5

Kosterlitz, R. W., 295, 295 n. 30, 340

Krieg, Laurence, 353 n. 46

L

Lady Margaret Hall, 239, 302

Last and First Men, 196, 201, 202, 204, 257, 258

Last Battle, The, 341

Law, William, 15, 16 n. 26, 31 n. 15, 342 n. 33

Lawrence, D. H., 14

Lazarus, 149, 162

Letters of C. S. Lewis, 93 n. 32, 97 n. 56, 97 n. 59, 128 n. 80, 129, 129 n. 85, 129 n. 89, 132, 142 n. 45, 147 n. 78, 149 n. 99, 151 n. 111-112

Letters to Malcolm, 266 n. 19, 281, 281 n. 94, 281 n. 96, 281 n. 98-99, 282, 282 n. 100-101, 284

Lewis, Albert, 75, 83, 91, 93, 99, 106, 113, 114, 114 n. 3, 119, 119 n. 33, 364 n. 8

Lewis, Cecil Day, 171, 172

Lewis, Flora, 75, 113, 113 n. 2, 114 n. 3

Lewis Papers, The, 74 n. 6, 76 n. 13, 77, 77 n. 20, 77 n. 26, 78 n. 34-35, 79 n. 40, 80 n. 43-45, 80 n. 47, 82 n. 62-63, 85 n. 72, 87 n. 89, 89 n. 6, 91 n. 15, 102 n. 99, 115 n. 10, 120, 120 n. 36, 124, 125, 128, 128 n. 80, 201 n. 45, 335 n. 2, 372 n. 73

Lindsay, David, 78, 201, 202

Lion, the Witch and the Wardrobe, The, 50 n. 28, 170

Little Lea, 73, 79, 83, 120

Lockhart, J. G., 74

Logical Positivism, 53, 54, 54 n. 50, 228, 228 n. 23

Loki Bound, 76, 77, 77 n. 20

Lucretius, 25

Lysenko, Trofim, 255

M

MacDonald, George, 14, 74, 75, 85, 141, 142, 142 n. 40, 161, 163, 195 n. 1, 269, 357, 365

Macrobius, 142, 163

Malory, Sir Thomas, 76, 77, 322, 327

Malvern College, 114, 118, 349 n. 23, 365, 367, 372 n. 69

Mascall, E. L., 139 n. 28, 268, 269, 356, 256 n. 65

Mathew, Gervase, 42, 44 n. 83, 128, 173, 352

Mauriac, François, 357

Maurice, F. D., 265 n. 10, 281

McClurg, William, 78, 83, 83 n. 68, 84

Merton, Thomas, 22, 161

Milton, John, 41, 81 n. 53, 189, 270, 318, 318 n. 9, 355 n. 64

Miracles: A Preliminary Study, 143, 143 n. 55, 144, 160, 163, 233 n. 55, 260 n. 42, 300, 339

Mitchell, Basil, 47, 304

Mitchison, Naomi, 74, 252

Moore, Paddy, 89, 90, 92, 93, 107, 110, 122, 124, 335, 354 n. 51, 363, 364

More, Henry, 16, 159

Muggeridge, Malcolm, 230, 283 n. 109

Murdoch, Jean Iris, 303

mysticism, 16, 22

myth/mythology, 14 n. 17, 31, 33-35, 135 n. 27, 49 n. 22, 60, 61, 61 n. 88, 61 n. 91, 62, 62 n. 92, 68, 69, 73, 74, 77 n. 20, 85, 142, 159, 202, 257, 258 n. 35, 260, 261 n. 33

Myths of the Norsemen, 74

N

Natural Law, 22, 228, 233, 261, 339

Naturalism, 14, 14 n. 20, 15, 232, 259

Nesbit, Edith, 313

Newton, Sir Isaac, 338

Newton, Katharine, 50, 50 n. 26, 52, 52 n. 38, 56-60, 58 n. 68, 209, 352

Newman, John Henry, 17

Nott, Kathleen, 161, 163

O

Officers' Training Corps, 89, 252, 335, 346, 354 n. 51, 363

Onions, C. T., 42

Ottley, Alice, 136, 145

Out of the Silent Planet, 78 n. 32, 139-141, 139 n. 28, 151, 159, 163, 188, 202, 219 n. 34, 251 n. 3, 256, 257, 350, 350 n. 27, 359

Oxford Union Society, 228, 228 n. 25, 239, 248

P

pacifism, 116 n. 18, 229, 268, 272, 347 n. 12

Patmore, Coventry, 142, 163

Paxford, Fred, 95, 98, 99

Perelandra, 78 n. 32, 143, 143 n. 53, 153, 159, 163. 165, 168, 168 n. 17, 202-204, 2-3 n. 57, 251, 251 n. 1., 251 n. 3, 257, 350

Phantastes, 16, 75, 85, 141, 159, 163

Phillips, Gordon, 47

Pilgrim's Regress, The, 20, 85, 107, 107 n. 127, 142, 159, 163, 218, 218 n. 32, 219, 270 n. 37, 351, 359 n. 83

Pitter, Ruth, 44 n. 83, 352

Plato, 13, 14, 93 n. 36, 270, 277, 288, 302 n. 56, 303

poetry, 31, 31 n. 15, 33, 62, 62 n. 97-98, 69, 76, 124, 127, 142 n. 40, 161, 171, 172, 180, 190 n. 69, 227, 236, 268, 270, 272, 285, 309, 318, 322, 322 n. 33, 326, 327, 330, 355 n. 61, 359 n. 82

Possible Worlds, 202, 203, 253, 253 n. 15, 256, 256 n. 29-30, 257, 258, 260 n. 43, 260 n. 45, 350

Prince Caspian, 165, 166

Prinknash Abbey, 10, 17, 18, 20

Problem of Pain, The, 29, 107 n. 123, 142 n. 49, 165, 169, 173, 234, 244, 260, 272 n. 50

Psalms, 138, 143, 147, 153, 156, 157, 160, 163, 346 n. 4, 358

Pseudo-Dionysus, 142, 163

Q

Quick, Oliver C., 52, 273, 357, 357 n. 61

R

Raine, Kathleen, 312, 313, 317

Realism, (the philosophical position), 62, 355 n. 61

reason, 54, 61, 107 n. 127, 202, 215 n. 15, 216 n. 18, 218, 219 n. 32, 225, 226, 226 n. 9, 232, 232 n. 46, 241, 252, 260, 292, 293, 299, 304, 350

Reflections on the Psalms, 62, 355 n. 61

Reid, Forrest, 83, 83 n. 67, 84

relativism, 228

"Religion and Rocketry," 235, 236, 236 n. 72

religionless Christianity, 281

resurrection, 15 n. 20, 56, 61, 213, 214, 216, 278, 279

Rice-Oxley, Leonard, 38

Robin Hood, 49

Robinson, John, 62, 278, 278 n. 76, 280, 336, 337

Royal Army Service Corps, 93, 101 n. 87, 103, 115, 117 n. 25, 120, 125

Royal Belfast Academical Institution, 83

Royal Hibernian Academy, 82, 82 n. 60-61

Royal Society, 255, 257, 321

Russell, Bertrand, 351

S

St. Anne's College, 52, 52 n. 38, 166, 302, 303

St. Hilda's College, 222 n. 52, 294, 300, 302

St. Hugh's College, 346, 348

St. Paul's Cathedral, 37, 48, 48 n. 10, 181

Salter's Shipyard, 171

Sayers, Dorothy L., 5, 5 n. 11, 69, 128, 169 n. 20, 274, 285, 289, 297

Scott, Sir Walter, 22 n. 65, 48, 356

scientism, 251, 257, 258, 261, 350

Screwtape Letters, The, 126, 135, 139, 153, 159, 161, 163, 232, 232 n. 46, 238, 238 n. 83, 245, 284, 290, 304, 304 n. 68, 307

Seaton, Ethel, 38

"Seeing Eye, The," 235, 235 n. 68

"Shadowlands," 59, 234

Shakespeare, William, 31, 32, 38, 39, 42, 45, 76, 101 n. 84, 272, 277, 310, 311, 317-319, 321, 321 n. 24, 321 n. 27, 322, 322 n. 33, 323, 364 n. 14

Shaw, George Bernard, 226 n. 3, 242, 246, 257, 258, 350

Shirreff's, 37

Shroud of Turin, 139, 159

Silver Chair, The, 95, 345, 345 n. 1, 349 n. 23

Skinner, Martyn, 17, 62

Slade School of Fine Art, 81, 81 n. 56, 81 n. 58

Brett-Smith, 36, 37

socialism, 229

Socratic Club, 47, 55, 56, 56 n. 61-62, 57, 57 n. 64, 60, 62, 63, 63 n. 103, 63 n. 105, 65, 65 n. 116, 66, 68, 165, 173, 170, 203 n. 61, 222, 225, 239, 239 n. 86, 241-242, 259, 259 n. 41, 282, 289, 289 n. 1, 290, 291, 291 n. 8, 292, 293, 293 n. 21, 294, 294 n. 23-25, 295, 295 n. 30, 297, 297 n. 35, 298, 298 n. 39, 298 n. 41, 299-301, 301 n. 49, 302 n. 56-57, 302 n. 60, 303, 303 n. 62-63, 302 n. 65, 304, 304 n. 71, 328, 335, 340

Socratic Digest, 61 n. 86, 62 n. 97-98, 63, 63 n. 104, 64 n. 110, 65 n. 111-115, 289 n. 2, 292, 292 n. 12-13, 292, n. 15-16, 293 n. 17, 295, 296, 296 n. 33, 299, 299 n. 43-44, 300 n. 46

Somerville College, 290, 290 n. 4, 291, 291 n. 10, 294, 295 n. 26, 302, 303, 307, 308, 312, 328 n. 14

Sophocles, 189, 310

soul, 18, 63, 64, 68, 149, 244, 339

Spencer, Herbert, 246, 255

Splendid Century, The, 41 n. 67, 128

Stalin, Joseph, 255

Stapledon, Olaf, 196, 201, 202-204, 257, 258, 350

Statius, 307, 309, 310, 310 n. 20, 317 n. 2

Stibbe, Philip, 43

Stock, Tom, 43

Strandtown, 80

Student Christian Movement, 50

Summa, 12, 12 n. 7,

Surprised by Joy, 11 n. 1, 13, 14 n. 17, 15 n. 21-22, 73, 74 n. 5, 80 n. 46, 81 n. 51, 107 n. 122, 113 n. 1, 127 n. 77, 180 n. 14, 184 n. 40, 201, 201 n. 47, 213 n. 1, 213 n. 3, 214, 214 n. 5-6, 216, 216 n. 17, 216 n. 22, 220 n. 43, 220 n. 45, 230 n. 35, 270 n. 43, 360 n. 92, 361 n. 93-94

symbolism, 145, 160, 357

T

Teresa of Avila, 16

Thackeray, William Makepeace, 48, 48 n. 7, 236, 356

That Hideous Strength, 78 n. 32, 143, 144, 160, 163, 202 n. 51, 204 n. 65, 251 n. 3, 257, 258, 258 n. 37, 260

Till We Have Faces, 59

Tillich, Paul, 265, 265 n. 10

Tizard, Sir Henry, 221

tolerance, 6

Tolkien, Christopher, 39-41, 40 n. 60, 44, 44 n. 83, 166

Tolkien, J. R. R., 4, 5, 5 n. 10, 14, 20, 29-31, 33, 34, 34 n. 25, 35, 35 n. 27, 36-40, 40 n. 60, 41, 42, 44, 44 n. 83, 45, 60, 128-130, 140, 150, 161, 166, 167, 169, 170, 172, 173, 195 n. 1, 207, 210, 234 n. 59

Traherne, Thomas, 357

"Transposition," 54

Trollope, Anthony, 48 n. 7, 227, 356

U

Universal Spirit, 11, 12

V

Virgil, 31 n. 15, 127, 310, 311, 364 n. 9

von Hügel, Friedrich, 238, 265 n. 10, 269, 342, 342 n. 32

Voyage to Arcturus, A, 78, 201, 202

W

Waddington, C. H., 64, 68, 203, 203 n. 61, 258

Wagner, Richard, 74, 76, 236

Wain, John, 129, 239, 300

Wakeman, Jean, 44, 60, 352

Waterman, Hugh, 17

"Weight of Glory, The," 3, 103, 274, 285, 291

Weil, Simon, 142, 161, 163

Wells, H. G., 74, 201, 201 n. 45,

202-204, 217, 225, 226 n. 3, 257, 342, 350

Wesley Memorial Church, 59

Whitty, Kathleen, 336, 368

Williams, Charles, 29, 32 n. 16, 37, 41, 130, 141, 142, 160, 163, 173, 238, 263, 267, 268, 272 n. 50, 285, 293, 328, 329

Willink, Stephen, 51

Wilson, F. P., 44

Windsor Sermons, 263, 275, 275 n. 65

wish fulfillment, 55, 293

Woolf, Leonard, 227, 227 n. 16

Wordsworth, William, 32, 127, 236, 355 n. 64

Wren, Christopher, 48, 278 n. 77

Wrenn, C. L., 37, 38, 38 n. 47

About the Author

Since 1998, Dr. Joel Heck has served Concordia University Texas first as Vice President of Academic Services and now as Professor of Theology. He has been a parish pastor in Missouri and Assistant Vice President of Academics and Professor of Theology for Concordia University Wisconsin. In 1984, he earned the Doctor of Theology from Concordia Seminary, St. Louis. He is the author or editor of fifteen books, five of them on C. S. Lewis, and an occasional speaker and workshop presenter on topics of practical ministry for the local church. His most recent book on Lewis before *No Ordinary People* is *From Atheism to Christianity: The Story of C. S. Lewis* (Concordia Publishing House, 2017). He and his wife Cheryl have three grown children, three grandchildren, and live in Austin, Texas.

Dr. Heck's teaching interests include the Old Testament, the life and writings of C. S. Lewis, Christian missions and outreach, and effective teaching methodology. Besides his books, he is the author of many articles, more than forty of them on C. S. Lewis, which have been published in denominational periodicals and scholarly journals, such as the *Journal of Biblical Literature*, *Bibliotheca Sacra*, *Sehnsucht*, *Seven*, and *CSL: The Bulletin of the New York C. S. Lewis Society*. He maintains a website on C. S. Lewis at www.joelheck.com.

OTHER BOOKS OF INTEREST

C. S. LEWIS

The Undiscovered C.S. Lewis: Essays in Memory of Christopher W. Mitchell
Bruce R. Johnson, Editor

Christopher Mitchell, former Director of the Marion E. Wade Center, delivered a lecture titled, "The Undiscovered C. S. Lewis," suggesting the path forward for future Lewis studies. In this collection, 18 leading scholars honor his vision and legacy with a wide range of essays.

The Leadership of C.S. Lewis: Ten Traits to Encourage Change & Growth
Crystal Hurd

This book is for readers interested in developing leadership traits by examining how C.S. Lewis became such an influential spiritual leader for our times. The chapters include: Humility, Morality, Vision, Courage, Intellect, Compassion, Duty, Inspiration, Resilience, and Creativity.

C. S. Lewis: Views From Wake Forest - Essays on C. S. Lewis
Michael Travers, editor

Contains sixteen scholarly presentations from the international C. S. Lewis convention in Wake Forest, NC. Walter Hooper shares his important essay "Editing C. S. Lewis," a chronicle of publishing decisions after Lewis' death in 1963.

> *"Scholars from a variety of disciplines address a wide range of issues. The happy result is a fresh and expansive view of an author who well deserves this kind of thoughtful attention."*
> Diana Pavlac Glyer, author of *The Company They Keep*

The Hidden Story of Narnia:
A Book-By-Book Guide to Lewis' Spiritual Themes
Will Vaus

A book of insightful commentary equally suited for teens or adults – Will Vaus points out connections between the *Narnia* books and spiritual/biblical themes, as well as between ideas in the *Narnia* books and C. S. Lewis' other books. Learn what Lewis himself said about the overarching and unifying thematic structure of the Narnia books. That is what this book explores; what C. S. Lewis called "the hidden story" of Narnia. Each chapter includes questions for individual use or small group discussion.

Why I Believe in Narnia:
33 Reviews and Essays on the Life and Work of C. S. Lewis
James Como

> Chapters range from reviews of critical books, documentaries and movies to evaluations of Lewis' books to biographical analysis.
> *"A valuable, wide-ranging collection of essays by one of the best informed and most accute commentators on Lewis' work and ideas."*
> Peter Schakel, author of *Imagination & the Arts in C. S. Lewis*

C. S. Lewis: His Literary Achievement
Colin Manlove

> "This is a positively brilliant book, written with splendor, elegance, profundity and evidencing an enormous amount of learning. This is probably not a book to give a first-time reader of Lewis. But for those who are more broadly read in the Lewis corpus this book is an absolute gold mine of information. The author gives us a magnificent overview of Lewis' many writings, tracing for us thoughts and ideas which recur throughout, and at the same time telling us how each book differs from the others. I think it is not extravagant to call *C. S. Lewis: His Literary Achievement* a tour de force."
> Robert Merchant, *St. Austin Review*, Book Review Editor

In the Footsteps of C. S. Lewis: A Photographic Pilgrimage to the British Isles
Will Vaus

Over the course of thirty years, Will Vaus has journeyed to the British Isles many times to walk in the footsteps of C. S. Lewis. His private photographs of the significant places in Lewis' life have captured the imagination of audiences in the US and UK to whom he has lectured on the Oxford don and his work. This, in turn, prompted the idea of this collection of 78 full-color photographs, interwoven with details about Lewis' life and work. The combination of words and pictures make this a wonderful addition to the library of all Lewis scholars and readers.

Speaking of Jack: A C. S. Lewis Discussion Guide
Will Vaus

C. S. Lewis Societies have been forming around the world since the first one started in New York City in 1969. Will Vaus has started and led three groups himself. *Speaking of Jack* is the result of Vaus' experience in leading those Lewis Societies. Included here are introductions to most of Lewis' books as well as questions designed to stimulate discussion about Lewis' life and work. These materials have been "road-tested" with real groups made up of young and old, some very familiar with Lewis and some newcomers. *Speaking of Jack* may be used in an existing book discussion group, to start a C. S. Lewis Society, or as a guide to your own exploration of Lewis' books.

Light: C. S. Lewis's First and Final Short Story
Charlie W. Starr
Foreword by Walter Hooper

Charlie Starr explores the questions surrounding the "Light" manuscript, a later version of story titled "A Man Born Blind." The insights into this story provide a new key to understanding some of Lewis's most profound ideas.

> "As literary journalism, both investigative and critical, it is top shelf"
> James Como, author of *Remembering C. S. Lewis*

> "Starr shines a new and illuminating light on one of Lewis's most intriguing stories"
> Michael Ward, author of *Planet Narnia*

C. S. Lewis & Philosophy as a Way of Life: His Philosophical Thoughts
Adam Barkman

C. S. Lewis is rarely thought of as a "philosopher" per se despite having both studied and taught philosophy for several years at Oxford. Lewis's long journey to Christianity was essentially philosophical – passing through seven different stages. This 624 page book is an invaluable reference for C. S. Lewis scholars and fans alike

C. S. Lewis' Top Ten: Influential Books and Authors, Volume One
Will Vaus

Based on his books, marginal notes, and personal letters, Will Vaus explores Lewis' reading of the ten books he said shaped his vocational attitude and philosophy of life. Volume One covers the first three authors/books: George MacDonald: *Phantastes*, G.K. Chesterton: *The Everlasting Man*, and Virgil: *The Aneid*. Vaus offers a brief biography of each author with a helpful summary of their books.

"*Thorough, comprehensive, and illuminating*"
Rolland Hein, Author of *George MacDonald: Victorian Mythmaker*

C. S. Lewis' Top Ten: Influential Books and Authors, Volume Two
Will Vaus

Volume Two covers the following authors/books: George Herbert: *The Temple*, William Wordsworth: *The Prelude*, Rudopf Otto, *The Idea of the Holy*.

C. S. Lewis' Top Ten: Influential Books and Authors, Volume Three
Will Vaus

Volume Three covers the following authors/books: Boethius: *The Consolation of Philosophy*, James Boswell, *The Life of Samuel Johnson*, Charles Williams: *Descent into Hell*, A.J. Balfour: *Thiesm and Humanism*.

C. S. Lewis Goes to Heaven:
A Reader's Guide to The Great Divorce
David G. Clark

This is the first book devoted solely to this often neglected book and the first to reveal several important secrets Lewis concealed within the story. Lewis felt his imaginary trip to Hell and Heaven was far better than his book *The Screwtape Letters*, which has become a classic. Readers will discover the many literary and biblical influences Lewis utilized in writing his brilliant novel.

C. S. Lewis Goes to Hell
A Companion and Study Guide to The Screwtape Letters
William O'Flaherty

The creator and host of "All About Jack" has written a guide to *The Screwtape Letters* suitable for groups or individuals, featuring an index of themes, summaries of each letter, questions for reflection, and over a half-dozen appendices of useful information.

Joy and Poetic Imagination: Understanding C. S. Lewis's "Great War" with Owen Barfield and its Significance for Lewis's Conversion and Writings
Stephen Thorson

Author Stephen Thorson began writing this book over 30 years ago and published parts of it in articles during Barfield's lifetime. Barfield wrote to Thorson in 1983 saying, ""*...you have surveyed the divergence between Lewis and myself very fairly, and truly 'in depth...'*". This book explains the "Great War" between these two friends.

Exploring the Eternal Goodness: Selected Writings of David L. Neuhouser
Joe Ricke and Lisa Ritchie, Editors

In 1997, due to David's perseverance, the Brown Collection of books by and about C. S. Lewis and related authors came to Taylor University and the Lewis and Friends Colloquium began. This book of selected writings reflects his scholarship in math and literature, as well as his musings on beauty and the imagination. The twenty-one tributes are an indication of the many lives he has influenced. This book is meant to acknowledge David L. Neuhouser for his contributions to scholarship and to honor his life of friendship, encouragement, and genuine goodness.

Inklings Forever, Volume X: Proceedings from the 10th Francis White Ewbank Colloquiunm on C. S. Lewis & Friends
Joe Ricke and Rick Hill, Editors

In June 2016, the 10th biennial Frances Ewbank Colloquium on C. S. Lewis and Friends convened at Taylor University with the special theme of "friendship." Many of the essays and creative pieces collected in this book explore the important relationships of Inklings-related authors, as well as the relationships between those authors and other, sometimes rather surprising, "friends." The year 2016 marked the 90th anniversary of the first meeting of C.S. Lewis and J.R.R. Tolkien – a creative friendship of epic proportions

> *What a feast! It is rare that a book of proceedings captures the energy and spirit of the conference itself: this one does. I recommend it.*
>
> Diana Pavlac Glyer, Professor of English at Azusa Pacific University and author of *The Company They Keep* and *Bandersnatch: C. S. Lewis, J. R. R. Tolkien, and the Creative Collaboration of the Inklings*

Mythopoeic Narnia: Memory, Metaphor, and Metamorphoses in C. S. Lewis's The Chronicles of Narnia
Salwa Khoddam

Dr. Khoddam offers a fresh approach to the *Narnia* books based on an inquiry into Lewis' readings and use of classical and Christian symbols. She explores the literary and intellectual contexts of these stories, the traditional myths and motifs, and places them in the company of the greatest Christian mythopoeic works of Western Literature.

Christian Living

Keys to Growth: Meditations on the Acts of the Apostles
Will Vaus

Every living thing or person requires certain ingredients in order to grow, and if a thing or person is not growing, it is dying. *The Acts of the Apostles* is a book that is all about growth. Will Vaus has been meditating and preaching on *Acts* for the past 30 years. In this volume, he offers the reader forty-one keys from the entire book of Acts to unlock spiritual growth in everyday life.

Open Before Christmas: Devotional Thoughts For The Holiday Season
Will Vaus

Author Will Vaus seeks to deepen the reader's knowledge of Advent and Christmas leading up to Epiphany. Readers are provided with devotional thoughts for each day that help them to experience this part of the Church Year perhaps in a more spiritually enriching way than ever before.

> *"Seasoned with inspiring, touching, and sometimes humorous illustrations .... I found his writing immediately engaging and, the more I read, the more I liked it. God has touched my heart by reading Open Before Christmas, and I believe he will touch your heart too."*
> The Rev. David Beckmann, The C.S. Lewis Society of Chattanooga

God's Love Letter: Reflections on I John
Will Vaus

Various words for "love" appear thirty-five times in the five brief chapters of I John. This book invites you on a journey of reading and reflection: reading this book in the New Testament and reflecting on God's love for us, our love for God, and our love for one another.

Jogging with G.K. Chsterton: 65 Earthshaking Expeditions
Robert Moore-Jumonville

Jogging with G.K. Chesterton is a showcase for the merry mind of Chesterton. But Chesterton's lighthearted wit always runs side-by-side with his weighty wisdom. These 65 "earthshaking expeditions" will keep you smiling and thinking from start to finish. You'll be entertained, challenged, and spiritually uplifted as you take time to breath in the fresh morning air and contemplate the wonders of the world.

> *"This is a delightfully improbable book in which Chesterton puts us through our spiritual and intellectual exercises."*
> Joseph Pearce, author of *Wisdom and Innocence: A Life of G.K. Chesterton*

GEORGE MACDONALD

Phantastes by George MacDonald: Annotated Edition
John Pennington and Roderick McGillis, Editors

Phantastes was a groundbreaking book in 1858 and continues to be a seminal example of great fantasy literature. Its elusive meaning is both alluring and perplexing, inviting readers to experience a range of deep feelings and a sense of profound truth. This annotated edition, by two renowned MacDonald scholars, provides a wealth of information to better understand and enjoy this masterpiece.

Crossing a Great Frontier: Essays on George MacDonald's Phantastest
John Pennington, Editor

> "This is the first collection of scholarly essays on George MacDonald's seminal romance Phantastes. Appropriately to the age of its hero Anodos, here we have twenty-one of the best essays written on Phantastes from 1972 onwards, in which straightforward literary analysis works together with contextual, psychological, metaphysical, alchemical and scientific approaches to the elucidation of this moving and elusive work."
> Colin Manlove, author of *Scotland's Forgotten Treasure: The Visionary Novels of George MacDonald*

Lilith by George MacDonald: Annotated Scholarly Edition
John Pennington & Roderick McGillis, Editors

Following the acclaim of their scholarly edition of MacDonald's *Phantastes*, these editors combine their expertise to create a foundational resource to enjoy *Lilith*, a masterpiece of fantasy literature. Hundreds of footnotes, many pages of reference material, reviews, and more.

Behind the Back of the North Wind:
Essays on George MacDonald's Classic Book
Edited and with Introduction by John Pennington and Roderick McGillis

The unique blend of fairy tale atmosphere and social realism in this novel laid the groundwork for modern fantasy literature. Sixteen essays by various authors are accompanied by an instructive introduction, extensive index, and beautiful illustrations.

Diary of an Old Soul & The White Page Poems
George MacDonald and Betty Aberlin

The first edition of George MacDonald's book of daily poems included a blank page opposite each page of poems. Readers were invited to write their own reflections on the "white page." Betty Aberlin responded to MacDonald's invitation with daily poems of her own.

> *Betty Aberlin's close readings of George MacDonald's verses and her thoughtful responses to them speak clearly of her poetic gifts and spiritual intelligence.*
> Luci Shaw, poet

George MacDonald: Literary Heritage and Heirs
Roderick McGillis, editor

This latest collection of 14 essays sets a new standard that will influence MacDonald studies for many more years. George MacDonald experts are increasingly evaluating his entire corpus within the nineteenth century context.

> *This comprehensive collection represents the best of contemporary scholarship on George MacDonald.*
> Rolland Hein, author of *George MacDonald: Victorian Mythmaker*

In the Near Loss of Everything: George MacDonald's Son in America
Dale Wayne Slusser

In the summer of 1887, George MacDonald's son Ronald, newly engaged to artist Louise Blandy, sailed from England to America to teach school. The next summer he returned to England to marry Louise and bring her back to America. On August 27, 1890, Louise died leaving him with an infant daughter. Ronald once described losing a beloved spouse as "the near loss of everything". Dale Wayne Slusser unfolds this poignant story with unpublished letters and photos that give readers a glimpse into the close-knit MacDonald family. Also included is Ronald's essay about his father, *George MacDonald: A Personal Note*, plus a selection from Ronald's 1922 fable, *The Laughing Elf*, about the necessity of both sorrow and joy in life.

A Novel Pulpit: Sermons From George MacDonald's Fiction
David L. Neuhouser

Each of the sermons has an introduction giving some explanation of the setting of the sermon or of the plot, if that is necessary for understanding the sermon. "MacDonald's novels are both stimulating and thought-provoking. This collection of sermons from ten novels serve to bring out the 'freshness and brilliance' of MacDonald's message." from the author's introduction

Through the Year with George MacDonald: 366 Daily Readings
Rolland Hein, editor

These page-length excerpts from sermons, novels and letters are given an appropriate theme/heading and a complementary Scripture passage for daily reading. An inspiring introduction to the artistic soul and Christian vision of George MacDonald.

Shadows and Chivalry:
C. S. Lewis and George MacDonald on Suffering, Evil, and Death
Jeff McInnis

Shadows and Chivalry studies the influence of George MacDonald upon one of the most influential writers of modern times, C. S. Lewis—the creator of Narnia, literary critic, and best-selling apologist. Without ever ceasing to be a story of one man's influence upon another, the study also serves as an exploration of each writer's thought on, and literary visions of, good and evil.

The Downstretched Hand:
Individual Development in MacDonald's Major Fantasies for Children
Lesley Willis Smith

Smith demonstrates that MacDonald is fully aware of the need to integrate the unconscious into the conscious in order to achieve mature individuation. However, for MacDonald, true maturity and fulfillment can only be gained through a relationship with God. By exploring MacDonald's major biblical themes into his own myth, Smith reveals his literary genius and profound understanding of the human psyche. Smith interacts with other leading scholarship and in the context of other works by MacDonald, especially those written during the same time period.

BIOGRAPHY

Sheldon Vanauken: The Man Who Received "A Severe Mercy"
Will Vaus

In this biography we discover: Vanauken the struggling student, the bon-vivant lover, the sailor who witnessed the bombing of Pearl Harbor, the seeker who returned to faith through C. S. Lewis, the beloved professor of English literature and history, the feminist and anti-war activist who participated in the March on the Pentagon, the bestselling author, and Vanauken the convert to Catholicism. What emerges is the portrait of a man relentlessly in search of beauty, love, and truth, a man who believed that, in the end, he found all three.

> *"This is a charming biography about a doubly charming man who wrote a triply charming book. It is a great way to meet the man behind A Severe Mercy."*
>
> Peter Kreeft, author of *Jacob's Ladder: 10 Steps to Truth*

Remembering Roy Campbell: The Memoirs of his Daughters, Anna and Tess
Introduction by Judith Lütge Coullie, Editor
Preface by Joseph Pearce

Anna and Teresa Campbell were the daughters of the handsome young South African poet and writer, Roy Campbell (1901-1957), and his beautiful English wife, Mary Garman. In their frank and moving memoirs, Anna and Tess recall the extraordinary, and often very difficult, lives they shared with their exceptional parents. Over 50 photos, 344 footnotes, timeline of Campbell's life, and complete index.

POETS AND POETRY

In the Eye of the Beholder: How to See the World Like a Romantic Poet
Louis Markos

Born out of the French Revolution and its radical faith that a nation could be shaped and altered by the dreams and visions of its people, British Romantic Poetry was founded on a belief that the objects and realities of our world, whether natural or human, are not fixed in stone but can be molded and transformed by the visionary eye of the poet. A separate bibliographical essay is provided for readers listing accessible biographies of each poet and critical studies of their work.

The Cat on the Catamaran: A Christmas Tale
John Martin

Here is a modern-day parable of a modern-day cat with modern-day attitudes. Riverboat Dan is a "cool" cat on a perpetual vacation from responsibility. He's *The Cat on the Catamaran* – sailing down the river of life. Dan keeps his guilty conscience from interfering with his fun until he runs into trouble. But will he have the courage to believe that it's never too late to change course? (For ages 10 to adult)

> "This book is a joy, and as companionable as a good-natured cat."
> Walter Hooper, author of *C. S. Lewis: Companion and Guide*

www.ingramcontent.com/pod-product-compliance
Lightning Source LLC
Chambersburg PA
CBHW030315100526
44592CB00010B/441